EXPLORING

WORLD

RELIGIONS

The Canadian Perspective

OXFORD

UNIVERSITY PRESS

OXFORD
UNIVERSITY PRESS

8 Sampson Mews, Suite 204, Don Mills, Ontario M3C 0H5
www.oupcanada.com

Oxford University Press is a department of the University of Oxford.

It furthers the University's objective of excellence in research, scholarship, and education by publishing worldwide in

Oxford New York
Athens Auckland Bangkok Bogotá Buenos Aires Cape Town
Chennai Dar es Salaam Delhi Florence Hong Kong Istanbul Karachi
Kolkata Kuala Lumpur Madrid Melbourne Mexico City Mumbai Nairobi
Paris São Paulo Shanghai Singapore Taipei Tokyo Toronto Warsaw

with associated companies in Berlin Ibadan

Oxford is a registered trade mark of Oxford University Press
in the UK and in certain other countries

Published in Canada
By Oxford University Press

National Library of Canada Cataloguing in Publication Data

Main entry under title:
Exploring world religions: the Canadian perspective

Includes index.
For use in grade 11.

ISBN-10: 0-19-541660-0
ISBN-13: 978-0-19-541660-2

1. Religions. I. DesRivieres, Dennis, 1947-
Quinlan, Don, 1947-

BL80.3.E96 2001   291   C2001-901573-9

Printed and bound in the United States of America
This book is printed on permanent (acid-free) paper ⊛.

14 15 16 —14 13 12

Acquisitions Editor: Patti Henderson
Developmental Editors: Elaine Aboud,
    Beverley Biggar, Maria Christopoulos
Production Coordinators: Sara Jane
    Kennerley, Tracey MacDonald
Copy Editors: Elaine Aboud, Ruth Chernia,
    Tracey MacDonald, Rachelle Redford,
    Coleen Young
Cover and text design: Joan Dempsey
Cover and text illustrations: Joan Dempsey
Text formatting, cartography, and
    illustrations: VISUTronX

Acknowledgements

In the development of *Exploring World Religions: The Canadian Perspective*, every care has been taken to ensure that the content within is authentic, thought-provoking, and most importantly, accurate. Our review team represents a broad spectrum of dedicated people who shared a vested interest in helping us produce such a text. Each chapter has been carefully reviewed by classroom teachers to ensure sound pedagogy; by academics specializing in world religions to ensure accuracy and balance; and by faith mentors to ensure that each religion is dealt with both fairly and authentically.

Oxford University Press would like to acknowledge the following dedicated group of reviewers for their valued contributions to the development of this text:

Syed Mumtaz Ali, Canadian Society of Muslims

Peter Ball, Teacher, Waterloo Collegiate Institute, Waterloo District School Board

Qazi Bashiruddin, Canadian Society of Muslims

Amila Buturovic, Division of Humanities, York University

Mary Ann Crossett, St. Joseph's High School, English Language Separate District School Board No. 38

Reverend Father Len Desjardins, Pastor, Sacred Heart Roman Catholic Church, Sarnia

Barry Elliot, Consultant, Windsor-Essex Catholic District School Board

Tim Evenden, Teacher, East Elgin Secondary School, Thames Valley District School Board

Tara Froman, Woodland Cultural Centre, Brantford, ON

Timothy J. Gianotti, Assistant Professor of Religious Studies, Pennsylvania State University

Doug Gordon, Consultant, Thames Valley District School Board

Silvana Gos, Teacher, St. Augustine Catholic Secondary School, Dufferin-Peel Catholic District School Board

Michael Harrison, Teacher, Our Lady of Mount Carmel Secondary School, Dufferin-Peel Catholic District School Board

Amir Hussain, Department of Religious Studies, California State University

Deo Kernahan, Vision TV

Bronek Korczynski, Consultant, Algonquin-Lakeshore Catholic District School Board

Rocky Landon, Sundance, St. Lawrence Youth Association, Kingston, ON

Rabia Mills, Canadian Society of Muslims

Tony Muhitch, Teacher, St. Elizabeth Catholic High School, York Region Catholic District School Board

Willard G. Oxtoby, Professor Emeritus, Department of Religious Studies, University of Toronto

Jack Palmer, Teacher, Catholic Central Secondary School, English Language Separate District School Board No.38

Jordan Pearlson, Founding Rabbi of the Temple Sinai Congregation of Toronto

Kelsang Phuntsog , Chandrakirti Buddhist Centre, Toronto, ON

John Podgorski, Consultant, Ottawa-Carleton Catholic District School Board

Carla Santomero, Consultant, Waterloo Catholic District School Board

Pritam Singh, President of the Sikh Cultural Centre, Toronto

Reverend William Steadman, St. Andrew's United Church, Sudbury

Dedications

Producing this text has been an "exploration" in itself. I have enjoyed an amazing team of colleagues: authors, editors, faith mentors, reviewers, production and sales staff. In particular, I would like to thank Elaine Aboud, Beverley Biggar, and Maria Christopoulos, the developmental editors; and Patti Henderson, Acquisitions Editor. Thanks to all for "keeping the faith."

—Don Quinlan, Senior Author

I am grateful for the support and direction of my wife Shirley, daughter Renée, friend Father Len DesJardins, and editor Maria Christopoulos. Thank you for showing the way in this exciting endeavour.

—Dennis DesRivieres

To Adam and Liam and Theresa, Fran, and Lorne

—Sean Dolan and
Sharon Goodland

I would like to thank the following people for their help in making this such a rewarding experience: my wife Barbara, for her constant support; the staff at Oxford University Press, including Beverley Biggar, Don Quinlan, and Patti Henderson; and Tara Froman at the Woodland Cultural Centre for her guidance.

—James Ellsworth

In dedication to my loving wife, Devi, and my charming daughter, Dhristi. Both have been a great support and inspiration to me throughout this stimulating experience.

—Deo Kernahan

To my children, Christopher and Elizabeth, for their input and constant encouragement.

—Peter Lawley

Exploring World Religions is dedicated to the memory of Deo Kernahan, author and friend.

Contents

Features

Today, one can explore world religions without ever moving beyond the borders of Canada.

Chapter One

The Religious Impulse

1

Look at the collage of photographs and consider the following questions:

1. What do you see when you first look at this collage?
2. What does it reveal about the nature of Canadian society? Be specific.

Introduction

Imagine a country where, on any given morning, young people rise to greet the day in the following ways. Many simply wash and dress, then eat a quick breakfast before heading off to school. Some turn to the rising sun and say a prayer of thanks, while others go to church to recite a series of prayers and sing hymns of worship. Still others walk to a neighbourhood **synagogue** to read excerpts from the **Torah**. A young girl rises, lays out a prayer rug—carefully placing it in the direction of **Makkah** (Mecca)—and begins a series of prayers and prostrations to God. A young boy spends several minutes expertly twisting his hair and covering it with a turban. A student preparing to write a set of exams takes an hour in the early morning to sit in the lotus position and quietly meditate, centring her thoughts before facing the hurly-burly of a busy day. Two brothers begin the day with a **smudge ceremony**, burning sweet grass and using it to cleanse their bodies and senses.

This multi-faceted description actually represents the religious and cultural reality in *our country*—Canada. The United Nations has declared Canada the most multicultural society on the planet and has declared Toronto the world's most multicultural city. In fact, because Canada is home to such a richly diverse group of people, it has become the platform for one of the great encounters of the modern world—the interaction of the world's major religious traditions. **Religious pluralism** is a central, ongoing, and definitive feature of contemporary Canadian society. The world's various religious traditions are now well established as important, even essential, threads in the fabric of Canadian life.

Learning Goals

At the end of this chapter, in addition to understanding the purpose and approach of *Exploring World Religions*, you will be able to:

- identify some of the diverse religions represented in Canada today and understand how religious pluralism is a defining feature of Canadian life
- know the major common features and questions associated with religion
- identify common problems and questions associated with the search for spiritual meaning
- know the relationship between religion and ethics
- evaluate religion's place in a highly technological and scientific age
- explore and employ primary and secondary research material appropriately in completing an assignment
- demonstrate an ability to recognize prejudice and bias in primary and secondary sources
- distinguish between fact, opinion, and argument as they apply to the study of religion
- identify the role of religion in human experience and culture
- differentiate between religion and ethnicity
- describe how misconceptions can influence people's views of various religions, beliefs, and practices
- differentiate between popular and religious symbolism associated with one major religious celebration in Canada
- understand the relationship of religion to the State in Canada

Figure 1.1

In December 2000, three great religions shared important religious observances during the same week. Christians *celebrated Christmas*, Jews *marked Hanukkah*, and Muslims *ended the holy month of Ramadan with Eid al-Fitr, a joyous feast of thanksgiving after a holy month of fasting from dawn to dusk. Each of these religions follows a different calendar, but at this particular time, these celebrations overlapped.*

THE RELIGIOUS IMPULSE

The truth is out there.

—*X-Files* slogan

Are you **religious**? What does the word *religious* suggest to you? Do you believe in a god or many gods? Do you feel that you have a **soul**? Is there a reality beyond that of the material world? Is death the end or a new beginning? Is there a purpose to life or is it just a series of random events? Is there really such a thing as right and wrong? What do you believe in?

The roots of religion appear to run deep and are clearly older than civilization and perhaps older than humankind (*Homo sapiens*) itself. Even early humans such as **Neanderthals** demonstrated an understanding of a supernatural force. Some observers believe that an essential characteristic of humankind is to have faith, and to have an intuitive sense of the supernatural—a force, power, or reality beyond the material world. The one common thread throughout countless diversities of human religion has been the instinct or impulse to worship *something*.

Many people would say that they have at least occasionally felt a sense of the supernatural or of a greater **spiritual** reality beyond the everyday world. Today, we live in an age of apparent religious revival. For some, it is a New Age where the threads of different religious traditions can be woven together to form a personal fabric of individual faith. The **religious impulse**, so apparent in traditional societies, seems to be thriving in the modern age of scientific advances and technological wonders.

What Is Religion?

Although religion is such a major part of the development of civilization, you might be surprised to learn that there is a considerable range of definitions for the term *religion*, as illustrated below. As you read these definitions, consider how you would define or explain the term *religion*. What common elements appear to exist in these definitions?

*There are, I realize, at least three aspects to every great religion: faith, hope, and charity. Faith is the **theology**, hope is the **ritual**, and charity is the **ethics**.*

—Lewis Browne, *The World's Great Scriptures*

Religion is the worship of higher powers from the sense of need.

—Allan Menzies, quoted in *World Religions*, by S. A. Nigosian

Religion is a unified system of beliefs and practices relative to sacred things— things set apart and forbidden—beliefs and practices which unite into a single moral community called a Church, all those who adhere to them.

—Émile Durkheim, *Elementary Forms of the Religious Life*

Religion had been defined as the attitude of individuals in community to the powers which they conceive as having ultimate control over their destinies and interests.

—J. Lewis, *The Religions of the World*

Religion is found in the field of the supernormal, and may be defined as a link between the finite and the infinite or as a grasping by [humans] toward something beyond [themselves] which gives [them] a reason for being.

—Gerald L. Berry, *Religions of the World*

The belief in a superhuman controlling power, esp. in a personal God or gods entitled to obedience and worship.

—*Canadian Oxford Dictionary*

Web Quest

In this introductory chapter, you might wish to visit the Web sites listed below for information on religion in general, interfaith dialogue, and current religious issues. Subsequent chapters in this book list Web sites devoted to the study and celebration of specific faiths. Vision TV broadcasts programs about Canada's religious communities. Its Web site provides program listings, as well as links to over twenty religious traditions that are a central part of contemporary Canada:

http://www.visiontv.ca

Ontario Multifaith Council on Spiritual and Religious Care:
http://www.omc.on.ca

North American Interfaith Network:
http://www.nain.org

Check Your Understanding

1. Why is Canada a good place to encounter the religions of the world?

2. What is the meaning of the phrase *religious impulse*?

3. What is your own personal definition of *religion*?

4. In general, how "religious" are you? Explain.

EXPLORING RELIGION

The Common Features of Religion

Rather than attempting to define a series of beliefs, experiences, and practices for each religion, perhaps it is easier to note the features that appear to be common to religious expression and practice. Most religions share many, if not all, of these characteristics:

- a belief in the supernatural and in a spiritual world beyond our physical material world
- a belief in the existence of a soul
- a collection of sacred writings or scriptures
- organized institutions
- a strong sense of family and community based on rituals and festivals that represent and celebrate shared beliefs and practices
- a set of answers about the most pressing human questions, for example, the meaning of suffering
- rules of conduct designed to help followers lead an honourable life and to provide order and purpose to individual and community life
- a system of ethics that offers a guide to moral behaviour
- significant founders or inspired leaders who introduced or spurred the development of the faith
- a search for perfection or salvation
- a life of faith and worship
- techniques for focusing or concentrating one's awareness
- an enriching impact on the lives of its adherents

Why Is Religion Practised?

Since the beginning of human existence, people have turned to religion in one form or another. The religious impulse seems to be part of being human and has many explanations. One aspect of the religious impulse is a recoiling from something, such as fear, while another is a search or quest for something better, yet somewhat unattainable. While we have physical needs that must be met, we also have a sense of something beyond the material world—a greater reality that we can barely sense but cannot easily verify with our formal knowledge and five senses. A number of factors may lead us to turn to religion or express ourselves spiritually. Let's consider the following factors:

Fear

For all of our development and sophistication, modern humans share the same deep-seated fears that our predecessors experienced throughout time. Our education, our riches, and our self-confidence are limited in the face of fears and insecurities about death, loneliness, and being or doing wrong. Often, our personal challenges or problems seem overwhelming. We feel physical or emotional pain from sickness, loss, and disease. At times, life may seem unbearably sad or hopelessly tragic. Life's trials are simply too difficult to bear or resolve on our own. Most of us struggle to be good and to become better people, but we are concerned that we may fall short of this goal. We fear the power of nature, our self-destructive tendencies, and internal and external conflict. We question the way we lead our lives. Are our lives pointless, or do they have meaning?

Wonder

For many people, this world is an unfathomable splendour. The stars in the sky, the power of storms, the beauty of nature, and the rich diversity and complexity of the natural world remain largely unexplained. The miracle of creation is rarely explained by science in terms that make real sense to the majority of people. Rather than actually explaining this miracle, science often describes it.

How and why did all this come about? Is there a plan? Was the development of earth a series of accidents, or can it really be neatly summed up in formulas and axioms? Is there an overall design to life and the universe? There seems to be so much that is unexplained in satisfactory terms. Some of us believe in a more spiritual realm of existence beyond everyday life. Much of the **New Age** movement is an attempt to experience the world more directly and to let our senses come in direct contact with the wonder of existence.

Questioning

Many of us refuse to accept that we are simply framed by birth, life, and death. The great insecurity of our lifespan is unsettling. It seems that our lives hang by a thread and can be cut short, perhaps by an accident, a genetic flaw, or a poor choice in a difficult situation. Some people point to the fact that so many individuals seem to live unrewarding lives. We are confronted by our failures and our weaknesses. The desire to be better, to be uplifted, and to be rescued from our condition is present in most people at some point in their lives. Few of us want to believe that we live our lives alone and face death alone. We don't want to believe that our lives are determined solely by chance or accident, much like a lottery, with some people winning long, happy lives and others facing shorter or more difficult ones.

For some people, religion offers the answers to these issues and provides an opportunity to celebrate the beauty of their lives and to enjoy a sense of belonging in their faith community.

Profile:
Rita Shelton Deverell

Figure 1.2

The new face of Canada is multicultural, multiracial, and, of course, multi-religious. A pioneer of this social revolution in Canada is Rita Shelton Deverell, "the face of Vision TV." Vision is Canada's only television station completely devoted to religious, spiritual, and moral issues. Ms. Deverell is the station's vice-president, new concept consultant, and executive producer of *Skylight*, the network's flagship series. She explains the unique character of the series in this way: "*Skylight's* deeper, more thoughtful approach to human affairs raises questions that are paradoxically tough and sensitive. Its reflection of the ethical and spiritual dimension ... provides viewers with a more life-affirming alternative to conventional current-affairs programming."

Ms. Deverell was born in Texas, and came to Canada in 1967. She has worked as an actor, broadcaster, writer, arts consultant, and university professor. As a woman of colour, she has experienced some discrimination but is a firm believer in Canada's diversity and future. She was cited by the Canadian Ethnic Journalists' and Writers' Club for "excellence in presenting Canada's racial and cultural diversity in a frank, courageous and truthful manner."

Ms. Deverell is enthusiastic about Canada's multicultural society: "Thank goodness that we live in a country where people of different faiths, skin colours, languages, genders, ages, and ethnicities live in relative harmony."

Questions

1. Why might Rita Deverell be considered to be a representative Canadian?
2. View Vision TV for a week, then write an analysis of its programming and explain your reaction.

Identity

Are humans simply a unique physical presence with a name and a set of experiences? Can we be summed up by our physical description as tall, short, fat, slim, strong, or weak? Do our tastes in music and clothes really sum up who and what we are? Many Canadians suffer from an identity crisis as we confront the questions about the meaning and purpose of our lives. Can human life be so neatly categorized by terms such as *student, jock, rocker, teacher, daughter,* etc.? At some point in life, most people sense a deeper, more lasting reality—something that is far beyond a mere physical or cultural description, something more permanent and purposeful. Some describe this reality in terms of a soul.

Intuition

Increasingly, people feel unfulfilled by the commercialism and materialism of modern life in Canada. Our rational minds have helped us to dominate the earth, but we may still feel that something is missing. Many religions were founded by leaders who felt inspiration or had revelations. They had a vision of a different reality. Some religious practices are designed to seek refuge from the so-called reality of the world and tune in to a deeper mystical truth.

Big Questions . . . No Easy Answers

Most people, and young people in particular, are curious about the difficult questions in life. What is right and what is wrong? Who are we? Why are we here? How was the world created? Is there a god or gods? What is the central meaning of life? Why is there suffering in the world?

Take a brief moment and list the "big questions" that you have considered or perhaps are actively considering at this moment in your life. Write out a list of at least five of these questions, then share them with your classmates.

Your Credo

Exploring World Religions: The Canadian Perspective looks at many aspects of religion, including personal belief. Take a moment to consider your beliefs carefully and quietly. Make a list of, write a paragraph about, or create a collage of your most cherished and deeply held beliefs. You are free to comment on whatever is important to you. This may include family, values, life, death, right and wrong, etc. Entitle your work "My Personal Credo." A **credo** is a statement of belief.

Purpose of the Textbook

The credo that you have written is central to your personality and life today. It is likely that some of your thoughts may change over time. Perhaps it was difficult to express some of your ideas. You may have

Figure 1.3
*Kensington Market is a multicultural neighbourhood in the old part of Toronto. Each December, the local residents celebrate the Kensington Market Festival of Lights, which is a mix of Christian, Jewish, and **pagan** traditions. Held on December 21, the shortest day of the year, this colourful community event celebrates Christmas, Hanukkah, and the winter solstice.*

more questions than answers at this time in your life. It can be frustrating to discover that your beliefs may be not only limited or uncertain but also in conflict with each other.

This textbook invites you to consider a stimulating range of belief systems, practices, and experiences. You are free to accept or reject them, but it is helpful to attempt to understand these faiths before making decisions on their merits or significance to your life. You might gain new perspectives on, or a new appreciation for, the traditions to which your parents may have exposed you. The religions explored in this textbook play a complex and central role in present-day Canada. They allow us to look deeper within ourselves and find answers to the mysteries of life. You will undoubtedly see common threads among these faiths and will also notice what appear to be walls dividing one faith from another. In your exploration of these great religious traditions, perhaps you will find personal answers and a personal credo.

Searching for Answers

Popular music sometimes deals with concerns and issues that many people face, including those relating to personal spirituality or ethics. Read these lyrics from a very popular song written and recorded by the Irish band U2, then answer the questions that follow.

"I Still Haven't Found What I'm Looking For"

I have climbed the highest mountains
I have run through the fields
Only to be with you
Only to be with you

I have run
I have crawled
I have scaled these city walls
These city walls
Only to be with you

But I still haven't found what I'm looking for
But I still haven't found what I'm looking for

I have kissed honey lips
Felt the healing in her fingertips
It burned like fire
This burning desire

I have spoke with the tongue of angels
*I have held the hand of a **devil***
It was warm in the night
I was cold as a stone

But I still haven't found what I'm looking for
But I still haven't found what I'm looking for

I believe in the kingdom come
Then all the colours will bleed into one
Bleed into one
Well, yes I'm still running

You broke the bonds and you
Loosed the chains
Carried the cross
Of my shame
Of my shame
You know I believed it

But I still haven't found what I'm looking for
But I still haven't found what I'm looking for . . .

QUESTIONS

1. What appears to be the central message of the song?

2. In your view, what is the overall tone of the song?

3. Do you think that many people feel that they "still haven't found what [they're] looking for"?

4. Have you found what you've been looking for? Explain.

5. What particular religious faith does the composer seem to be referring to in the lyrics? How do you know this?

Religion and Ethics

Most of us are concerned with being good and doing what is right. Life presents us with many choices, some of them complex and difficult. If we do something wrong, we often feel guilt or shame. While we may project our anger and disappointment with ourselves toward others, we may still suffer with the negative emotions that come from doing wrong.

Both religion and ethics are concerned with being good or doing the "right thing." Ethics may be defined as the search for good judgment about how to act or behave. Daniel Bonevac, William Boon, and Stephen Phillips wrote about it in the following way in their book *Beyond the Western Tradition.*

> *It is a* practical *discipline focussing on such questions as:*
> *What should I do?*
> *What kind of life should I lead?*
> *What kind of person should I try to become?*
> *How can I tell right from wrong?*
> *What obligations do I have to other people?*
> *When am I justified in criticizing others?*
> *When are they justified in criticizing me?*

Many people feel that ethics and religion are the same or, at least, inseparable. Others hold that ethics do not necessarily depend on religion or on being religious. *Can We Be Good Without God?* is the title of a book by Canadian **humanist** Robert Buckman. Humanists believe that leading a good and useful life should be the central goal of our existence. Buckman claims that how one lives between birth and death is ultimately what matters in life.

The religions that you will encounter in this textbook offer a wide range of ideas and experiences designed to help individuals lead a good and useful life. In time, you will likely note some important differences among these faiths, but you may also notice a number of basic commonalties. Whether one feels that ethics and religion are separate or fundamentally and eternally entwined, the challenge of doing good is a significant concern for most people.

Science and Religion

Some people, today and in the past, view science and religion as rivals and antagonists. They appear to be competitors in the race to understand and explain the true nature of the world, and its origins, purpose, and future direction. In the past, the **evolutionary** theories of Charles Darwin, suggesting that all living things have evolved from a few simple forms, seemed to signal a head-on clash between science and religion, in spite of the fact that Darwin himself continued to be a religious man. The literal truth of religion, particularly Christianity, appeared to contradict the measurable, quantifiable discoveries of science. Much of the nineteenth and twentieth centuries was consumed by a bruising battle as scientists and religious people put forth their competing explanations of the world.

While one might expect that in the twenty-first century, this struggle will continue, so far this does not appear to be the case. Instead, the similarities of science and religion seem to offer a complementary partnership and mutual respect. For instance, both science and religion are concerned with truth and understanding; specifically, the search for purpose and meaning, as well as practical questions about the origins of the earth and the guiding forces that regulate it. For many people, the truths of science and religion can be mutually supportive and complementary. While some religious adherents may accept and heed scientific fact and discoveries, others do not. Science, on the other hand, has learned to be aware of its limitations. The

Living My Religion

Sandy Mackellar

Figure 1.4

Sandy Mackellar is a Grade 11 student in Scarborough, Ontario. Read about her views on religion, and consider the questions that follow.

I have never been an extremely religious person, but I have often questioned if there is a God or one true religion. I have studied a few religions in school, however, none of these faiths ever said exactly what I believed. I felt it was becoming more and more important to me to know in what I believed, as I had not really considered it before. There were a few aspects of a couple of religions that I could believe in or relate to but I never found one religion to which I could completely devote myself. I do believe in a higher power, and I figure that the fact that I have faith is more important to me than being able to classify that faith into one specific religion.

My dilemma with religion is that I have a hard time putting so much trust and belief into something that I have no proof exists. It used to be very important to me to find the religion that would suit me best. Now I am happy feeling that I do not need to be part of an organized religion in order to prove that I believe.

There are many things about life that I believe in, but I cannot tie them all down to one religion in particular. I believe that each person has a purpose in life and that everything happens for a reason. I believe that fate is ultimately what chooses the paths our lives take, and I believe that life does not necessarily end after death. This is a comforting thought, but I often contemplate whether or not this is why religion was originally created.

Religion can be so overwhelming because there are so many to look into but no "evidence" proving the truth of any one religion in particular. This is why right now I just believe what I believe without devoting myself to any specific religion.

QUESTIONS

1. Which of Sandy's views about religion do you share? Which do you disagree with? Explain.

2. Do you think that Sandy is a "religious" person? Explain.

unending stream of scientific knowledge continues to suggest some sort of order to the world. Generally, for adherents of science and religion, there appears to be a growing acceptance of the value of the other and an understanding that both disciplines play a role in understanding the universe.

Technology

We are living in the Technological Age—a time when humankind's ingenuity and effort have created vast new opportunities and possibilities. Technology has not only made the world a global village but has also, in a sense, shrunk the universe. Space exploration has progressed from speculative science fiction to recorded history. New inventions and discoveries are moving humans far beyond the initial wonders of the Industrial Revolution to a digital, wireless world, whose central feature is dynamic, wholesale change. Biotechnology and genetic research are challenging the limits of the human lifespan and reducing the threats of age-old diseases that once ruled humans' time on earth. For many, the increasingly technological future heralds an era of tremendous wealth, health, and happiness.

For others, technology does not provide all the answers nor does it meet all their needs. Some people point out that environmental destruction is one of the negative by-products of technological development; others remark that humans need to look far beyond our basic needs for true meaning and happiness. The search for meaning, especially in a technological web that is difficult to understand and master, continues. Despite all the promise of the new technologies, many individuals believe the central questions that are at the heart of most religions still need answers. Some of these questions include

- Who am I?
- Why am I here?
- How should I live my life?
- What is my relationship to others?
- Is there life or existence after death?
- How and why was the universe created?

GOD'S VOICE MAIL

"Thanks for calling, if you want a miracle, press 1, if you want a sin check-up, press 2, if you want to leave a prayer, please wait until after the beep..."

Figure 1.5
Even in such a dizzying technological age, when communication is instantaneous and constant, many people still feel the need to communicate with another reality—a higher power, a god. The religious impulse is deep within most human beings. Why do you think this is so?

Check Your Understanding

1. Identify five common features of religions.

2. In your view, which two reasons best explain why people throughout time have turned to religion? Why?

3. What is the essential difference between religion and ethics?

4. Do you think that science and religion can coexist? Explain.

Skill Path

In any field of study, people need tools to facilitate their work. For example, a graphic designer uses a computer and graphic software, and a biomedical scientist uses a microscope and biological specimens. Someone studying world religions would use primary and secondary sources of information as their research tools.

Primary sources include first-hand evidence, such as eyewitness accounts, photographs, videos, and artifacts. Secondary sources are second-hand accounts created by people who did not actually experience a given event, but instead based their findings on primary sources. Secondary sources could include documentaries, books (other than autobiographies or diaries), and other forms of print media such as newspapers, magazines, and Web sites.

A researcher choosing primary and secondary sources must view each through a critical eye to make sure the information is reliable and accurate, and also to recognize any bias in the material.

Bias

An individual demonstrates bias when he or she forms a fixed opinion about someone or something without examining the facts thoroughly and fairly. While a bias may be positive or negative in nature, the important point is that it is often an inaccurate or limited view of something or someone. In its worst form, it is a slanted, one-sided position.

Bias usually develops out of our frame of reference—experiences, family, friends, religion, occupation, etc. This frame of reference may predispose us to certain opinions and values and may blind us to people, ideas, and information that are unfamiliar or that challenge our central beliefs. If we are biased at the start of our research, it will shape and twist all the information that we find. The goal of research is to be critical of, but also open to, new information. If we don't recognize or restrain our bias, we may not learn new information and may actually reinforce our bias. This will result in a research report that presents a seriously distorted, ill-informed point of view.

Recognizing Bias

The first step is to understand that most people are biased to a certain degree. We are not blank slates; we come to our work with a set of preconceptions and, perhaps, prejudgments. The challenge is to recognize our biases and not to become their prisoner.

When researching, you must be able to identify an author's frame of reference and be equipped to quickly recognize bias in a source, whether it is a book, a Web site, or a resource person. In some cases, bias may be easy to detect, but often it is more subtle and implicit. Even when information is biased, it may still have value depending on how you use the information, thus, you must become adept at separating information from conclusions. In extreme cases, a source may be completely unreliable because it is blatantly biased. When validating your sources, be alert for features that may indicate bias or prejudice:

- The ratio of fact to opinion in the material. (See the following section.)
- The amount of simplification and generalization. If the source offers sweeping, simple answers to complex questions, be wary.
- The tone of the source. Screaming titles, wild claims, and charged, emotional language may be interesting to read but may mask a seriously prejudiced position. If the source

appears to be too "persuasive," it is probably biased.

- Who and what is included or excluded from the text and documentation. A narrow frame of reference does not usually result in a balanced account.
- Who? When? Why? What? Where? Does the source cover the five Ws in its presentation of material? If not, it may be omitting important information.

Facts, Opinions, and Arguments

A fact is something that is exact and specific; we know it exists or happened, and can prove it is true. For example, as stated on page 4, it is a fact that, in December 2000, three great religions shared important religious observances during the same week. Christians celebrated Christmas, Jews marked Hanukkah, and Muslims ended the holy month of Ramadan with Eid al-Fitr.

Opinions are views, thoughts, and feelings that may or may not be based on facts. In this chapter, for example, the authors of the book expressed the following opinion: "We believe that the rich variety of religious traditions born across the globe, and practised in Canada today, offers positive experiences open to all Canadians."

Arguments are explanations or reasons that support or reject a viewpoint or opinion. They are based on facts, and try to offer an explanation for an event and then draw some conclusions. Arguments often include words such as *because*, *since*, and *therefore*. For example, in the introduction to this chapter, the authors explain that "*because* Canada is home to such a richly diverse group of people, it has become the platform on which one of the great encoun-

ters of the modern world is taking place— the interaction of the world's major religious traditions."

Practise It!

1. In the list below, identify each source as either primary or secondary, and explain the reason.

- a photograph of a member of the Algonquin nation
- the Web site of the Canadian Society of Muslims
- an interview with a Roman Catholic priest
- a digital map of world religions
- an Aboriginal artifact
- an article on the history of Hinduism
- a diary belonging to the Dalai Lama
- a documentary on the Prophet Muhammad
- a poster of a Shinto festival
- a video on Joseph Brant
- statistics on world religions

2. Read the following paragraph and identify each of the sentences as F (fact), O (opinion), or A (argument).

Multicultural and religious pluralism are features of Canadian society. Canadians are far more tolerant and understanding of cultural and religious differences. Canada is the best place in the world to study religions. In such a vast country, it is likely that some Canadians may not be aware of the extent of Canada's cultural and religious diversity. Since Canada is so diverse, it is likely to hold a key position on the world stage during the twenty-first century.

UNDERSTANDING RELIGION AND CULTURE

Religion and Ethnicity

It is common for people to confuse religion with ethnicity. While religion is primarily concerned with beliefs, rituals, and practices, ethnicity refers to a person's origins, race, or culture but not necessarily to his or her religion. For example, there are South Asians who are Christians, and there are North Americans from many different cultural backgrounds who are Buddhists. One cannot assume to know a person's religion other than through his or her personal declaration. The key elements in determining religious adherence are belief and practice, not ethnicity.

Religion and Popular Culture

It is also easy to confuse the beliefs and practices of religion with what we see reflected in popular culture. Consider how many books, television programs, movies, and songs deal in some way with religious themes or the supernatural (Figure 1.6). Take a moment to write down as many pop culture references to religion as you can.

Popular culture is an exciting, stimulating, and pervasive phenomenon that has gained tremendous power and acceptance in modern societies. It has also gained a level of respect and acceptance that it may not deserve. Stereotypical images, often negative in tone, may be superimposed on certain groups of people. For example, Canada's Muslim community has often defended itself against the simplistic images of "the Arab terrorist" perpetuated by films and television

Figure 1.6
Popular culture—especially films—often presents powerful, but inaccurate, views of religion. What do these images suggest about religion?

programs. Music videos, late-night talk shows, movies, and so on are major sources of information for many of us. Our understanding of the world is heavily influenced by our exposure to popular culture. Popular culture is here to stay, but it is too often a poor substitute for genuine understanding.

As we explore some major faith traditions practised by Canadians today, we need to be willing to drop our preconceptions and encounter these faiths on their own terms. We also need to realize that some features and qualities associated with a religion may, in fact, be more cultural in origin. As a religion spread to other parts of the world, it often became associated with new beliefs and practices rooted in the welcoming culture, even though they were not really part of the religion's original core beliefs or values. This can make it difficult for the observer to actually know what the central message, rituals, and values of the religion might be. This complex point might be illustrated best by investigating one of the most popular North American religious traditions, Christmas.

Christmas

Christmas is, perhaps, the most well-known communal celebration in North America. Virtually everyone is familiar with and influenced by this event, regardless of his or her religious affiliation. The Christmas season has a huge impact on the economy since the shopping period associated with it can make or break the financial success of a company over an entire year. In fact, some economists estimate that 40 per cent of annual purchasing takes place during this time. Some people go into debt for months or even years after a Christmas "blowout." Most people take holidays at this time, and many firms and organizations shut down for a period ranging from a few days to a couple of weeks. Cultural arts centres feature Christmas concerts and plays. Movie theatres release a number of new films for the Christmas season, some with Christmas themes. Television and radio play Christmas music that is both **sacred** and **secular**, or having to do with the material world.

People tend to act differently during the Christmas season. They give more to charities in terms of money, goods, and their most precious commodity—time. They are often more light-hearted and are quick to offer a cheery "Merry Christmas," "Happy Holidays," or "Season's Greetings." The postal system and the Internet are swamped with the exchange of Christmas cards. Whatever your religious affiliation, it is hard not to be caught up in the swirl of excitement that is Christmas. While many children and adults eagerly await Christmas and the rich array of Christmas traditions and practices that are celebrated in so many homes, not all may be knowledgeable about the origins and purely religious meaning of Christmas.

Although it is one of the central Christian celebrations, many faithful Christians worry that the religious significance of Christmas is lost in the non-religious hoopla sweeping society. As well, followers of non-Christian faiths are sometimes troubled by seeing their families and friends get caught up in a celebration that is so central to another religious tradition. They may worry about the future of their own faith, the unity of their families, or the confusion of Christmas messages.

Christmas is a powerful example of a celebration with deep religious roots that over time has adopted a vast array of **symbols**, practices, traditions, and ideas having little to do with Christianity. For example, the exact date of Christ's birth is actually unknown, and December 25 is not the likely date. However, through time, it became the appointed day to celebrate the birth of Christ by most Christians.

The Essential Christmas

The annual tide of Christmas cheer that swamps North America in December can be a difficult experience for a non-Christian. Modern celebrations of Christmas are both spiritual and secular, and participants themselves may often be unaware of which aspect they are celebrating.

Christmas is, in its origins, about the miraculous birth of Jesus Christ, the founder of Christianity. Jesus was born to Mary and Joseph. This poor, young couple witnessed the birth of their son in a lowly stable in the town of Bethlehem, attended by shepherds and three **Magi**, sometimes referred to as "wise men." (These wise men were possibly Zoroastrian priests who had followed a heavenly star to the miraculous event.) Adding to the drama, the tiny baby was being sought by King Herod, who had instructed his agents to slay the child because he feared prophecies that the child would become a king.

Across Canada and around the globe, Christmas is celebrated in ways that have nothing to do with the sacred origins of the tradition. In fact, much of Christmas is a curious mixture of global tradition, popular cul-

Figure 1.7
*Two views of Christmas: the sacred (the **Nativity**) and the secular (Santa Claus). Which one most closely represents your personal view? Explain.*

ture, and sheer commercialism (Figure 1.7). Let's look at the tradition of Santa Claus, as an example.

Although Santa Claus has become a central part of Christmas tradition, particularly for children, this figure has no real connection to the birth of Jesus Christ. Saint Nicholas had origins in Turkey as the patron saint of children. In Holland, he became known as Sinter Cleas. The tradition of hanging stockings by the fire and waking to find them full of gifts and food was brought to North America by Dutch settlers.

In 1822, Clement Moore, an American, wrote the poem "The Night Before Christmas" for his children. This poem, well-known to many North Americans, described the popular image of Santa Claus as we know him today. It was a successful attempt to create an American gift-giver distinct from the British Father Christmas.

Later, the Coca-Cola Company presented a striking image of a chubby, happy fellow dressed in fur and carrying sacks of presents for children around the world. While his sleigh, pulled by eight reindeer, flew across the evening sky bringing joy and gifts to children everywhere, Santa proclaimed, "Happy Christmas to all, and to all a good night!"

The Future of Christmas

The way Christmas is celebrated will likely continue to adapt and change in the years to come. For Christians, the concern is that the important origins of this holy event may be smothered by commercialism and the addition of traditions that are alien, and perhaps hostile (in the rampant commercialism and materialism of Christmas shopping), to the celebration of the original event. In some parts of England, the season is referred to as "Winterval" to render it more open to people of other faiths and traditions. In many schools in Canada, Christmas celebrations have been replaced with interfaith celebrations, sometimes called "Winterfests," featuring songs and traditions from other religious and cultural traditions. As Canada and the world become more multicultural, it is likely that religious traditions will become somewhat blurred and that traditions and customs will increasingly overlap. Author Ellie Tesher, who lives in a **multi-faith** family in Toronto, makes this observation about the holiday season:

*Today, I live, as do countless other people, in this polyglot city of colour and light, in a mixed union with grown children and stepchildren whose friends and relationships cover the map. There'll be a Hanukkah menorah and a Christmas tree inside our home, not to mention a photo of the **Dalai Lama**, pungent incense and Buddhist texts, and still no confusion—because everyone knows who they are and who they come from.*

Check Your Understanding

1. Carefully explain the difference between ethnicity and religion.

2. How has popular culture influenced your view of religion?

3. What examples of multi-faith practices or customs are you aware of? Describe at least one.

Fundamental Freedoms

- *freedom of conscience and religion*

- *freedom of thought, belief, opinion and expression, including freedom of the press and other media of communication*

Equality Rights

- *the right to equal protection without discrimination based on race, national or ethnic origin, colour, religion, sex, age or mental or physical disability.*

RELIGION IN CANADA TODAY

Religion and the State

In Canada, religion and the State are separate institutions. Religion is a personal, not a political, matter or a federal responsibility. Canadians are free to follow and celebrate any religious tradition that they choose. They are also free not to observe any religion. Canadians may be **atheists,** and believe that there is no God, or **agnostics,** by believing that nothing can be known about the existence of God, just as easily as they may be Hindus, Muslims, Christians, Buddhists, Jews, etc. This freedom of religion is specifically entrenched in the Canadian Charter of Rights and Freedoms, as shown in these brief excerpts:

However, freedom of religion and the separation of Church and State are not absolute, nor probably would a majority of Canadians wish it that way. The existence of a god is explicitly recognized in many important national institutions such as the Canadian constitution and the national anthem:

Whereas Canada is founded upon principles that recognize the supremacy of God and the rule of law: . . .

From the Constitution Act, 1982

God keep our land glorious and free!
From "O Canada"

Representatives of different religions are often asked to open or close ceremonies at important events held by the three levels of government—federal, provincial, and municipal.

These ceremonies are becoming increasingly interfaith in character and involve participants from a variety of religious traditions. For example, when representatives of Aboriginal groups attend federal government events, they often present Aboriginal traditions and rituals.

Interestingly, statistics seem to suggest that attendance at religious services is in a serious downward spiral. A Statistics Canada study indicates that regular attendance (at least once a month) by Canadians at religious services declined by almost 10 per cent between 1988 and 1998. The study also revealed that the most regular worshippers were married couples with children, senior citizens, recent immigrants (especially those from Asia), and residents of rural areas.

Many Paths . . . One Direction

By dialogue, we let God be present in our midst. For as we open ourselves to one another, we open ourselves to God.

—Pope John Paul II

Exploring World Religions takes the view that the pursuit of truth is a worthwhile goal and that most people are eager to understand themselves and life's mysteries in greater depth. The authors of this book believe that the rich variety of religious traditions born across the globe and practised in Canada today offer positive experiences, open to all Canadians.

By exploring the different religions in this book, we can examine how each of these faiths defines and arrives at the truth. In discovering the beliefs and practices of world religions in Canada, we can learn more about other Canadians and our country. In fact, it is through dialogue and understanding that we discover ourselves.

We cannot afford to be ignorant of what our next door neighbours (some just an e-mail away) may believe about the nature and destiny of mankind.

—Jordan Pearlson, founding rabbi of Temple Sinai, Toronto

Our Approach

The measure of a religion is its best ideals. We expect others to estimate our religion by its best expression; and in turn, as an elemental courtesy, we should judge others by their best.

—Floyd H. Ross and Tynette Hills, *The Great Religions*

The authors of *Exploring World Religions* see Canada's diversity as a sign of strength and richness. We invite you to share our wonder, curiosity, and respect for different ways of understanding and encountering our world. In this textbook, we search for the best elements in these faiths while being mindful of the difficult history of religious conflict that has coloured too much of the past. Our approach is comparative, not competitive. We seek no hierarchy. We believe that Canada is one country in one world.

The origins of most of the religions that we shall study are far from the borders of Canada and are often shrouded in history. However, *Exploring World Religions* regards these religious traditions as vibrant and alive, and playing an integral part in the daily lives of their followers in Canada. While we are mindful of the origins and roots of these faith traditions, our emphasis is on the current Canadian context and the religious fabric of Canada today.

Figure 1.8
Canada's increasingly multicultural character has prompted one Canadian, Sheena Singh, to create what is perhaps the world's first multicultural calendar. Singh's calendar includes all of the major world religions, including faiths such as Zoroastrianism. It indicates virtually all of the major cultural and religious holidays of the world's peoples. According to Singh, "The calendar opens dialogues between peoples from different backgrounds and encourages them to share what makes them what they are." To learn more about this calendar, visit http://www.multicultural. calendar.com.

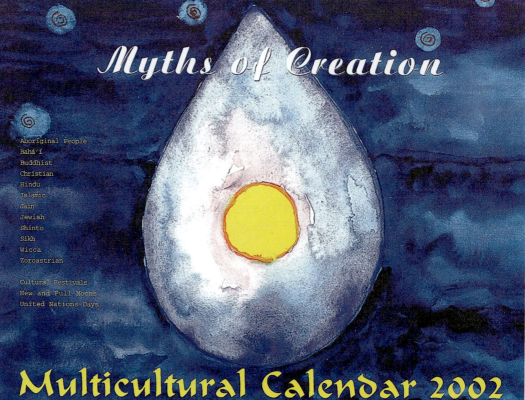

Myths of Creation

Aboriginal People
Bahá'í
Buddhist
Christian
Hindu
Islamic
Jain
Jewish
Shinto
Sikh
Wicca
Zoroastrian

Cultural Festivals
New and Full Moons
United Nations Days

Multicultural Calendar 2002

Check Your Understanding

1. How is religious freedom protected in Canada?

2. How would you account for the fact that married couples, senior citizens, recent immigrants, and rural Canadians are most likely to attend religious services? Comment briefly on each category.

Activities

Check Your Understanding

1. Define and provide examples of the phrase *religious pluralism.*

2. Describe four reasons why people turn to religion. Which of the four, if any, apply to you?

3. Explain why ethnicity may not be a reliable indicator of a person's religion.

Think and Communicate

4. Do you believe in a god or gods? If so, and you were given the chance to speak to this higher power, what would you say?

5. In small groups, discuss what you believe to be the major ethical questions facing Canadians today. On chart paper, list the various answers to these questions. Be prepared to share your findings with the class.

6. Working in pairs, discuss the following: How do you decide what is right and what is wrong? Do you think that you always try to do what is right? Explain.

7. Write a poem that summarizes or expresses what you are searching for in your life.

Apply Your Learning

8. Visit the multicultural calendar Web site http://www.multiculturalcalendar. com, then report on the upcoming religious observances for the week.

9. Review a TV program schedule for the coming week, and circle all the programs with religious themes. Report your discoveries and conclusions to the class.

10. Assume that you have just been appointed principal of a very multicultural school, with representatives of most of the world's religious traditions among the student body. How would you organize the school, e.g., celebrate special events, to reflect the different traditions and values of the students?

11. Find examples of popular songs that deal with religious themes. Write out the lyrics and offer a brief interpretation. For lyrics, you might visit the Web site http://www.lyricsworld.com.

Glossary

agnostic [ag NOSS tik]. A person who doubts that humankind can know the existence of a possible god and the possible existence of anything beyond this life.

atheist [AY thee ist]. One who holds that no god exists.

credo [CREE do]. A philosophy or a set of beliefs.

Dalai Lama [DOLL eye LOMMA]. The ruler and spiritual leader of Tibet. *Dalai* means "great ocean" and *lama* means "teacher."

Devil. The supreme spirit of evil in Jewish and Christian belief.

ethics. A system of morals; rules for human conduct.

evolutionary [ev va LOO sh'n ary]. A person who believes that evolution explains the origin of species.

humanist. An adherent of humanism—an outlook or system of thought that views humankind, rather than spirituality or religion, as the source of all value or meaning.

Magi [MAY jie]. The "Three Wise Men" who attended the birth of Jesus Christ. They may have been Zoroastrian priests.

Makkah [MECCA]. A city in Saudi Arabia. It is the most important Muslim pilgrimage site.

multi-faith. Of many faiths.

Nativity [nuh TIV VA tee]. The birth of Jesus Christ, the founder of Christianity.

Neanderthal [nee ANDER tholl]. An early form of human being who lived in Europe during the Ice Age.

New Age. A broad movement characterized by alternative approaches to traditional Western culture, particularly in relation to spirituality, mysticism, holism, etc.

pagan [PAY g'n]. A person holding religious beliefs other than those of any of the other main religions of the world. In the past, this term was sometimes used by Christians to describe non-Christian faiths.

religious. Devoted to religion.

religious impulse. The universal urge to believe in something beyond ourselves.

religious pluralism. A positive attitude toward the existence of many faiths in one society.

ritual. A prescribed religious procedure or performance.

sacred. Connected with religion.

secular. Concerned with or belonging to the material world.

smudge ceremony. A spiritual cleansing ritual performed by members of Aboriginal religions.

soul. The spiritual or immaterial part of a human being or an animal.

spiritual. Concerned with sacred or religious things and related to the human spirit or soul.

symbol. A mark, character, or object that serves to represent an idea, process, or function.

synagogue [SINNA gog]. A Jewish place of worship.

theology. The study of religion, especially religions with a belief in God.

Torah [TORE uh]. The first five books of the Hebrew Bible.

1990: As the Manitoba Legislature moved to vote on the issue of constitutional reform, the honourable member Elijah Harper sat stoically holding an eagle feather and steadfastly refused to give the Manitoba Legislature the vote it needed.

In March 1997, Melissa Labrador, a Mi'kmaq girl from Nova Scotia, was removed from the House of Commons because she carried an eagle feather. The security guard who escorted her from the House thought the feather might be a weapon.

Chapter Two

Aboriginal Spirituality

2

Examine the photos and captions on the opposite page and read the introductory text below. Answer the following questions:

1. What evidence is there that the eagle feather is considered important by Aboriginal peoples?
2. Describe the symbolism of the eagle feather. Identify a symbol that you use in your life to represent connections to other things. Why did you choose this symbol?
3. Write a headline that captures what happened to Melissa Labrador, the Mi'kmaq girl from Nova Scotia, when she visited the House of Commons in Ottawa.

Introduction

The eagle feather, a symbol of strength, gives the holder the power to represent others. It is often presented as recognition to someone who defends, fights for, or negotiates on behalf of **Aboriginal** peoples or people of native ancestry.

Some believe that because the eagle flies closest to the Creator, it can see over all the land. When the eagle is flying overhead, it means that Mother Earth will prosper. Some Aboriginal peoples believe that the Creator loves the eagle the most because it symbolizes the duality, or contradictions, of life—man and woman, light and darkness, summer and winter. Even its feathers are divided in two parts—light and dark—reminding humans of the duality of life. Some **elders**, or respected members of the community, describe the eagle feather as a symbol of healthy relationships. The spine of the feather holds relationships together. It is widest at the bottom symbolizing a relationship's beginning, a time when learning is greatest.

Learning Goals

- understand the differing views on the origins of Aboriginal peoples
- compare and contrast beliefs, practices, and rituals among Canada's Aboriginal cultural groups
- identify influential figures in the development of Aboriginal spirituality and explain their contributions
- identify key passages from The Great Law and the Code of Handsome Lake, and explain their meaning
- understand the role and influence of Indigenous oral teachings on Aboriginal spirituality
- identify and interpret important oral stories in Aboriginal spirituality
- examine the role and significance of symbols in Aboriginal spirituality
- understand and interpret the meaning of the supernatural in Aboriginal spirituality
- identify the origin and importance of Aboriginal practices, rituals, and festivals
- demonstrate an understanding of meditation, prayer, and fasting in Aboriginal spirituality
- examine the impact of key events in the development of Aboriginal spirituality
- interpret Aboriginal works of art
- use primary documents effectively
- communicate effectively through oral presentations

1800 CE The code of Handsome Lake is developed

1815 CE Handsome Lake dies, Aug. 10

1000 CE The first recorded meeting between Europeans (Norse) and Aboriginal peoples in Newfoundland

1830s CE Creation of residential school system

35 000– 15 000 BCE Scientists theorize that people migrated from Asia to North America over the Bering land bridge

1784 CE Under the leadership of Joseph Brant, Mohawks settle on the Grand River after being displaced following the American Revolution

- Many Aboriginal peoples contend that they have always inhabited North America and offer a range of creation stories

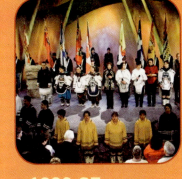

Woodland Cultural Centre

•**1999 CE** The new territory of Nunavut is created

•**1996 CE** National Aboriginal Day is instituted on June 21

•**1998 CE** Canadian government expresses profound regret to Canada's Aboriginal peoples for past mistreatment and issues Statement of Reconciliation

•**1970 CE** A residential school is turned into the Woodland Cultural Centre in Brantford, Ontario

•**1990 CE** Elijah Harper stops Meech Lake Accord process

•**1990 CE** The Oka Crisis explodes when plans for a golf course clash with Aboriginal sacred burial grounds

•**1884 CE** Potlatch ceremonies are banned by the federal government

•**1876 CE** Indian Act is passed

Timeline

Aboriginal Spirituality

ORIGINS

It is impossible to pinpoint an origin or a founder of Aboriginal spirituality. Occasionally, a significant person rises to the forefront during a crisis and renews the faith, but there is no single founder.

Figure 2.1

This wampum of parallel purple and white shells is made from Atlantic seashells. Used by many different Aboriginal nations, it has been used to record history and sacred agreements dating back 400 years.

Figure 2.2

Pictographs on rock outcrops depict Aboriginal beliefs and practices.

Aboriginal spirituality around the world has a long history. Some **Indigenous** peoples, or Aboriginal inhabitants of a region, believe that they "came out of this ground," a theory that essentially means their origins are ancient beyond record. While there exists considerable disagreement on origin, some archaeological evidence supports a second theory that Aboriginal peoples migrated from Asia to North and South America by crossing a land bridge over the Bering Strait (situated between Alaska and Russia) approximately 35 000 years ago.

Regardless of theory, Aboriginal peoples have clearly been in the Americas longer than anyone else. Archaeologists, who study human history, have found Aboriginal artifacts dating back beyond 10 000 years. They have discovered **wampum**, or beaded belts (Figure 2.1), animal paintings on rock outcrops (Figure 2.2), bones representing different burial rites, and wooden carvings all attesting to Aboriginal spiritual practices and beliefs from centuries ago. Aboriginal traditional stories about **genesis**, or origins, carry a great deal of spiritual power. These creation stories are important vehicles for conveying Aboriginal beliefs.

Aboriginal Spirituality Around the World

Although we will be focusing in this chapter on North America, specifically Canada, it is important to note that there exists a huge diversity of Aboriginal spirituality throughout the modern world. Indigenous peoples live in virtually every area of the globe. Some are well known, such as the Aboriginal groups of Australia, the Maori of New Zealand, or the Guarani of Paraguay, who were featured in the film *The Mission*. Although some groups are now extinct, such as the Beothuks of Atlantic Canada, or the Caribs of the Caribbean Islands, millions in the world still claim Indigenous status, even though they do not necessarily practise their Indigenous religion. Today, 80 per cent of the world's approximately 300 million Aboriginal peoples live in Asia, while 13 per cent live in North and South America (Figure 2.3).

Anthropologists, who study societies and customs, estimate that at the time of Columbus about 100 million Indigenous peoples inhabited the Americas, which in 1500 CE would have accounted for one-fifth of the human race. Some lived in huge cities (present-day Mexico City had 250 000), and others were farmers, or nomadic hunters. To this day, twelve million still speak Quechua, the language of the Incas of South America. In Central America, there are six million who speak the ancestral language of the Maya, comparable to the number of French speakers in Canada. Currently, over 800 000 Aboriginal people live in Canada, some in every province.

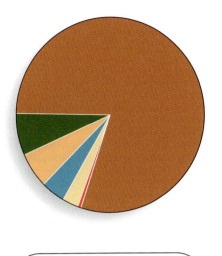

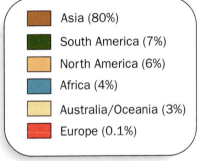

Asia (80%)
South America (7%)
North America (6%)
Africa (4%)
Australia/Oceania (3%)
Europe (0.1%)

Figure 2.3
World Distribution of Indigenous Peoples. China, India, Mexico, Peru, Pakistan, and the Philippines all have Indigenous populations over five million.

Not all, but many Aboriginal peoples around the world still believe in and practise aspects of their traditional religions. Aboriginal people of the Canadian Arctic, who in their language call themselves Inuit, share a cultural identity with two other large populations in Alaska and Greenland. Although most of the over 100 000 Inuit in these three jurisdictions practise Christianity, a growing number are returning to their religious and cultural heritage. For example, the drumming and chanting with ancient prayers that once accompanied official occasions experienced a comeback in the recent celebrations surrounding the proclamation of Nunavut, Canada's new territory.

Whether Aboriginal peoples migrated from Asia to the Americas and developed as **First Nations,** or were here from the earliest of times, the fact remains that they developed into several large cultural groups in North America. The geographical environment in which they lived defined them. Canada has at least six distinct cultural groups of Aboriginal peoples:

- Northeast Woodlands
- Great Plains
- Northwest Pacific Coast
- Plateau
- Subarctic
- Arctic

Each culture has several nations in it. As a group they have similar aspects of belief, although different practices of form represent those beliefs. For example, each culture has familial clans represented by animals who protect them, such as the Raven or Wolf, but the animals vary and have different regional significance. Furthermore, a cultural group may share common characteristics that identify it with a specific environment, but there is often great diversity among nations within that large cultural environment. The Northeast Woodlands, for example, is divided into two linguistic groups, Algonquin and Iroquois. The Algonquin and Iroquois nations differ according to their religious beliefs and practices.

Figure 2.4
Aboriginal Cultural Groups in Canada

The Subarctic

The Subarctic region runs the breadth of Canada and includes the thick forests and mountains in the East, the Canadian Shield of rock and swamp, and the sparsely-wooded northern Prairies with their many lakes and rivers. The Innu, the Montaignais, the James Bay Cree, and the Dene were nomadic hunters of deer and caribou.

In the 1990s, Cree Grand Chief Matthew Coon Come was instrumental in persuading Quebec to cancel plans for James Bay Project 2 after he witnessed the harmful environmental effects of Quebec's James Bay Project 1. Coon Come is currently the National Chief of the Assembly of First Nations.

The Plateau

The Aboriginal peoples of the Plateau live in the foothills of the Rocky Mountains, separate from the Plains and Pacific Coast nations. The Kootenay mountain chain takes its name from one of the many Plateau nations. The Plateau were once nomadic hunters of elk, bear, and caribou.

In 1995, at Gustafsen Lake in British Columbia, several campers used ranch land for a sun dance ceremony. When the owner asked the campers to leave, they refused, saying the land was unceded, no treaty had been signed, and it was a sacred site. After a four-month period, the standoff ended with a negotiated settlement led by an Alberta medicine man.

The Northwest Pacific Coast

For generations, Haida, Tlingit, and Salish nations depended on the sea and lived in cedar plank houses on the beaches. They harpooned whale and trapped salmon. They used the cedar to make houses, baskets, and dugout canoes that could carry up to seventy people.

The Northwest Pacific Coast culture carved several **totems** in one long pole, commonly known as a **totem pole**. A totem is a protective entity, often in the form of an animal, that is associated with a cultural group or nation. Today, magnificent examples of totem artwork can be seen in parks and museums throughout British Columbia.

In 1998, the Nisga'a, a First Nation living in northwestern British Columbia, signed an historic agreement with the British Columbia and federal governments. The Nisga'a Treaty was the first land claims treaty in British Columbia since 1871. It granted land, a financial settlement, and a model for self-government to the Nisga'a nation.

Cultural Areas

- ARCTIC
- SUBARCTIC
- NORTHWEST PACIFIC COAST
- PLATEAU
- GREAT PLAINS
- NORTHEAST WOODLANDS

The Arctic

The Inuit, which means "the people," live in a region above the treeline that is snow covered for eight months of the year. For generations, nations, including the Mackenzie, Labrador, and Caribou, hunted and depended on the seal. Seal skin provided boots, bags, kayaks, igloo linings, and clothing. Seal oil was used for heating, cooking, and light.

Today, many people in these groups live in a modern world, connected globally through technology and educated in schools. Some Inuit refer to their traditional ways using the past tense.

The Great Plains

There are seven distinct languages and over thirty nations of the Great Plains including the Sioux, the Cree, and the Siksika, or Blackfoot. In the past, these people generally depended on the buffalo. In fact, when the buffalo numbered in the millions, they were used for almost everything. The hide provided coverings for moccasin soles, for shields, and for their homes, which were cone-shaped tents called **tipis**. The buffalo ribs became sled runners. The skull was used for the Sun Dance altar—a ceremony that involves chants and purification, which is still practised today.

Northeast Woodlands

The Iroquois live along the St. Lawrence River and the Great Lakes, and were once farmer-hunters. They lived in **longhouses** in villages of approximately 1500 people and farmed corn, squash, and beans, which they named "the Three Sisters." A typical Iroquois longhouse was cigar-shaped, about fifty metres long and ten metres wide, and would hold several related families.

The Iroquois formed a confederacy of Six Nations, including the Cayuga, Mohawk, Oneida, Onondaga, Seneca, and Tuscarora nations. Displaced after the American Revolution, the Six Nations, under the leadership of Joseph Brant, relocated to a reserve southwest of Brantford, Ontario. Other well-known reserves are at Kanesatake, near Oka, northwest of Montreal, and Akwesasne, near Cornwall, Ontario.

Today, the Iroquois practise the **Longhouse** religion in a building that replicates a traditional longhouse. **Faithkeepers** are community members selected to maintain the spiritual traditions of the Iroquois.

The Algonquin of this region were nomadic hunters who depended on the forests, rivers, and sea for their livelihood. The forests, in particular, played an important role in their survival. They used the needles of the white pine to make a tea that prevented scurvy and relieved colds. They made another tea from dandelion roots and leaves to treat heartburn.

Animals were an important resource for the maintenance of physical and spiritual needs. In many communities, clans (family groupings) were defined by the attributes of their associated animal.

The Algonquin nations include the Beothuk who are now extinct, Mi'kmaq, Ottawa, Cree, and Ojibwa. Collectively, there were no identifiable spiritual movements. Instead, some nations such as the Ojibwa were spiritually united with the Grand Medicine Society (Midewinin). Spiritualism within Algonquin communities was deeply personal and was defined by the individual community.

Today, the connection to their natural environment continues to be a source of their spiritualism.

Profile: The Peacemaker

The nations of each North American cultural group have their own interpretation of how to live their lives. For some, the Creator gives directions for a better way of life. The Iroquois of the Northeast Woodlands tell the story of the Peacemaker, a central figure to their culture and religion. Members of the Iroquois nation believe one should never say the Peacemaker's name, Dekanawida, until the end of the world when his name will be called.

The Peacemaker was born of a virgin Huron maiden. His grandmother was ashamed because there appeared to be no father, so she ordered her daughter to drown the baby in icy water. The girl could not. When the grandmother herself tried to kill him without success, she realized he was special and would grow to be a great man. The Huron people abused the young boy. They beat him, kept him in isolation, and ridiculed him. As foretold in a dream, he went to live with another Iroquois nation, the Mohawk.

The Iroquois nations were constantly feuding, and the evil wizard, Tadodaho, seemed to be the instigator of the lawlessness. The Peacemaker chanted songs of peace before the lodge of the crooked, snake-haired sorcerer. The moment the Peacemaker was able to touch Tadodaho, the wizard's body became straight and his mind healthy. With evil overcome, the Peacemaker gathered the Five Nations and planted the Tree of Peace in the Onondaga nation. He said its roots would go north, south, east, and west. At the top he placed an eagle that would see afar and warn the nations of danger. *He then delivered to them a message called "The Great Law of Peace," and the warring nations were reconciled. The message included one hundred laws governing funerals, clans, adoption, and emigration, among other things. One law said that the rites and festivals of each nation shall remain undisturbed "...for they were given by the people of old times as useful and necessary for the good of men."*

The Peacemaker's message can be broken down into three main parts. He said to the woman, Jigonsaseh, or New Face, who was the first to accept what he proclaimed, "The message has three parts: Righteousness, Health, and Power. Righteousness means justice, Health means soundness of mind and body, and Power means the authority of law and custom, and religion, for justice enforced is the will of the Holder of the Heavens."

Questions

1. What contributions did the Peacemaker make to the Five Nations?

2. Describe how the message of "righteousness, health, and power" is a good rule by which to live one's life.

3. Is the story of the Peacemaker similar to other stories you have been told? Explain.

Check Your Understanding

1. Explain the disagreement concerning the origins of Aboriginal peoples.

2. Describe the six cultural groups in Canada and their connection to their environment.

3. List three things you learned about the traditional culture of Aboriginal peoples. Choose the one that impressed you the most and explain why.

BELIEFS

Animism

Many adherents of Aboriginal spirituality believe that everything in the world is alive. All living things reside in close connection and harmony with one another, and move in cycles (Figure 2.5). Even in afterlife, their spirits return to the environment. Aboriginal peoples recognize the powers around them: in the heavens, in human ghosts and spirits, in animals and plants, and in the weather.

Aboriginal spirituality expresses a belief in **animism**, which holds that all things, human and non-human, have spirits or souls, and that the person or animal lives on after death through the presence of that spirit.

Some observers have claimed that Aboriginal spirituality is **polytheistic**, believing in many gods, rather than **monotheistic**, believing in one. Most Aboriginal peoples believe in a supreme Creator. However, power in the universe is also given to other per-sonified spirits who are less powerful than the Creator, but also guide human activity. The Inuit call the sea "Sea Woman"; the Iroquois call the sky "Sky Woman"; and the Algonquin call the sky "Grandfather."

Aboriginal spirituality turns to many spirits because Aboriginal people believe they have more than one specific need in nature or in life. For example, a fisher strives to be on good terms with the spirit of the sea; a farmer wishes to please the spirit of the rain or the sun. A faith in supernatural and natural forces that connect human beings to all other living things permeates the life of almost all Aboriginal societies.

Black Elk, born in 1863, was a Sioux holy man from the Great Plains (Figure 2.6). He said, "We know that we all are related and are one with all things of the heavens and the earth...May we be continually aware of this relationship which exists between the four-leggeds, the two-leggeds, and the wingeds..."

Figure 2.5
Thunder Bay Art Gallery houses a collection of Aboriginal art as well as creations like masks, baskets, and other natural artifacts. Relationship to Nature, this painting by Ojibwa artist Roy Thomas, shows the interconnection of humans to the environment. Note that it overlays several animals in an "x-ray" style around a human figure. Can you identify the birds, fish, bear, beaver, and tipis? Explain animism in the painting.

Figure 2.6
Black Elk, spiritual elder of the Sioux, 1863–1950

Figure 2.7
Birth of the Earth by Arnold Jacobs, an Onondaga artist. In this painting, a woman falls from the sky and creates the earth, with the assistance of the animals. It depicts the Aboriginal belief that humans and nature are connected.

Creation Stories

Creation stories, which were often oral, play an important role in Aboriginal cultures by offering a response to questions of existence, such as where we come from, why certain things in the environment are the way they are, and where we go when we die.

Each cultural group has their own identity and creation stories. Some believe that they were born from a clam and were helped by the Raven or some other animal. Many recount a legend of a person falling from the sky (Figure 2.7).

The Northeast Woodlands

One Aboriginal creation story is "Turtle Island" (Figure 2.8). The people of the Northeast Woodlands believe that after a great flood, water covered the Earth. Several water animals and birds tried to bring some mud to the surface of the water. Eventually, a muskrat succeeded. Sky Woman then spread the mud on the back of a turtle and created North America, or Turtle Island.

The Northwest Pacific Coast

A renowned Haida artist, Bill Reid, depicted his culture's creation story of the Raven coaxing the original people out of a clamshell onto the land (Figure 2.9). The famous carving is at the Museum of Anthropology at the University of British Columbia.

Death and the Afterlife

A basic element of most religions is the belief in the afterlife. Many Aboriginal legends recount stories of **reincarnation**, or rebirth. The Sioux of the Great Plains believe that four souls depart from a person at death. One of them journeys along the "spirit path," and it is judged by an old woman. She determines whether the spirit should carry on to reconnect with its ancestors or return to Earth as a ghost. The other souls enter fetuses and are reborn into new bodies. In the Northeast Woodlands, the Iroquois believe that souls or spirits can enter man-made objects like fishing nets or spears. Other groups believe the souls inhabit the many stars of the Milky Way.

The Arctic

The Inuit pay homage to the souls of killed animals by facing the animal in the direction from which it came so that its soul can return. Upon killing a seal they give it a drink of water so that its spirit can re-enter the sea. During an annual festival, the Inuit collect all the seal bladders caught the previous year and throw them back to the sea, so that the seals can reproduce.

Totems

Totems link Aboriginal peoples to their mythical ancestors. Totems are protective entities—plant, animal, or mythological being—of a clan or individual. The Ojibwa identify each totem group by the name of a bird, fish, animal, or reptile. Persons of the same totem are considered to be close relatives and may not marry.

Figure 2.8
Turtle Island *by Stanley R. Hill, a Mohawk artist. This wooden sculpture depicts the creation of the world and features the sacred Tree of Peace. Notice the eagle, representing strength and power, is at the top of the tree.*

Figure 2.9
The Raven and the First Men *by Bill Reid*

Figure 2.10
Peace Doe-dem (totem) *by Blake Debassige. The Anishnawbek have different totems to which families belong. One of these is the seagull, which is the symbol of peace.*

Check Your Understanding

1. Explain animism in the following sentence: "Some believed they should walk on soft shoes or no shoes at all during the spring because Mother Earth is pregnant and they must not harm her body."

2. Recount one story about creation or the afterlife that reflects the Aboriginal view of boundaries easily crossed between the human and supernatural worlds.

3. Although there is tremendous variety among Aboriginal cultures, describe three common beliefs in their religions.

4. Explain the importance of totems in Aboriginal spirituality.

Figure 2.11
Powwows, Algonquin for cultural gatherings, are currently experiencing a revival. Attendees eat food of Sioux, Iroquois, or Haida origin. They witness traditional dancing, drumming, and chanting, all integral parts of many Aboriginal practices and rituals.

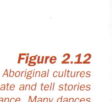

Figure 2.12
Aboriginal cultures communicate and tell stories through dance. Many dances interpret events or customs from the past. Today, Aboriginal peoples use dance to rediscover their past, and share with the world their knowledge and their culture.

PRACTICES, RITUALS, SYMBOLS, AND FESTIVALS

Practices and Rituals

Today, Aboriginal peoples are keeping their spiritualism alive by participating in traditional festivals and by depicting their beliefs through their art and symbols. The willingness to relearn the ancestral beliefs and practices illustrates the strength and pride Aboriginal peoples gain from their cultural revival.

Some religious practices, although regional, over time have become common to all Aboriginal peoples. Many of the rituals of the Great Plains people have crossed cultural boundaries and been adopted into Aboriginal spirituality. These practices provide a means by which all cultural groups can demonstrate their connectedness in spiritual ways.

The Morning Dance

Every spring, the Ojibwa of southern Ontario perform the Morning Dance, also known as the Wabeno. The dance pays homage to the "tree of the universe." All the participants fast and cleanse themselves beforehand, then a male elder plays a drum and leads the dance in a clearing around the selected tree. Children, adults, and the elderly dance from dawn to noon. As each dancer passes the tree, the drummer signals the dancer to touch the trunk to give thanks. At midday, a huge feast of meat and fish is served.

The Sun Dance

The Great Plains nations hold an important summer festival that takes place over a period of eight to sixteen days and includes the Sun Dance (Figure 2.13). This festival of the Great Plains is so powerful, and the dance so symbolic a ritual, that the Canadian government banned it in the late 1880s.

The ceremony identifies the circle as an important symbol, and acknowledges and respects the sun as the giver of life. Performed in early summer, the participants dance for long periods around a central cottonwood pole, or "tree of the universe." They face the sun and pay homage to the sun's life-giving powers. During the ceremony some of the dancers embed sharp wooden hooks deep into their chest, then connect the skewers to leather thongs that trail from the top of the cottonwood pole. As they dance, they pull back on the thongs and tear their flesh. The resulting scars bear witness to their faith. The dancers perform this ritual because they believe that the body is the only thing they control and can offer as a sacrifice to the Creator. They believe that by enduring pain, others will not have to suffer famine, war, or disease. During the Sun Dance, prayers are said for all peoples and vows are made to the Great Spirit.

This celebration of renewal and reconnection with all creation, including the piercing dance, once again is practised today.

Figure 2.13
Sun Dance on the Reserve by Allen Sapp

The Potlatch Ceremony

The Northwest Pacific Coast nations practise the Potlatch ceremony (Figure 2.14), which the Canadian government made illegal in 1884. Government officials thought that the Potlatch contributed to idleness and seemed "backward" and wasteful. The government lifted the ban in 1951.

Feasting, distributing wealth, and sharing songs and dances are all part of a Potlatch. The host gives a feast to celebrate an important event, such as a marriage, the naming of an heir, or to atone for a humiliation. The more wealth the host gives away, the more that person gains in status and greatness. Thus, the hosting clan grows in prestige. Songs and dances are performed to honour the Great Spirit.

Many of the early Potlatch traditions, including dancing and singing, continue today.

Figure 2.14
The potlatch ceremony, an important spiritual practice among Aboriginal peoples, was banned in 1884. The Canadian government lifted the ban in 1951.

The Sweat Lodge

The sweat lodge ceremony, common among the Great Plains nations renews the soul and helps to regain focus. The sweat lodge cleanses both the physical and spiritual body. Under the direction of a **shaman**, who is both a medicine man and spiritual leader, the participants make a sauna-like construction, called a sweat lodge. The sweat lodge is a dome made of saplings. A covering of animal skins, cedar, or a tarpaulin make it dark and airtight. Heated stones are placed in the centre of the interior, and water is sprinkled on the stones. The participants crouch and crowd around the stones in the confined space. The intense heat and steam cause them to perspire profusely, thus cleansing the body both physically and spiritually. Usually prayers and a sacred pipe are shared. An elder or a shaman assists by coordinating the ceremony.

The Shaking Tent

The shaking tent a ritual used by Aboriginal groups fron the subarctic to the Great Lakes region, represents the beliefs and values of some Aboriginal people about the supernatural world and its close relationship to the living. Through the shaking tent, one can communicate with the spirits. It is constructed using four to eight poles, which are placed deep in the soil to form a circle about a meter in diameter. A wooden hoop encircles the poles at the top and sometimes at the bottom. The cylindrical shape, left open to the sky to allow the spirits to enter, is wrapped in birch bark or hide. The individuals who have requested the ceremony make a trade with the shaman. He enters the tent and intercedes with the spirits. He asks the spirits to solve problems such as finding a lost object, communicating with an ancestor, locating a missing person, or predicting the outcome of an event. The ceremony always takes place at night.

Symbols and Icons
The Tree of Peace

A central symbol for some Aboriginal religions is the tree, connecting Earth to Heaven. It is integral to some practices like the Sun Dance. The dance centres around a cottonwood pole to which the dancers attach themselves with leather thongs.

The white pine is a key symbol for the Iroquois. The hero, Peacemaker, said that whenever the Iroquois gathered by the Great Tree, they "...shall offer thanks to the earth...to the streams of waters...to the maize and the fruits, to the medicinal herbs and trees, to the animals that serve as food and give their pelts for clothing...to the messengers of the Creator who reveal his wishes and to the Great Creator...ruler of health and life."

For West Coast groups, the cedar tree is an important carrier of symbols since it is used in the creation of totem poles.

QUESTIONS

1. The tree is a common global symbol. Academics call this the *axis mundi*, or core of the world. Describe the attributes of the tree that make it an appropriate global symbol.
2. How does the tree reflect the central beliefs of some Aboriginal peoples?
3. Describe the role of the tree in any other religions of which you are aware.

Figure 2.15

Festivals

Figure 2.16

The Northeast Woodlands Iroquois have a series of Ceremonies connected to the agricultural cycle: The Midwinter Ceremony held in January; The Maple Syrup and Seed Planting Rituals held in April; The Strawberry, Bean, and Green Corn Celebrations held in summer; and The Thanksgiving or Harvest Festival held one day in November.

Pictured here are flint corn and squash, foods associated with The Thanksgiving Festival. Iroquois regard the harvest and food as gifts from the Creator.

Profile: *faithkeepers*

Figure 2.17
Dorothy Green

"The Creator is watching and listening and the people are looking to you for help and guidance."

Traditionally, the Iroquois women have had great power in society. They lived in a matrilineal society where the mother had control. The matriarch's extended family lived in the longhouse, and she nominated **sachems**, or clan chiefs. Other clan mothers, or mothers of the same family group, would confirm the sachem's appointment.

Today the Longhouse clan mothers still appoint faithkeepers—three men and three women—to assist with their ceremonies. The faithkeeper preserves and passes on the spiritual belief system by conducting the ritual ceremonies. Usually one man and one woman are chosen for their leadership and their public-speaking ability. A chosen faithkeeper of a Longhouse must accept the appointment.

Dorothy Green is the oldest member of the Onondaga Longhouse and served as a Cayuga faithkeeper for many years. She is also a member of the Turtle clan. As a faithkeeper, she attended all the ceremonies, singing the songs and dancing the dances, until arthritis stopped her. She keeps busy today making moccasins, jackets, and leggings. She is called Kiduwitu, which means "Walking in Gardens."

Question
1. Describe three ways in which Dorothy Green helps to keep her religion meaningful for the people.

Check Your Understanding

1. Explain the procedure and the significance of the Sun Dance and the Morning Dance.

2. What are some "cyclical" festivals that you share with the Iroquois? Compare and contrast one festival.

MILESTONES

The Vision Quest

The rite of passage to adulthood, often ritualized in a coming-of-age ceremony, includes the **vision quest**, or dream. The vision quest is a ceremony common to most Aboriginal religions.

The seeker of the vision quest is first purified, which involves a confession, or at least a desire to atone. This usually occurs at a sweat lodge (Figure 2.18). The medicine man then instructs the youth to go to a place far from the camp. The youth prays, fasts from food and water, and endures the elements for several days while awaiting a "vision." At the end of a period of fasting and prayer, the seeker of the vision hopes to receive a message from a guardian spirit, who may appear in an animal, object, or other natural form. However, the person might not see the vision, and would have to try again. Often the shaman helps to interpret the vision and its message.

Figure 2.18
An Aboriginal youth participates in a sweat lodge ceremony.

John Fire Lame Deer (1903–1976), a Sioux holy man, described the vision quest he had as a young man. The dream solidified the beliefs and values of his religion, as well as confirmed for him the balance and harmony between Heaven and Earth.

The old man left me on the top of the hill. He had been with me in the sweat lodge and prayed, "Oh holy rocks, we receive your white breath, the steam. It is the breath of life. Let this young boy inhale it. Make him strong." I was still lightheaded from the purifying sweat bath and my skin tingled. It seemed to make my head empty but maybe that was good...plenty of room for the vision. Sounds came through the night but suddenly I became aware of a huge bird flying around me. I could hear its cries and feel its feathers. All at once I was up in the sky with the bird. I heard a voice say, "We are the fowl people, the winged ones, the eagles and the owls. You shall be our brother. You are going to understand us whenever you come to this hill to seek a vision. You will learn about herbs and roots and heal people. A man's life is short. Make yours a worthy one."

I felt that the voices were good and I was no longer afraid. I lost all sense of time. Then I saw a person coming out of the darkness and swirling fog. It was my great-grandfather who had been shot by a white soldier. I saw the blood dripping from his chest. Then I understood that he wanted me to take his name, Lame Deer, and it made me extremely happy. I felt my soul within me, and a power surge through me like a flood. I knew then that I would become a medicine man and I wept with happiness.

Finally the old man was gently shaking me. He said I had been on the hill for four days and nights. He gave me water and food and I told him what I heard and saw. He told me I was no longer a boy but that I had become a man. Now I was Lame Deer.

Check Your Understanding

1. What is the role of purification in preparing for a vision quest?

2. Why is it important to have an elder or shaman involved in a vision quest?

3. Who would you select to accompany you if you participated in a vision quest?

SACRED WRITINGS

Oral Teachings

In Aboriginal cultures, prayers are passed to new generations by the telling and retelling of events. Members, such as elders or shamans, memorize the stories and become the keepers who pass on the words. They communicate their stories and lessons by speaking fluently, listening, and understanding, an ability known as **oracy**. Sometimes the speaker uses an aid, like a necklace of beads or wampum, or even a totem pole, to help retell the event.

An effort was made in the early part of the twentieth century to record the Aboriginal oral stories. Handsome Lake, an Iroquois prophet, told six members of his nation about his "Good Message," or Gaiwiio. The six holders memorized what Handsome Lake had taught them and twice a year would recite the message to their people. It took three days to recite all of the Gaiwiio. In 1912, A.C. Parker, an archaeologist, listened to a holder and transmitted the words to text.

Handsome Lake (1735–1815)

The life of an Iroquois holy man of the Seneca nation, Handsome Lake, coincided with the decline of Iroquoian power after the American Revolution. He had been a warrior in the Turtle clan but, after losing his homeland in New York in 1783, he suffered from several debilitating illnesses and became an alcoholic. In 1799, he swore off alcohol and returned to his sick bed. In June of that year, a remorseful Handsome Lake experienced death and was revived. Upon recovery, he explained that he had seen visions and had received a Good Message, called the Gaiwiio. It resulted in a reforming movement, with a renewed moral code designed to reverse the social decline of the remaining Iroquois, who had dwindled to approximately 4000.

Handsome Lake reported seeing four heavenly messengers from the Creator who said: "...four words tell a great story of wrong, and the Creator is sad because of the trouble they bring, so go and tell your people." The four words were alcohol, witchcraft, black magic, and abortion. Other evils he attacked were adultery, child and wife abuse, and desertion.

Sacred Text

The Code of Handsome Lake

Handsome Lake's teachings were recorded forty years after his death by his brother Cornplanter, who in 1905 told them to a nephew, A.C. Parker.

The Good Message has two main themes. The first part contains a prophecy of impending disaster if people do not mend their ways. The second part states that only those who do not repent and change will suffer and perish and go to the House of the Punisher, who is the brother of the Creator. There are over 130 "messages."

The first word is one'ga (whiskey). It seems that you never have known that this word stands for a great and monstrous evil and has reared a high mound of bones. Alas many are too fond of it. So now all must now say, "I will use it never-more. I now stop." So must all say when they hear the message.

Section 1, The Code of Handsome Lake

The Creator has ordered that man and wife should rear their children well, love them and keep them in health. This is the Creator's rule.

Section 7, The Code of Handsome Lake

Now another message to tell your people. The married often live well together for a while. Then a man becomes ugly in temper and abuses his wife. It seems to afford him pleasure. Now because of such things the Creator is very sad. So he bids us to tell you that such evils must stop. Neither man nor woman must strike each other.

Section 10, The Code of Handsome Lake

QUESTIONS

1. What message could you follow according to the Code of Handsome Lake, and where would you find difficulty? Explain your answer to a peer.

2. Do you think a code of ethics is good for all time or should it be revised to change with the times?

3. If you had to select four words that would be basic to your personal code of ethics, what would they be?

Sour Springs Longhouse

Sour Springs, situated on the Six Nations Reserve, near Brantford, Ontario, received its name because of the sulphurous taste in the water. The old squared-log construction has been a ceremonial centre since 1855. The followers practise the teachings of Handsome Lake, and their ceremonies are conducted according to his influence.

The concept of "duality" guides the strict organization of the Longhouse and represents a symbolic view of the universe. There are two main clan groupings: the Turtle and the Wolf. Those within a clan are brothers and sisters, and those of the other clan are called cousins. When entering the longhouse, the members of the Wolf clan go in through the west door, and the members of the Turtle clan enter by the east. Seating changes according to the ceremony and depending on the longhouse. In one setting, the women sit on one side opposite their clan men. Each side, or clan, then participates in the longhouse ceremony. For instance, a speaker of one clan may open the proceedings and a speaker of the other clan may close, thus both contribute to the community of the longhouse.

QUESTIONS

1. Explain the meaning of duality in the universe. How does the longhouse represent the concept of duality?
2. Describe how the ceremonies of Sour Springs Longhouse reflect the concept of community.

Figure 2.19

Check Your Understanding

1. What are the four words from the messengers? Select one and explain how Handsome Lake addresses it in his Code.

2. Describe the development of the Code of Handsome Lake.

3. Explain the term "oracy."

4. How can a wampum or totem pole aid a speaker in retelling an event?

GROUPS AND INSTITUTIONS

Elders

"Knowledge was inherent in all things. The world was a library and its books were the stones, leaves, grass, brooks..."

Luther Standing Bear

Figure 2.20
Today in Aboriginal communities, elders are helping young people connect with their heritage.

An elder is a man or woman who is recognized by his or her community to be a wise person, full of knowledge and experience (Figure 2.20). Elders pass on practical, daily knowledge, and are also the keepers of tradition. They tell the stories of their religion, and act as spiritual guides. For example, an elder might teach animism by telling a young child not to kick an animal, even if it is dead, because it is food and must be given respect. They might instruct young people about natural herbs and medicines. Elders are important touchstones to the past. They impart knowledge and skills for the present and future, and are highly valued in their communities.

Elders Today

In Aboriginal communities, the role of the elder is experiencing a cultural rebirth. To meet the challenge of the future, many Aboriginal people are looking back to their past and to the leadership, wisdom, and knowledge of elders. The following demonstrates the heightened interest in elders:

- Traditional Knowledge, the knowledge of the elders, is now taught at many Aboriginal schools and consulted by governments in Nunavut and the Northwest Territories when politicians make important decisions;

- In many communities, elders act as counsellors and teachers to Aboriginal youths coping with the challenges of contemporary society. In Toronto, councils of elders serve as courts for small-time offenders. These councils are concerned with healing, not just punishment;
- The Assembly of First Nations, a powerful political organization of Aboriginal peoples in Canada, is advised and guided by a council of elders;
- Many Canadians, both Aboriginal and non-Aboriginal, engage in the preservation of teachings of Aboriginal elders. They are busily taping, filming and recording elders' stories and advice.

The False Face Society

The False Face Society is a respected Iroquois group whose members are knowledgeable in the natural powers of herbs, and who perform ritual prayers. They are named "False Faces" because the members wear quizzical and grimacing masks that have been carved from living trees. The masks represent powerful beings that live in the forest. Many of the masks have bent noses, which reflect a legend in which the Creator causes the Great False Face to break his nose after a contest.

The man-like being, Hadui, challenged the Creator to see who could move a mountain. Hadui did move it a little. Then it was the Creator's turn. Hadui heard rumbling behind him and when he turned, he hit his face into the mountain, thus breaking his nose. The Creator had more power and moved the mountain that fast and far. "I am beaten...but I still have great power. I do not want to be banished from this earth. If you let me stay, I promise to help the people who are still to come. Your people will carve masks in my likeness to remind them of this occasion and of my promise to cure the sick and drive out evil spirits."

Web Quest

If you are interested in reading more teachings of the elders, the Internet is a modern vehicle to access the teachings of the past. Visit Virtual Circle at http//:www. vcircle.com/elders and click on "Current Elders Teachings." Consider how relevant these teachings are for your life today.

Community Study

The Woodland Cultural Centre

Figure 2.21
A wall mural created by Six Nations artist, Bill Powless, for the Woodland Cultural Centre. This scene depicts an elder (right) leading Aboriginal peoples who have fallen away from their traditions into a never ending circle where all are equal.

The Woodland Cultural Centre in Brantford, Ontario displays Aboriginal art by well-known artists, such as Tom Hill and Norval Morriseau. When one looks at the logo of the Centre with the two eagles reaching for the star (see page 29), it is evident that animism and spiritualism are still strongly present in Aboriginal values.

The Woodland Cultural Centre, located on reserve land, was once a residential school. Since 1972, it has followed its mandate to preserve and promote the cultural heritage of both the Algonquian and Iroquoian nations. Visitors learn about the history and heritage of the First Nations, contemporary lifestyles, and social and cultural issues of local and national First Nations. The museum displays include an Iroquoian village, a mystical evening forest showing the typical environment of the Northeast Woodlands, and the interior of a nineteenth century longhouse. The research library currently maintains over 6000 volumes.

Today, elders and speakers of the language work diligently on projects that reflect the renaissance of the Northeast Woodlands cultures. Indeed, "...the Centre is the bridge from the past to today and poses questions for the directions of the future which will provide for the 'Seventh Generation,' or those who will follow our generation's generation; in other words, the future for our children... The Centre validates the past, celebrates the present, and seeks answers for the future from Elders and our children."

QUESTIONS

1. Explain what the Woodland Cultural Centre's logo means for spiritualism and animism.

2. Describe three ways the Woodland Cultural Centre is maintaining Aboriginal heritage and religion.

3. The "Seventh Generation" refers to those generations that follow us. "What we do in our lives should reflect our responsibility to future generations." Do you agree with this? What are you doing to practise this belief?

Living My Religion

Chris Warner and Courtney Thomas

Figure 2.22

L.E. Raths, an American educator who studied values and beliefs, said there are four steps or phases in the process of believing. In the first stage, we are "aware," and we know our beliefs; in the second stage we "prize" our beliefs; in the third stage, we "choose" them from among several others; and in the fourth stage we "act" on them consistently and with integration.

Two Aboriginal students at Pauline Johnson Collegiate and Vocational School in Brantford, Ontario, clearly have moved through Raths' four stages. Courtney Thomas (19) and Chris Warner (20) attend Longhouse ceremonies regularly on the Six Nations Reserve. They go to school in the city, but try to maintain their religion, language, and culture on and off the reserve. Courtney belongs to the Turtle clan, and Chris to the Wolf. They both say that members of the clans are their teachers and protectors.

Members of the same clan do not intermarry. They believe that three or four guardian spirits, usually ancestors, watch over them. Keeping clan connections is very important. Strict traditions rule the Longhouse religion, like which door to enter, and where to sit.

The beliefs and values spoken at the longhouse are the ones of the Peacekeeper and Handsome Lake. But the longhouse is also the place for community socials such as weddings, funerals, raising money for a special event, or sending someone off on a dance or drum competition. The Longhouse offers support during rites of passage. Humour, as well as a sense of community, provide guidance. At puberty, the community might warn the boy not to swim or whistle, or his voice will never change. When a girl first menstruates, there are those to help with the "healing time." One custom requires the girl to wash her hands in ashes to connect with the fireplace so she can still cook. Chris is learning his language—Cayuga—so he can pray and chant properly when, and if, he burns tobacco. Courtney has learned that food must be covered to protect it and keep its nourishment. Their sense of spiritualism and animism is strong.

When asked what they get from their Aboriginal religion, both say they get strength and energy. When they go to the longhouse, they must think good thoughts, which purifies them. They certainly feel that it is easier to communicate with fellow adherents, and that there is a bonding. If they didn't have the religion and community of the Longhouse, they both feel their traditions would be lost, their language would suffer, and their identity would disappear. "It would be like a kind of death."

QUESTIONS

1. Identify three ways Courtney and Chris have integrated traditional beliefs and values into their daily lives.
2. Explain which of Raths' four stages Courtney and Chris would be in with regard to their beliefs.
3. Describe a spiritual belief you have, and explain how Raths' stages apply to you and your belief.

Web Quest

If you are interested in reading more about the Woodland Cultural Centre visit www.woodland-centre.on.ca Click on "What's Cool" to find out about upcoming events.

Check Your Understanding

1. Are museums and galleries important factors in keeping Aboriginal spirituality alive? Explain.

2. Describe the importance of elders and shamans in Aboriginal spirituality.

3. How important are elders in your social group?

CULTURAL IMPACT

The Europeans and the Aboriginal Peoples

There can be no question that the Europeans and the Aboriginal peoples had both positive and negative impacts on each other. The Aboriginal peoples exposed the early explorers to new agricultural techniques and new ways of coping with the challenges of survival, while the Europeans provided tools that fostered the development of Aboriginal culture.

In 1755, the British created the first Indian Department of Canada. Its purpose was to maintain good relations with the Aboriginal peoples and to secure their support of Britain. Their allegiance was crucial during the years when Britain was fighting against the French, or the Americans. By 1900, however, Indigenous cultures had suffered near extinction because of the many years of warfare and disease. Often smallpox, measles, and tuberculosis carried away the old and the young—the past and the future.

Before the Europeans' arrival in North America, the Aboriginal peoples were self-governed. Over the centuries, their government has been weakened through policies of control and assimilation. The Indian Acts in both 1876 and 1895 encouraged Aboriginal peoples to give up their culture and adopt "white ways." Policies that established reservations or encouraged assimilation have had mixed results.

Residential Schools

By the mid 1800s, the Canadian government was funding a residential school system for the Aboriginal peoples. Children were removed from their reserves and were placed, often far away from their communities, in boarding schools run mainly by Catholic, United, and Anglican religious orders. From the turn of the century to the 1960s, Aboriginal children in Canada were often taught that it was wrong to practise their cultural ways. Sometimes the punishments for trying to maintain traditional ways were severe, such as having a needle stuck in the tongue for speaking their Aboriginal language, or making a boy wear a dress if he tried to contact a female relative. The residential schools broke the connection between children, parents, and their culture. Many children, isolated for years and instructed to forget their traditional ways, often rejected their past.

The Assembly of First Nations report, *Breaking the Silence*, claimed there were seventy-seven residential schools in 1909, and that sixty were still open in the 1960s. The Mohawk Institute, which is now the Woodland Cultural Centre, closed its doors in 1970. In 1996, the Report of the Royal Commission on Aboriginal Peoples pointed to residential schools as the major factor in the high rates of substance abuse and suicide. At that time, however, many students had already begun the healing process by rediscovering their Aboriginal culture and traditional spirituality.

Throughout the 1990s, many important changes occurred for Aboriginal peoples in Canada. The decade began with a lands claim standoff and ended with the birth of the new Inuit territory and homeland, Nunavut.

Standoff at Oka

Sometimes, the cultural impact of mainstream society on Aboriginal life erupts into violence. Where the Ottawa River joins the Lake of Two Mountains and the St. Lawrence, there is a Mohawk reserve called Kanehsatake, which borders the resort town of Oka. At the edge of town, in the woods called the Pines, some Oka businessmen acquired title to the land and in 1959 built a nine-hole golf course. In 1989, they wanted to expand the golf course to eighteen

Figure 2.23
Oka, 1990: a Mohawk and a Canadian soldier stand face-to-face during a tense stand-off.

holes. The land they wanted was the ancestral burial grounds, considered sacred by the Mohawks. The courts, however, had rejected the Mohawks' claim. The Mohawks decided not to stand by and let the land be taken. They erected a barricade across the road, and the eleven-week armed standoff began. During the standoff, the Mohawks drummed and sang around a sacred fire in order to gain strength from the ritual power of False Faces. One of the Mohawk protesters showed how Aboriginal spirituality was involved: "...We had medicine pouches that we wore around our necks: the ashes from the sacred fire. The guns were nothing. We didn't have enough ammunition to stand off the army for ten minutes. It was all symbolic."

National Aboriginal Day

Indigenous cultural revival is growing, and the surviving elements of Aboriginal religions play an important role. In 1996, Canada declared June 21 to be National Aboriginal Day. Each year, Aboriginal people celebrate their past and future together in pan-Aboriginal activities.

Reconciliation

In 1998, the Canadian government acknowledged its role in the cultural and spiritual impact on Aboriginal cultures. It issued the "Statement of Reconciliation," in which it formally expressed its profound regret for past actions. It also included an action plan to help with healing for residential school students, to improve health conditions, and to speed up land claims. In recent years, Christian Churches have also accepted some of the guilt and have made attempts to reconcile with Aboriginal communities.

Nunavut

For some Aboriginal groups, one way to protect their heritage and religious values is through self-government. With control over their own lands and laws, Aboriginal societies might have a better hope of protecting and preserving traditional values. On April 1, 1999, Canada established its most recent territorial government in the eastern half of the region formerly part of the Northwest Territories (Figure 2.24). Nunavut is home to a population of over 27 000 which is 80 to 85 per cent Inuit. It spreads over almost two million square kilometres of Arctic wilderness, passes through three time zones, and is larger than any other territory or province in Canada. In Inuktitut, the Inuit language, "Nunavut" means "Our Land." The residents of Nunavut hope that by controlling their own affairs they can modernize their society while at the same time maintaining the essential values of their Aboriginal culture. The government pledged to respect and apply IQ (Inuit Qaujim-ajatuqangit), or traditional Inuit knowledge—the knowledge of the elders. In fact, in the legislature, unelected elders have seats right behind the elected leaders of the government.

Figure 2.24
Performers and Inuit Junior Rangers carry the flags of Canada's ten provinces and three territories at the inaugural celebration in Iqaluit, Nunavut on April 1, 1999.

Exploring Issues:
Smudging Ceremony

Figure 2.25 *A Métis woman conducts a smudging ceremony.*

A teacher who had invited two guest speakers to his Aboriginal Studies class worried when the guests took out some sweet grass and a smudge pot, and invited the class to participate in a **smudging ceremony**. There were explicit rules about no smoking on school property and yet this was a cultural ceremony of purification and symbol of unity. (At a university in 1999, five students were banned* when it was discovered that they gathered weekly to purify themselves in the smoke of sage and sweet grass. School officials thought they were using marijuana or causing a fire hazard, and therefore banned it.) Clearly the teacher was allowing a law to be broken in favour of allowing a ritual practice to occur.

The two guests put some tobacco and sweet grass into a small bowl, lit the contents, blew gently on it until fragrant smoke began wafting in the room. They explained that this was a religious belief and practice that they wanted to conduct before they began telling their stories. They invited Aboriginal and non-Aboriginal students to "smudge" by taking the bowl and with one hand, drawing the smoke over their faces and bodies, and inhaling the smoke. There was some nervousness about breaking the rules, but students said afterwards that they felt peaceful, more empathetic to the speakers, and more unified with their classmates than ever before.

* The students at the university fought their suspension, used the hearing to educate the officials about the beliefs and symbolism behind smudging, and got their ban overturned.

AT ISSUE: Should a "smudging ceremony," which is an Aboriginal purification ritual, be banned from schools?

Purification of the mind and spirit plays an important role in Aboriginal spirituality. Burning sweet grass and tobacco in a smudge pot and drawing the smoke ritually over one's face, head, arms, and torso, and inhaling the smoke, is all part of a smudging ceremony of cleansing. Tobacco is considered a sacred plant and the smoke is a spiritual way to clear one's thoughts, to wash away impurities, to help focus on the task with freshness and with renewed zeal, and to bond with co-smudgers. Although the sweet grass ceremony and smudging is a Great Plains cultural and religious act connected to the vision quest, many Aboriginal peoples have adopted the practice.

Every institution has rules of health and safety. Schools are no different. There are anti-smoking bylaws that state there can be no smoking on school property. Also, smoking poses a problem of addiction and health that educators and governments are trying to address. Students can be suspended for smoking on school property and certainly for starting fires, especially in classrooms. It is both a health issue and a fire hazard. School administrators and teachers are liable by law if they allow smoking or fires of any kind in schools.

QUESTIONS
Which statement would you support? Explain.
1. **In a multicultural setting, Aboriginal practices are valid and allowable.**
2. **Students should be suspended for participating in a smudging ceremony and the ritual should be banned.**

Skill Path Oral Presentations

The ability to make effective oral presentations is an important skill, particularly in today's workplace, where many jobs involve public speaking and presentations.

Making an effective oral presentation requires planning, organization, knowledge of the subject, and practice. The more presentations you do, the easier this skill will become. If you are prepared and enthusiastic, your audience will show interest and involvement.

The following are some helpful hints to get you started:

Step 1: Plan your Presentation

- Choose a topic and subtopics. Conduct research to identify issues related to your main topic.
- Create a written plan of the presentation. Start by identifying the main theme. Develop a powerful opening to catch the attention of your audience. Consider using a quotation, a visual, an interesting statistic, or a moving personal experience. Develop each subtopic individually. Your audience will be more interested in your presentation if you provide examples and visuals. Create a summary that reinforces your message. You might use a quote, a question, or an interesting anecdote.
- Consider your audience. Who are they and how many will be in attendance?

Step 2: Rehearse

- Rehearse your presentation in front of a mirror. Use gestures that come naturally.
- Time your presentation. Leave time for questions or discussion.

- Listen to professional speakers, such as TV announcers, and note their pace and tone of voice. Listen to yourself on tape.
- Use visuals strategically. They can help to control and vary your pace.
- Create cue cards that you can refer to during your presentation.

Step 3: Deliver the Presentation

Do

✔ Arrive early to organize your presentation and to ensure equipment is available and in good working order.

✔ Ensure you have enough handouts for all members of the audience.

✔ Be well-rested so you can think on your feet.

✔ Have cue cards that you can refer to occasionally.

✔ Stand to make your presentation so you can be both seen and heard.

✔ Speak clearly and loudly.

✔ Establish eye contact with members of the audience so that everyone feels included.

✔ Use carefully prepared visuals (graphs, charts, pictures, etc.) to enhance your presentation.

✔ Make use of memorization strategies to help you avoid simply reading from your cue cards.

✔ Smile and be animated.

Tips to help you remember

- **Mnemonics is the skill of improving memory by using a formula, code, or associative artifact. One such way is to develop an acronym, where a word or phrase is formed from the first letters of what is to be remembered. For example, in a presentation about the Aboriginal cultural groups in Canada, you might develop an acronym (THEN) to help you remember the order of your subtopics (today, history, environment, nations).**

Don't

✔ Arrive late and ask for additional time.
✔ Just read your presentation. Look away from your cue cards as much as possible.
✔ Look at the teacher throughout. The students are your audience.
✔ Speak in a monotonous tone of voice.
✔ Display poor posture.
✔ Chew gum or eat candies.
✔ Simply talk, with no visual references.

Practise It!

Do some research, and prepare an oral presentation on one of the following:

• one of the six Aboriginal cultural groups in North America
• an Aboriginal creation story, its meaning and significance
• an Aboriginal cultural centre
• The Peacemaker
• Handsome Lake
• developments in Nunavut since its creation
• the Oka Crisis
• the Statement of Reconciliation

Check Your Understanding

1. Describe one example of cultural conflict related to Aboriginal spirituality.

2. How can Aboriginal religious values play a positive role in the future development of Canada's Aboriginal peoples?

3. Which elements of Aboriginal spirituality might benefit all Canadians? Explain.

Activities

Check Your Understanding

1. Select five terms from the Glossary on page 59 and explain the meaning and importance to Aboriginal spirituality for each.

2. Describe how each of the following contributed to Aboriginal spirituality: Handsome Lake, elders, Elijah Harper, shaman, Lame Deer, The Peacemaker, animism, Melissa Labrador.

3. What were the challenges to Aboriginal spirituality for each of the following: Smudging, Potlatch, Sun Dance?

4. Describe what the following pairs have in common:
• Handsome Lake–The Peacemaker
• Sun Dance–Morning Dance

Think and Communicate

5. Briefly describe one Aboriginal belief or practice that you feel might be essential to a balanced life in today's society.

6. Describe an appropriate way to commemorate June 21, National Aboriginal Day. Give at least three reasons for your decision.

7. Interview or conduct research on one of the following to identify and analyze his or her spiritual beliefs and practices: an elder, someone who attended a residential school, a faithkeeper, Matthew Coon Come. Present your findings to a peer for editing and appraisal.

8. Develop a collage or poster that would represent where and how Aboriginal spirituality fits in today's world.

9. Prepare an announcement or advertisement that promotes the protection of an Aboriginal sacred place, such as a burial ground or disputed land **or** that recognizes a sacred event, such as the death of Handsome Lake.

10. Explain the challenges for someone practising an Aboriginal religion today.

11. Do some research on the medicine wheel and the dream catcher to identify their significance as symbols in Aboriginal spirituality. Present your findings to the class in an oral presentation.

12. Conduct research on other Aboriginal groups, such as the Midewiwin Society, which is an Ojibwa spirituality group.

Apply Your Learning

13. Adopt an environmental issue, e.g., the protection of an endangered species, the preservation of green space, disposing toxic waste, logging, etc. Research the evidence surrounding the issue. Explain to an environmental group, city council, or Member of Parliament, what action should be taken using at least three Aboriginal spiritual references.

14. Explain how one world problem might be solved by applying an Aboriginal spiritual viewpoint.

15. If you or a friend were feeling "lost" or "depressed," what Aboriginal beliefs, practices, or values might help you deal with your problems?

Glossary

Aboriginal. Of Native ancestry, inhabiting or existing in a land from the earliest times and before colonists.

animism [ANNA mism]. The attribution of a living soul to plants, animals, inanimate objects, and natural phenomena.

elder. A person (male or female) venerated for age and wisdom.

faithkeeper. Member of a nation selected to maintain the traditional ceremonies and rituals.

First Nations. An Aboriginal band, or a community functioning as a band, but not having band status. The term First Nations does not include the Inuit or Métis.

genesis [GENNA sis]. The origin, the beginnings, the formation of something.

indigenous [in DIDGE a nus]. Originating naturally in a region, belonging naturally to an environment (of people) born in a region.

longhouse. Iroquois home, cigar-shaped, about fifty metres long and ten metres wide, a dwelling shared by several nuclear families.

Longhouse. Religion of the Iroquois.

monotheism [monna THEE ism]. The belief in one God.

oracy. The ability to express oneself fluently in speech and to understand a spoken language.

polytheism [polly THEE ism]. The belief in or worship of more than one god.

powwow. A gathering of Aboriginal people with ritual dances, drumming and chanting.

reincarnation [re in car NAY sh'n]. The belief in the rebirth of a soul in a new body or form.

sachems [SAY chum]. The supreme chief of a clan.

shaman [SHAY min]. Medicine man or spiritual leader.

smudging ceremony. A purification ritual that includes the burning of sweet grass and drawing smoke ritually over body.

tipi. Cone-shaped tent and dwelling found in the nations of the Great Plains.

totem. A protective entity in the form of an animal, natural object, or plant.

totem pole. A long pole in which several totems are carved, used to recount history.

vision quest. The process of purifying and fasting in order to be sensitive to a vision or voices that might guide a person; a sacred ceremony.

wampum [WOM pum]. A belt of coloured beads used to confirm a treaty, or to help with the skill of oracy.

The Story of the Bell Stand

Khing, the master carver, made a bell stand
Of precious wood. When it was finished,
All who saw it were astounded. They said it must be
The work of spirits.

The Prince of Lu said to the master carver:
"What is your secret?"
Khing replied: "I am only a workman:
I have no secret. There is only this:
When I began to think about the work you
commanded
I guarded my spirit, did not expend it
On trifles that were not to the point.
I fasted in order to set
My heart at rest.

"After three days of fasting,
I had forgotten gain and success.
After five days
I had forgotten praise and criticism.
After seven days,
I had forgotten my body
With all its limbs.

"By this time all thought of your Highness
And of the court had faded away.
All that might distract me from the work
Had vanished.
I was collected in the single thought
Of the bell stand.
Then I went into the forest
To see the trees in their own natural state.
When the right tree appeared before my eyes,
The bell stand appeared in it, clearly, beyond doubt.

"All I had to do was to put forth my hand
And begin.

"If I had not met this particular tree
There would have been
No bell stand at all.

"What happened?
My own collected thought
Encountered the hidden potential of the wood;
From this live encounter came the work
Which you ascribe to the spirits."

Paula R. Hartz, *Taoism*

Chapter Three
Early Religions

3

Read "The Story of the Bell Stand," and consider the following questions:

1. Why did people think that the bell stand was "the work of spirits"?
2. The master carver is a model of humility. What does the word *humility* mean? Give three examples from the story that show the master carver's humility.
3. Did the spirits make the bell stand? Explain your answer.
4. What does the word *spirit* mean to you?

Introduction

Religion begins with questioning. Individuals feel the need to understand the world more concretely, so they ask questions like, Why is the sky blue? or Why does the tree grow? As time passes, the questions become more complex and the answers more difficult to find. A religious person is someone who takes nothing for granted and seeks answers to these complex questions.

The quest for these answers often begins with a puzzle, like the one faced by Chuang Tzu in the following story:

Chuang Tzu had a dream that he was a butterfly. He was filled with bliss as a butterfly, floating gracefully and effortlessly. He was pleased with himself and he was satisfied with who he was. He knew nothing of what it was to be Chuang Tzu. However, shortly after waking, he recognized that he was Chuang Tzu and did not know whether he had dreamed he was a butterfly or if the butterfly had dreamed he was Chuang Tzu.

With the advent of civilization and the growth of nations, humanity was confronted with the puzzle of life. People were pressed into questioning the nature of their being and the nature of existence. Some say there was no greater period of religious and philosophical thinking than between 700 and 200 BCE.

The early religions represent a departure from the **myth**-driven belief systems that preceded them. Instead, one can see the emergence of systems of philosophy, belief, and ritual that are consistent with a different sense of what it is to be human. With the emergence of Zoroastrianism, Jainism, Taoism, Confucianism, and Shinto, humans placed their most fundamental questions before creation. Some profound answers began to emerge.

Learning Goals

At the end of this chapter, you will be able to:

- identify the origins of Zoroastrianism, Jainism, Taoism, Confucianism, and Shinto
- identify how and where they emerged as religions
- identify and state the significance of Zoroaster, Mahavira, Lao Tzu, Chuang Tzu, Confucius, and Mencius
- identify major historic events in the development of these early religions
- demonstrate an understanding of the supernatural in Zoroastrianism, Jainism, Taoism, Confucianism, and Shinto
- identify the origins and significance of the various practices, rituals, and symbols of Zoroastrianism, Jainism, Taoism, Confucianism, and Shinto
- demonstrate an understanding of the role of sign and symbol in these early religions
- analyze the practices and rituals of these early religions
- read and evaluate excerpts from the sacred writings and oral teachings of these religions
- review the political, social, ideological, and geographic impact of these early religions on their respective cultures
- evaluate the pros and cons of Jain vegetarianism
- describe ways in which these early religions are represented in Canada
- identify religious groups associated with Zoroastrianism, Jainism, and Taoism in Canada
- define key terms from Zoroastrianism, Jainism, Taoism, Confucianism, and Shinto
- use the Internet in researching topics in the study of these early religions

●142 CE Taoism: Way of the Celestial Masters emerges

●456–536 CE Taoism: Assembling of the Three Caverns; acknowledgement of the three truths—Taoism, Confucianism, and Buddhism

●300 BCE (approx.) Jainism: sky-clad and white-clad sects are formed

●200 CE (approx.) Shinto: Chinese religions arrive in Japan

●1700-600 BCE? The date of Zoroaster's birth is still debated by scholars

●371–289 BCE (approx.) Mencius (390–305), Chuang Tzu (369–286), Hsun Tzu (298–238)

●604–479 BCE Lao Tzu (*c.* 604–*c.* 532 approx.), Mahavira (599–527), Buddha (563–483), Confucius (551–479); early signs of Shinto belief

1991 CE 100 000 people attend the first Earth Spirit Festival, a celebration of the Aboriginal, Chinese, and Japanese Canadian communities in Toronto

1971 CE Zoroastrian Society of Ontario founded

1995 CE Fung Loy Kok International Institute of Taoism opens in Toronto

1964 CE Japanese Canadian Cultural Centre opens in Toronto

1970 CE Master Moy Lin-Shin establishes International Taoist Tai Chi Society

1945 CE Shinto: Defeat of Japan in the Second World War; State Shinto abolished

1130–1200 CE Confucianism: Four Books assembled by Chu Hsi

1869 CE Shinto: State Shinto founded

Timeline

ZOROASTRIANISM

ORIGINS

Figure 3.1
According to tradition, Zoroaster was born in Azerbaijan, in northern Persia.

Ancient Persia was a loosely organized, polytheistic community. A polytheistic community believes in many gods. This proved troubling to a man named Zoroaster, who some scholars claim lived some time between 1700 and 600 BCE. (These dates are vigorously debated.) He became convinced that **polytheism** was failing to meet the needs of the people of Persia. To deal with this, Zoroaster did what all great sages do—he went off on his own to think. He hoped that by spending time contemplating the way the world worked, he might arrive at some answers. While meditating, he received a revelation that confirmed his suspicions: a multitude of competing gods did not dominate the spirit world; instead, the universe was ruled by one God. This God's name was **Ahura Mazda**, and Zoroaster spent the rest of his life preaching, teaching, and fighting to convince people of the power of the one God. His early efforts met with failure, but some claim, by the time of his death at the age of seventy-seven, Zoroastrianism, the "Good Religion," was the state religion of Persia.

Zoroaster's life has been presented to the world as legend, since the historical record is largely unreliable. Legend has it that instead of crying when he was born, Zoroaster laughed. He apparently tamed wild beasts in his youth, performed miraculous healings, and fought off evil by reciting simple prayers and hymns. People who follow Zoroastrianism cherish the legend of Zoroaster.

Zoroaster's life also bears a striking resemblance to the life of Jesus of Nazareth (see Chapter 7). Once again, according to tradition, Zoroaster was conceived by a flash of light and born to a young virgin. His ancestry could be traced back forty-five generations to the Persian version of Adam. He engaged wise men in debate at a young age and, like Jesus, at the age of thirty, he went into the desert and received the revelation that changed his life and the lives of so many others.

Check Your Understanding

1. What did Zoroaster discover after he went off to think about the way the world worked?

2. What similarities are there between the life of Zoroaster and the life of Jesus of Nazareth?

BELIEFS

Zoroastrians believe that Ahura Mazda is the governing Lord of the Universe. His main rival is **Angra Mainyu**, a God of similar power who denied the truth and came to represent the forces of evil. Ahura Mazda and Angra Mainyu represent the battle between good and evil, a 12 000-year battle in which Ahura Mazda has been able to maintain the upper hand because he is slightly more powerful than Angra Mainyu.

This central belief is significant for two reasons. First, it parallels the battle between good and evil that exists in every person. Temptation to do what is evil can often be curtailed by the presence of good within the human conscience. Second, it provides an answer to the following fundamental theological question: If God is good, why is there evil in the world? In Zoroastrianism, the answer is quite simple. There is evil in the world because there are really two deities: one is supreme and represents good, the other is almost as powerful and represents evil. Thus, an important near balance between good and evil exists in the world, with good prevailing for the benefit of humanity.

MILESTONES AND SYMBOLS

The Death of the Body

One of the more interesting elements of Zoroastrianism is the ancient ritual relating to death. Still today in India, and until 1971 in Iran, the bodies of the dead were given back to nature in a compelling fashion. When a person died, the family held a three-day vigil. After the mourning period, the body was taken to a *dakhma*. A *dakhma* is a round, open-air structure with high walls, where the body of the dead person is placed. A combination of natural elements (such as the sun's rays) and scavenging birds (such as vultures) that descend on and consume the corpse results in the disposal of the dead person's remains. Later, when the body is reduced to bones, they are swept into a specially constructed well in the centre of the *dakhma*. It is important to note that *dakhmas* are built on high, rocky ground, away from population centres.

This manner of corpse disposal is criticized today for two reasons: there are health issues associated with leaving decaying bodies in the open air, and it is said that the vulture population cannot consume the number of corpses produced by the human population. The manner of dealing with the body of a dead person is a reflection of Zoroastrian values. First, rich and poor alike are left in the *dakhma*, reflecting the equality of all before Ahura Mazda. Second, Zoroastrians believe that the soul of the person is bound for something much greater and that the body should be given back to the earth.

Today, Zoroastrians adapt to the body-disposal procedures of the society in which they live. Funeral services are normally presided over by a priest during a four-day period. In Canada, the body is taken to a funeral parlour where it is prepared for the funeral ceremony. This involves ritual washing of the body, dressing the deceased in a *sudreh* (a white undershirt with a symbolic bag to gather good deeds), and the untying and retying of the sacred thread (*kusti*) several times daily. Since the body is considered to be unclean once the soul has departed, Zoroastrians do not touch it. The body is disposed of by either burial or cremation. If the body is cremated, the ashes are dispersed at a scattering ground owned and maintained by the Zoroastrian community.

The Journey of the Soul

While the body is left to nature, the soul engages in a very different experience. It is said that when a person dies, a guardian spirit accompanies the soul to the "Bridge of the Separator." This is the bridge of judgment where individuals' good deeds are weighed against their evil deeds. As a person progresses, the bridge widens for the righteous deeds and narrows for the evil deeds. A wider path allows the person to cross to heaven, accompanied by Zoroaster himself. A narrow path eventually causes the person to tumble off the bridge into the abyss of hell.

Symbols and Icons

Fire

Fire is the most important symbol in Zoroastrianism. Often, images of fire will appear on Zoroastrian relics. Fire represents divine presence and is the organizing principle behind the place of worship for Zoroastrians—the fire temple. The fire temple is more of a shrine than a congregational meeting place. Within the sanctuary is a square fireplace with grill work and a vent to allow smoke to escape. The fire burns continuously on a large metal urn and is maintained by a Zoroastrian priest. Once again, the continuous burning of the fire signifies the continuing divine presence of Ahura Mazda. Figure 3.2 shows a priest standing at the central altar of fire in Toronto's Zoroastrian temple.

QUESTION

1. What does fire symbolize for Zoroastrians?

Figure 3.2

SACRED WRITINGS

The main body of sacred writing for Zoroastrians is known as the Avestan Scriptures. The Avesta in its present form comprises five parts: the Yasna, the Yashts, the Visperad, the Vendidad, and the Khordeh Avesta (the minor Avesta). This collection of sacred writings is a combination of hymns, laws, prayers, and theological teachings. One book, the Yasna liturgy, includes seventy-two chapters, seventeen of which were composed by Zoroaster. These chapters, known as the **Gathas**, are combined into five hymns that deal specifically with religious matters relating to Ahura Mazda. The Gathas are the spiritual core of the Yasna liturgy.

Sacred Text

Zoroastrian sacred texts place a great deal of importance on the battle between good and evil. It is important to remember that Zoroastrians believe that a battle between Ahura Mazda, the governing Lord of the Universe, and Angra Mainyu, the one who denied the truth, will last for 12 000 years. This battle can be seen in the following passage:

Yasna 30: 3–6

Now, these are the two original Spirits who, as Twins, have been perceived by me through a vision. In both thought and speech, and in deed, these two are what is good and evil. Between these two, the pious, not the impious, will choose rightly.

Furthermore, the two spirits confronted each other; in the beginning each created for himself life and non-life, so that in the end there will be the worst existence for the Drugwants [liars or evildoers], but the best Mind for the Righteous.

Of these two Spirits, the deceitful chose the worst course of action, while the most beneficent Spirit who is clothed in the hardest stones chose Truth, as also do those who believingly propitiate Ahura Mazda.

Between these two spirits, the daewas [demons] did not choose rightly at all since, while they were taking council among themselves, delusion came upon them, so that they chose the worst Mind. Then, all together, they ran to Wrath with which they infect the life of man.

QUESTIONS

1. Based on your study of Zoroastrianism, who were the two original spirits?

2. What happened when the two spirits confronted each other?

3. Do you believe that a battle between "good" and "evil" sometimes takes place when you make a decision? Explain your answer.

4. How do you personally explain the existence of evil in the world?

Living My Religion

Sherna Bharucha

Figure 3.3

Sherna Bharucha goes about her business like many high-school students. She likes socializing with her friends, but when it is time to get serious about her schoolwork, that is exactly what she does. Every once in a while the topic of religious practice comes up in one of her classes at Markham District High School in Markham, Ontario. When Sherna is asked about her faith, she confidently tells her classmates that she is Zoroastrian. Their curiosity piques, and they ask her to explain aspects of her faith tradition. Sherna thinks that because Zoroastrianism is new and different to the minds of many people, they are curious about her faith and interested in learning more about it.

When she was five years old, Sherna was enrolled in religious education classes; at the age of eight, she was officially initiated into the faith. This event, known as **navjote**, is a community celebration of the entrance of a child into the world of Zoroastrianism. Sherna's *navjote* began at her house. In the presence of her family, a Zoroastrian priest said prayers and made offerings to prepare her for the event. Then she went upstairs to take a ritual bath, known as a *nahn*. The prayers are believed to provide cleansing of the spirit, and the *nahn*, cleansing of the body. Thus, in a purified state, Sherna was ready for the next step in her *navjote*.

In Sherna's case, her parents rented a hall for her *navjote* celebration. When Sherna arrived at the hall, she was met by her mother, who greeted her by circling a coconut and an egg around Sherna seven times and then breaking them. This is symbolic of the meeting between the inner and outer world that the *navjote* is initiating. Next, Sherna was escorted to the hall's stage where the priest, using items symbolizing good (such as flowers, sugar crystals, and rice), offered prayers for the young initiate. Sherna joined the priest in prayer and then was given her *sudreh* (a sacred undergarment that she wears everyday) and her *kusti* (a woollen string made of seventy-two strings of lambswool). The *kusti* must be tied in a special way, and, every time Sherna puts it on, she must say certain prayers from the Khordeh Avesta. At the end of the prayers, the *navjote* was complete, and Sherna was a true Zoroastrian.

Sherna's strong religious background has inspired her to become one of the assistant teachers with the Zoroastrian Religious Education Committee. From October to May, Sherna and ten other teachers work with young Zoroastrians to help them develop a sound knowledge of their faith and traditions. Sherna says her parents have always emphasized her religious background. A possible explanation for this is the fact that the Zoroastrian community is relatively small and, therefore, is motivated to work hard to maintain its identity. There is little doubt that the emphasis on religion, passed down to Sherna by her parents, has had a profound effect on her.

Questions

1. How does Sherna Bharucha say people react when they find out she is a Zoroastrian?

2. What is the *navjote* ceremony? What are the *sudreh* and the *kusti*?

3. Sherna is involved in the faith life of her community. Why do you think it is important for someone to become actively involved in his or her religion? How can serving others contribute to a deeper understanding of one's faith?

CULTURAL IMPACT

There are approximately 140 000 Zoroastrians in the world today, with the majority living in India and Iran. The Zoroastrians living on the Indian subcontinent are called Parsis. The centre of Zoroastrian culture is in Mumbai (Bombay), India.

Recent estimates put the North American Zoroastrian population at around 12 000. In Ontario, the Zoroastrian community is a small, but noticeable, religious group. In fact, some say that outside of Iran and India, Ontario has the next largest population of Zoroastrians, with a community of about 4000 people. The main community gathering place is the Darbe Meher at Bayview and Steeles Avenues in Toronto. The Darbe Meher is the centre for religious ceremonies, religious education classes, and community receptions. It houses a fire-altar room for special Zoroastrian services.

Scholars have approached the study of Zoroastrianism from the perspective of its historical contribution to other great religions. For example, the historical record suggests that the concepts of life after death, final judgment, redemption, and the idea of Satan as God's rival, so prominent in Judeo-Christian culture, were likely influenced by the Zoroastrians around the time of the Babylonian exile. It was during this period that the Jews, then subject to Babylonian rulers, were uprooted from their homeland and held in captivity. In 538 BCE, Cyrus the Great, a Persian, conquered the Babylonians and encouraged the Jews to return to Israel and pursue their faith. At the time, Jews saw Cyrus as a liberator and a part of God's plan. Cyrus may have opened the hearts and minds of the Jews to aspects of Zoroastrianism. While this position is subject to debate, the fact remains that the post-Babylonian exile period influenced the development of Jewish theology.

Check Your Understanding

1. State two reasons why the battle between Ahura Mazda and Angra Mainyu is relevant to your everyday life.

2. a) What is a *dakhma*?
b) With reference to the *dakhma*, outline the way Zoroastrians deal with the death of a member of their community.

c) Where does the soul of an individual journey after physical death?

3. What part of the section on Zoroastrianism has appealed to you the most? Explain your reasons.

JAINISM

The spirit of Jainism is captured in **ahimsa**, the noble art of non-violence, as expressed in the sacred Jain scripture called the Agam:

> *Some kill living beings for sacrificial purposes, some kill for their sins, some kill for their flesh, some for the blood, heart, liver, fate, feathers, or teeth, some with specific reasons, some without reason, some out of fear (defence).*
>
> *He who is disinclined from killing the smallest living beings knows what suffering is because he who knows his own happiness and pains knows others' too, and he who knows others' feelings knows his own feelings. This is the way one must compare himself with others. He who has obtained this knowledge would not wish to live at the expense of other living beings.*

Acharang Sutra, stanza 1.6.55

Figure 3.4
This statue of Mahavira stands in the Vimalsha Temple in Rajasthan, India, one of the holy places of Jainism.

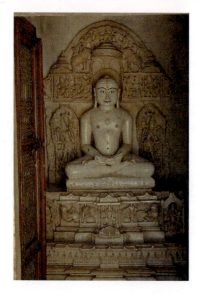

ORIGINS

Some time after Zoroaster received the revelation regarding Ahura Mazda, a child was born in the north of India who would grow into a living model of non-violence. Vardhamana Mahavira (599–527 BCE) was the man who came to "reorganize" the way people approached religious life. Mahavira (Figure 3.4) grew up in India where Hinduism was the dominant religion. However, while he accepted aspects of Hinduism, Mahavira felt that changes needed to be made.

Jains believe that Mahavira was one of twenty-four holy teachers who came to teach people the way of self-mastery. Therefore, Mahavira is not seen as a religious founder but as a teacher who came to re-establish what had been previously taught. Mahavira was a **jina**, or "conqueror," who sought to give his followers a clear path to enlightenment.

Mahavira's life and teachings were dedicated to the art of ahimsa, or non-violence. The process by which he came to embrace ahimsa is a compelling one. At the age of thirty, the same age that Zoroaster and Jesus began their ministries, Mahavira decided to abandon Hinduism and pursue his spiritual ambitions as an ascetic. **Asceticism** was a common Hindu practice in India at the time. Ascetics are people who deprive themselves of pleasure for the purpose of achieving union with their spirit. Many Hindus chose a path of asceticism, including a contemporary of Mahavira, Siddhartha Gautama (563–483 BCE), who came to be known as the Buddha. In Mahavira's case, his first step as an ascetic was to give up all worldly possessions except for one piece of clothing. He also became a strict vegetarian soon after pursuing the ascetic way of life.

One of the main spiritual practices of ascetics is **meditation** (Figure 3.5). Meditation is the process of eliminating self-centred thinking and becoming united with the spirit that governs the universe. Mahavira lived a life of intense meditation until he reached enlightenment, becoming a "conqueror" at the age of forty-two. For the next thirty years, the enlightened Mahavira taught, ordained male and female ascetic monks, and built the philosophy that formed the foundation of Jainism. Mahavira achieved "liberation" at the age of seventy-two, when he died of gradual fasting.

Figure 3.5
Meditation is considered essential in Jainism because it is believed that this practice enables individuals to free themselves from worldly attachments and gain the understanding and enlightenment necessary for salvation.

BELIEFS

Ahimsa

The central Jain belief is ahimsa. In fact, some say ahimsa can be described as the noblest form of religious conduct. Ahimsa is more than just agreeing to avoid physical violence. It involves commitment to all life forms on earth, as well as to the survival of the planet by not engaging in practices that may bring the earth harm. It also involves avoiding conduct that can be mentally and emotionally damaging to oneself and others. In other words, ahimsa encompasses the entire lifestyle of the individual, and, according to Jain tradition, it is the clearest and most intelligent path to liberation.

Check Your Understanding

1. What is the connection between Jainism and Hinduism?

2. What do you think of Mahavira's lifestyle of asceticism? How did you react when you read that he "gave up all worldly possessions"?

Figure 3.6

Jain monks and nuns wear muslin cloths over their mouths to keep out flying insects. They also carry small brooms to gently brush away living creatures from their path, so as not to crush them accidentally.

Ahimsa can be seen in many aspects of Jain life. Jain monks often sweep off their seats with a light brush before sitting down so as not to kill insects that may have landed there. Others wear masks while walking to avoid breathing in an insect. In fact, the holiest time of year for monks is a four-month period of solemnity known as Caturmas. During this time, travel is restricted to avoid the accidental deaths of insects and animals. While these examples may seem extreme to a North American reader, they do express the seriousness with which Jains approach ahimsa.

The concept of ahimsa has been embraced widely in Canada. Some peace and social justice organizations, drawing inspiration from champions of non-violence like Mohandas K. Gandhi and Martin Luther King, Jr., use the open-palm symbol of non-violence (Figure 3.7) as their logo. Advocates for the rights of poor and oppressed people affiliate themselves with organizations like Interfaith Voices for Peace and Justice, whose membership includes the Jain Society

of Toronto. Clearly, ahimsa, the organizing principle of Jainism, is becoming an internationally recognized ideal. People are discovering the far-reaching consequences of violence among humankind, as well as violence toward the environment.

Karma, Reincarnation, and the Five Practices

Karma is the belief that, for every action, there is a consequence. Karma affects people while they live their life on earth and also has an impact on their next life. Jains believe in **reincarnation**, the concept that one has an eternal soul that is reborn into different bodies over the course of many lives. The goal of the present life is to pay one's karmic debt in order to achieve salvation, or **moksha**. Moksha results in the elimination of the effects of karma in one's life and is achieved through meditation and right conduct. Right conduct involves demonstrating a commitment to ahimsa and can be seen in the Five Practices of Jainism. Jains are encouraged to make a vow to conduct themselves according to the following principles:

1. non-violence (ahimsa)
2. truthfulness
3. non-stealing
4. celibacy
5. non-possession

Following the Five Practices focuses a person's life on proper conduct. One can see that the five practices are interrelated, indicating a holistic focus on righteousness. Consequently, the life of a Jain involves proper conduct that results in either moksha in

Web Quest

To find out more about the philosophy of Interfaith Voices for Peace and Justice, go to http://www. interfaithvoices. org/ifv.cfm

this life or an improved rebirth in the next life.

Atomism

Jains also believe that every living thing on the planet possesses a soul, or *jiva*. Even the building blocks of nature, atoms, possess individual souls. When atoms are combined to form a larger object—a human perhaps—a soul encompassing the size of that object also emerges.

The teaching of **atomism** demonstrates how the elements of earth, water, air, and fire are composed of atoms, each possessing a soul. When combined, the atoms make objects, which also have souls. Therefore, a clear link between the physical and spiritual world is established within the framework of the Jain belief system. Viewing this belief from the perspective of ahimsa, Jains believe that people are bound to act more compassionately if they acknowledge that everything is composed of a spirit or soul. To accentuate this point, one Jain sect avoids using flowers as part of its sacred rituals because the plucking of a flower could injure the soul of the flower.

No Absolutes

In Jainism, all truths depend on the perspective from which they are observed. When different individuals look at a particular river, the following perspectives may emerge:
- The river flows into Lake Huron.
- There is a variety of fish and plant life living in the river.
- I could canoe down that river.
- We should build a dam and harness hydroelectric power from the river.

All four perspectives are valid. No perspective is wrong despite the fact that different perspectives have different effects on the life of the river. The fact remains that no one is absolutely correct in his or her statement of perspective. Extending this theory to all observable natural phenomena, one can see that nothing can be stated that is absolutely correct or absolutely incorrect. Thus, Jains take the position that there are no absolutes; one should live a life in accordance with ahimsa and avoid bold declarations that reveal certainties that are really just illusions.

Check Your Understanding

1. a) What is ahimsa? Why is it so important to the Jains?
b) Give two examples of how Jain monks or nuns practise ahimsa.

2. According to Jain tradition, what is *jiva*? Where does the *jiva* reside?

3. What changes would you have to make in your life if you were to follow the Five Practices of Jainism?

MILESTONES AND SYMBOLS

Sallekhana

As mentioned previously, Mahavira died of gradual fasting at the age of seventy-two. This practice is called

Symbols and Icons
Swastika and Open Palm

Parasparopagraho Jivanam
Figure 3.7

A symbol to represent the Jain community was adopted in 1973, 2500 years after the emancipation of Mahavira. The symbol summarizes the principles of Jainism. The outline of the symbol is that of the Jain description of the shape of the universe, resembling a person standing with feet apart and arms rested on both hips.

The swastika represents four types of birth into which a soul can reincarnate during its journey in the universe. The three dots above the swastika are the three jewels of Jain philosophy by which liberation can be attained: Right Faith, Right Knowledge and Right Conduct. The half-moon indicates the abode where liberated souls reside, and the dot within represents the liberated pure soul.

The stylized hand is in a gesture of blessing and protection. The palm with a wheel of 24 spokes represents Jinas and is inscribed with the word *ahimsa*—the essence of Jain ethical teaching. The phrase at the bottom of the symbol means "the purpose of living beings is to assist each other."

QUESTIONS

1. What was your initial reaction when you first saw the swastika symbol on this page?
2. How does the symbol capture the spirit of Jainism? Be specific.

sallekhana. A person who dies from an eating disorder like anorexia is not considered to be participating in *sallekhana*. Nor is *sallekhana* considered to be a form of suicide, even though people participating in it are willingly proceeding to their own deaths. While it may be difficult for many people to understand the rationale behind such an act, *sallekhana* is considered to be a sacred and holy practice, and not a form of self-destruction.

Sallekhana is only to be undertaken by spiritually fit individuals, usually monks or nuns, and must be supervised by religious authorities. It is viewed as death with dignity and dispassion. The Jain attitude toward the *sallekhana* of Mahavira is captured in the following passage from the Kalpa Sutra:

In the fourth month of that rainy season . . . the Venerable Ascetic Mahavira died, went off, quitted the world, cut asunder the ties of birth, old age, and death; became a Siddha, a Mukta, a maker of the end (to all misery), finally liberated, freed from all pains . . .

The death of Mahavira is seen as liberation and achievement, not suicide and dread. Voluntary death by fasting indicates complete renunciation of worldly possessions. It allows the participants the opportunity to die in full meditative awareness, maintaining their vows until the end of their earthly existence.

SACRED WRITINGS

The sky-clad (Digambaras) and the white-clad (Svetambaras) sects each hold different books as sacred (these sects are discussed further on page 76). The skyclad sect treats the Satkandagama and Kasay-aprabhrta collections as sacred, while the white-clad sect refers to the Āgama (tradition) collection as sacred. Other books outside these collections, like the Kalpa Sutra, are also revered.

Sacred Text

The sacred scriptures of Jainism are called the Āgama, comprising of different aspects of philosophical and religious system. Originally, they were passed down orally through the generations. In the third century BCE, these were reconstructed into 12 limbs (Angas) and twelfth Anga consisted of 14 purvas. Some of the scriptures translated into English include Acharanga, Tattvartha Sutra, Kalpa Sutra, Samana Suttam and Uttaradhyayana.

Kalpa Sutra 1
Obeisance to the Arhats!
Obeisance to the Liberated Ones!
Obeisance to the Religious Guides!
Obeisance to the Religious Instructors!
Obeisance to all Saints in the World!

QUESTIONS

1. Define *obeisance* and *benediction*.

2. Why do you think the passage calls for a demonstration of reverence to the great spiritual teachers of the world?

3. Do people today give respect to spiritual teachers? Why or why not?

Web Quest

For a detailed look at the world of Jainism, visit Jainworld at http://www.jainworld.com/ Click on "History of various sects" to find out more about the Digambaras and the Svetambaras.

GROUPS AND INSTITUTIONS

Digambaras and Svetambaras

The Jain community is composed of monks, nuns, laymen, and laywomen. Within the community there are two distinct religious groups: the **Digambaras** (sky-clad, or unclothed) and the **Svetambaras** (white-clad). While both sects agree on the religious doctrine deemed essential to Jainism, their practices differ. The division between the sky-clad Jains and the white-clad Jains likely occurred around 300 BCE over two issues: the nature of Mahavira and monastic nudity. Sky-clad Jains hold the position that Mahavira was more godly than human. White-clad Jains believe that Mahavira lived a relatively ordinary life and achieved liberation as a natural part of his life. Although this area of disagreement is significant, it is monastic nudity that has proven to be the real dividing point.

According to one account, the group that came to be known as the sky-clad sect followed a Jain leader south when he predicted a famine in the north. This group was gone for quite some time. By the time the group returned, the white-clad sect had begun wearing a few articles of white clothing, a seeming contradiction to the previous practice of nudity for monks. And so the debate began. The sky-clad group claimed that the wearing of clothing by monks was not in keeping with the renunciation of earthly possessions, a key aspect of the Five Practices. The white-clad group, while holding monastic nudity as an important ideal, did not see the wearing of some clothing to be a problem. These differences proved to be insurmountable, and, to this day, the sky-clad Jains are a separate and distinct sect from the white-clad sect.

A few points need to be raised before leaving the discussion of these sects. First, sky-clad monks are covered from view today when they are in public. Second, women have never been permitted to go sky-clad. As a result, according to the sky-clad sect, females are not able to reach liberation. The white-clad sect acknowledges the ability of women to achieve liberation regardless of monastic nudity.

CULTURAL IMPACT

There are approximately four million Jains in the world today. Most Jains live in India, with smaller populations in Canada, the United Kingdom, and the United States.

The most important contribution of Jainism to global thinking is the concept of ahimsa. There is little question that this belief influenced the great Hindu Mohandas Gandhi (see page 127). Gandhi believed that the British were playing the role of masters in India's house and that they must be forced to leave. He decided to do this by embarking on a non-violent campaign to force out the British. When British batons struck Indian protesters, the Indians simply took the blows, forcing the British to consider the fact that they were beating people who were not striking back. In the end, Gandhi's campaign of non-violent

Figure 3.8
Dr. Martin Luther King opposed discrimination against African Americans by organizing non-violent resistance and peaceful mass demonstrations. In 1965, King (front row, fourth from the right) led over 10 000 civil-rights demonstrators on the last leg of their march from Selma to Montgomery, Alabama.

non-co-operation led to the British withdrawal from India. Gandhi, in turn, influenced Martin Luther King, Jr. King's civil-rights campaign had a powerful effect on the U.S. His non-violent protests and inspirational speeches appealed to the American sense of conscience. Eventually, the American public admitted to the injustices done to the African American community, and dramatic civil-rights reforms were initiated. It is clear that while Jainism may not be the most well-known world religion, it has certainly affected the spiritual development of the world.

Check Your Understanding

1. Explain the ritual of *sallekhana*. What is your considered opinion of this spiritual practice?

2. What is the significance of the swastika in Jainism?

3. What disagreement led to the formation of the two Jain sects?

4. Do you think non-violent protests can be effective? Explain your answer.

Exploring Issues: Vegetarianism

The Jain community follows a strict vegetarian diet. This diet is an expression of ahimsa, designed to act as a physical demonstration in the belief in the sanctity of all life forms. Thus, a Jain engages in vegetarianism as a moral responsibility or imperative.

Jains refrain from drinking wine and eating meat, eggs, and honey. They do not drink wine because germs are killed during the fermentation process, and because of the intoxicating impact it has on a person. This intoxication clouds people's judgment and makes them more likely to act in a manner contrary to the moral teaching of ahimsa. Meat-eating is prohibited because the flesh of the body of a "mobile being"—an animal—has to be obtained by killing. Since the meat is obtained through killing, meat-eating would make a person party to the murder of the animal and, subsequently, would contravene the principle of ahimsa. Eggs are not eaten because the consumption of eggs contributes to the death of the embryo of the chicken. Finally, honey is forbidden because it is formed from the regurgitation of bees. Compounding the problem of honey is the fact that bees rob plants of some of their essential nutrients.

Jain vegetarianism does not come without its problems. For example, where do you draw the line? If the idea of atomism is true, and every individual atom has a soul, or *jiva*, then why would it be permissible to harvest certain vegetables for consumption? After all, the eating of the vegetable leads to the death of the vegetable in the same way that eating meat is a by-product of the killing of the animal. The facts that a plant is immobile and the animal is mobile have little effect on this outcome.

Jains argue that vegetarianism minimizes the amount of suffering in the world, and that the consumption and harvesting of meat put a tremendous strain on the earth's resources. EarthSave Canada, a Canadian organization that promotes vegetarianism, claims that cattle must consume 12 pounds (5.4 kg) of grain to produce one pound (0.5 kg) of hamburger. Alternatively, the same amount of grain could be used to make eight loaves of bread or twenty-four plates of spaghetti. While complete elimination of suffering is not an achievable goal, a vegetarian diet does promote ahimsa and results in less suffering in the world.

The vegetarian movement has become quite popular in Canada. While some vegetarians say they "won't eat anything with a brain," others go as far as Jain vegetarians by eliminating eggs and milk from their diets. Many Canadians practise a vegetarian diet in the interests of personal health and, in some cases, to promote a culture that places less strain on the resources of the planet. Restaurants and grocers have tried to accommodate vegetarians by adding vegetarian dishes to their menus and improving the selection and quantity of vegetables in grocery stores. Regardless of the reasons for the increased popularity of vegetarianism, it is clear that several of these reasons are making their way into the daily lives and diets of many Canadians.

QUESTIONS

1. How is Jain vegetarianism different from North American vegetarianism?

2. Name four things that are forbidden in the Jain diet. Why are they forbidden?

3. Evaluate the practice of Jain vegetarianism. Where do you stand on this issue? Does vegetarianism contribute to less suffering in the world?

4. Is it possible to practise a vegetarian diet in your home and in school? Explain your answer.

TAOISM

The Tao Te Ching (sometimes spelled Daodejing) makes the following proclamation:

> *The Tao gives birth to the one*
> *One gives birth to two*
> *Two gives birth to three*
> *Three gives birth to all things*

Tao is the force that existed before all things. By giving birth to the one, Tao gave the world a mechanism for balance. The birth of two means the birth of opposites. The birth of three refers to the existence of heaven, earth, and humanity. Thus, all creation can be related back to Tao, the great silent source of harmony.

ORIGINS

While Zoroastrianism was rising to prominence in Persia and Jainism was gaining strength in India, China was sitting on the brink of a major religious era. The reigning folk religions of China were ready for a movement that would bring them focus. That focus would arrive with the recognition of Tao as the force governing the universe.

Huang Di

Before discussing the emergence of Taoism (sometimes spelled Daoism)—and Confucianism, for that matter—we'll consider an emperor of China named Huang Di. Legend has it that, in the nineteenth year of his reign,

Huang Di visited a hermit and asked him a question. The hermit refused to answer Huang Di's question, but the emperor persisted and, eventually, the hermit spoke. The wisdom that Huang Di received from the hermit was so profound that it changed the way the emperor governed his people. His people called him the "Yellow Emperor" because of his compassionate and benevolent leadership. He was seen as a healer and a magician and was eventually recognized as the greatest emperor that China had ever seen. So what was the secret that the hermit shared with Huang Di? The secret was Tao.

Tao literally means "way." To follow the Tao is to practise the way of nature. Tao has been described as being like water; water is fluid and soft, but it can also demonstrate great force, wearing down the hardest rock. In a world of opposites, the Tao is the balance between opposing forces. Huang Di took the wisdom of the Tao and created harmony within himself and then created harmony within his kingdom.

Lao Tzu

Traditionally, the founding of Taoism is ascribed to Lao Tzu (sometimes spelled Laozi). However, scholars are uncertain whether or not Lao Tzu (Figure 3.9) actually existed. There are several reasons for this: first, Lao Tzu means "old master," which is a title and not an actual name; second, scholars speculate that the wisdom associated with Lao Tzu seems to be an amalgam of the work of three different people. If Lao Tzu did exist, he may have been a man named Li Erh, an archivist at the royal palace of Luoyang, the capital city of the Chou dynasty.

Figure 3.9
According to legend, Lao Tzu was head librarian of the imperial archives at Luoyang. In this position, Lao Tzu became very knowledgeable about history, philosophy, and literature, gaining wisdom and insight in the process.

Relying on the theory that Lao Tzu was Li Erh, we can put together a rough biography of the father of Taoism. According to some traditions, Lao Tzu was an older contemporary of Confucius. He kept his job at the royal court until he was very old, leaving when he had tired of working in government. As Lao Tzu was on his way out of the province of Ch'u, a border guard, recognizing the wise old master, asked him to leave some reckoning of his wisdom behind. It was at this point that Lao Tzu wrote the Tao Te Ching, a short collection of wise verses that encapsulated the heart of the "way."

Chuang Tzu

In many ways, the Tao Te Ching was more appealing to the educated and wealthy members of society. Something needed to be done to bring the Tao to life for the common people. This responsibility fell to Chuang Tzu (369–286 BCE), the next great sage of Taoism (Figure 3.10). From the perspective of biography, little is known about the life of Chuang Tzu (sometimes spelled Zhuangzi) other than the fact that he was one of the authors of the book that bears his name. *Chuang Tzu* is a collection of stories, written in prose form instead of poetry, that seeks to teach the Tao from the perspective of active, everyday life.

By the time of Chuang Tzu's death in 286 BCE, the groundwork had been laid—the great secret of Huang Di's encounter with the hermit had been given form, and philosophical Taoism was born.

Philosophical Taoism

Taoism continued to grow after the death of Chuang Tzu with the founding of the Huang Lao School in the fourth century BCE. The Huang Lao School was named in honour of Huang Di (the Yellow Emperor) and Lao Tzu (the author of the Tao Te Ching). One of the greatest contributions of the school was to clarify the teaching of **wu wei**. *Wu wei* means "not acting." Specifically, Taoists believe that action is not to be wasted and that no action should be undertaken that goes against nature. Therefore, non-action is often preferable to action because action can disturb the delicate balance of nature. The Huang Lao School taught that individuals should pursue action that was consistent with the historical period in which they were born and with the position they held in society.

Religious Taoism

By the second century BCE, the Huang Lao School was flourishing, and Taoism had become the dominant philosophy of the Han dynasty (206 BCE–220 CE). A shift was about to take place, moving Taoism from a largely philosophical movement into the realm of religion. China had been a predominantly polytheistic nation as far back as the time of the Yellow Emperor. Taoism had introduced a philosophy that challenged the mythology of the ancients. However, polytheism and folk religion never died out, and, with the emergence of Chang Chiao and Chang Tao-ling, folk religion was about to take new form in religious Taoism.

The Way of the Celestial Masters

Taoism was transformed by two events early in the first millennium. First was the emergence of Chang Tao-ling (34–156 CE) and the "Way of the Celestial Masters." As Chang Tao-ling was growing up in southwest China, he could not help noticing the growing appeal of Buddhism to the local people. They were attracted to the rituals and deities of a new faith that possessed quite a few parallel beliefs with Taoism and Confucianism. However, Chang, a Confucian who had turned to Taoism, wanted to ensure the survival of a strong Chinese religious tradition. After immersing himself in Taoist literature

Figure 3.10
In his writings, Chuang Tzu maintained that all things are united through the processes of nature, thus humankind should try to live in harmony with nature and not impose on it. He believed that individuals could accomplish more by doing nothing.

and teachings, Chang received a revelation from Lord Lao the Most High— the deified spirit of Lao Tzu. The revelation directed Chang to organize Taoism into a formal faith in order to compensate for the rise of Buddhism in China. Chang travelled the countryside, teaching, healing, and establishing places of worship. Eventually, Chang and his followers came to represent what came to be known as the Way of the Celestial Masters. It has survived until today, with the sixty-third Celestial Master currently residing in Taiwan.

The "Yellow Turban" Rebellion

The second development was the "Yellow Turban" rebellion of 184 CE. The rebel leader, Chang Chiao, wanted to see a new spiritual dominion that followed the Tao of the yellow heaven of Lao Tzu and the Yellow Emperor. Chang Chiao's band of rebels, wearing yellow turbans as a sign of their loyalty to the "way," tried to overthrow the ruling Han authorities but were suppressed by the military. Their brief rebellion was put to rest. However, the seeds of religious Taoism had been sown.

Over the centuries, Taoism would prosper and decline but never disappear. It continues to hold a key role in Chinese culture, sharing prominence with Confucianism and Buddhism. It should be noted that Taoists, Confucians, and Buddhists all recognize the inherent strengths in each faith and have seldom acted in a manner that would compromise the other.

Check Your Understanding

1. What is Tao?

2. Identify and state the significance of Huang Di, the Yellow Emperor.

3. What two events transformed Taoism early in the first millennium?

4. Do you think it is possible to model one's life on the "way of nature"? Explain.

BELIEFS

Wu Wei

As mentioned earlier, a central belief in Taoism is *wu wei*, or "not doing." *Wu wei* is not an invitation to laziness or sloth. Rather, it is a spiritual request to leave things alone and let nature take its course. Thus, a person should not manipulate others' thoughts and minds into thinking in a certain manner. Instead, one should have faith in the Tao and allow people to find their own way based on the eternal Tao that underlies all existence. The Huang Lao School brought greater definition to the concept of *wu wei* in the book *Huai Nan Tzu*, in which *wu wei* is described as follows:

> . . . wu wei *means that selfish motives cannot be allowed to disturb public business; wild wishes cannot be allowed to destroy right principle* . . . (Wu wei) *doesn't mean that one should have no reaction to feelings, or no response to pressure. If one wants to boil away a well, or irrigate a mountain by the Huai River, these are stubbornly against nature, hence they are called "taking action* (yu wei)." *If you take a boat when you come upon water, or take a special cart when you walk in the desert or take a special sledge when you move on mud . . . these are not what is called "doing* (wei)."

Therefore, *wu wei* is more than just sitting idly by in apparent communion with nature. Instead, individuals are vitally involved in what is going on around them. Their actions are based on a sense of effortlessness, wherein they are acting in a manner that does as little harm as possible to the natural world.

PRACTICES, RITUALS, AND SYMBOLS

Physical Well-Being

Taoists place a tremendous emphasis on physical health and longevity. This dates back to the time of Liu An (d. 221 BCE) and the Huainan Masters. Liu An's court was active with sages studying and teaching Tao. Soon, the medical arts started to flourish as Liu An encouraged his scholars to discover a potion that would give a person physical immortality. While the sages failed to discover the magic elixir, they did transform the Taoist understanding of physical health. Balance and harmony within the body became as important as the spiritual quest for the same goal.

The efforts of Liu An and the Huainan Masters had far-reaching consequences. Thousands of years later, early Taoist practices have made their way into mainstream Canadian culture. The three most notable are described below.

Tai Chi

Taoism encourages physical activities designed to bring a person into harmony with Tao. This harmony is expressed, and continues to be expressed, in martial arts like Tai Chi (also spelled Taiji). Founded in the twelfth century CE by Chang San Feng, Tai Chi harmonizes the flow of energy (*chi*) through the body. This is accomplished through a series of movements that bring the physical system of the person into a state of harmony. Tai Chi is said to have a positive effect on a person's nervous system, blood circulation, and muscle tone. Tai Chi movements are also said to massage a person's internal organs.

Chinese Medicine and Acupuncture

As with Tai Chi, Chinese medicine seeks to bring a balance to the flow of energy (*chi*) within a person. Balance is disrupted when there is a disruption or blockage in the flow of *chi* within a person's body. The blockage can be remedied through physical exercises, herbal remedies, or procedures like acupuncture.

Acupuncture is a procedure that targets pressure points within the body in order to maintain a proper flow of *chi*. Practitioners apply tiny needles to the acupuncture points of a person's body. Traditionally, there were 365 major points; as a result of the growing body of research on acupuncture, the total number of acupoints is now believed to exceed 800.

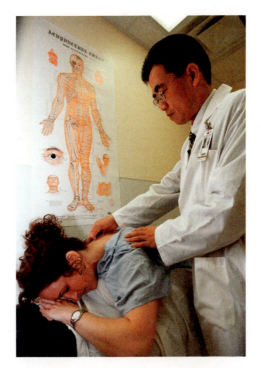

Figure 3.11
The growing acceptance and popularity of Chinese medicine and acupuncture in Canada have led to the formation of a number of organizations. The Chinese Medicine and Acupuncture Association of Canada (CMAAC) was formed in 1983 to bring practitioners into a professional organization and to inform the public on issues surrounding these ancient practices. In 1990, the Canadian Academy of Acupuncture and Chinese Medicine was established to train and certify practitioners of acupuncture and Chinese medicine.

Feng Shui

Drawing on the ancient Chinese ideal of living in harmony with the environment, the art of constructing buildings in accordance with Tao emerged. This style of design is called feng shui, and it dates back thousands of years. A traditional practitioner of feng shui seeks to bring a building into alignment with the environment in order to ensure the best possible use of spiritual energy. This is accomplished by placing doorways, staircases, windows, and rooms in certain geometrical locations. All choices are made with the optimal use of the spiritual energy in mind. Feng shui practitioners also consider things like road configurations, environmental features, and the location of entrances to the building. A building—whether an office or a home—designed with feng shui in mind is constructed with the idea of balance and the positive flow of energy.

Symbols and Icons
Yin-Yang

Figure 3.12

The central symbol in Taoism is the **yin-yang**. The symbol itself suggests the balance and harmony inherent in Taoist philosophy. This is seen in the contrasting black and white areas, with a small white dot in the black area and a small black dot in the white area. Some people interpret the small opposing dots in each area to represent the fact that in all evil there exists some good, while in all good there exists some evil. However, more than anything, the symbol itself points to the existence of pairs of opposites like dark and bright, night and day, dry and moist, aggressive and passive, and sun and rain. The curves in the symbol suggest movement, representing the Taoist belief that everything is subject to change.

Each side also carries with it a specific meaning. The white side of the symbol is yang. It represents the heavenly force and is akin to movement, light, fire, warmth, and life. Yang is seen as the breath that formed the heavens. The literal meaning of yang is "sunny side." The black side of the symbol is yin, and it represents the "shady side" of existence. Yin is seen as the breath that formed the earth. Note that the two elements are inseparable—one cannot exist without the other.

QUESTIONS

1. How does the yin-yang reflect the elements of balance and movement?
2. What is the difference between yin and yang?
3. Is your life "balanced" or not? Explain.

Check Your Understanding

1. What contributions did Liu An and the Huainan Masters make to the medical sciences?

2. What is acupuncture? Would you go for treatment? Explain.

3. What evidence is there that Chinese medicine and acupuncture have been accepted in Canada?

4. What is feng shui?

SACRED WRITINGS

As mentioned previously, the Tao Te Ching and *Chuang Tzu* are the most sacred books of Toaism. The Tao Te Ching is a collection of eighty-one short poems. The topics vary from advice to leaders to paradoxes about life. *Chuang Tzu* uses a prose writing style. The stories focus on uniting with the Tao by abandoning the conventions of society. Whereas the Tao Te Ching provides advice for kings, *Chuang Tzu* indicates a disdain and distrust for government.

Lu Xiujing (406–477 CE) developed a system of classifying a vast body of scripture that came to be known as the "Three Caverns." He did this to encourage scholarly examination of Taoist scripture as well as to make Taoism more appealing to the sovereigns of his day.

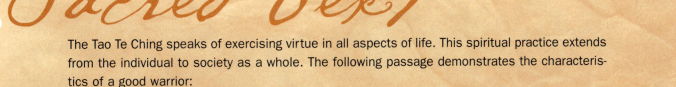

The Tao Te Ching speaks of exercising virtue in all aspects of life. This spiritual practice extends from the individual to society as a whole. The following passage demonstrates the characteristics of a good warrior:

Tao Te Ching, 68
Good warriors do not arm,
good fighters do not get mad,
good winners do not contend,
good employers serve their workers.
This is called the virtue
of non-contention;
this is called mating with
the supremely natural and pristine.

QUESTIONS

1. According to the Tao Te Ching, what are the qualities of a good warrior?

2. Explain the "virtue of non-contention" in your own words.

Community Study

International Taoist Tai Chi Centre
Orangeville, Ontario

Today, thousands of Canadians practise Tai Chi. In fact, Orangeville, Ontario, is home to the International Taoist Tai Chi Centre. The centre was founded by Master Moy Lin-Shin, a Tai Chi master and Taoist monk who immigrated to Canada from Hong Kong in 1970. Master Moy's goal was to demonstrate the health benefits of Tai Chi to as many people as possible. He felt that Tai Chi was effective in bringing people to a sense of internal calm because of its emphasis on natural movement. He combined this vision with cease-less service to his community, with particular emphasis placed on teaching Tai Chi to senior citizens and people with various illnesses. After a lifetime of work, Master Moy left an incredible legacy, establishing the Canadian-based International Taoist Tai Chi Society, with over 500 locations worldwide. He is also credited with helping to found the Fung Loy Kok Institute of Taoism in Toronto. Master Moy died in 1998, but his work continues under the guidance of the board of directors of the society, as well as an international team of

Web Quest

To learn more about Master Moy and the activities of the International Taoist Tai Chi Society, go to http://www.taoist.org/

Figure 3.13

volunteers who share his vision of health and happiness through Tai Chi.

One aspect of the International Taoist Tai Chi Society worthy of special attention is the establishment of the Taoist Tai Chi Health Recovery Centre in Orangeville. While studying Tai Chi, Master Moy was concerned that instruction in this martial art was too oriented toward self-defence, while the health component was not being emphasized enough. To deal with the situation, Master Moy founded Taoist Tai Chi, which focused primarily on health improvement. This goal came to full realization with the purchase of land and buildings just outside of Orangeville, Ontario. This location would become the international home of Taoist Tai Chi and, in addition to being a Tai Chi centre, would be of service to people with health problems like stroke, heart disease, multiple sclerosis, Parkinson's Disease, high blood pressure, and diabetes. Master Moy believed that people suffering from various ailments could benefit greatly from Tai Chi. Based on this assumption, residences were established and programs were set up for people to improve their heath through Tai Chi at the Health Recovery Centre. Today, people can apply to attend one of the monthly sessions offered by the centre in the hope of channelling the energy of their body into a pattern of growth, rejuvenation, and recovery.

The contribution of Tai Chi to Canadian society is not easily measured. Master Moy's efforts have set an example of incredible compassion and generosity. The International Taoist Tai Chi Society has inherited this example and continued his work. In the meantime, Tai Chi, along with the other martial arts, has grown in popularity. The practice of Tai Chi has become "common" in the best sense of the word.

QUESTIONS

1. Who was Master Moy? What did he do to establish Canada as an international centre for the development of Taoist Tai Chi?

2. What function does the Health Recovery Centre serve?

3. What aspects of Tai Chi interest you the most? Explain.

CULTURAL IMPACT

Taoism has gone through three distinct periods of development. The first period of growth happened with the founding of Taoism by Lao Tzu and Chuang Tzu as well as with the emergence of the Huang Lao School. This period of development gave Taoism form and identity. The second period of development was marked by the emergence of religious Taoism. Faced with challenges from Buddhism and Confucianism, Taoism needed to define itself as a faith. Chang Tao-ling's Way of the Celestial Masters, in particular, provided Taoism with a religious foundation that would grow exponentially over the centuries, followed by the formation of groups like the Highest Purity Sect.

The third developmental period was marked by the decline of the traditional Chinese religion early in the twentieth century. In 1911, the collapse of the Ch'ing dynasty saw the end of state support for Taoism and Confucianism. Between 1911 and 1949, Taoism and Confucianism fell victim to warlords and vandals. The treasures of these two religions were attacked in a new era of Chinese nationalism that eventually resulted in the victory of the Chinese Communist Party in 1949. This was followed by the Great Cultural Revolution (1966–1976) when Mao Zedong attempted to eliminate the legacies of Taoism and Confucianism. The result was a period of tragedy that saw Mao fail to meet his objective, China begin to move away from anti-religious policies, and the rest of the world suddenly become interested in ancient Chinese spirituality.

Many Chinese have left their homeland and settled in countries such as Korea, Vietnam, Indonesia, and Malaysia. Currently, Taiwan is the most active Taoist nation in the world, providing a home in exile for the Celestial Master. The island of Taiwan is an example of a thriving Taoist community.

Recent estimates put the global population of Taoists at 20 million, with 30 000 Taoists living in North America, many of whom reside in Vancouver and Toronto. The most evident signs of Taoist impact on Canadian culture can be seen in the areas of the martial arts, herbalism, holistic medicine, meditation, and acupuncture.

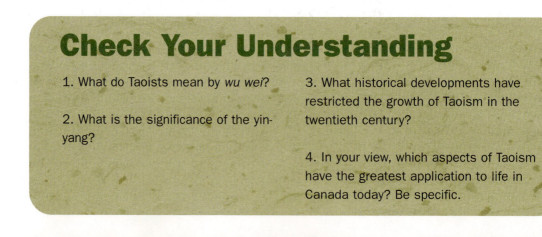

Check Your Understanding

1. What do Taoists mean by *wu wei*?

2. What is the significance of the yin-yang?

3. What historical developments have restricted the growth of Taoism in the twentieth century?

4. In your view, which aspects of Taoism have the greatest application to life in Canada today? Be specific.

CONFUCIANISM

ORIGINS

The Master said, "Clever talk and a pretentious manner are seldom found in the Good."

—The Analects of Confucius, Book 1

The Master said, "He who learns but does not think is lost. He who thinks but does not learn is in great danger."

—The Analects of Confucius, Book 2

Confucius was a younger contemporary of Lao Tzu, and his philosophy, while distinct in its application, shares some of the main components of Taoism. For example, the idea of harmony, yin-yang, and ancestral roots tied to the great Yellow Emperor are essential to Confucianism. With the emergence of Confucius, the Tao of Lao Tzu was about to face a challenge from the Tao of the "Heavenly Way."

Scholars often have difficulty determining whether Confucianism is simply a philosophy or a philosophy and a religion. On the one hand, Confucianism is a philosophical movement, with all of its emphasis on studying and scholarship. On the other hand, Confucianism teaches the "Way of Heaven" and provides consistent moral training that is quite religious. It is this combination of philosophy and religion that has caused the misunderstanding.

Confucianism is so practical and reasonable that often people dismiss it as being a simple list of suggestions on how to live a balanced life. However, it

Figure 3.14
In The Analects of Confucius, Confucius's disciples describe him as such: "Confucius was completely free from four things: He had no forgone conclusions, no dogmatism, no obstinacy, and no egotism." How might these traits help an individual acquire wisdom and insight?

is the practical nature of Confucianism that makes it a great religion. Besides asking adherents to develop an alert mind, a healthy body, and a pure soul, Confucius also taught people to live in accordance with the Way of Heaven. For Confucians, heaven exists in the here and now, a position that is strikingly similar to the proclamation of Jesus of Nazareth 500 years later regarding the kingdom of God. In the end, scholars must concede that Confucianism is both philosophy and religion—two traditions that are not seen as separate in Chinese culture.

Confucius

What of the man who came to be known as Confucius? Confucius was born in the Chinese province of Lu in 551 BCE. His mother was his first and most important teacher, providing him with rigorous training that eventually led to his mastering of the six arts: ritual, music, archery, charioteering, calligraphy, and arithmetic. His father was the commander of a district in Lu, but he died three years after Confucius was born. By the time he was nineteen, Confucius was a well-educated young man. He got married and started a family with his wife. However, in his early twenties, Confucius suffered through the loss of his mother. After a period of mourning, Confucius became a teacher and built a reputation as a man of virtue who cherished Chinese culture and values.

Confucius was upset by the lack of morality in the province of Lu. The decline of the Chou dynasty brought with it a wave of cynicism and corruption that greatly disturbed him. Like the Taoists, Confucius revered the Yellow Emperor and longed for the days of virtuous leadership and political stability of days gone by. Eventually, he became convinced that the only way to remedy the malaise of society was to teach people the ways of the Yellow Emperor and encourage people to take responsibility for their conduct.

By the age of fifty, Confucius was appointed magistrate of the town of Chung-tu, before moving to the position of Minister of Justice for Lu. Under Confucius's guidance, Lu became an icon of justice and fairness. However, the power of Confucius caused others within the imperial court to become envious, and, in 496 BCE, he felt compelled to leave office. He travelled and taught beyond the borders of Lu for eleven years before returning home at the age of sixty-seven. He studied and taught until he died in 479 BCE. By the time he died, Confucius had seventy-two disciples (each of whom mastered the six arts) and 3000 followers.

Mencius

Confucianism was the subject of criticism in its early development. Mozi, a Chinese philosopher (479–380 BCE), took exception to the apparent godlessness of Confucianism, claiming that Confucians were preoccupied with music, ritual, and determinism. Mencius (390–305 BCE) disagreed with Mozi's position. He claimed that people needed to remain grounded, to avoid the trap of dwelling on the gods, and to live in the present moment. He stated that " . . . the true great man dwells in humanity and walks the path of righteousness for the sake of the way." Mencius believed that people are naturally good and that evil is learned. He suddenly became the great defender of the Way of the Heaven, and in doing so gave Confucianism a clarity that had been missing since the death of its founder.

Hsun Tzu

Confucius and Mencius solidified the foundation of Confucian philosophy; however, it was Hsun Tzu (298–238 BCE) who brought Confucianism to life with clarity and precision. Through a process of systematic scholarship, he was able to explain the philosophical importance of living virtuously. He warned that human nature was inherently evil and easily corrupted unless people were taught otherwise. Over the course of his life, Hsun Tzu would write thirty-two essays that clarified the Confucian belief system.

Web Quest

To learn more about the life of Confucius, go to http://www.confucius.org/ebio.htm

Profile: *Mencius:* (371?–289 BCE)

Figure 3.15

The second great sage of Confucianism was Mencius. Born in Chao, Mencius spent his youth studying under the direction of his mother and, according to legend, the grandson of Confucius. By the time he reached maturity, he had developed an appreciation for the teachings of Confucius. He soon came to determine that human nature is inherently good and that practising goodness was the best way to achieve fulfillment. Eventually, he focused on political theory and, like Confucius, travelled from province to province trying to teach local rulers how to govern justly. His efforts were not greeted with enthusiasm because he challenged the sense of superiority engendered by many kings. His teachings have survived in the Book of Mencius, a collection assembled by his disciples after his death.

The philosophy of Mencius emphasizes the Confucian concept of *jen*, or virtue. He was concerned with teaching the merits of humaneness and benevolence. This virtue is expressed in relationship to other people. In other words, based on the fact that people are in relationship with one another, they are obligated to act virtuously with one another for the sake of the relationship. Acting virtuously is the natural response for a person seeking to create harmony with another person. To act with virtue is to recognize a person's humanity and treat him or her with kindness and benevolence.

This concept can be extended to the manner in which rulers govern their subjects. Mencius claimed that people need peace of mind to develop *jen*. This is necessarily dependent on material security like food, shelter, and work. Therefore, if rulers do not provide for their people, they should be forced out of office.

Mencius also believed that wise people surface out of blood, sweat, and tears. He said:

Heaven, when it is about to place a great responsibility on a man, always first tests his resolution, wears out his sinews and bones with toil, exposes his body to starvation, subjects him to extreme poverty, frustrates his efforts so as to stimulate his mind, toughen his nature and make good his deficiencies.

Mencius, Book VI, Kao Tzu, Part II, 15

Despite these hardships, Mencius pointed out that the companion of wisdom is joy. He said, "There is no greater joy than to find, on self-examination, that I am true to myself. Try your best to treat others as you would wish to be treated yourself, and you will find that this is the shortest way to humanity." Once again, the Confucian golden rule of propriety and reciprocity is advocated—this time by the second great sage, Mencius.

QUESTIONS

1. Why weren't the teachings of Mencius greeted with enthusiasm by local rulers?

2. How does the Confucian ideal of *jen* (see page 93) fit into the philosophy of Mencius?

3. According to Mencius, what obligations do rulers have in order to properly serve their subjects? What if they do not meet these obligations?

Check Your Understanding

1. Is Confucianism a philosophy or a religion? Explain.

2. What impact did Confucius have on the lives of his disciples?

3. What contributions did Mencius and Hsun Tzu make to the growth of Confucianism?

4. Do you agree with the position of Mencius that states that humans are naturally good? Explain.

BELIEFS

Wisdom

The Master said, "Do I regard myself as a possessor of wisdom? Far from it. But if even a simple peasant comes in all sincerity and asks me a question, I am ready to thrash the matter out, with all its pros and cons, to the very end."

—The Analects of Confucius, Book 9

One day Confucius was asked if a person should always be kind. Confucius responded, " . . . return malice with justice, but return kindness with kindness." On another occasion, Confucius advised his disciples to conduct themselves according to the Confucian "golden rule": "Do not do to others what you would not want to have done to you." Precision and wisdom were the defining features of his advice. He encouraged people to conduct themselves in a manner that did not compromise their own sense of virtue or the virtuousness of others. Therefore, he demonstrated that a person who defended virtue needed to be firm with those who acted in a cruel or malicious fashion. The key was to know how and when to use the power of justice, always keeping the well-being of others in mind. In terms of a general rule of conduct, Confucius advised people to employ empathy in their thoughts, deeds, and expressions. The clarity of his message left no doubt in the minds of those who listened.

But where did this great wisdom come from? It seems that for every question, Confucius had a clear answer. Confucius claimed that he was merely a transmitter of wisdom and that everything that he said had been said before. Once he declared, "I transmit but do not create. Being fond of truth, I am an admirer of antiquity." He simply acquired information through intense study of the ancients and, as a result, appeared to be wise. Confucius never conceded to any degree of originality; the wisdom of his sayings, advice, and teachings rested on what his ancestors had given him. Like Mahavira, the "reorganizer" of Jainism, he worked with the legacy of those who had come before him.

This sense of humility added to the power of his teachings. People started to listen to him because, like the master wood carver from "The Story of the Bell Stand" (see page 60), Confucius seemed lost in the purity of nature—a purity consumed by virtue. He sought no credit for what he said; instead, he let the things that he said stand on their own merit. Thus, when Confucius gave his disciples the golden rule, they were prepared to accept it because they knew that the words were coming from someone who practised the virtue that he preached. Sounding very Taoist, Confucius proclaimed, "Nature's way is to be genuine. To be genuine is to act truly without effort, to attain without thinking about it, and automatically and spontaneously to realize one's nature. Such a man is wise." The wisdom of Confucius is truly genuine and effortless.

Virtue

While Taoism sought to teach the Tao of nature, Confucianism emphasized the Tao of Heaven. The difference between the two rests in the Confucian emphasis on transforming the individual into a living example of virtue as a strict duty to heaven.

Confucius believed this transformation rests in the potential for perfection that exists in each individual. This perfection is achieved through teaching the person the Way of Heaven and encouraging a process of continual self-improvement. Confucius was a lover of learning. He always sought self-improvement and did so by studying the ways of the ancients, specifically the early Chou dynasty and the rule of the Yellow Emperor, Huang Di. In the end, Confucius determined that humans have a duty to act as guardians of heaven's creation. As guardians of creation, humans determine the course of history and of nature based on their ability to live virtuously in the context of a community.

The Five Virtues

Fan Ch'ih asked about Goodness. The Master said, "In private life, courteous, in public life, diligent, in relationships, loyal. This is the maxim that no matter where you may be, even amid the barbarians of the east or north, may never be set aside."

—The Analects of Confucius, Book 13

Confucianism is the active pursuit of Tao. It involves choosing actions that are in accordance with one's sacred duty to follow the Way of Heaven. For a Confucian, this is achieved by practising the Five Virtues.

The Five Virtues are *jen, yi, li, chih,* and *hsin.* Like yin-yang, they correlate and are necessary for the individual to achieve a sense of peace and balance. **Jen** means goodwill, sympathy toward others, politeness, and generosity. It also involves diligence and perseverance. **Yi** means rightness; in the case of Confucians, to respect their duty as guardians of nature and humanity. **Li** is the art of right conduct wherein Confucians practise propriety in all that they do. Propriety involves demonstrating their inner attitude in their outer expression. **Chih** is wisdom. Wisdom is expressed by demonstrating *jen, yi,* and *li.* The final virtue is **hsin**. *Hsin* is faithfulness and trustworthiness. It indicates how the wise person has come to be a visible example of goodwill, loyalty, and propriety.

Confucian Leadership and the Virtues

The Master said, "He who rules by moral force is like the pole-star, which remains in its place while all the lesser stars do homage to it."

—The Analects of Confucius, Book 2

Both Confucius and Mencius demonstrated a concern for the way in which people were governed. They extended the Taoist belief in the "way" by claiming that people can follow their natural inclination to be good more readily if they have a living example in their king. People can find these examples either by studying the leaders of the time of the Yellow Emperor or, more ideally, their own ruler. According to Confucius, rulers should practise the Five Virtues. They should do this simply because they are a son or daughter of heaven. Confucius felt that virtue was a requirement of leadership and was essential if individuals hoped to develop a sense of dignity and solidarity within a community. Practising the Five Virtues is a natural inclination since, according to Confucius and Mencius, human nature is naturally inclined to do good.

The Five Relationships and Ancestor Veneration

The Master said, "A young man's duty is to behave well to his parents at home and to his elders abroad, to be cautious in giving promises and punctual in keeping them, to have kindly feelings toward everyone, but seek the intimacy of the Good. If, when all that is done, he has any energy to spare, then let him study the polite arts."

—The Analects of Confucius, Book 1

Two commonly misinterpreted Confucian beliefs are the teaching of the Five Relationships and ancestor veneration. The five relationships are

- father/son
- ruler/citizen
- husband/wife
- older brother/younger brother
- friend/friend

Mencius created the teaching of the Five Relationships in an effort to show people the importance of mutuality in dealing with others. Each relationship involves mutual respect and recognition in order for it to work. Thus, rulers have a moral obligation to rule their citizens with justice, and the citizens have a responsibility to obey and remain loyal to their rulers. Problems arise when people forget the Mencian emphasis on mutuality. If a ruler becomes authoritarian and oppressive, the citizens are likely to respond with disobedience and rebelliousness.

Ancestor veneration involves honouring and remembering the members of one's family who have died. It is considered to be an expression of *hsin* (faithfulness), in which loved ones are remembered for the contributions they made to the people they touched. Some critics have equated ancestor veneration with ancestor worship, where ancestors would be seen as gods who have passed on. Confucianists practise veneration—the honouring of one's ancestral roots as an act of sincere remembrance.

MILESTONES AND SYMBOLS

Birth and Conception

Confucianism is rich in rituals and ceremony relating to the movement from one life era to the next. At birth, the spirit of the fetus (*T'ai-shen*) is believed to protect the mother from harm. After the birth, the placenta is disposed of in a special manner, and the mother is given one month to rest and recover. The mother's family provides everything the child needs on the first-, fourth-, and twelfth-month anniversary of the birth.

Marriage

The marriage process is another interesting Confucian ritual (Figure 3.16). The process starts with the proposal. It involves an exchange of the details surrounding the couple's respective births (hour, day, month, year). If anything unfavourable happens in the family of the bride-to-be over the three days after the initial exchange, the proposal is rejected. If nothing unfavourable happens, and the proposal is accepted, the engagement is formalized, and details of a dowry are arranged. It is interesting to note that the dowry paid by the bride's parents is matched by gifts given to her family by the groom's parents. The wedding day involves a procession to both families' homes, a ceremony and reception, and a breakfast gathering where the bride serves the groom's parents, and the groom's parents reciprocate.

Figure 3.16
As part of the Confucian wedding ceremony, the bride offers cups of tea to the wedding guests. The bridal headdress is made of a framework of bamboo with braces angled up to a high-vaulted point and covered with rectangular-shaped embroidered cloths, usually family heirlooms. A red cloth with tasselled corners is placed over this frame, with the tassels forming a veil over the bride's face.

Death

When a Confucian dies, the relatives of the deceased cry aloud in order to inform the neighbours of the person's death. The body is washed and placed in a coffin, along with food and objects that are significant to the deceased. The family of the dead person wears clothing made of coarse material, and mourners bring incense and money to offset the cost of the funeral. A priest performs the burial rituals, leading the coffin to the grave. Family members follow, carrying a willow branch that represents the soul of the deceased. Later, they return to a shrine in their home, placing the willow branch on an altar to signify the presence of the spirit of the deceased in their home. The seventh, ninth, and forty-ninth days after the burial are recognized through a liturgy, as are the first and third anniversaries of the person's death.

Symbols and Icons
Confucius and the Five Virtues

禮 義 信 仁 知

Figure 3.17

Hong Kong artist, was inspired by the statue of the Sage in the Temple of Confucius in Ch'u Fu. The statue dates back to the Ch'ing dynasty. The robes and headdress worn by Confucius in the portrait signify the Confucian declaration of 739 CE, which named him the Exalted King of Culture. Declaring Confucius a king demonstrates his exalted status in the "Way of Heaven."

Symbols are difficult to come by in Confucianism. While a great deal of reverence has been paid to Confucius himself in the form of statues and paintings, there is a reluctance to turn these images into icons. Over the course of the history of Confucianism, fears have surfaced that if Confucius were made the symbol of the faith, followers might resort to honouring his image more than his teachings.

Thus, the Chinese characters for the Five Virtues, which surround the portrait of Confucius above, can be used to bring one closer to the spirit of Confucian teachings. Described in detail on page 93, the Five Virtues are

Over the centuries, artists have been inspired by the teachings of Confucius and have produced beautiful portraits like the one by Peter Mong shown above. Mong, a

jen 仁   *yi* 義   *li* 禮   *chih* 信   *hsin* 知

QUESTIONS

1. Why is a portrait or statue of Confucius the most appropriate symbol of Confucianism?

2. How does the artist effectively demonstrate the majesty of Confucius in the portrait?

SACRED WRITINGS

Confucianism has developed a rich tradition of scholarship. Consequently, the body of literature available is vast. However, it is generally agreed that the sacred writings of Confucianism are the Five Classics (Wu Jing) and the Four Books (Si Shu).

The Five Classics existed before Confucius's time. As such, they offer background detail into the ritual, social, political, historic, and poetic philosophy of Confucianism. The Five Classics include the I Ching (sometimes spelled Yi Ching), or "Book of Changes." The I Ching could best be described as instruction in the art of divination, or fortune-telling. Through a process of forming hexagrams with yarrow sticks, the diviner is able to get a general read on the potential shape of things to come. Divination was used to help kings make decisions about their future and the future of their kingdom. The I Ching dates back to the time of the Yellow Emperor.

The Four Books were given status by Chu Hsi (1130–1200 CE). The Four Books include The Analects of Confucius, a collection of wise sayings and stories related to Confucius and his disciples. Confucius's disciples compiled the Analects after his death. The Four Books also include the sayings of Mencius.

Web Quest

To view more Confucian art, visit http://www.confucius.org/plate/english/cplate.htm

Sacred Text

These passages capture much of the spirit of Confucius's own work. They emphasize leadership and obligation, or duty. True leaders despise people who divide the kingdom through slanderous speech. Therefore, leaders must take action to prevent this division by combating those who seek to divide. They do this because it is a sacred duty entrusted to them by heaven.

From the Counsels of Yu (in the Book of History, one of the Five Classics)
The Tî said, "Lung, I abominate slanderous speakers and destroyers of the (right) ways, who agitate and alarm my people. I appoint you to be the Minister of Communication. Early and late give forth my orders and report to me, seeing that everything is true."

The Tî said, "Ho! you, twenty and two men, be reverent; so shall you be helpful to the business (entrusted to me by) Heaven."

QUESTIONS

1. A true leader seeks to oppose those who use slanderous speech and gossip to divide the group. How can you oppose slander and gossip in your everyday life?

2. In your view, what are some other qualities of a good leader?

CULTURAL IMPACT

During the past millennium, Confucian teaching became influential in Korea and Japan. Some Koreans today continue to identify themselves as Confucians. Like Taoism, Confucianism suffered persecution in the twentieth century at the hand of Chinese revolutionaries, specifically the Communists. In mainland China, Confucian practices have been severely restricted, although there has been some relief under the leaders of the post-Mao Zedong era. It is difficult to establish how many Confucians there are around the world; some estimates put the figure at about 6 000 000, with 26 000 living in North America.

The philosophy of Confucius has become popular in Canada and the rest of the Western world. The succinct nature of Confucian wisdom is appealing to both young and old. Calls for virtuous leadership and responsible use of authority are important to Canadians. This accounts for the recent swing in popular exposure to Confucian ethics and ideals. As Canadian students study the wisdom of the ancient philosopher, perhaps they will be reminded of Confucius himself studying the ways of the Yellow Emperor. Being fond of truth, they will become admirers of antiquity.

Check Your Understanding

1. Which Confucian beliefs do you find most inspirational?

2. Confucius called himself a transmitter of wisdom. What did he mean by this? How could you be a "transmitter of wisdom"?

3. How could you incorporate the Five Virtues into your own life?

4. According to Confucius, what are the characteristics of a great leader? Name a great leader that you have heard of. What makes this leader great?

5. Why have the Five Relationships and ancestor veneration been misinterpreted? Be specific.

6. What is divination? Does divination still exist in our world today? Give examples.

7. How are Confucian rituals a reflection of the philosophy of Confucius?

SHINTO

ORIGINS

The difficulty in examining Shinto as an organized, early religion rests in the fact that it has no founder, no ritual use of scripture, and no organized teachings. What is known is that, about 2500 years ago, early evidence of Shinto practice and ritual began to emerge. This is roughly the same time period that Zoroastrianism, Jainism, Taoism, and Confucianism were founded.

Early Shinto focused on mythology and nature worship. It was fundamentally polytheistic, using many gods to express religious beliefs. The belief in many gods was not a problem for participants in Shinto since this seemed to provide adherents with a wider variety of answers to their spiritual questions. The name *Shinto* comes from the Chinese term *shin Tao*, which means "the way of the divine." In Japanese, the same characters have the pronunciation *kami no michi*.

As time passed, Shinto demonstrated tremendous ability to coexist with other religious movements. When the religions of China made their way into Japan around 200 CE, Shinto embraced the positive aspects of both Taoism and Confucianism. Similarly, after 552 CE, when Buddhism arrived in Japan, Shinto adopted many of its tenets. Equating of the three faiths eventually led to a situation where Shinto appeared to have been absorbed into Buddhism. This was intolerable to some members of the imperial family, and, in 1868 CE, Emperor Meiji directed government money to Shinto shrines (Figure 3.18) and priests. This led to a resurgence in Shinto worship and the founding of State Shinto. It also provided the people of Japan with a sense of patriotism and obedience, as well as a belief that the emperor was a direct descendant of the gods.

These values and beliefs lasted up until the defeat of the Japanese in the Second World War. The fierce patriotism of State Shinto was condemned by the Allied powers at the end of the war, and the Japanese were forced to abolish State Shinto in 1945. Humiliated by the Japanese defeat, Emperor Hirohito went to the shrine at Ise to apologize to the sun goddess, Amaterasu, for what had happened.

Figure 3.18 *One of the most significant Shinto shrines, the Grand Shrine at Ise, houses the Imperial Shrine (also known as the Naiku, or inner shrine) as well as the Toyouke Shrine (also known as the Geku, or outer shrine). To gain access to the shrine, one must cross the Uji Bridge over the Isuzu River and pass through the large torii gate. The Naiku is extremely important to the family of the Japanese emperor because it is said to enshrine Amaterasu, the ancestral goddess of the imperial family.*

Check Your Understanding

1. What difficulties exist in determining the origins of Shinto?

2. Which religions have influenced the development of Shinto?

3. In your view, should governments become associated with religions? Explain.

BELIEFS

Kami and Shinto Mythology

Figure 3.19

In Shinto mythology, Izanagi and Izanami were given the task of creating the world. Standing on the Floating Bridge of Heaven, Izanagi dipped his jewelled spear into the ocean and churned the water. When he pulled the spear free, the water that dripped from it congealed and formed the first island of the Japanese archipelago.

According to Shinto tradition, the spirits that exist everywhere are known as **kami**. Literally, *kami* means "high" or "superior," but it is commonly used in relation to the words *god* or *deity*. More often than not it is used to refer to spirits.

The *kami* pervade everything. They are found in anything from rocks and trees to animals and thunder. The emergence of the *kami* is explained in the story of two key deities: Izanagi and Izanami, a brother and a sister who descended from the rainbow-striped Floating Bridge of Heaven. When Izanagi dipped his sword into the sea, the mythical process that resulted in the formation of the Japanese islands began (Figure 3.19).

Izanagi and Izanami eventually married and gave birth to a number of other deities, each reigning over a different aspect of nature. While giving birth to the fire god, Homu-subi, Izanami died and descended to the land of darkness. Izanagi, overcome with grief, chopped Homu-subi into pieces with his sword. Each piece of the fire god formed a new deity. Then Izanagi made his way to the land of darkness in search of Izanami. He eventually found her hidden away in the shadows. She did not want him to see her because she had eaten the food of the underworld and was sentenced to remain there. Izanagi implored her to appeal to the gods for release from the land of darkness. She agreed but only if Izanagi agreed not to look at her. Izanagi grew impatient with the process and found Izanami deep in the underworld. She was surrounded by ugly hags, and her maggot-infested body was in the process of rotting. Izanami became enraged and chased Izanagi out of the land of darkness. Izanagi blocked the gateway back to earth with a rock so that Izanami could not escape.

Feeling unclean, Izanagi dove into a river, and, as he bathed, new deities were born. It is said that, as he washed his face, three significant deities emerged. When he washed his nose, Susano-o, goddess of the sea and storms was born. When he washed his right eye, Tsuki-Yomi, the moon god was born. Finally, from the cleansing of his left eye came **Amaterasu**, the sun goddess. Amaterasu is the most significant deity in Shinto belief. She represents hope and prosperity. The sun on the Japanese flag (Figure 3.20) is representative of how important Amaterasu is to the people of Japan. The emperor of Japan is also believed to be a direct descendant of Amaterasu.

PRACTICES, RITUALS, AND SYMBOLS

Purification

Two key components of Shinto ritual are purity and pollution. Ritual purity is critical if the appeal to the *kami* made by a priest or believer is to be successful. A person can become ritually impure in a variety of different ways. For example, a victim of an act of violence can become ritually unclean simply by bleeding. It does not mean that the person is at fault. However, it does mean the victim should take measures to become ritually clean again.

Figure 3.20
Amaterasu, the sun goddess, is the supreme deity of the Shinto religion and is queen of all the kami. *The rising sun, Amaterasu's emblem, is displayed on Japan's national flag. In Japan, festivals are held in her honour on July 17 during the Great Festival of the Sun Goddess, and on December 21, the winter solstice, when she is celebrated as the birth of light.*

Yutate

Purification rituals are extremely important in Shinto. One ritual, called the **yutate**, involves a priest dipping the branch of a sakaki tree, which symbolizes the *kami*, into a cauldron of hot water. The priest then waves the branch over the heads of those assembled and says a prayer called a **norito**. This is followed by a ritual dance that is part of the process leading to the purification of the water. At one point, a shrine maiden takes a wooden bowl and scoops the air above the cauldron, inviting the *kami* into the bowl, which she in turn pours into the cauldron. Later, the members of the gathering drink from the cauldron, receiving the purified water, which allows them to receive purification as well.

The Great Purification

One significant Shinto ritual is the Great Purification. This ritual symbolically recreates the act of purification that led to the birth of Susano-o, Tsuki-Yomi, and Amaterasu. The ritual happens twice a year, once at the New Year's Festival and the other at the beginning of summer. During the ritual, the priest recites the Great Purification *norito* while waving a purification wand over the worshippers. Each word of the *norito* is said to have its own *kami*, so precision is of the utmost importance if the purification ritual is to be successful. The rhythm of the prayer is said to wash away the impurities within people and is the key to the event.

Symbols and Icons

Torii

Figure 3.21

The **torii** is the Shinto symbol representing the way to the *kami*. The symbol looks like a gateway with two vertical beams intersected by two horizontal crossbeams at the top. Torii means "bird dwelling," and the horizontal crossbeams leave the viewer with the impression of a bird stretching its wings across the sky. A torii stands at the gateway of every Shinto shrine; it is also a feature of some Japanese Buddhist temples.

QUESTION

1. Why do Shintoists use the torii as a gateway to all of their shrines?

SACRED WRITINGS

Shinto has two highly revered sacred texts. Early in the eighth century CE, Emperor Gemmyo ordered that the oral histories of Japan be put into writing. Two volumes were produced: one was called the Record of Ancient Matters (Kojiki) and the other was called Chronicles of Japan (Nihongi). The Chronicles of Japan, in particular, captures the mythical nature of Shinto sacred writings.

Sacred Text

It is the language of mythology that Shinto utilizes to communicate its origins. Shinto texts are rich with imagery and symbolism. The following excerpt from the Nihongi speaks of the creation of heaven and earth.

Nihongi, The Age of the Gods, Book 1

Of old, Heaven and Earth were not yet separated, and the In and Yo [yin and yang] not yet divided. They formed a chaotic mass like an egg which was of obscurely defined limits and contained germs.

The purer and clearer part was thinly drawn out, and formed Heaven, while the heavier and grosser element settled down and became Earth.

The finer element easily became a united body, but the consolidation of the heavier and grosser element settled down and became Earth.

Heaven was therefore formed first, and Earth was established subsequently.

Thereafter divine beings were produced between them.

Hence it is said that when the world began to be created, the soil of which lands were composed floated about in a manner which might be compared to the floating of a fish sporting on the surface of the water.

At this time a certain thing was produced between Heaven and Earth. It was in form like a reed-shoot. Now this became transformed into a God, and was called Kuni-toko-tachi no Mikoto.

Next there was Kuni no sa-tsuchi no Mikoto, and next Toyo-kumu-nu no Mikoto, in all three deities

These were pure males spontaneously developed by the operation of the principle of Heaven.

QUESTIONS

1. What is the significance of heaven being composed of the "finer element" while earth is composed of the "grosser element"?

2. What is the main distinction between heaven and earth in the passage?

Skill Path On-Line Research

The ability to transform large amounts of information into useful material is rapidly becoming an all-important skill in today's world. Preparing for the future involves learning how to adapt to ongoing change. Often, this requires learning new things quickly and knowing where to get and how to disseminate information easily. The recent explosion of readily accessible information will only increase in years to come. As a result, it is important to develop the necessary skills to cope with the inevitable information-overload and the constant pressure of time.

Good research requires the use of many resources. Books, magazines, newspapers, television and radio documentaries, and news programs are all considered valuable sources of information. As well, the Internet continues to gain popularity as a necessary and important research tool for people all over the world who are seeking quickly accessible information.

One of the biggest challenges for on-line researchers is to find good, reliable material and avoid useless, and possibly fraudulent, Web sites. Since the Internet contains enormous amounts of information, a researcher may find it difficult to locate relevant information. Once the information has been located, it may be poorly organized or fail the information reliability test (see #3). The important skills of thinking, analyzing, and evaluating become crucial when you are faced with information overload. It is important to develop a critical eye and to be able to identify what your different sources are actually telling you.

Steps in On-Line Research

Following are a few helpful hints about effective on-line research:

1. Use several search engines.

A search engine is a program that searches the Internet for information on your requested topics. There are currently over 3000 search engines to choose from (see http://www.searchengineguide.com). Experts advise researchers to use several search engines because even the best engines cover approximately only one-quarter of available sites!

2. Master the Boolean search technique.

The Boolean search technique is based on a system of logic in which the words *and*, *or*, and *not* are used to search for information. For example:

- Let's say you want to find Web sites that mention both Taoism and Shinto. You would then input "Taoism AND Shinto."
- Let's say you want to find Web sites that mention Shinto or Jainism. You would then input "Shinto OR Jainism."
- Let's say you want to find Web sites that mention Confucianism but not Taoism. You would then input "Confucianism NOT Taoism."
- Let's say you want to find a Web site where the word *religion* appears close to, but not right next to (i.e., separated by only a few words) the word *early*. You then input "early NEAR religion."

3. Know how to evaluate your Internet sources.

Just about any individual or organization can set up and list a Web site. Most sites have a commercial purpose, although they might also have an educational function or, at least, appear to be educational in nature. Some sites are purely personal and reflect the thoughts, feelings, biases, and experiences of the Web site author. Others may have a political perspective or represent a particular lobby or interest group. For the researcher, it is vital to be able to quickly evaluate the reliability and nature of the Web site.

Use the following checklist when you evaluate a site:

- What appears to be the purpose of the site? Who is the intended audience? Is the site appropriate or useful for your purposes?
- Who is the sponsor, if any, of the site? The Web site of a government, cultural, or educational organization generally presents more reliable information than commercial, political, or personal Web sites.
- Who authored the site? What qualifications does the author(s) have? Is the author a professional or an amateur? Does it matter?
- When was the information compiled and presented? Does the site show signs of updating or ongoing revision? Is current information important to your research?
- How is the material presented? Is it reasonable and balanced or inflammatory and simplistic?
- Is the material well written and is the presentation logical? (Web sites with obvious grammatical and spelling errors should be avoided as research sources!)
- Are there hyperlinks to other Web sites? What do these other sites reveal about the reliability, accuracy, and purpose of the original site? For example, a site about Shinto that provides links to commercial travel or publishing ventures may not be the most reliable and unbiased source of information.

4. Create bookmarks (a personalized URL list).

When conducting your research, you may not always have time to fully explore a site or download information. Sometimes, your goal may be to simply make a whirlwind visit to a number of sites or work through a number of hyperlinks. These sites should be bookmarked for future reference. Simply use the bookmark command supplied with your browser software. By bookmarking, you will be creating your own personalized URL list organized for the successful investigation of your research topic. If you bookmark many sites, place them in separate folders for easy referral. The folders might be organized by chronology, sub-topic, individuals' names, question, category, etc.

5. Conduct careful personal research.

Many researchers do not really understand the full scope and power of Internet technologies. While these technologies allow you to roam the world in search of information, they can also be used to track you, your preferences, your itinerary, and any personal information that you provide. For your protection, follow these "safe surfing" hints when using this powerful research tool:

- Observe your school's, family's, or organization's rules for Internet use.
- Keep all passwords, phone numbers, and addresses confidential.
- Never share your account.
- Treat all Internet information as copyrighted material and never plagiarize sources.
- Avoid any links to questionable Web sites.
- If any information or personal contact that you receive seems questionable, inform an adult immediately.

PRACTISE IT!

1. Assume that you are researching one of the religions in this chapter and its practice in Canada.
   a) List the Boolean search techniques that you might try.
   b) After reviewing your possible research strategies with a peer, choose one strategy to try, and report on the results. As part of your report, rank from 1 to 5 the utility of the first five sites that you visited (1—very useful, 5—not useful at all). Explain the reasons for your ranking.

GROUPS AND INSTITUTIONS

There are four distinct varieties of Shinto. They are State Shinto, Sect Shinto, Shrine Shinto, and Folk Shinto.

Emperor Meiji proclaimed **State Shinto** in 1868. It emphasized patriotism and obedience. It also claimed that the emperor of Japan was a descendant and representative of the gods. State Shinto was abolished in 1945 with the defeat of Japan in the Second World War.

Sect Shinto emerged around the same time as State Shinto. Sect Shinto amounted to granting official status to religious movements that were popular among peasants and farmers. Some of these drew on the teachings of Shinto, Buddhism, Confucianism, and Taoism, and there were eventually thirteen recognized sects.

Shrine Shinto rose to prominence after the Second World War. In an effort to preserve the shrines of State Shinto, the Japanese embraced Shrine Shinto. With over 80 000 shrines to maintain, the Japanese banded together to save the structures that they felt were a vital and living example of the Shinto faith. Today, Shrine Shinto is a dominant aspect of the Shinto tradition.

Folk Shinto is most closely aligned with the ancient practice of Shinto and focuses on personal worship of local *kami*. Because of the individual nature of the practices of this sect, rituals and prayers vary greatly. Thus, while one Folk Shinto family worships at a home shrine, another might worship at a shrine on a farm. Many of the rituals of Folk Shinto seek tangible goals of purity, fertility, health, and prosperity.

CULTURAL IMPACT

It is difficult to determine how many adherents Shinto has since many Japanese participate in both Shinto and Buddhism. Once again, the incredible tolerance inherent in the Shinto tradition demonstrates that identifying oneself as a Shintoist is secondary to recognizing the reality of the *kami*. Some sources claim that there are about 3 000 000 people who follow Shinto. Other sources claim that the number could be close to 107 000 000, virtually the entire population of Japan. As with other traditions, the real number of followers of Shinto is difficult to determine. In Canada, the Japanese Canadian Cultural Centre in Toronto is a particularly active and informed presenter and preserver of Shinto traditions.

Figure 3.22
San Francisco's Japanese American community holds a parade as part of the annual Cherry Blossom Festival. The cherry blossom (sakura) is the national flower of Japan. Held in early spring, the Cherry Blossom Festival is the most famous of Japanese celebrations. Although there is no specific religious significance to the festival, many of the finest examples of the cherry blossom can be found around Shinto shrines or holy mountains.

Check Your Understanding

1. Why is it difficult to determine the origins of Shinto?

2. Give two examples of Shinto tolerance of other religions. Why is tolerance an important part of any religion?

3. What are the *kami*? Why are they important?

4. What is a torii? Why is it important?

5. What is the significance of mythology in Shinto belief?

6. Identify and explain the significance of the four types of Shinto.

7. Why do you think Shinto places so much importance on purification rituals?

CONCLUSION

The Chinese called the era of Lao Tzu, Confucius, Chuang Tzu, and Mencius the era of 100 philosophers. They would never know how history would be able look back at their celebratory proclamation and confirm their conclusion from a global perspective. Besides the great Chinese sages, Zoroaster, Mahavira, and Buddha emerged to lead new spiritual movements. Meanwhile, in Japan, the rich mythology of Shinto began to flourish. The world sought explanations for things spiritual. They received some of those answers from Zoroastrianism, Jainism, Taoism, Confucianism, and Shinto.

Thousands of years later, these spiritual movements are alive in Canadian communities and studied by students in Canadian schools. The answers are evident in the wealth of wisdom that each religion offers.

Zoroaster

Religion: Zoroastrianism.

- *Given name:* Zarathrustra (Zoroaster is the anglicized version of his name).
- *Dates:* sometime before 600 BCE
- *Major compositions:* the Gathas—17 of the 72 chapters in the Yasna.
- *Views on human nature:* One should live a life of virtue for the benefit of oneself and others, and in accordance with the wishes of Ahura Mazda, the one Supreme God.
- *Zoroastrian holy place:* Ateshgah Temple, Surakhany, Azerbaijan. The temple was built over a pocket of natural gas, fuelling a holy flame. The original construction date is disputed, but the existing temple dates from the 18th and 19th centuries.

Mencius

Religion: Confucianism.

- *Given name:* Meng K'o/ Meng-tzu, which means "Master Meng" (Mencius is the Latinized version of this title).
- *Dates:* 371(?)–289 BCE.
- *Major compositions:* none (The Book of Mencius was written by his followers).
- *Views on human nature:* Humans are inherently good and evil is learned.

Buddha

Religion: Buddhism. (See Chapter 5.)

- *Given name:* Siddhartha Gautama (Buddha is his title).
- *Dates:* probably 563–483 BCE.
- *Major compositions:* none (His followers collected what they understood to be his sermons and lectures).
- *Views on human nature:* One can overcome suffering in life by pursuing a life of virtuous selflessness.
- *Buddhist holy place:* Mahabodhi Temple, Bodh Gaya, India. See page 166 in Chapter 5.

Mahavira

Religion: Jainism.

- *Given name:* Vardhamana (Mahavira is his title).
- *Dates:* 599–527 BCE.
- *Official scripture:* Āgama.
- *Views on human nature:* One should practise ahimsa (non-violence) to reach the goal of liberation.
- *Jain holy place:* Jalmandir Temple, Pawapuri, India. Mahavira died in Pawapuri and was cremated there. The temple was built near the site of his funeral pyre and is now a major pilgrimage site.

AZERBAIJAN
Surakhany
(Ateshgah Temple)

TURKMENISTAN

IRAN

AFGHANISTAN

PAKISTAN

SAUDI ARABIA

TIBET

BHUTA

NEPAL

Pawapuri
(Jalmandir Temple)

BANGLĀ

Bodh Gaya
(Mahabodhi Temple)

INDIA

SRI LANKA

Figure 3.23

Early religions: great spiritual leaders and holy places. What are the similarities and differences among the religious leaders you studied in this chapter?

Lao Tzu

Religion: Taoism.

- *Given name:* Li Erh (Lao Tzu is his title and means "old master").
- *Dates:* possibly 570–490 BCE (disputed).
- *Major compositions:* Tao Te Ching.
- *Views on human nature:* One should live in accordance with Tao in order to maintain a sense of personal and communal harmony with the world.
- *Taoist holy place:* Mao Mountain, Jiangsu, China. The three Mao brothers, who were born at Jun Qu Mountain, dedicated themselves to Taoism and became famous as mystics and healers. They are believed to have ascended to immortality after their physical deaths. The mountain was renamed in their honour.

Shinto

Religion: Shinto.

- *No founder:* Its practices and rituals began to emerge about 2500 years ago.
- *No official scripture:* The Record of Ancient Matters (Kojiki) and Chronicles of Japan (Nihongi) are highly revered.
- *Shinto holy place:* Itsukushima Shrine, Miyajima, Japan. First constructed in 593 CE and enlarged in 1168, the shrine is dedicated to three Shinto goddesses of the sea, who are believed to live within the inner sanctum of the shrine.

Confucius

Religion: Confucianism.

- *Given name:* K'ung Ch'iu/K'ung Fu-tzu (Confucius is the Latinized version of this title).
- *Dates:* 551—479 BCE.
- *Major compositions:* none (The Analects were his sayings but were written by his disciples. He is said to have edited and compiled the Spring and Autumn Annals).
- *Views on human nature:* Tao, or balance, can be achieved by governing oneself and a nation with virtue. Once, when asked if human nature was inherently good, Confucius refused to answer.
- *Confucian holy place:* Confucius Temple, Qufu, China. A year after his death, a temple was constucted at Confucius's house so that followers could offer sacrifices to him. The temple, now 2 km in length, was continually expanded up until the Ming Dynasty.

Chuang Tzu

Religion: Taoism.

- *Dates:* 369–286 BCE.
- *Major compositions: Chuang Tzu* (Chuang Tzu apparently wrote the first seven chapters of the book bearing his name).
- *Views on human nature:* The human quest should be subject to Tao (the way of harmony and balance) and *wu wei* (effortless action).

Hsun Tzu

Religion: Confucianism.

- *Dates:* 298–238 BCE.
- *Major compositions: Hsun Tzu*; 32 essays.
- *Views on human nature:* Humans are inherently evil and easily corrupted unless taught otherwise. (These views posed a challenge to the teachings of Mencius and Confucius.)

Activities

Check Your Understanding

1. Make the following organizer in your notebook and fill in the appropriate information:

Spiritual Leader / Religion / Main Teachings

2. How is the concept of Tao a significant teaching in both Taoism and Confucianism?

3. How is Tao similar to *kami*?

4. Why do many Canadians find the philosophies of Confucius to be so appealing?

5. Define the term *myth*. Are myths just as valuable as historical accounts of events? Explain your answer.

Think and Communicate

6. Compare the Zoroastrian teaching regarding Ahura Mazda and Angra Mainyu with the Taoist teaching of yin-yang. How are these teachings similar? How are they different?

7. Debate the ethics of the Jain practice of *sallekhana*. Complete this assignment either as a class project or as a position paper.

8. Conduct a newspaper study. Using Confucius's teaching on leadership, prepare a class presentation that demonstrates how Canada's leaders are or are not employing a virtuous approach to governing.

9. Shinto myth is rich in imagery and symbolism. Referring to the Shinto creation myth, write your own creation story. Be sure to use plenty of imagery and symbolism.

10. Which of the five religions described in this chapter has had the most profound effect on you? Write a reflection paper outlining your experience in learning about this religion.

Apply Your Learning

11. Conduct an Internet study of the religions you have studied in this chapter. Visit the Web site http://www.religioustolerance.org/. Use the links listed at this site to visit other Web sites related to the five religions discussed in the chapter. Make a comparison organizer like the one below to keep track of your findings.

Name of Religion	Origins	Main Beliefs	Scriptures

12. What religious organizations affiliated with the religions you have studied in this chapter exist in your community? Use the Internet, the yellow pages, or resources in the library to find this information. See if you can arrange a classroom visit from one of the representatives of these groups.

13. Invite practitioners of feng shui, Tai Chi, acupuncture, etc., to visit the class to discuss these practices. Prior to the presentation, prepare a set of questions to ask your visitors.

14. Practising ahimsa, or non-violence, on a daily basis is a challenging concept.
a) Working in small groups, discuss the practice of ahimsa in terms of daily activities in your school or community. Brainstorm a list of changes that would have to be implemented in one of these areas in order to achieve ahimsa.

b) Working independently, think of five actions that you could take to bring about ahimsa in your personal life.
c) Is it possible to incorporate ahimsa in the activities of your school or community? Is it possible to practise ahimsa in your own life? Explain.

Glossary

Introduction

myth. A traditional story, usually involving supernatural or imaginary persons, that serves to reveal the world view of a people on natural or social phenomena, etc.

Zoroastrianism

Ahura Mazda [ah hurra MAZDA]. The Wise Lord; the God of Righteousness; revealed to Zoroaster when he was meditating.

Angra Maniyu [ang rah MINE you]. The Evil One; denier of truth and rival of Ahura Mazda.

dakhma **[DOCK ma].** A circular, open-air structure for the disposal of dead bodies.

Gathas [GA thus]. Seventeen of the seventy-two chapters in the Yasna; composed by Zoroaster.

navjote **[NAV jote].** The initiation of a child into the Zoroastrian religion.

polytheism. The belief in more than one god.

Jainism

ahimsa [ah HIN sa]. A doctrine of non-violence toward all living beings.

asceticism [a SETTA sism]. The process of self-deprivation; denying oneself of food, clothing, cleansing, and pleasure in order to achieve a higher spiritual goal.

atomism. The belief that all aspects of nature, including atoms, possess a soul.

Digambaras [dig UM bar ah]. The "sky-clad" sect in Jainism, which practises ascetic nudity.

jina **[GEE na].** A conqueror; one who defeats his or her desires and achieves enlightenment.

jiva **[GEE va].** The soul. Jains believe that both animate (e.g., a human) and inanimate (e.g., a rock) beings have a soul.

karma. The law of cause and effect—for every action, there is a consequence.

meditation. The process of eliminating self-centred thinking and becoming united with the spirit that governs the universe.

moksha [MOOK shaw]. The salvation from the cycle of rebirth.

reincarnation. The rebirth of a soul over many lives until it achieves release.

sallekhana **[selleh KENNA].** A holy ritual of gradual fasting to the point of death.

Svetambaras [shway TAM bar ah]. The "white-clad" sect in Jainism in which monks wear white clothing.

Taoism

chi **[GEE].** Energy; the spiritual breath of life that moves all existence.

Tao [DOW]. The way; to practise the way of nature and to understand how to achieve balance between opposing forces.

wu wei [wu way]. Not doing; leaving things alone and letting nature take its course.

yin-yang. The sunny side and the shady side; the symbol of balance between opposing forces.

Confucianism

chih [JU (with *u* of cup)]. Wisdom—the product of virtuous living.

hsin [SHIN]. Faithfulness and trustworthiness—virtues to be practised.

jen [RUN]. Virtue, goodwill, empathy, politeness, generosity—personal qualities to be developed in a person's encounters with others.

li [LEE]. Propriety; right conduct; treating others with dignity and honour.

yi [YEE]. Rightness; Confucius taught that a person has a duty to "heaven" to live a life of justice, compassion, and integrity.

Shinto

Amaterasu [ah motta ROSSU]. The sun goddess; the most revered deity in Shinto.

Folk Shinto. A variety of Shinto closely aligned with the ancient practice of Shinto and focused on personal worship of local *kami*.

kami [commie]. The spirits that underlie all existence.

norito [noh REE toh]. A prayer, often used as an invocation for purification; precision in use and in pronunciation of words is essential if the prayer is to work.

Sect Shinto. A variety of Shinto that gave official status to religious movements popular among peasants and farmers; there were thirteen recognized sects.

Shrine Shinto. A variety of Shinto that rose to prominence after the Second World War in an effort to preserve the shrines of State Shinto. Shrine Shinto is a principal part of the Shinto tradition.

State Shinto. A form of Shinto that emphasized patriotism and obedience, and maintained that the emperor of Japan was descended from and represented the gods.

torii [TORY ee]. A symbol shaped like a gateway; the gateway to heaven.

yutate [YOU tah teh]. A Shinto purification ritual.

Thousands in Toronto See Ganesha Miracle

Thousands of Hindus, non-Hindus, believers, non-believers, and sceptics last month flocked to the Vishnu Mandir in Richmond Hill and the Vaisno Devi Mandir in Oakville to witness a miracle.

Carved in marble, Shri Ganesha, Lord [Remover] of all Obstacles, son of Shiva, was 'drinking' milk fed to Him in a spoon…

News of this miracle hit the Toronto media, and through word of mouth it spread like wildfire. By midnight thousands had witnessed the elephant-headed God of the Hindus absorbing milk through its tusks and trunk….

Explanations ranging from science's capillary action in marble and stone, to the divine revelation in stone are suggested.

Some just don't know what to believe or disbelieve....

And should the capillary theory be true, what about the saturation capacity of the image? What is certain is that a miracle is a miracle because it confounds science and baffles the mind...

- Indo Caribbean World, Oct 4, 1995

Chapter Four

Hinduism 4

Read the article "Thousands in Toronto See Ganesha Miracle," and consider the following questions:

1. Describe the "miracle" reported in the article.
2. Identify the possible explanations for the phenomenon proposed by the article.
3. Do you believe in miracles? How would you explain the "miracle" presented in the article?
4. Describe any other miracles that you have witnessed or of which you are aware.

Introduction

Any attempt to define Hinduism through one system or set of beliefs can be a frustrating, if not impossible, task. The name *Hindu* is universally accepted as the word that refers to the indigenous religion of India. *Hindu*, however, is not of Indian, but of Persian, origin. The early Persians used the term *Hindus* to speak of the inhabitants on the other side of the Sindhu River, and today we use the word *Hinduism* to refer to their religion. As the religion of the Hindus spread throughout India, it experienced many modifications but ultimately retained at its core the teachings from which it had originated along the banks of the Sindhu River.

For thousands of years, foreigners who settled in India left their own mark on Hinduism, as the religion assimilated many of their customs and practices. Over the course of time, Hinduism's resilient nature has enabled it to bend with the course of history, while, at the same time, not become overwhelmed by it. The result has been a multitude of religious sects, each with its own rituals and customs, which share a unity of spirit. Hindus share a common literature, a history of religious thought, and a world view that places spiritual values above earthly concerns.

Many Canadians are quite familiar with some elements of the Hindu faith. Vegetarianism is increasingly popular, especially among young Canadians. Many of us are generally aware of the theory of reincarnation, which suggests that we may live many lives and that our position in the next life is determined by our deeds, or karma, in the present. Meditation and yoga are very popular pastimes among Canadians, and many communities have teachers and practitioners of these activities, which originated in Hindu tradition. Hinduism's roots run deep and far from Canadian shores, but its modern face is a vibrant part of the current Canadian reality.

Learning Goals

At the end of this chapter, you will be able to:

- describe the role of faith in Hinduism
- describe how symbols are used to represent Hindu beliefs
- identify significant sacred writings, for example, Vedas, Ramayana, Bhagavad-Gita, and describe their importance
- identify key passages from a variety of Hindu scriptures and explain their significance
- identify how Hinduism is reflected in art, architecture, music, literature, dance, and cuisine
- analyze the role of women in Hinduism
- describe how Hinduism is reflected in Canada's pluralistic society and identify challenges that Hindus face within this society
- identify the role and responsibility of the Hindu within his or her religion, as well as the stages of his or her development
- describe how Hindu rites of passage reflect Hinduism's central beliefs
- analyze how and why certain rites of passage may have changed over time
- identify how Mahatma Gandhi used religion to oppose prejudice and discrimination
- understand the characteristics and functions of a guru
- evaluate Hinduism's place in the modern age
- identify topics on Hinduism that require quantitative research
- organize, interpret, and evaluate information on Hinduism gathered through research

•2700–1500 BCE
Indus Valley civilization

•1500–1200 BCE
Aryan settlement

•1200–900 BCE (approx.)
Composition of Rig-Veda

•400 BCE–400 CE
(approx.) Compilation of
Mahabharata

•200 BCE (approx.)
Composition of Ramayana
in Sanskrit

•1500 CE
Composition of
Ramayana in Hindi

•300 CE (approx.)
Compilation of the code of
Manu

● **1960s CE** Hare Krishna movement founded by Swami Bhaktivedanta in the US; Beatles popularize yoga and meditation in the West

● **1947 CE** Mahatma Gandhi negotiates India's independence from Britain

● **1948 CE** Mahatma Gandhi assassinated

● **1875 CE** Arya Samaj movement founded by Dayanand Saraswati

● **1858 CE** Britain takes control of India

● **1893 CE** Swami Vivekananda attends the World's Parliament of Religions in Chicago

● **1869 CE** Birth of Mahatma Gandhi

● **1838–1917 CE** Hindus taken as labourers to other parts of the world as a result of European colonialism

Timeline

Hinduism

ORIGINS

Unlike other religious traditions, for example, Christianity and Buddhism, Hinduism was not founded by a particular individual. Because it was not limited by the influence of any one person, Hinduism absorbed ideas and practices that suited its social and cultural framework as it evolved over thousands of years. This accommodation of new thoughts may account for the generally, inclusive nature of this religion.

Hinduism is the product of the various peoples that have occupied the region of India through time, which might explain its diverse and complex nature. However, the foundation of Hinduism was probably laid by two groups of people—the Indus Valley civilization and the Aryans.

The Indus Valley Civilization

The earliest evidence of religious thought in India was uncovered during archaeological excavations along the banks of the Indus River (Figures 4.1 and 4.2) in 1926. Archaeologists discovered the remains of a civilization that arose in the Indus Valley between 3000 and 2500 BCE at

Mohenjo-Daro and Harappa (located in present-day Pakistan). This civilization, which extended over the area that is now Pakistan and northwestern India, is referred to as the Indus Valley civilization or the Harappa culture. Evidence shows that the people of this civilization were impressive builders and town planners. They lived in cities that included a central area for civic activities as well as large residential zones. Remarkably, some of the houses in these zones contained a drainage and sewer system that included bathrooms on both the first and second floors.

Some of the buildings in the central and residential areas of Mohenjo-Daro have been identified as worship houses. In these buildings, archaeologists have uncovered stone sculptures that seem to represent a mother goddess and may, in fact, be early depictions of the Hindu goddesses Parvati and Kali (see page 122). Discoveries around the Indus River include many amulets, or charms that protect against evil, and thousands of flat seals. Some of the seals depict a man wearing a headdress seated in a yoga-like position, surrounded by animals. This male figure may be an early representation of the Hindu god Shiva (see page 122). Other evidence of the religious nature of the Indus Valley civilization includes fire altars and pits lined with bricks, containing ashes and animal bones. These discoveries suggest that this culture participated in religious activities like fire rituals and animal sacrifices.

Figure 4.2
Excavations along the banks of the Indus River have uncovered remains of the ancient Harappa culture. What do we know about this culture?

The Arrival of the Aryans

Around 1500 BCE, thousands of people migrated into India from the northwest, destroying the Indus Valley civilization. It is believed that these people, known as Aryans, hailed from Central Asia and spoke an early form of the ancient language of Sanskrit. The Aryans settled near the river Sindhu and later migrated to the area along the Ganges River.

The Aryan settlers created poems and, later, texts on rituals and philosophy. Aryan religious thought flourished between 1500 to 500 BCE and was embodied in a collection of hymns, ritual texts, and philosophical works called **Vedas**, which are considered Hinduism's earliest sacred writings (see page 141). To this day, Hindus consider the Vedas to be authoritative scripture. The earliest of these texts is the Rig-Veda, which constitutes the earliest record of sacred knowledge on Hinduism. These

Vedas, written in verse, gave rise to prose interpretations called Brahmanas and mystical texts on human existence known as Upanishads (see page 141).

The Aryans lived in awe of the magnificent, yet destructive, forces of nature and worshipped them in the form of deities, or gods. They also worshipped fire, called **Agni**, and believed that it was a link between gods and humans. Worship and prayer rituals to honour and please these deities formed the core of early Hindu practice. The Upanishads combined this notion of prayer with philosophical inquiry about **atman**—the human soul. Closely related to Vayu, the god of wind or air, the atman was considered to be the "breath" of human life and became one of the fundamental principles of Hindu philosophy.

Check Your Understanding

1. Hinduism has no founder. Explain this statement.

2. What did the Indus Valley and Aryan cultures contribute to Hindu thought?

3. What evidence is there that, from a very early stage, Hinduism was a complex web of religious ideas?

BELIEFS

Hinduism is often described as a non-dogmatic religion where one is free to worship any set of doctrines or rules as his or her conscience dictates. It does not impose its religious beliefs on others, nor does it believe in conversion. However, Hindus are expected to follow certain rules in their personal conduct and in their performance of daily duties; in fact, there is a vast body of rules and rituals for the Hindu to follow for almost every station and stage of life.

Hinduism is a complex web of diverse beliefs and practices generally held together by considerable mutual tolerance and respect. The Hindu view of an unreal world, varied conceptions of god, and a unique view of reality represent a challenging vision for many Canadians.

The Hindu Concept of God

It may not be easy for non-Hindus to understand the Hindu concept of God. Some describe Hinduism as *polytheistic*, meaning a religion of many gods; others describe it as *monotheistic*, which means believing in only one god; it might also be described as *monistic*, where God is an impersonal and unknowable entity. The unique nature of Hinduism seems to reconcile these three different concepts of God, and this quality is what scholars refer to as Hinduism's "tolerant characteristic." The early hymns of the Rig-Veda (1200–900 BCE) praise the spirits of natural forces such as Fire, Thunder, Dawn, Water, Earth, and the Sun. The hymns praised individual deities, but the Vedic sages believed that they represented different manifestations or aspects of the same supreme being.

Brahman

The Upanishads refer to this supreme being as Brahman. **Brahman** is an entity without form and quality. It is the soul of the universe from which all existing things arise and into which they all return. It is everything and everywhere. The essence of Brahman is divine, invisible, unlimited, and indescribable. Although Brahman is an entity without form, Hindus are free to imagine Him or Her in any way that is meaningful to them. Thus, Hindus worship different deities that they consider manifestations, or expressions, of Brahman. Brahman is described in the Upanishads as follows:

As a spider envelops itself with the threads [of its web],
So does he, the One God, envelop himself with [threads]
Sprung from primal matter out of his own essence.
May he grant us entry into Brahman.
The One God, hidden in all creatures.
Pervading all, the Inner Self of all contingent beings,
The overseer of karma abiding in all creatures...
Eternal among eternals, conscious among conscious beings...

Svetasvatara Upanishad

Hindu Deities

The most prevalent manifestations of Brahman are the gods Brahma, Vishnu, and Shiva, who are often depicted together as one concept, called the **Hindu Trinity**. They each have a female counterpart, the most prominent one being Parvati, the consort of Shiva.

Brahma

Brahma is the creator of the universe. He has four faces and is seated on a lotus. He holds a book, a rosary, and a gourd. Although he is an important element of the Hindu Trinity, he is not as widely worshipped as Shiva and Vishnu. His female counterpart is Saraswati.

Saraswati

She is the goddess of learning and the arts, which is why she is depicted holding a book and a musical instrument called a veena (Figure 4.3). Her vehicle is a peacock or a swan. Although she is the consort of Brahma, she is often portrayed alone.

Figure 4.3
A statue of Saraswati, the Hindu goddess of learning and the arts

Vishnu

He is the preserver of the universe and is, therefore, a loving and forgiving figure who brings salvation. **Vishnu** (Figure 4.4) has four arms in which he holds a conch shell, a discus, a lotus, and a mace. His vehicle is a divine eagle. This god has many **avatars**, or incarnations, and appears on earth in the form of an animal or a human in order to conquer evil and establish righteousness. Many Hindus believe that one of his incarnations is that of Siddartha Gautama, the founder of Buddhism, which is the subject of the next chapter. In many of his manifestations, Vishnu is accompanied by his companion Lakshmi.

Figure 4.4
This ivory statuette depicts the Hindu god Vishnu, the preserver of the universe.

Lakshmi

She is the goddess of wealth, happiness, and good fortune. Lakshmi blesses her worshippers with wealth and liberation. She is often shown rewarding worshippers with gold.

Shiva

He is the destroyer and restorer of the universe and is associated with creative energy. He is considered a great **yogi**, or spiritually evolved individual, and holds a trident, a rosary, and a gourd in his hands. His vehicle is a bull. **Shiva** is also depicted as Nataraj, the god of dance, and is shown holding a drum, serpent, and sacred fire in his hands while performing the dance of creation. He holds water from the sacred Ganges River in his hair. His wife is the goddess **Parvati**.

Parvati

She is a mother goddess whom Hindus worship as **Shakti**, or female energy. She takes on many forms including that of Durga, the warrior goddess, in which she is portrayed riding a tiger and holding many weapons in her hands. She is also depicted as Kali, the fierce destroyer of evil.

Other Hindu Deities

Other popular gods include Ganesha, Subrahmanya, and Hanuman. Ganesha (featured on pages 114-15) is the son of Shiva and Parvati. He has a human body and an elephant's head with only one short tusk. The other tusk is used as a pen to write the wisdom of the scriptures. Hindus worship him as the remover of all obstacles.

Subrahmanya is the second son of Shiva and Parvati. He is also called Kartikeya and is widely worshipped by the Tamil population in southern India. Hanuman is the monkey god. He is a model of devotion and everyone's protector.

Atman

Atman is the human soul or spirit. It is the part of our innermost self that is identical to Brahman, the universal soul. A Hindu's goal in life is to reunite the atman with the Brahman. The famous Sanskrit phrase *tat twam asi*, meaning "you are that" in English, expresses the idea that the atman and the Brahman are inseparable. In that statement, *you* refers to atman while *that* refers to Brahman. The atman is eternal and immortal; when one dies, the atman lives on, shedding the lifeless body to enter a new one. This immortal nature of the atman is described in Hindu scriptures as follows:

> He [atman] is not born, nor does he die at any time; nor, having once come to be will he again come not to be. He is unborn, eternal, permanent, and primeval; he is not slain when the body is slain . . .
>
> Just as a man, having cast off old garments, puts on other, new ones, even so does the embodied one, having cast off old bodies, take on other, new ones.
>
> He is uncleavable, he is unburnable, he is undrenchable, as also undryable. He is eternal, all-pervading, stable, immovable, existing from time immemorial.

Reincarnation

As described in the passage above, Hindus believe that the soul does not die along with the body but enters another body to carry on its existence.

This endless cycle of rebirth, or reincarnation, is called **samsara**. In Hindu thought, the physical world in which we live is temporary, ever-changing, and artificial. This imperfect world is referred to as **maya**, and life in it is considered meaningless. Hindus believe that the universe moves through endless cycles of millions of years, subject to the constant themes of creation and destruction. All life is caught in this cycle of birth, death, and rebirth. The goal of Hindus is to achieve **moksha**, or liberation, from the endless cycle of rebirths into this world, and to unite the atman with the Brahman.

Karma is the totality of one's actions in life, and it determines the form that an individual will take when he or she is reborn. The accumulation of bad karma will result in rebirth at a lower station in life or as a lower form of life, such as an animal. The accumulation of good karma will result in rebirth at a higher station in life, which is closer to attaining salvation. In order to achieve salvation, Hindus must work their way up the ladder of existence; they do so by trying to secure rebirth at a higher level. The traditional levels of Hindu society are dictated by the caste system, which is discussed on page 125 of this chapter.

Paths to Salvation

In Hinduism, there are four paths to salvation. The path a Hindu follows generally depends on his or her nature and inclinations. Each path can lead to salvation if the follower is sincere.

Web Quest

To view more images of Hindu deities, go to http://www. hindunet.org/god/

Bhakti Yoga (The Path of Devotion)

Bhakti yoga is one of the simpler paths to salvation and involves devotion and love toward a personal deity, for example, Shiva, Vishnu, or Lakshmi. This is a popular path among Hindus because it provides the opportunity to worship Brahman in a concrete way rather than as an abstract notion. Representations of the chosen deity help followers to focus their devotion through prayer and rituals. Devotees surrender themselves to the deity and delight in hearing and singing praises to him or her.

Karma Yoga (The Path of Action)

The key to this path is good deeds and thoughts, which will lead to the accumulation of good karma. Good deeds are unselfish actions that are done not for a reward but because they are morally right or the duty of an individual.

Jnana Yoga (The Path of Wisdom)

This difficult path calls for the guidance of a **guru**, or teacher. Followers learn about the relationship between the Brahman and atman and about the nature of the universe as explained in the scriptures. By knowing the scriptures, following the guru's teachings, and meditating, followers gain the insight necessary to achieve salvation.

Raja Yoga (The Path of Meditation)

Followers of this path achieve salvation through meditation, or deep contemplation, on Brahman. Intense meditation leads to a trance-like state in which the individual acquires knowledge of the Truth and becomes one with the Brahman. This is a difficult path because it requires strict physical and spiritual discipline.

Dharma

Hindus refer to their religion as **dharma**, which means code of moral and righteous duty. The concept of dharma pertains to the duties and responsibilities of the individual, and it is considered essential to the welfare of the individual, the family, and society. Essentially, there are two kinds of dharma mentioned in the scriptures: *sanatana dharma* and *varnashrama dharma*. Simply translated, *sanatana dharma* means "eternal religion" and refers to universal values and principles that apply to all people regardless of religion, nationality, age, sex, or profession. *Varnashrama dharma* concerns the specific duties of each individual with respect to age, sex, and status in society.

The Caste System

By the end of the Vedic period, Indian society was organized into categories commonly known as castes. The basic structure of the **caste system** seems to have its roots in Vedic hymns on creation, which divide humanity into four classes, or varnas. The four varnas are as follows (from highest to lowest): **Brahmins**, **Kshatriyas**, **Vaishyas**, and **Sudras**.

As discussed earlier in the chapter, people are born into each varna according to the karma they have accumulated in their previous lives. People of different castes live very different lives and are not allowed to dine together or marry each other. Figure 4.5 illustrates the occupations, goals, duties, and required characteristics of each varna, according to *The Laws of Manu*, an early Indian law book.

Untouchables

There is a fifth group outside the traditional four castes. The people of this group are called "untouchables" because they engage in what are considered "unclean" occupations, such as tanning leather, removing dead animals, or washing toilets. Degraded by the nature of their work, they have lived separately from those in the other castes.

Mahatma Gandhi, India's most influential political, spiritual, and social leader, fought to have these people included in the mainstream of Indian society.

The Caste System Today

Today, India's Charter of Rights bans discrimination on the basis of gender, caste, race, or religion. The Indian government has introduced a number of social welfare programs and economic initiatives to improve the living conditions of those who have suffered as a result of the caste system. The president of India, K. R. Narayanan, is

Varna (Caste)	Occupations	Goals	Duties	Required Characteristics
Brahmin	priests, religious teachers	knowledge, education	• performance of rituals and sacrifices • pursuit of arts, sciences, ethics, philosophy, and religious study • research and teaching	highly developed intellect, discipline
Kshatriya	warriors, rulers	political power, diplomacy	• government • maintenance of law and order • protection from foreign invaders	physical strength and courage, governing skills
Vaishya	merchants, farmers	wealth, commerce	• management of wealth • trade with other societies	management and entrepreneurial skills
Sudra	servants, labourers	manual skills	• service to other castes	ability to acquire particular skills

Figure 4.5 The caste system. What determines a person's placement in one of the above castes?

a member of this fifth caste, which is popularly known today as the *dalits*. The late Dr. B. R. Ambedkar, who is the principal author of modern-day India's constitution, also hailed from this oppressed group.

Stage	Responsibilities
Student	• discipline mind and body • gain knowledge • learn rules and rituals of Hinduism • show respect toward elders
Householder	• marry and have a family • provide for the family • give to charity • care for family elders • practise social and religious traditions
Forest Dweller	• retire and transmit household duties to wife or son • read and study • participate in religious pilgrimages
Ascetic	• give up worldly life • wander • meditate • attain salvation

The Four Stages of Life

The caste system and the Four Stages of Life, outlined in Figure 4.6, represent the social aspect of karma since they define the actions for which people are responsible in society. Women normally do not enter the last two stages, and very few men enter the stage of ascetic.

Four Aims or Goals of Life

The Four Goals of Life outlined in this section constitute for a Hindu a personal value system that incorporates his or her material desires and spiritual needs. These goals are as follows:

Dharma: conducting one's duties with compassion toward all beings, forbearance, absence of jealousy, purity, tranquility, goodness, absence of cruelty, and absence of greed

Artha: earning money by honest means to provide for the family; acquiring wealth and power

Kama: pursuing love and physical pleasures to balance life and to sanctify marriage

Moksha: leading the soul toward salvation through honest and moral actions

Profile: *Mahatma Gandhi* (1869–1948)

Figure 4.7

Mahatma Gandhi is, perhaps, the best-known Hindu in the world and is considered the father of his country. He has been called one of the most influential figures of the twentieth century and has had a profound impact on the religious conscience of humankind. Born in India in 1869, he married when he was fifteen and his wife was thirteen. He studied law in England and practised law in South Africa between 1893 and 1914, where he fought against colonial laws that discriminated against the Indians who settled there. Guided by the teachings of the Bhagavad-Gita (see page 144) and the New Testament, he showed great admiration and tolerance for all religions. He gained solace and inspiration from the teachings of the Bhagavad-Gita and based his religious ideals on the concepts of dharma (duty), **satya** (truth), **ahimsa** (non-violence), and moksha (spiritual liberation).

When he returned to India in 1915, he immediately embarked on a non-violent mission to end British rule. He entered politics in 1919 and became the leader of the Indian National Congress. He used his theory of satyagraha, or insistence on truth, as a political weapon and insisted that his followers be guided by the following four religious principles: truth, non-violence, self-control, and penance. By practising spiritual values, Gandhi was trying to change the governance of India as well as

peoples' lives. He negotiated the independence of India in 1947. Gandhi spent most of his life opposing social injustice in Hindu society and working to improve the condition of minority groups in India, such as Muslims, women, and the "untouchables" of the Indian caste system. Gandhi accepted the caste system on a spiritual level, but did not accept its social implications because he opposed the privileges of the high-caste Hindus. He fought passionately for the rights of the "untouchables," and, as a result of his efforts, discrimination against this group was eventually outlawed. He demonstrated the principle of ahimsa by respecting all living things, and he was prepared to die for a righteous cause. In 1948, he was assassinated by a fanatic Hindu.

Quotes by Gandhi

Real education consists in drawing the best out of yourself. What better book can there be than the book of humanity?

An eye for an eye only ends up making the world blind.

I know of no greater sin than to oppress the innocent in the name of God.

QUESTIONS

1. How did Mahatma Gandhi use religion to oppose prejudice and discrimination?

2. Which quotation by Gandhi appeals to you the most? Why?

Women in Hinduism

The Hindu law book, *The Laws of Manu*, which was written at the beginning of the Common Era, provides contradictory views on the status and duties of Hindu women. The two following passages illustrate these opposing views:

> *Women must be honoured and adorned by their fathers, husbands, and brothers, and brothers-in-laws who desire welfare/Where women are honoured, there the gods are pleased, but where they are not honoured, no sacred rite yields reward.*
>
> The Laws of Manu, 3.56.
>
> *By a girl, by a young woman, or even by an aged one, nothing must be done independently, even in her own house. In childhood a female must be subject to her father, in youth to her husband, when her lord is dead, to her sons; a woman must never be independent.*
>
> The Laws of Manu, 5.147–148

Figure 4.8
Indira Gandhi was prime minister of India from 1966 to 1977 and 1980 to 1984.

The first passage suggests that women hold a place of honour in the home, and that it is the sacred duty of men to honour and provide for them. The second passage portrays women as subordinate to and dependent on the men in their life. The latter passage seems to reflect the reality of most Hindu women, especially those in the lower levels of society, who are deprived of an education.

Divorce is not encouraged but it is allowed in today's Hindu world. As more women work outside the home, gender roles are changing, but women still carry the bulk of household duties. Government and other educational and religious institutions are now providing better opportunities for women to develop literacy skills and participate in the work force.

Conversely, Hindu women from the privileged classes have been working and excelling in their fields for some time. They are doctors, professors, authors, lawyers, parliamentarians, officers in the armed forces, ambassadors, etc. One of the first three women prime ministers in the world was a Hindu woman named Indira Gandhi (Figure 4.8). She was the prime minister of India from 1966 to 1977 and again from 1980 until her death in 1984. Her aunt, Vijaya Lakshmi Pandit, became the first woman president of the United Nations in 1953.

Check Your Understanding

1. Explain the difference between the following terms:
   - Brahman, atman
   - dharma, karma
   - *samsara*, moksha

2. Indicate the significance of the Hindu deities listed below. How are they portrayed and why?
   - Saraswati
   - Lakshmi
   - Shiva
   - Ganesha

3. Review the material on the caste system, and, working with a partner, create a list of the positive and negative aspects of caste. Summarize your view of the caste system in a written paragraph.

4. Summarize the responsibilities of a Hindu at each stage of his or her life. Each of these stages roughly corresponds to twenty-five years. How are your responsibilities at each of these stages similar? How are they different?

5. Write a letter to a female Hindu goddess such as Lakshmi or Parvati, and outline your views and concerns about the role of women in Hinduism.

PRACTICES, RITUALS, SYMBOLS, AND FESTIVALS

Practices and Rituals

The Hindu lives his or her religion through worship rituals that have been transmitted from one generation to another. Hindus worship in many different ways, and there is no standard form. Daily worship takes place mainly at home; going to the temple for prayer is not absolutely necessary. A Hindu child learns about the religion and its festivals by observation and by taking part in rituals at home. Many Hindus begin their day with some kind of religious ritual, for example, greeting the sun; others perform their rituals in the evenings or on weekends. Most Hindus purify themselves with water before participating in a religious ritual, usually by taking a bath.

The syllable **om** (see page 133), which represents the supremacy of Brahman, is chanted at the beginning and end of all Hindu prayers and readings of scripture. In a practice called *japa*, worshippers chant the names of deities repeatedly as well as sacred phrases called **mantras**. The following mantra, which Hindus chant to greet the sun, is considered one of the most important: "I meditate on the brilliance of the sun; may it illumine my intellect."

Worship at Home

A peek in a Hindu home reveals an elaborately decorated shrine that serves as an altar for worship. The shrine is adorned by images of deities, which are usually in the form of framed pictures or copper and marble statues. These images serve as points of focus to help the mind concentrate on the abstract ideals that the deities represent.

The most common form of home worship is called **puja**, a form of thanksgiving in which offerings are made to the deities. Devotees place all of the offerings on a tray near the shrine and present them to the deities at certain points in the worship. Offerings include flowers, fruits, incense sticks, water, milk, clarified butter, and a lamp. A traditional puja follows sixteen steps, and it is usually performed by worshippers on festival days and special occasions. All pujas conclude with the waving of a lamp, called *arati*, around the altar while worshippers sing hymns and verses of praise. After the final prayers are recited, some of the food that has been offered to the deities—and is now considered blessed—is redistributed to those present at the ceremony as a gift from the deities; this gift is called ***prasad***. ***Homa*** is a ritual that involves the burning of offerings in a fire that has been blessed by a priest. At special pujas, families invite a priest, who is from the Brahmin caste in most cases, to perform the ceremony.

Figure 4.9

A Hindu family performs a puja, with the help of a priest. What kinds of offerings are shown in the picture?

Worship in Temples

Worship in a Hindu temple is not a requirement, nor is it a necessity. Hindus usually visit temples during festivals or for special functions. Worship in a temple is conducted by a priest and his helpers. The priest leads the devotions each day. In the morning, he rings the temple bells, prepares the deities, and offers fresh flowers, incense, and food on behalf of devotees. In the evening, devotees sing sacred hymns and share in *arati* and *prasad*. Images of deities in temples are treated like royalty. The deities are given ritual baths, adorned, and taken on procession on special occasions. Worshippers revere and bow to them in prayer.

On festival days and on other special occasions when the reading of the scriptures takes place over several nights, many families join in worship. Hindus in the West also go to the temple to learn more about their religion. Many temples offer classes that teach children Hindu prayers and hymns, called *bhajans*.

The Significance of the Cow

Most Hindus refrain from eating beef since they consider the cow sacred to their culture and beliefs.

"Holy cow" is a familiar expression that refers to Hinduism's reverence of cows. Hindus adore the cow as a manifestation of all that is good and precious. They attribute its docility to its vegetarian nature, and aspire to a vegetarian lifestyle.

Yoga and Meditation

To Hindus, yoga and meditation are spiritual disciplines. **Yoga**, in the strict Hindu sense, means "yoke," that is, the atman in union with the Brahman. To achieve this union with God, **meditation** is necessary. The practice of meditation requires a sitting posture, which meditators can comfortably maintain for long periods of time.

Meditators try to control their breathing so that it is regular and will not break their concentration. They then concentrate on a single object, sound, or idea until they are in a deep meditative state and are experiencing the divine presence. Undoubtedly, the real experts are the **swamis**, or holy men of India, who have dedicated their lives to meditation. Many of them travel from India on a regular basis to lecture and teach in Canada.

Pilgrimages

Pilgrimages, or journeys to holy places as acts of devotion, are an important element of Hinduism. One holy place that all Hindus strive to visit, at least once in a lifetime, is the holy city of Varanasi (formerly known as Benares), which is located along the west bank of the holy Ganges River. It is believed that the Ganges River fell from heaven to earth, giving life to people and watering the plains that produce much-needed food. Bathing in the river is the first thing pilgrims do when they arrive, and it is a daily rite for local residents. Hindus believe that bathing in the Ganges cleanses them of their sins.

Holy Places
The City of Varanasi

Benares [Varanasi] is older than history, older than tradition, older even than legend, and looks twice as old as all of them put together.

—Mark Twain

Varanasi (formerly called Benares) is India's holiest city and one of the oldest cities in the world. It is situated on the west bank of the holy Ganges River, and is also known to Hindus as Kashi, the City of Lights. Varanasi is the home of God Shiva. Of the 1500 temples in the city, the Vishvanatha Temple (Figure 4.10), which is dedicated to Shiva, is perhaps the most revered. What is most significant about Varanasi is the belief that virtually every step of the city is marked by a *linga*, a symbol that represents the creative energy of Shiva. According to Hindu mythology, the entire sacred zone of Varanasi is one great *linga* of light that once burst through the earth and pierced the heavens in the presence of Brahma and Vishnu—the other deities in the Hindu Trinity. Pilgrims walk around this great *linga*, which is about 40 km long. It usually takes five days to complete this holy rite.

Today, Varanasi is home to many *ashrams*, or Hindu learning centres, that have housed famous poets, mystics, and itinerant holy men. The city continues the tradition of education through the Benares Hindu University, founded in 1905.

Hinduism is not the only religion that considers Varanasi a holy place. Varanasi is the birthplace of Tirthankara Parsvanatha, a spiritual teacher of Jainism, who was born there during the eighth century BCE. Three hundred years later, the Buddha gave his first sermon in the groves of Sarnath, in Varanasi, and so started the Buddhist sangha, or community of monks. Today, it is an important pilgrimage destination for Buddhists from around the world.

Figure 4.10

QUESTIONS

1. Why is Varanasi an important pilgrimage destination for Hindus?
2. Assume that you are a Canadian Hindu who has just visited the holy city of Varanasi. Write a half- to one-page journal entry describing the experience.

Symbols and Icons

There are many symbols in Hinduism, and they are all considered sacred. These symbols are concrete representations of abstract religious thought. Some of the most important Hindu symbols are presented in this section. In Hinduism, symbols that represent an aspect of Brahman serve as personal aids and reminders of this divine spirit. By focusing on these symbols, Hindus try to gain an awareness of this all-mighty entity and its universal presence.

Swastika

This Hindu good luck symbol represents "well-being." The Hindu swastika is usually illustrated in red and is used on wedding invitations, decorative drawings, textiles, and in rituals to bring good luck and protect against evil. Unfortunately, a modified version of this symbol (with the arms bent in a clockwise direction) was adopted by the Nazi regime of Adolf Hitler and has negative connotations in the non-Hindu world.

Figure 4.11

Symbols and Icons

Om

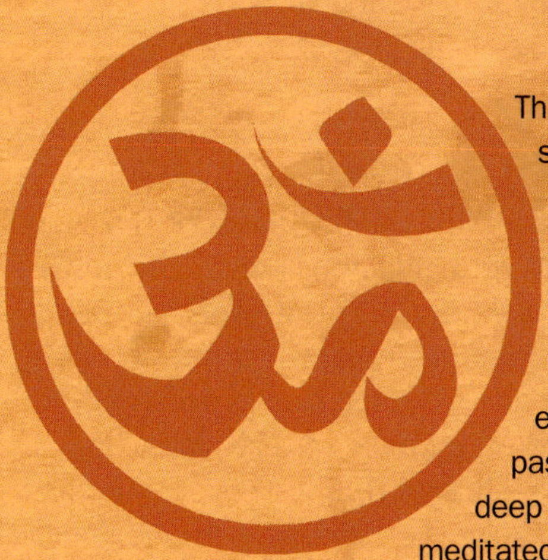

This important Hindu symbol represents the sacred syllable om. This syllable is made up of three sounds: *a-u-m*. When *a* and *u* come together, they make the sound *o*. The sound of the syllable begins deep within the body and ends at the lips. Hindus use this syllable as a mantra to evoke the supreme essence of Brahman. Om is believed to contain the secrets of the universe and is chanted at the beginning of prayers, blessings, and meditation. It is considered the first and most sacred sound and is believed to contain the essence of true knowledge. Om symbolizes the first three Vedas—the present, past, and future—and the three states of consciousness—waking, dreaming, and deep sleep. The symbol and the sound that it represents are not worshipped but meditated on as a means to gain enlightenment.

Figure 4.12

QUESTIONS

1. What does om represent to Hindus?

2. Make the room quiet, and try gently chanting "om" for a few minutes. Describe what happens.

Nataraj

Figure 4.13

The image representing Shiva as Nataraj, the Lord of Dance, is a prevalent Hindu icon (Figure 4.13). It shows the four-handed Shiva whirling and playing the drum with his upper right hand. The drum symbolizes sound, speech, and the divine truth heard through revelation. His dance symbolizes energy and the endless cycle of creation and destruction.

Forehead Marks

Figure 4.14

Some Hindu men and women mark a symbol, called a *tilak*, on their foreheads to indicate the deity that they worship. Devotees of Vishnu (Figure 4.14) use sandalwood paste, those of Shiva use ashes, and those of the goddess Parvati use red powder. The signs are worn on the forehead, between the eyebrows, to symbolize the third eye of wisdom.

Many married Hindu women mark their foreheads with a red dot called *bindi*. It signifies that a woman is married and should be respected as such. It is applied daily after a bath and puja, as well as on special occasions.

Festivals

There are many Hindu festivals, and they are joyous, colourful occasions. Among other things, these special events celebrate the birthdays of important deities and seasonal changes. The occurrence of Hindu festivals is based on the lunar calendar.

Diwali

This festival of lights is Hinduism's most popular celebration. In India, it is normally celebrated over five days at the end of October or the beginning of November. In most other countries, like Canada, **Diwali** is observed on only one evening, but is preceded and followed by days of festivities (Figure 4.15). During this festival, Hindus set off fireworks, decorate their houses with lights, give gifts, and wear new clothes to celebrate the triumph of good and knowledge over the dark forces of evil and ignorance. Lavish vegetarian dinners are prepared, and a traditional puja is performed at dusk before the feast begins. Diwali honours Lakshmi, the goddess of wealth and good fortune, and Vishnu, who defeated the demon Naraka. This festival also commemorates Rama's return to his kingdom after defeating Ravana, the evil king who had abducted his wife, Sita, in the Ramayana.

Holi

Holi is a spring festival that Hindus usually celebrate sometime in March, on the full-moon day of the last month in the Hindu calendar. The night before, worshippers light a bonfire that signifies the burning of evil. According to Hindu legend, the young Prahalad was resented by his wicked father for being pious and God-fearing. His evil aunt took Prahalad away and tried to burn him in a fire. Instead, she was burned to ashes. To mark this festival, Hindus of all ages join in the merriment of squirting coloured water on friends and family members. They distribute and eat sweets and other foods.

Mahashivaratri

This event takes place on the day before the new moon, during the month of February. Strictly speaking, Mahashivaratri is not a festival nor a feast. It is a special event dedicated to the devotion of Shiva. Devotees worship him, keep vigil, and fast for twenty-four hours; those who are unable to fast eat light vegetarian meals. Between midnight and sunrise, devotees worship him by repeating his name and placing flowers and grains on his image. Water is poured in a steady stream from a copper vessel suspended over the image.

Navaratri

This "Nine Nights" festival is held in the spring and autumn. On the first three nights of Navaratri, Hindus worship the goddess Durga, a manifestation of Parvati, who washes away laziness and evil thoughts. The next three nights, with a mind better prepared for spiritual guidance, they offer puja

Figure 4.15
Canadian Hindus celebrate Diwali with a parade. What is the origin of this festival?

to Lakshmi, the goddess of wealth and good fortune. The final three nights are dedicated to Saraswati, the goddess of knowledge and learning. On the tenth day, worshippers observe Vijayadasami, or the Day of Victory.

Check Your Understanding

1. Describe the following Hindu practices and indicate their significance:
   - puja
   - yoga and meditation
   - the distribution of prasad

2. How does the practice of vegetarianism reflect Hindu beliefs and principles? Are you or any of your friends vegetarian? Why or why not?

3. Briefly identify and describe any two Hindu symbols.

4. Identify the significance of the Hindu festivals listed below, and describe how Hindus celebrate them.
   - Diwali
   - Holi
   - Navaratri

5. Assume that you are a reporter for the local community paper or, perhaps, your school newspaper. Write a feature article introducing your readers to the central elements of Hindu worship.

MILESTONES

Life is a series of events and steps from birth to death or, as the Hindu would say, "from conception to crema-tion." In Hinduism, each step, or rite of passage, is called a *samskara*. There are forty such rites, which illustrates the importance of these rituals to the development of the individual within Hindu society. Of the approximately forty rituals, sixteen are central to the religion. However, in actual practice, few people observe them all. Some of the most important rites are presented below. Priests officiate at all these rites, which are attended by relatives and friends.

Naming a Child

Traditionally, in Hinduism a child is named by a priest ten days after birth. While orthodox Hindu families continue this tradition today, for most Hindus, this ceremony has become a symbolic gesture. Many parents choose a name even before their baby is born. Nevertheless, because a baby is considered a blessing and an occasion for celebration, most Hindu parents continue to hold some sort of informal naming ceremony performed by a priest.

A Child's First Outing

The purpose of the first formal excursion outside the home is to expose the child to the environment and the neighbours. The occurrence of this event depends on the health of the baby as well as the climate and weather conditions of his or her surroundings. The parents and child take a bath and wear new clothes. The parents apply a dab of soot to the baby's forehead for protection from the evil eye. With the infant in their arms, the mother and father offer a simple prayer to the deities and then take the baby out for a short walk. Special care is taken to avoid overexposure to the sun or other weather-related conditions.

First Solid Food

This ritual takes place about seven to eight months after the birth of the child, depending on his or her health. On the day of the ceremony, parents recite a special prayer asking the deities to bring good health and long life to the child. The father then begins the feeding by giving the child a small portion of boiled rice mixed with ghee (clarified butter) and honey.

First Haircut

Between the ages of six to eight months, the hair of a baby boy is cut by the local barber. The barber completely shaves the head, except for a small tuft of hair at the front. In southern India, some girls are given a haircut as well.

Thread Initiation Ceremony (Upanayana)

Upanayana is a sacred initiation ceremony performed by boys of the Brahmin, Kshatriya, and Vaishya castes between the ages of eight to twelve. It marks the boy's transition into the student stage of life, where he is expected to begin his studies of the sacred texts. During this ceremony, which takes place over two days, the boy wears a sacred thread over his left shoulder and chants a mantra.

Marriage

Marriage is a sacred milestone that marks the bride and groom's entry into the householder stage of life, described on page 126 of the chapter. This stage of life, called *grihasta*, sanctifies the bond between the bride and groom and the future fulfillment of their social responsibilities.

In India, arranged marriages are a common practice. Among Hindus born in the West, love matches are more common. Whatever the route to marriage, parents scrutinize the other family to make sure that the bride and groom are socially, culturally, and financially compatible. When the parents agree on a marriage, they arrange an engagement, where the father of the groom formally asks for the woman's hand in marriage to his son. Most of the family elders are present at this ceremony because a marriage is not only a union of two people but also of two families. After the engagement, an auspicious, or favourable, date is set for the wedding.

The wedding ceremony lasts for approximately three hours. It is performed by a priest, who is usually assisted by another priest. A traditional Hindu wedding (Figure 4.17) can be an elaborate affair consisting of about fifteen rituals. In today's busy world, these rituals are shortened. Some of the most important include the giving away of the bride by the father, the giving of auspiciousness to the bride by the groom's family, the clasping of hands by the couple, and the couple taking seven steps around a sacred fire. During the giving of auspiciousness, the groom's family gives the bride a necklace or string that she wears around her neck for the rest of her married life.

Exploring Issues:

The majority of Hindu marriages in India are arranged. This custom is not strictly followed by Hindus living outside of India. In Canada, traditional Hindu families are caught in the social battle of arranged marriages. For many Hindu girls, it is not a matter of choice, but a matter of honour or shame. Families feel disgraced and devastated if a girl does not marry or if her marriage fails. To Hindu families who place importance on status, caste, colour, and creed, resistance to arranged marriages is becoming a growing social problem.

AT ISSUE: Are arranged marriages a good idea?

Hindu Brahmin parents seek tall, slim, beautiful university educated match for handsome son, 29, 5'10". Computer professional, management position. Please e-mail biodata and photo.

Figure 4.16 *Advertisements like this one for suitable marriage partners are common in South Asian magazines and newspapers.*

The following article "First Comes Marriage, Then Comes Love" was written by Ira Mathur, an Indian-born journalist living in Trinidad, who writes for the Trinidad Guardian, the island's leading daily newspaper.

First Comes Marriage, Then Comes Love

by Ira Mathur

A suitable boy is first spotted by Bharati Narvani's uncle at a wedding in New Delhi, India. Bharati then lived in Trinidad where her parents migrated some 25 years ago from the Gujarat region of India. The 21-year-old university graduate was brought up with the customs and values of India. The boy, Manoj Solanki, 29, a civil engineer, is also of Gujarati parentage. Born in Liberia and educated in England, he went to India with his parents to find a bride.

Soon after that New Delhi wedding, Bharati accompanies her parents to India on one of their regular visits. She knows that her parents are making this trip with the hope of finding a groom for her. She is amenable to the idea. Bharati was never allowed to date, or mingle freely with boys her age. She didn't rebel, unlike some of her peers in Trinidad's Indian community.

Her friend, Sujata, the daughter of a well-known surgeon, reluctantly agreed to marry the son of a family friend in India. Before the wedding, she committed suicide by drinking gramoxone, a poisonous pesticide. Sujata was in love with a young man in Trinidad, and was too afraid to tell her parents. There is speculation that she might have been pregnant, and saw no other way out.

That will not be Bharati's fate. She will follow the ancient script of courtship and marriage that still prevails widely throughout India.

Once the Narvanis arrive in New Delhi, the uncle—the closest senior male relative in India—arranges a meeting of the two families. Manoj is accompanied by his mother and aunt, Bharati by her mother and uncle. A discreet discussion takes place among the elders: Is Manoj able to support a wife? Can Bharati adapt to a foreign country? . . .

Arranged Marriages

Finally the couple are given a chance to talk alone in another room. Manoj, being more confident, breaks the awkward silence with a joke. In between light bantering, the two manage to ask and answer serious questions about one another. Asking whether Bharati likes Indian movies, for instance, tells him how strong her cultural ties are. She wants to know whether Manoj expects her to be a housewife or will he be happy with her working? Will she live with her in-laws? His answers reassure her that they will live alone, that she is free to work, and that she can visit her parents whenever possible.

The attraction between the couple is immediate...

A month later, there is an elaborate engagement ceremony. Soon after, the wedding takes place in the couple's ancestral home of Baroda, Gujarat....

Earlier this year, the newlyweds visited Trinidad with their infant son for a huge reception given by the Narvani family. Bharati is radiant in her traditional bridal outfit. Manu, as she affectionately calls her husband, looks smugly satisfied. Those of us who knew Bharati before she was married have to admit she has gained confidence, matured and looks very happy.

Bharati's mother, Manju, misses her daughter tremendously, but is satisfied that the arranged marriage was the best she could have done for her.

It can also go horribly wrong. Meena, a 20-year-old high school graduate from Hyderabad in India, ended up—through an arranged marriage—with a computer analyst ten years her senior. Sharing their home in Los Angeles, California, was her husband's American girlfriend.

Indian society is quick to reject divorced, separated or abandoned women. If Meena went home, her parents' status in society would be shattered. Their pride and honour—on which the highest premium is placed—would make them societal rejects. She had no choice but to accept her husband's mistress and live as a semi-servant in his house.

Many Indians contend that arranged marriages are more successful than marriages in the West, particularly given the latter's staggering divorce rates. Romantic love does not necessarily lead to a good marriage, and often fails once the passion dissipates, they argue. Real love flows from a properly arranged union between two individuals...

QUESTIONS

1. Make a list of arguments supporting and opposing arranged marriages. Do you think arranged marriages are a good idea? Present your opinion in a letter to the author of this article.

2. What advice would you give to a devout Hindu friend who respects his or her parents but does not want to be involved in an arranged marriage?

A Hindu wedding ceremony is followed by a grand feast. Festivities can be quite extravagant and may include singing, dancing, drumming, fireworks, and, even, riding on a white horse.

Death and Cremation

When a Hindu dies, a solemn ceremony, which includes cremation by fire, is performed. Under the direction of a priest, family members bathe and dress the body in new, but traditional, clothing, leaving the face uncovered. Light and flowers are offered to the spirit of the deceased before the procession to the crematorium takes place. The name of Lord Rama is chanted, and hymns, or holy songs, are sung.

The priest recites passages from the holy scriptures to sanctify the fire. Then the oldest son, or a male member of the family, lights the pyre or, in a modern crematorium, pushes the button to begin the cremation. The family collects the ashes in an urn and scatters them in the holy rivers of India or any other body of water. On the tenth and thirteenth days after the funeral, relatives, friends, and neighbours gather for a special prayer and a feast.

Death Anniversary (Shraddha)

This ceremony marks the anniversary of a death. The priest performs religious rites, and family members, friends, and other guests are invited to witness the ceremony and enjoy a meal.

Check Your Understanding

1. a) Identify five Hindu milestones.
   b) What is the significance of the thread and the marriage ceremonies?

2. How have the rites below changed over time? How would you explain these changes?
   - naming a child
   - marriage ceremony
   - cremation ceremony

3. In your view, which of the rites of passage presented in this section is the most significant? Why?

SACRED WRITINGS

Unlike many other religious traditions, which have a single source of scripture, for example, the Bible, Hinduism has a number of sources, or books, that it considers sacred texts. Hindu scriptures consist of over 200 books that were composed from about 1500 BCE until about 1500 CE. Hindu scriptures are classified as being *shruti* or *smriti*. *Shruti* is knowledge that is revealed or "discovered" by the rishis, or seers of Hinduism. This wisdom is contained in the Vedas. *Smriti* is "human-made" literature, or knowledge that is "remembered."

The Vedas

The four **Vedas**, composed around 1500 BCE, are considered the oldest and most authoritative Hindu scriptures. They are a collection of writings on subjects ranging from the divine spirit to medicine and the sciences. Before 1500 BCE, these compositions were memorized and transmitted orally from teacher to student.

The four Vedas include the Rig-Veda, which comprises 1028 hymns (contained in ten books) that praise the ancient deities; the Yajur-Veda, a priest's "handbook" for the performance of fire sacrifices; the Sama-Veda, which consists of melodies, chants, and tunes for the singing of hymns; and the Atharva-Veda, which contains magical formulas, chants, spells, and charms. Each Veda contains the following types of compositions:

- **Mantras:** psalms of praise that constitute the main body of Vedas

- **Brahmanas:** prose manual for priests on prayer and ritual

- **Aranyakas:** "forest books" for saints and hermits

- **Upanishads:** philosophical commentaries that appear at the end of each Veda

The Upanishads

These concluding sections of the Vedas, which are collectively called Vedanta and form the basis of Hindu philosophy, have dominated Indian life and thought for 3000 years. There are over 200 Upanishads; of these, sixteen are considered to be the most important. Some of these include Isa, Katha, Prasna, Kena, and Mandukya. The Upanishads discuss topics such as the mind, the senses, worship, meditation, and the various means of liberation. They also discuss concepts that represent Hinduism's most central beliefs, including Brahman, atman, karma, samsara, moksha, and maya.

The Ramayana and the Mahabharata

India's two great epics, the **Ramayana** and the **Mahabharata**, are popular vehicles for spreading Hindu ideals of moral conduct. These *smriti* texts have such a grip on the Hindu imagination and such wide appeal that they have both been produced for television in over 100 episodes. The Ramayana even appears in comic-strip format in magazines and on the Internet (Figure 4.18). The Ramayana was written in Sanskrit around 200 BCE, about 200 years after the Mahabharata. However, the Ramayana deals with incidents that took place before the events of the Mahabharata.

The Ramayana

There are about twenty-six different versions of the Ramayana, but the most popular one was written around 1500 CE by Tulsidas, a contemporary of Shakespeare. It was the first scripture to be translated into Hindi from Sanskrit. This epic contains 24 000 verses. It is the story of Prince **Rama**, who is worshipped throughout the Hindu world as the seventh avatar, or incarnation, of God Vishnu. He was exiled to the forest for fourteen years so that his half-brother Bharata could become king. Sita, Rama'a wife, and his other half-brother Lakshmana followed the prince in exile. Unprotected in the forest dwelling, Sita was abducted by the wicked Ravana, who was disguised as a beggar. A battle ensued where Rama, assisted by Hanuman (king of the monkeys), defeated Ravana, rescued his wife, and returned triumphantly to his kingdom. Taken as a whole, the epic represents the constant struggle between good and evil, where good eventually prevails. The following is an excerpt from the Ramayana:

> *Forcing his way past Lakshmana, Raavana [Ravana] precipitated himself against Raama [Rama] with all the pent-up fury of hatred and revenge and strove to overwhelm him with a spate of arrows.*
>
> *Raama easily baffled these arrows with his own and struck Raavana repeatedly, without however being able to penetrate his Armour. Thus they fought, these supreme bowmen, each bent on slaying the other and using increasingly potent missiles of secret power, while the gods in heaven looked on in marvel and admiration. Neither hero had met such another opponent before and on both sides admiration was mingled with wrath. . . .*

Figure 4.18
The Ramayana appears in comic-strip format in magazines and on the Internet. Is this a good way to present an epic?

The Mahabharata

This monumental work, which is the longest poem in the world and comprises about 100 000 verses, appears to be the work of many authors. It was probably compiled between 400 BCE and 400 CE. The Mahabharata is the story of two forces: the Pandavas, who represent good, and the Kauravas, who represent evil. There is a war between the Kuru princes and the five Pandu princes, and after many intrigues and adventures, the evil forces of the Kauravas are defeated by the Pandavas, who rule for many years.

The Puranas (Myths)

The word *Purana* means "old narrative." They are *smritis* that form a distinct category of Sanskrit religious literature. This literature describes the exploits of the deities in thirty-six volumes, eighteen of which are widely used. Each Purana usually begins with the name of the god or incarnation it glorifies, for example, Vishnu Purana, Bramha Purana, and Shiva Purana. These legends are mostly used by temple priests and were composed between the sixth and sixteenth centuries CE.

Manusmriti (The Laws of Manu)

This Hindu law book affirms the Hindu concepts of dharma, caste, and the four aims of life. It deals with religious practice, law, customs, and politics. Brahmins accept this book as authoritative, but it is rejected by other castes. The present text, compiled around 300 CE, contains 2600 verses. In India, Hindus refer to this text for guidance on matters such as family property, inheritance, marriage, adoption, and guardianship. All other legal matters are subject to Indian secular law.

Check Your Understanding

1. a) What is the difference between shruti and smriti scriptures?
   b) Identify five sacred texts of the Hindu tradition and classify them as shruti or smriti.
   c) Describe the importance of each text.

2. Provide at least one example that illustrates the influence of Hinduism's ancient sacred writings on modern Hindu society.

3. Why are the Ramayana and Mahabharata so popular in your opinion?

4. Which of the Hindu scriptures mentioned would you most like to read? Explain your choice.

Sacred Text

One very important component of the Mahabharata is the Bhagavad-Gita, which is the one text that can claim to be the Hindu bible. This text, commonly called the Gita, is set in the Mahabharata war. Its 700 verses, contained in eighteen chapters, discuss the central beliefs of Hinduism and include teachings on dharma, reincarnation, and paths to salvation.

The text of the Gita is in the form of a dialogue. **Krishna**, the eighth incarnation of Vishnu, is explaining to his confused friend, Arjuna, the importance of performing one's duty in this world. Arjuna, who is a Pandu army leader, is reluctant to fight because he believes it is wrong to wage war against his own relatives and citizens, who are fighting for the opposing side. Krishna patiently and logically reasons with Arjuna about his role in life as a defender of human rights. These verses, spoken by Krishna, illustrate the fundamental importance of devotion to God.

Bhagavad-Gita
Chapter 9, verses 3–8

3. *Whosoever offers to Me with devotion a leaf, a flower, a fruit, or water—that offering of love, of the pure of heart, I accept.*

4. *Whatever thou doest, whatever thou eatest, whatever thou offerest, whatever thou givest away, whatever austerities thou practise—do that, O son of Kunti [Arjuna], as an offering to Me.*

5. *Thus shall thou be freed from the good and evil results, which are the bonds of action. With this mind firmly set on the way of renunciation, thou shall become free and attain to Me.*

6. *I am the same to all beings, none is hateful or dear to Me. But those who worship Me with devotion—they are in Me and I also in them.*

7. *Even if a man of the most vile conduct worships me with undistracted devotion, he must be reckoned as righteous for he has rightly resolved.*

8. *Swiftly does he become a soul of righteousness and obtain lasting peace. O son of Kunti [Arjuna], know thou for certain that My devotee perishes never.*

QUESTIONS

1. Why is Krishna using the first person to talk about God in the quotation?

2. What is Krishna's message to Arjuna? Do you agree or disagree with this message? Explain.

3. How does this passage illustrate the importance of faith in the Hindu tradition?

GROUPS AND INSTITUTIONS

The overwhelming majority of Hindus fall into three main groups: those who worship Vishnu and his incarnations, for example, Rama and Krishna; worshippers of Shiva; and devotees of Parvati, the consort of Shiva, who is identified as the Mother Goddess. The deity that a Hindu worships depends on family tradition, however, these classifications are not rigid and exclusive. Devotees of a particular deity also worship other deities and install images of many deities in home shrines and temples.

Shaivism

The worshippers of Shiva, in his various forms, are called Shivites, and the sect is known as **Shaivism**. Shivism is predominantly practised by Hindus in southern India and among the Tamils in Sri Lanka. This sect is more closely identified with the strict disciplines of fasting and meditation. Many adherents cover their bodies with ashes, and others make three horizontal marks across their foreheads to indicate their devotion to Shiva. However, all devotees of Shiva worship him as the great yogi, sitting in meditation on the snow-covered Himalayan Mountains. Followers revere him as the destroyer and creator of the universe. His creative power is symbolized by the *linga* (a cylindrical shaft).

There are many scriptures that are especially significant to Shivites. Among the Upanishads, the Svetasvatara is the most important.

The Shiva Puranas include the myths of Shiva and his consort, Parvati. They also contain ritual and ethical instructions on the performance of pujas and penances in order to gain salvation.

Shakti

Hindus recognize the feminine aspect of energy, known as *shakti*, as equally

Shiva et sa femme Parvati.

Figure 4.19
The goddess Parvati (shown seated beside Shiva) is a manifestation of shakti.

important, and they believe that a male deity's strength comes from his female consort. Thus, Shiva is incomplete without Parvati (Figure 4.19). In fact, Shiva is often depicted as Ardhanari, a manifestation whose right half of the body is male and whose left half is female.

Shakti is the generic name for all manifestations of female energy, which may be represented in various forms ranging from very gentle to fierce. The various manifestations of

Web Quest

To read about current issues that are of interest to Hindus all over the world, go to *Hinduism Today Magazine* online at http://www.hinduismtoday.com

Shakti include Sati, Parvati (Figure 4.19), Durga, and Kali. An affectionate name used collectively for all the manifestations of female energy is Devi, or Great Goddess. Sati and Parvati are deities that represent mild forms of energy, including patience, obedience, and compassion. Durga and Kali are deities that represent fierce energy and are depicted with many arms, bloodshot eyes, and destructive weapons. Durga and Kali use their destructive power to defeat evil forces and negative tendencies.

Vaishnavism

The followers of Vishnu are called Vaishnavites. This sect of Hinduism, which is more prevalent in northern India, is known as **Vaishnavism**. As preserver of the universe, Vishnu sometimes appears in human form to restore order and righteousness in the world. There are ten avatars, or incarnations, of Vishnu; nine are believed to have taken place, and the tenth is yet to come. The seventh and eight avatars, Rama and Krishna, are the most revered throughout the Hindu world.

The primary sacred text for devotees of Rama is the Ramayana. Guided by the virtues of Hindu dharma, Rama defeats the evil forces of nature and restores peace in a troubled world.

Devotees of Krishna are greatly influenced by the Mahabharata—the other Hindu epic, in which Krishna, also called Hari, is the great warrior. However, the most famous account of Krishna's teachings appears in the Bhagavad-Gita. The doctrine central to all Vaishnavites is *bhakti*, or intense devotion to a particular, personal god.

The Arya Samaj Movement

Unlike the three mainstream sects of Hinduism mentioned above, the followers of this movement are non-ritualistic and do not worship any deities. The **Arya Samaj** movement was founded by Swami Dayanand Saraswati in North India in 1875. He preached a reformed version of Hinduism that rejected the worship of images as symbols of the Supreme God.

The central teachings of the Arya Samaj movement are based on the Vedas, and the most important form of worship for followers of this sect is a fire ceremony known as *havan*.

Smaller Movements Within the Hindu Mainstream

Within the mainstream of Hinduism, there exist many sects and institutions that follow particular gurus, or teachers. The following are some of the movements that have active groups operating in Canada.

Hare Krishna Movement

The International Society for Krishna Consciousness (ISKCON) was first started in the U.S. during the early 1960s by Swami Bhaktivedanta, a Hindu guru from India who based his teachings on the earlier tradition of Vaishnavism (the worship of Vishnu). The followers of this movement (Figure 4.20) must follow a strict code of belief and practice. They are vegetarians and do not use tobacco, drugs, or alcohol.

Satya Sai Baba Movement

The disciples of this movement seek guidance from their living guru, Satya Sai Baba. Satya Sai Baba lives in South India and proclaims that he is a person who serves all religions. He believes that all religions are valid paths to God. His disciples follow five principles—*satya* (truth), dharma (righteous conduct), *shanti* (peace), *prema* (love), and ahimsa (non-violence).

Swami Narayan Movement

This sect of Hinduism was founded by Sahajananda Swami in the early nineteenth century in Gujarat, India. His followers declared him Swami Narayan, another name for Vishnu, and believed that salvation could also be granted through him. This movement, which emphasizes clean living, prayer, and good works, has grown in Canada. Followers in Toronto are presently building the largest Hindu temple in Canada.

Vedanta Society

This group, as the name implies, bases its teachings on the philosophy of the Vedas. It was founded by Swami Vivekananda, who attended the World's Parliament of Religions in Chicago in 1893, where he made a great impact. On his second visit to America, he established the Vedanta Society of San Francisco. This movement grew across India, the U.S., and Canada. The Vedanta Society of Toronto began in 1968 and has regular lectures on the Upanishads, the Bhagavad-Gita, and the teachings of Swami Vivekananda. The value of interfaith dialogues is a cornerstone of this group's philosophy.

Figure 4.20
Followers of the Hare Krishna movement celebrate a summer festival.

Check Your Understanding

1. Identify and describe the three main Hindu sects.

2. What is the Arya Samaj movement, and how does it differ from mainstream Hindu sects?

3. a) What is a guru?
b) Identify the significance of the following Hindu gurus, and describe the movements that they have founded:
• Sahajananda Swami
• Swami Bhaktivedanta
• Swami Vivekananda

4. Which of the streams of Hinduism described in this section most appeals to you? Why?

Community Study

The Swaminarayan Organization
Toronto, Ontario

Figure 4.21

Charitable work is a key component of this organization. In 1997, it donated over $100 000 to the flood disaster in Los Angeles. In India, it has adopted five villages and provides medicine, eyeglasses, and financial assistance. In Canada, the group also assists other Hindu groups during major festivals and fundraising drives.

Inspired by their spiritual leader, his Holiness Pramukh Swami Maharaj (Figure 4.21), members have embarked on a grand millennium project—to build a Hindu temple and cultural centre that will change the skyline of Toronto. The complex will be the largest Hindu structure in Canada, standing on 2 ha of land. The site is at Highway 427 and Finch Avenue in Toronto. In addition to an enormous temple, the complex will include a large permanent museum devoted to Hinduism that will exhibit ancient artifacts and the holy scriptures. It will also feature a community centre that will accommodate the numerous charitable and cultural activities in which the organization is involved. These include regular blood donor clinics, food drives, health and financial management seminars, family counselling, classical music and dance, yoga, meditation, drug and alcohol awareness, career planning, and language instruction.

In 1975, ten Hindu families who had recently emigrated from East Africa met in Toronto to form the Shree Swaminarayan group. Many had fled the racial reprisals waged against South Asians in eastern African countries, especially Uganda, and Canada opened its doors to them. By 1988, this religious group had grown to include approximately 100 families from Africa, India, and England. They eventually purchased four industrial units in the west end of Toronto, which today function as a temple. They meet at the temple every day for pujas, but the largest congregations take place on Sundays. A resident priest conducts all the religious ceremonies from pujas to birth and death sacraments.

QUESTIONS

1. What is the history of the Swaminarayan Organization?

2. How is this group contributing to the Hindu community in Canada and abroad?

CULTURAL IMPACT

During the European colonization of India in the nineteenth century, the British, French, and Dutch imperial powers shipped Indian people overseas to work in plantations that were once worked by African slaves. Most of these Indians were Hindus, and so Hinduism was transplanted in places like Fiji, Mauritius, Trinidad, Guyana, Suriname, and other territories.

Large pockets of Hindus can be found in most cosmopolitan centres of the Western world, such as London, Birmingham, Amsterdam, New York, Sydney, Toronto, and Vancouver. In these major centres, there are well over one million Hindus.

One of the most influential aspects of Hinduism on modern Western culture is the discipline of yoga. The impact of yoga and meditation can be judged by the multitude of classes and courses offered everywhere, and mainly by non-Hindu teachers.

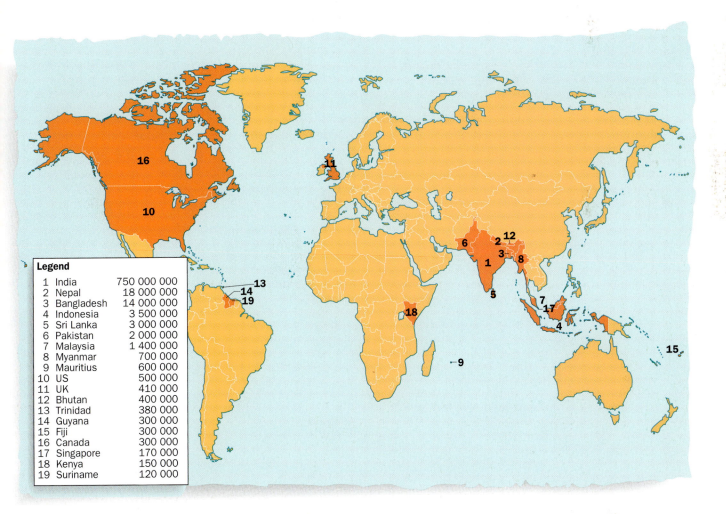

Legend

1	India	750 000 000
2	Nepal	18 000 000
3	Bangladesh	14 000 000
4	Indonesia	3 500 000
5	Sri Lanka	3 000 000
6	Pakistan	2 000 000
7	Malaysia	1 400 000
8	Myanmar	700 000
9	Mauritius	600 000
10	US	500 000
11	UK	410 000
12	Bhutan	400 000
13	Trinidad	380 000
14	Guyana	300 000
15	Fiji	300 000
16	Canada	300 000
17	Singapore	170 000
18	Kenya	150 000
19	Suriname	120 000

Figure 4.22
This map shows the world population of Hindus (approximately 800 million). Where has Hinduism taken root beyond the borders of India?

Living My Religion

Chaaya Raghunanan

Chaaya Raghunanan was born of Hindu parents in a predominantly Hindu village in Trinidad in 1970. She immigrated to Canada with her parents when she was

Figure 4.23

four years old and has since lived in Toronto. She attended the University of Toronto where she graduated with a degree in sociology. Today, she is employed as an executive assistant with an organization involved in industrial and workers' safety. She has recently completed a diploma course in human resources and labour relations at the University of Toronto. As part of her personal development, Chaaya is a student of Indian classical dancing. She pursues this interest under the guidance of her guru.

Chaaya writes the following regarding her religion:

I follow much of my Hindu tradition in my daily life. On many evenings, I pray at my home shrine and light a lamp. On weekends, I do my prayers on mornings and offer flowers to the deities. I have learned these rituals from my parents who are not really religious but like to offer puja to the gods and goddesses as a form of thanksgiving. We sometimes attend temples, not any one in particular, and we honour all the divine images. During festivals like Diwali, we fast as a family, that is, we do not eat any meat, fish, or poultry for several days and do our puja to the particular deity we are honouring. We sing bhajans and perform the havan, or fire ceremony.

During elementary school, I did not particularly enjoy hot dog and pizza days. You see, at home, we do not eat beef and pork. Most Hindus do not eat beef, so my mother prepared chicken dogs for me. This saved me from being singled out. At Christmas time, my parents allowed me to take part in activities relating to Jesus and Christianity. In fact, Christmas is a great time for my family. We have Christmas dinners, exchange gifts, and put up lights as we do for Diwali, the Hindu "festival of lights."

I would not call myself a religious person, but I ardently follow my Hindu practices. The strength it has given me in difficult times illustrates that Hinduism has useful and practical things to offer me in life. I find great solace in listening to Hindu hymns that are emotionally and spiritually satisfying. Beyond rituals, Hindu philosophy forces me to look with reason and faith at and within myself, as well as at others and the world around me. Lighting a simple lamp and offering a small flower make me feel like a child of God.

QUESTIONS

1. What elements of Hinduism are important to this Canadian woman?

2. What evidence is there that Chaaya has adopted other religious traditions while living in Canada?

3. a) What aspect of growing up Hindu in Canadian society did Chaaya find somewhat challenging?

   b) Why was it challenging, and how did she deal with it?

Hinduism in Canada

In Canada, the Hindu population exceeds 300 000. The majority of Hindu Canadians live in the Greater Toronto Area. Vancouver has the second largest concentration, and smaller populations are scattered among the larger cities of the eastern and western provinces.

Today, the Hindu community in Canada is very diverse, with origins in India, Sri Lanka, Guyana, Trinidad, England, and many east African countries. They have all brought with them different values and customs native to their countries, and they embrace different deities.

Their differences are also evident in the way they perform ceremonies, rituals, and sacraments. Sermons, lectures, and other discourses are delivered in the language particular to each linguistic group.

Southern Ontario is unique in Canada with regard to the Hindu population. Over 200 000 Hindus, representing about 70 per cent of the Hindu population in Canada, reside in this corridor, which stretches from Oshawa in the east to Niagara Falls in the west. In Markham and neighbouring Richmond Hill alone, there are four Hindu temples that reflect different styles and cultures (Figure 4.24). In addition to providing a place of worship, these temples are the cultural hub of Canada's Hindu communities, as well as learning centres where interested members are tutored in traditional vocal and instrumental music and dance.

Figure 4.24

The architecture of the Vishnu Mandir temple, located in Richmond Hill, Ontario, reflects both modern and traditional northern Indian Influences.

Check Your Understanding

1. How has Hinduism influenced Western culture?

2. Hinduism in Canada is as diverse as Canada's religious landscape. Explain.

3. Where is most of Canada's Hindu population located? Why do you think this is the case?

4. What elements of Hindu belief and practice do you personally find attractive or interesting? Why?

Web Quest

For a list of Hindu temples in Canada, go to http://mandirnet.org/canada/area

Quantitative research emphasizes experiments, numbers, and measurement and relies on the use of numerical scores and relationships to summarize data.

A quantitative research study is always designed to answer a specific question.

Characteristics of Quantitative Research

Hypothesis

Quantitative research begins with a hypothesis—an unproven statement that forms the basis for the investigation. The data collected by a researcher may or may not support the hypothesis.

Role of the researcher

Quantitative researchers decide what problem or topic to investigate, but once the investigation begins, his or her personal opinion does not play a role in the process.

Numerical Data

The quantitative researcher always expresses numerically the data collected from interviews, tests, questionnaires, or experiments. He or she may summarize the quantitative data using a variety of graphs such as the pie chart, bar graph, or scattergraph.

Topics That Lend Themselves to Quantitative Research

In general, quantitative research topics or problems

- are easily summarized using numerical results, graphs or charts;
- can be observed in artificial settings such as a laboratory;
- involve the investigation of groups over a very short period of time;
- involve the use of statistics and hard data.

Steps in Quantitative Research

The steps involved in quantitative research are outlined below. The topic of Hindu priests in Canada is used as an example.

1. Identify the topic or problem to be investigated.

Quantitative researchers begin their investigation with a statement (in declarative or question form) identifying the topic or problem and/or the subjects or group(s) of people involved.

Sample Topic: What is the country of origin of most Hindu priests living in Canada?

2. Identify the hypothesis.

The statement identifying the problem is always followed by a hypothesis that includes definitions of the variables, or important factors. The purpose of the hypothesis is to give direction to the research. In the example below, the variables include the two locations, Canada and Guyana.

Sample Hypothesis: Most Hindu priests living in Canada are originally from Guyana.

3. Design all elements of the investigation.

Before quantitative researchers collect any data, they outline all elements of their proposed study. The researcher provides a detailed description of the procedures for testing the hypothesis. The choice of appropriate technique or method is important. For example, a questionnaire might be an appropriate method to determine the origin of Hindu priests.

4. Select the participants in the study.

As in all research, identifying the participants is an important step in the process. A sampling of those who represent the whole population must be selected. To locate Hindu priests, one might contact Hindu temples.

5. Collect data.

• Experiments

Experiments may be conducted in a laboratory, allowing the researcher total control over the conditions of the experiment.

Experimental research is often used for comparison: If two situations or groups are essentially equal except for one variable, that one variable is added or deleted from the appropriate situation and the researcher observes the consequences.

• Surveys

In collecting data for a survey, the researcher can use a number of methods, including the interview, the questionnaire, and the use of measuring tools such as tests.

a) The Interview: For more information on Interviews, see Chapter 7.

b) The Questionnaire: The written questionnaire is a popular method in survey research because it can be distributed to a large number of people. A good questionnaire

- is brief, well-worded, clear, and concise;
- asks questions that elicit answers which are not easily accessed elsewhere;
- seeks facts, not opinions or impressions;
- takes a minimum amount of time to complete;
- includes clear instructions.

c) Tests: Tests are valuable measuring tools in survey research. In order to elicit facts, tests should be designed to avoid elements that lend themselves to a subjective evaluation.

6. Analyze data and draw conclusions.

In quantitative research, conclusions are drawn at the end of the study. The researcher organizes and displays the collected information using graphs, which transform the data into a "readable" form.

PRACTISE IT!

1. Conduct a quantitative research study into the national origins of Hindus living in your community and/or attending your school. Make sure to do the following:

- Formulate a hypothesis, e.g., The country of origin of most Hindu Canadians in my school is India.
- Design the elements of your investigation; you may wish to use a questionnaire or survey to collect the data for this particular study.
- Select the participants of your study.
- Collect your data.
- Display your results in a graph, and analyze your findings. Be prepared to support your analysis.

Activities

Check Your Understanding

1. Briefly describe what you consider to be three of Hinduism's most important beliefs.

2. It is interesting to note that many Hindu beliefs and practices are presented in fours. Describe at least two beliefs and practices that are based on the number four.

3. Yoga is very much a part of our society. How does the general practice of yoga in North America differ from yoga as understood by Hindus?

4. Symbols play an important role in Hindu ceremonies and rituals. Show how this statement is true by using fire worship and the *om* symbol as examples. Why are these symbols important in Hinduism?

Think and Communicate

5. You are probably familiar with the sayings below. Choose one of these phrases and discuss it with a partner. Do you accept the statement? How does the statement reflect Hindu teachings?
   - "What goes around comes around."
   - "As you sow, so shall you reap."
   - "I have a sense of déjà vu."
   - "Life is a merry-go-round."

6. Create a word web with the term *faith* at the centre. Add five spokes emanating from the centre. For each spoke, identify a way in which Hindus express, or show, their faith.

7. Dharma (duty) is a very important concept in Hinduism. In your opinion, what is the essential dharma of each of the following: teacher, parent, friend, police officer, politician, soldier, yourself. Record your answers in your notebook.

8. Assume that you have reached the last Hindu stage of life. Write a diary entry of at least half a page stating what you have learned about the world.

9. Working individually or with a partner, create a colourful poster of a Hindu deity. Be sure that the characteristics associated with your particular deity are clearly represented.

10. Hinduism is an ancient religion facing the challenges of the modern, scientific age. Working with a partner, try to determine which aspects of Hinduism will likely help it thrive in the contemporary world and which aspects might challenge its survival.

Apply Your Learning

11. Ahimsa is a significant concept to Hindus. Working in small groups, create media ads that promote this concept in our somewhat violent society. Use words, images, music, film, etc., to best promote this ideal.

12. Hinduism suggests that you are a result of your past actions. Describe at least five past actions that have had an important effect on the person that you have become.

13. Review the last ten years of your life, and note how you have changed under the following headings: Physically, Emotionally, Skills and Knowledge, Interests, Behaviour. In what ways have you remained the same?

14. Vegetarianism is increasingly popular among Canadian youth. Visit the school or community library for more information on the subject. You might also consult the Internet, visit health food stores, or chat with a friend who is vegetarian. Complete and present a brief report on the topic. Why is vegetarianism growing in popularity? What are the positive and negative aspects of a vegetarian diet?

15. Using the information and techniques presented in this chapter's Skill Path, complete a quantitative analysis of the Hindu population in your community.

Glossary

Agni [UGH nee]. The god of fire; the link between gods and humans.

ahimsa [a HIM sa]. The doctrine of non-violence toward all living creatures.

Arya Samaj movement [AR ee ya suh MODGE]. A reformed version of Hinduism that rejects the worship of images and the caste system; founded in 1875 by Swami Dayanand Saraswati.

atman [OT man]. The human soul; part of our innermost self that is identical to Brahman, the universal soul.

avatar [AVVA tar]. An incarnation, or manifestation, of a deity in earthly form.

bhakti [BOCK tee]. Intense devotion to a particular deity; often expressed through music.

Brahma [BROMMA]. A deity who is considered the creator of the universe; part of the Hindu Trinity.

Brahman [BRA mun]. The universal soul and sup-reme being; the eternal spirit from which all things originate and to which they return.

Brahmin [BRA min]. A member of the highest Hindu caste.

caste system. The organization of Hindu society into four groups, each with its own duties and expectations.

dharma [DARR muh]. Religious or moral duty.

Diwali [dee WOLLY]. The Hindu festival of lights that takes place at the end of October or beginning of November; celebrates the triumph of good over evil.

guru. A spiritual teacher or guide who can help one achieve moksha, or salvation.

Hindu Trinity. A concept that unites the gods Brahma, Vishnu, and Shiva into one entity.

__homa__ **[hoe MA].** A ritual that involves the burning of offerings in a fire that has been blessed by a priest.

karma [KUR ma]. The totality of one's actions; the accumulation of good or bad karma determines one's birth in his or her next life.

Krishna. The eighth incarnation of the god Vishnu.

kshatriya [ka SHAW tree ya]. A member of the military caste.

Mahabharata [maha BARRA tuh]. A Hindu epic poem comprising about 100 000 verses, probably compiled between 400 BCE and 400 CE. It tells the story of the struggle between two forces—the Pandavas and the Kauravas.

mantra. A sacred word or phrase that is chanted during worship or meditation.

maya [MY uh]. A word used to refer to the temporary and imperfect nature of the physical world.

meditation. Deep contemplation that leads to a trance-like state in which the individual tries to become one with the Brahman.

moksha. Liberation of the soul from the endless cycle of rebirths; attained by uniting the atman with the Brahman. It is the ultimate goal of Hindus.

om [OME]. A sacred syllable that invokes the essence of Brahman when chanted. It is believed to be the sound of all reality.

Parvati [PARVA tee]. A mother goddess who represents female energy.

prasad **[PRA sad].** A practice that involves redistributing to devotees food that has been offered to the deities.

puja [POO juh]. A common thanksgiving ritual that involves offerings of flowers, food, and other articles to the deities.

Rama [RAMMA]. The seventh incarnation of God Vishnu; the hero in the Hindu epic the Ramayana.

Ramayana [RA MY anna]. A Hindu epic of about 24 000 verses, composed around 200 BCE.

samsara **[sam SARA].** The endless cycle of rebirths.

Shakti [SHUCK tee]. The generic name for all manifestations of female energy, which may be represented as gentle or fierce.

Shiva [SHIVVA]. A deity who is considered the destroyer and restorer of the universe; part of the Hindu Trinity.

Shivism [SHY vism]. A sect of Hinduism whose followers worship the god Shiva. It is practised predominantly in southern India.

shruti **[SHROOTY].** Knowledge that is revealed to, or "discovered" by, the wise men of Hinduism, e.g., the content of the Vedas.

smriti **[SMEERTY].** human-made literature, or knowledge that is "remembered," e.g., the content of the Mahabharata and the Ramayana.

Sudra [SOO dra]. A member of the lowest Hindu caste.

swami [SWOMMY]. The holy men of Hinduism.

Vaishnavism [VIE ish na vism]. A sect of Hinduism whose followers worship the god Vishnu. It is practised predominantly in northern India.

Vedas [VAY duh]. Hinduism's earliest sacred writings, composed around 1500 BCE.

Vishnu [VISH NOO]. A deity who is considered the preserver of the universe; part of the Hindu Trinity.

yoga. A practice or discipline combining philosophy with physical exercises and meditation; union with God.

yogi. A spiritually evolved individual who practises meditation.

Chapter Five

Buddhism

5

Look at the photograph and consider the following questions:

1. Describe the setting of the photograph. What is the mood of the picture?
2. A Buddhist monk is walking up a path through trees.
   What symbolism is being presented?
3. What impressions about Buddhism do you get from this photograph?
4. Does this picture appeal to you? Explain.

Introduction

In the last four decades of the twentieth century, Buddhism—a religion that has its origins in the East—has become increasingly popular in the West. In their quest to "find themselves" and the meaning of life, more and more people are looking outside the conventional Western view, and towards Buddhism, for answers to life's questions. What is the appeal of this religion, and why are so many people in the West, particularly in North America, looking to Buddhism to fulfill their spiritual needs?

Buddhism emphasizes *things to do* rather than *things to believe* and does not recommend that anyone accept its teachings without experimentation. A Buddhist is not asked to accept teachings on blind faith but through direct religious experience. If this religious experience helps followers to find the truth, they should accept it; if it does not, they should seek the truth elsewhere. In fact, a central idea in the teachings of Buddhism is that everyone has the right to find the truth for himself or herself, even if it means finding it outside of Buddhism. This tolerance and the general calmness and serenity that is exhibited by many followers of this religion may help to explain Buddhism's growing appeal.

The ultimate goal of Buddhism is to end suffering and, thereby, attain absolute peace and joy. In western society, we try to achieve happiness by acquiring material possessions. However, in the midst of plenty, suffering and unhappiness are rampant. Buddhism offers an alternative way to end suffering.

What challenges do you face in your life? What types of suffering have you experienced? As you read this chapter, consider these questions to gain a more personal understanding of Buddhism and a deeper understanding of yourself.

159

Learning Goals

At the end of this chapter, you will be able to:

- understand the origins of Buddhism and recount significant events in its history
- identify important figures in the development of Buddhism and explain their contribution to the religion
- evaluate the importance of key concepts like nirvana and enlightenment
- identify key passages from the Tripitaka and explain their significance
- examine the importance of sacred writings in Buddhism and identify their influence on society
- identify the origin and significance of Buddhist practices, rituals, symbols, and festivals
- understand the role of symbols in Buddhism and their connection to practices
- review the political impact of Buddhism on various cultures
- analyze the role of women in Buddhism
- understand the differences between sects of Buddhism and between Buddhism and Hinduism
- understand how Buddhism has influenced individuals in Canadian society
- identify observances associated with Buddhist festivals and celebrations
- identify topics on Buddhism that require qualitative research
- use primary and secondary sources to conduct research on a topic related to Buddhism
- write newspaper articles and written reports on topics related to Buddhism

•**278 CE** Buddhism enters Myanmar, Cambodia, Laos, Vietnam

•**200 BCE** (approximately) Beginnings of Mahayana Buddhism

•**100 CE** (approximate) Buddhism enters China

•**531-486 BCE**
Teaching period of the Buddha

•**486 BCE**
Parinirvana, or death, of the Buddha

•**563 BCE** (approximately)
Birth of Siddartha Gautama (who later becomes the Buddha)

•**530 BCE**
Enlightenment of Siddartha

1990s CE
Appearance of the movies *Seven Years in Tibet, Kundun*, and *The Little Buddha* in the West spur international interest in Buddhism

1989 CE Dalai Lama receives Nobel peace prize

1992 CE The Falun Gong movement is first made public

1893 CE Beginning of Buddhist activity in the West

1959 CE Chinese takeover of Tibet; Dalai Lama flees

538 CE Buddhism spreads into Japan

750 CE (approximately) Buddhism spreads into Tibet

327 CE Buddhism introduced to Korea from China

Timeline

Buddhism

ORIGINS

Buddhism was founded approximately 2500 years ago in India. The man who was to become the Buddha, Siddhartha Gautama, was born around 563 BCE into a family of the Kshatriya caste in a kingdom called Shakya. The kingdom of Shakya was located in the foothills of the Himalayas, inside present-day Nepal (Figure 5.1). Siddhartha's father was King Shuddhodana, who belonged to the Gautama clan. The king's principal wife, and Siddhartha's mother, was Queen Maya. The story of the Buddha's early life varies from one Buddhist tradition to the other and was not recorded in written form until hundreds of years after his death. Later versions of the story are longer and include more miraculous events.

The Early Life of the Buddha

According to Buddhist literature, Siddhartha's birth was miraculous. Siddhartha's mother, Queen Maya, conceived her son when Siddhartha descended from Heaven and entered his mother's womb in the form of a baby white elephant—a symbol of purity. She carried him for ten months and could see the baby within her womb.

She gave birth from her side on the full-moon day of May, while standing and holding on to a tree. According to some Buddhist stories, the tree lowered a branch to assist her while she gave birth. Although he was born clean and unstained in any way, water poured from the sky to wash the mother and child. His mother died a week after giving birth, and Siddhartha was raised by his aunt. It is written that when Siddhartha was born, he immediately took seven steps and said, "This is my last birth." The meaning of this was that the child would be a great ruler or a great religious teacher. His father, King Shuddhodana, wanted him to be a ruler and was disturbed by the suggestion that he would be a religious leader. He vowed to make life as pleasant as possible for his son so that Siddhartha would not want to leave the palace.

At sixteen, Siddhartha married Princess Yasodhara, and together they had a son named Rahula. They lived in luxury in the three palaces that King Suddhodana built for them.

The Four Sights

Even though life was comfortable, Siddhartha craved spiritual satisfaction. His father, fearing that his son would leave home for a religious life,

Figure 5.2
This eighteenth century Tibetan painting depicts the events surrounding Siddartha's miraculous birth. Identify one of these events.

arranged for the streets of the city to be filled with healthy and happy people so that Siddhartha would not see any unpleasantness that might trouble him.

The King's plan went awry when, at the age of twenty-nine, Siddhartha visited the city four times with his charioteer, Channa, and experienced what Buddhists refer to as the **Four Sights**. On the first excursion, he saw an old man—his body broken by life—leaning on a staff. During the second visit, Siddhartha saw a sick man lying by the roadside. On the third trip, he saw a corpse being prepared for cremation. Siddhartha asked Channa for the meaning of these three sightings and was told that "these come to all men." On the fourth outing, Siddhartha's attention was drawn to an **ascetic** Hindu monk, that is, a monk who practises severe self-denial. The monk's head was shaven, and he wore a tattered yellow robe and was holding a bowl. When Siddhartha asked Channa for the meaning of this sighting, the charioteer answered, "This is a man living the homeless life in order to seek the answer to life's riddle." Siddhartha became inspired by the thought of finding a spiritual solution to the problems of human life. That night, he decided to leave the palace, and his privileged life, to become a homeless beggar.

This story may not be literally true: It may be a fable, where palace life represents complacency and self-delusion, and the vision of the four signs represents the realities of human life. It might also represent the idea that although these realities are all around us, most of us put up mental barriers to keep them at a distance.

Renunciation and Austerities

Siddhartha became a wandering seeker of spiritual knowledge. His first teacher taught him to meditate and attain a state of deep trance. The experience was good but did not produce the permanent solution he sought, since after the trance the same problem still existed. Siddhartha then tried controlled breathing, which involved retaining breath for longer and longer periods of time; this, however, resulted in headaches. Next, he tried reducing food intake to just one grain of rice a day. Siddhartha became emaciated and ill and gave up this form of asceticism, or self-denial, as he realized that extremes of any kind were not productive. He found that self-denial was as unsatisfactory as life in the palaces, so he came to the conclusion that the best course was the **Middle Way**, or a path between both extremes. Siddhartha concluded that the best lifestyle was one of moderation.

Enlightenment

Siddhartha began to take food again and returned to meditation. He sat under a tree (Figure 5.3), and in a state of higher consciousness, something comparable to a psychic state, remembered all of his previous lives in detail. He saw the death and rebirth of all types of beings as a consequence of their good and bad deeds; good deeds brought a better life in the next rebirth, while bad deeds brought unpleasantness. In realizing this, he removed craving and ignorance for himself. In that moment, he achieved **nirvana**, a state of supreme realization and **enlightenment**, an understanding of the truth of life and the freedom from ignorance. By attaining enlightenment, Siddhartha experienced the end of suffering and was released from the endless cycle of rebirth; he had now attained perfect wisdom and absolute peace.

Nirvana is a difficult idea to fully comprehend, and the Buddha suggested it had to be experienced to be understood. However, most observers suggest that nirvana is a state of total liberation and serenity. Some claim it is permanent truth, tranquility, and peace. It is a goal, difficult to put into words, whose promise of peace and liberation from suffering continues to be attractive to many around the world today.

Siddhartha stayed in this state for seven days (or seven weeks according to other versions), pondering his future and deciding to publicize his teachings and ideas about the nature of reality, the **dharma**, to the world.

Figure 5.3 *The Bodhi Tree, located at the site of the Mahabodhi Temple in Bodh Gaya, India, is believed to be the site where the Buddha achieved enlightenment. Describe this "enlightenment."*

The Mahabodhi Temple

The Mahabodhi Temple in Bodh Gaya, India, commemorates the enlightenment of Siddhartha Gautama and is one of Buddhism's most sacred sites. Because it was built at the site of the Bodhi tree, under which the Buddha attained enlightenment, it marks the birthplace of the religion. The structure is considered Buddhism's oldest and most revered temple.

The base of the temple is 15 m^2 and 52 m high. The top of the temple is a tapering pyramid; four smaller towers at the corners of the base give balance to the structure. The temple houses an immense 1700-year-old statue of the Buddha, which is facing in the same direction as the Buddha when he attained enlightenment.

During the third century BCE, King Ashoka, the king of the Mauryan Empire of India and a Buddhist, built a fence around the Bodhi tree to commemorate the enlightenment of the Buddha. It is believed that he built a monastery at the site and eventually the Mahabodhi Temple. In the twelfth century CE, Muslim invaders destroyed the temple completely. In 1891, the Maha Bodhi Society of India was formed. One of the goals of this organization was to restore the Mahabodhi Temple, which it has done with the financial help of Buddhists from around the world.

Today, the Mahabodhi Temple is an active pilgrimage site and learning centre. Buddhists from all over the world visit the temple to seek the enlightenment of the Buddha.

Figure 5.4

QUESTIONS

1. Why is the Mahabodhi temple such a revered place for Buddhists around the globe? Would you like to visit this site? Explain why or why not.

2. How do you think the Buddha would view the Mahabodhi site? Why?

3. Does this temple resemble any religious or secular buildings that you have seen? Explain.

The First Sermon

Siddhartha came to be known as the **Buddha**, which means "the Enlightened One" or "One Who Has Awakened." He went to Sarnath, in India, and, in a park reserved for royal deer, he preached his first sermon. This event is referred to as the "Setting in Motion the Wheel of the Dharma." In Deer Park, he shared his new understanding of life with five Hindu ascetics who accepted his insights and became **bhikkhus**, or Buddha's monks. This was the beginning of the Buddhist community. His teachings spread quickly, and after five years, an order of monks, the **sangha**, was established. An order of nuns, called the **bhikkhuni sangha**, was also established, and the Buddha praised the work of the nuns in preaching the dharma. For the next forty-five years, the Buddha travelled all over northern and central India preaching his philosophy.

Parinirvana

When he was eighty years old, the Buddha was in poor health. The question came up as to whether or not he would have a successor. Since he never considered himself the "leader," the Buddha declared that the dharma, together with the rules of monastic life, would be the people's spiritual guide when he was gone. He believed that each person should decide, for himself or herself, which teachings to follow, based on personal evaluation and that, ultimately, each person is responsible for his or her own salvation. He expressed this view on his deathbed, where he is believed to have spoken the following words to his followers:

Hold firm to the truth as a lamp and a refuge, and do not look for refuge to anything besides yourselves. A monk becomes his own lamp and refuge by continually looking on his body, feelings, perceptions, moods and ideas in such a manner that he conquers the cravings and depressions of ordinary men and is always strenuous, self-possessed, and collected in mind. Whoever among my monks does this, either now or when I am dead, if he is anxious to learn, will reach the summit.

The Buddha died in 486 BCE, resting between two trees. Upon his death, he reached the state of **parinirvana**, or complete nirvana, which released him from the cycle of involuntary rebirth.

Buddhism's Hindu Origins

The Buddha was born into the Kshatriya caste, and was therefore born a Hindu. In fact, some Hindus believe that the Buddha is an incarnation of the god Vishnu. The religion founded by Siddhartha Gautama grew out of Hinduism, and while there were many aspects of the Hindu religion to which the Buddha objected, there were some elements that he retained. These include the notions of reincarnation, *samsara*, karma, dharma, and nirvana.

There were several aspects of the Hindu religion, as it existed in his day, that the Buddha rejected. The first was the caste system—particularly the power of the Brahmin caste. The caste system was contrary to the Buddhist notion of the equality of all individuals. The Buddha also believed that people were responsible for seeking their own spiritual fulfillment rather than being dictated to by the Brahmins.

The Buddha objected to Hindu rituals, which he saw as insignificant activities that dominated the religion. These included making offerings to the gods, chants, and sacrifices. Brahmins often collected money for performing these rituals. The Buddha was determined to keep Buddhism free of meaningless rituals.

He considered questions and theories about the creation and eternity of the world futile. The Buddha believed that these questions could not be answered and that it was pointless to try. The religion he preached was practical and free of such mystical obsessions.

The Buddha disapproved of the language of Hinduism. The Brahmins continued to use Sanskrit, a language that, at the time of the Buddha, few spoke or understood. This left the Hindu religion under the control of the priests. The Buddha gave all his talks in Pali, the language common to the people of his region. This made Buddhism accessible to all.

Finally, the Buddha disagreed with the Hindu notion that an individual can achieve nirvana only after thousands of lifetimes and upon reaching the Brahmin caste. He believed that this prospect made nirvana virtually impossible for most Hindus. Buddhism preaches that through self-effort, enlightenment could be achieved in one lifetime, regardless of one's position in society.

Check Your Understanding

1. Describe Siddhartha's origins. How are the circumstances of his birth different from those of other religious founders? How are they similar?

2. What are the Four Sights? Why are they so important?

3. What is the meaning of the term *Buddha*? How did Siddhartha earn that name?

4. Which aspects of Hinduism did the Buddha accept? Which did he reject and why?

5. Assume you were present at the Buddha's funeral. Write a brief eulogy in which you share your thoughts about this great religious leader.

BELIEFS

Many of Buddhism's teachings are challenging, and it can be difficult to grasp such a different and unique view of the world. To understand this religion, it is helpful to remember its ultimate goal: the end of human suffering. If we concentrate on what

Buddhism is addressing, perhaps we will find it easier to comprehend its answers to life. As you read this section, consider the following personal questions: How happy are you? What are the most important goals in your life? What makes us suffer? How do we deal with suffering?

Every religion has its own defining characteristic or distinguishing nature. Buddhism is in many ways an introspective religion, with the single most important aspect being personal responsibility for one's own salvation.

Unlike Christianity or Islam, Buddhism does not have a single, central source of beliefs such as the Bible or the Qur'an. There are, however, a number of sources for the Buddhist to use in the search for spiritual truth. Taken together, these sources form a guide to a proper life. All Buddhist teachings show the way to end the suffering of life and to stop **samsara**. *Samsara* is the endless cycle of uncontrolled rebirths. These rebirths, referred to as **reincarnation**, involve the transference of one's mind or consciousness into new bodies after death. As explained earlier in this chapter, when one achieves nirvana, one has attained perfect wisdom and is released from the endless cycle of *samsara*.

Women in Buddhism

In Buddhist thought, there is no distinction made between men and women because gender is part of those delusions that we have as unenlightened humans. All humans have had past lives as both males and females. Rebirth as a female entails more suffering because of experiences like childbirth, menstruation, and pregnancy. However, in Buddhism, suffering is not necessarily considered an obstacle since it may lead someone to live a more spiritual life (Figure 5.5).

In Buddhism, women are not considered to be the property of men. Since Buddhism is opposed to violence toward any living creatures, the physical abuse of women and children is not tolerated. In some Buddhist countries, attitudes toward women reflect the culture of that particular region rather than the philosophy of Buddhism.

Web Quest

For detailed information and colourful visuals on many aspects of Buddhism, visit www.buddhanet.net.

Figure 5.5 *Buddha Tara, a figure in Buddha's teachings, vowed to take rebirth as a woman until she became a Buddha. Are women and men considered equal in Buddhism? Expain your answer.*

The Three Characteristics of Existence

The Buddha's thoughts on the nature of existence represent a radically different view of the world than the one accepted by most Canadians today. Through observation and meditation, the Buddha came to a conclusion regarding the natural existence of things that represents one of the most important concepts in Buddhism. He believed that all things, outside of nirvana, had three fundamental characteristics: *anicca* (impermanence), *dukkha* (dissatisfaction), and *anatta* (selflessness).

Anicca, or impermanence, represents the idea that the world is in constant flux and that nothing stays the same for long. Impermanence is a fundamental feature of everything—the environment changes, our clothes wear out, our cars break down, and our bodies age. Today, we live in a world that is constantly changing and that may, in fact, be more impermanent than the one the Buddha experienced in his own lifetime.

Dukkha, or dissatisfaction, represents the idea that all humans and animals experience suffering. Physical and mental pain are extreme examples of this characteristic. We can contract painful illnesses such as cancer, or we may experience the mental distress of a death in the family. The Buddha knew that there was no such thing as continuous happiness or pleasure since these feelings only last for a limited amount of time. In this sense, *dukkha* touches everything that exists.

Anatta, or no-self, is more difficult to understand. The notion of *anatta* is connected to the idea that we cannot point to any one thing in ourselves that we can say is self. No single part of the body, for example, an eye, an arm, or a foot, is the person. Only when we put all the parts together do we collectively call them a person. When the body is dead, we do not call it a person any more. The mind is also made up of parts, including moods or states of mind. There is no permanent independent self, only changing parts that we designate as self. For young Canadians struggling with self-concept and self-image, the Buddha's concepts may offer some insights.

The Five Precepts

These are the rules followed by Buddhist lay people to control improper, or non-beneficial, physical and verbal behaviour that might cause suffering. **The Five Precepts** are listed in Figure 5.6. Consider which of these precepts you may already practise. The first precept, which is referred to as **ahimsa**, is of paramount importance and accounts for Buddhists' non-violent behaviour. It is explained in the scriptures as follows:

> *All tremble at violence, all fear death. Putting oneself in the place of another, one should not kill nor cause another to kill... One who, while oneself seeking happiness, does not oppress with violence other beings who also desire happiness, will find happiness hereafter.*
>
> Dhammapada, section 10, verses 130–145

The last precept is crucial because if an individual disregards it, he or she could lose control and end up breaking all of the other precepts.

Ordained monks and nuns, who have taken the vows of poverty and chastity, observe the additional precepts outlined in Figure 5.7. In some sanghas, a monk or nun might have as many as 200 precepts to follow.

The Five Precepts

1. Abstain from killing or harming living beings

2. Abstain from stealing

3. Abstain from improper sexual conduct

4. Abstain from false speech, e.g., telling lies, setting people against each other, and gossiping

5. Abstain from taking alcohol and harmful drugs

Figure 5.6

Additional Precepts

6. Abstain from eating after noon

7. Abstain from looking at dancing, singing, or drama

8. Abstain from the use of perfumes and things that tend to beautify and adorn a person

9. Abstain from using comfortable beds

10. Abstain from accepting gold or silver

Figure 5.7

The Four Noble Truths

The Buddha observed that no one can escape death and unhappiness. If people expect only happiness in life, they will be disappointed. When people are sick, they go to a doctor. As a doctor tries to find out the cause and treatment of an illness, so the Buddha looked at the cause of unhappiness and its treatment. The result was the doctrine of the **Four Noble Truths**, which he explained to his earliest followers during his first sermon in Deer Park. These "truths" are central to an understanding of Buddhism. Most observers can relate to the central themes of suffering and desire, but while many people feel that the Buddha accurately understood existence, others find some of these "truths" to be rather dark and dismal.

1. The Noble Truth of Suffering

To live is to suffer. On a very basic level, this suffering includes the experiences of birth, old age, disease, death, sorrow, and frustration. Other types of suffering include being around those whom we dislike, being apart from loved ones, and not getting what we want. These are all experiences we do not want, we try to avoid, and, at times, we even pretend do not exist. Buddhists do not believe that there are no moments of happiness in life, but they do believe that these moments do not last forever.

2. The Noble Truth of the Origin of Suffering

The cause of suffering is negative desire. Every kind of suffering has its origins in craving or selfish desire, which is the result of ignorance or delusion. People, greedy for the wrong kind of pleasures, do harmful things to their bodies and peace of mind. The possessions that people desire most cause them the most suffering. Everyone has basic needs, that is, food, clothing, and shelter; when these needs are met, one should enjoy them without becoming greedy.

3. The Noble Truth of the Extinction of Suffering

The goal of Buddhism is to end suffering. Reaching nirvana will be possible only when the urge to possess more and more things is destroyed. To cut off greed means changing one's views and living a more natural and peaceful life. The person attaining nirvana is in a blissful, happy, and content state where nothing whatsoever causes any kind of suffering, physical or mental. Nirvana is difficult to properly describe in words. Many Westerners think that it is Buddhist heaven, but it is not a place; it is a state of being.

4. The Noble Truth of the Path Leading to the Extinction of Suffering

To end suffering, one must adopt the Middle Way by following the **Noble Eightfold Path**, which is explained below. Adopting this path is to live the Buddhist way of life—a life of self-improvement. For some people, The Noble Eightfold Path is a blueprint for a happier life.

The Noble Eightfold Path

When the Buddha gave his first sermon in Deer Park, he "set in motion the wheel of the Dharma." The symbol of the eight-spoke wheel (Figure 5.8) was chosen by him to represent the eight steps of the path. The centre of the wheel represents nirvana, which is the only fixed point. As the spokes of a wheel are needed for the wheel to keep turning, Buddhists need to follow each step of the path to reach the end of suffering. These steps are not to be followed one after the other; they are to be used together as a way of life along a path of self-conquest that ultimately leads to real happiness, peace, and nirvana. Many people relate to the image of life as a "wheel," and the "path" provides suggestions that we might consider for our own life. The steps are as follows:

1. Right View

We need a "blueprint" to guide us through life; therefore it is essential that we know the doctrine of the Four Noble Truths.

2. Right Thought

The mind has to be freed from sensuous desire, ill-will, and cruelty. We are what we think, so nurture good thoughts because they produce good, strong character.

3. Right Speech

By using kind speech, we will be respected and trusted; therefore, we should not lie, criticize unjustly, use harsh language, or engage in gossiping.

4. Right Conduct

This is also called Right Action, and it is accomplished by observing the Five Precepts (see page 171). People will judge a person according to his or her behaviour.

5. Right Livelihood

Earn a living through occupations that do not cause harm to living things. Trades that should be avoided include the butchering of animals, lending money at excessively high interest rates, and trading in weapons, liquor, or poison.

6. Right Effort

Conquer all evil thoughts and strive to have good thoughts. Individuals must do their best at all times and have goodwill toward others.

7. Right Mindfulness

A person has to recognize what is important and must not to be led astray by unwholesome acts or thoughts. Full attention must be given to proper thoughts, words, and deeds, as explained in the Five Precepts. Doing something mindfully is not necessarily good; a person can steal and cheat mindfully, but these actions are the result of incorrect mindfulness.

8. Right Concentration

The final step involves focusing the mind on one thought or object at a time. This concentration leads to true peace of mind and tranquility. Deep meditation will lead to enlightenment.

The Three Refuges (The Triple Jewel)

A refuge is a place of safety from danger. In order to make it easier to follow his teachings and take refuge from a difficult existence, the Buddha established the Three Refuges. The purpose of the refuges is to guide

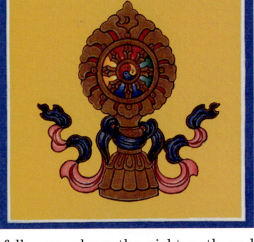

Figure 5.8 *The Dharma Wheel represents the Noble Eightfold Path. Why is the wheel an appropriate Buddhist symbol?*

followers along the right path and help them on their journey. They are

- the Buddha (the guide)
- the dharma (the path)
- the sangha (companions and teachers).

The scriptures say the following about taking refuge:

People, driven by fear, go for refuge to many places—to hills, woods, groves, trees and shrines. Such, indeed, is no safe refuge; such is not the refuge supreme. Not by resorting to such a refuge is one released from all suffering. Those who have gone for refuge to the Buddha, his Teaching and his Order, penetrate with wisdom the Four Noble Truths—suffering, the cause of suffering, the cessation of suffering, and the Noble Eightfold Path leading to the cessation of suffering. This indeed is the safe refuge, this is the refuge supreme. Having gone to such a refuge, one is released from all suffering.

Dhammapada, section 14, verses 177–192

For a Buddhist, taking refuge is the first step to enlightenment. In special ceremonies, lay people take refuge with the "Triple Jewel" by reciting the following in front of an ordained monk or nun: "I go to the Buddha for refuge; I go to the dharma for refuge; I go to the sangha for refuge."

The Six Perfections

A **Bodhisattva** is a person who has attained nirvana but chooses to be reborn within *samsara* in order to help others on their path to enlightenment. A Bohdisattva practises the **Six Perfections**: giving, morality, patience, vigour, meditation, and wisdom. The last is the most important because it indicates full awareness.

Check Your Understanding

1. When people have reached enlightenment, what have they achieved? What is nirvana? Why is the attainment of nirvana an important goal for Buddhists?

2. Describe the three elements of existence. How applicable are they to the world in which you live? Explain.

3. a) Identify the Five Precepts. What purpose do they serve? Why is the fifth precept so crucial?
b) Rank the Five Precepts according to their relevance in your life. Begin by identifying the Precept that is most relevant.

4. What is the Noble Eightfold Path, and why is it so important? How is it represented by the Dharma Wheel?

5. Make an organizer with the following headings: "I Agree," "I Disagree, and "I Do Not Understand." Review the beliefs presented in this section (starting on page 168), and classify them in the appropriate columns of your organizer. Be prepared to discuss the placement of these beliefs within your organizer.

Skill Path Qualitative Research

When researchers want to acquire detailed information about a particular situation or individual, they use **qualitative research.** Qualitative research differs from quantitative research, which we examined in the previous chapter. Unlike quantitative research, which relies on the use of numerical scores, qualitative research relies on detailed description to summarize data.

In conducting qualitative research on a particular topic, the researcher employs at least three different methods, which are used together to achieve credible results. These research methods might include the following: observation, field notes, interview, case study, and focus group.

Characteristics of Qualitative Research

Natural Settings
Qualitative researchers conduct their research where it occurs naturally.

Non-Numerical Data
Collected data might be in the form of summary notes, interview transcripts, personal comments, diaries, photographs, or audio and video recordings.

Focus on the "how" and "why"
Qualitative researchers observe how people interact and how and why people are affected by others' actions.

No Hypotheses
In qualitative research, there is rarely an hypothesis stated at the beginning for which researchers collect data to prove or disprove. There is a general belief that an hypothesis will limit the information that researchers gather, and will most certainly reflect bias.

Triangulation
Triangulation crosschecks, or compares, the results of the various research methods used in the study to confirm the validity of findings.

Topics That Lend Themselves to Qualitative Research

In general, these topics
- are not easily summarized using numerical results;
- can be observed in a natural setting;
- involve the investigation of groups over a period of time;
- involve the study of activities;
- involve the study of organizations or groups.

Steps in Qualitative Research

The steps involved in qualitative research are outlined below. The topic of Buddhist monks in the modern world is used as a sample research topic.

1. Identify the topic of study.
Qualitative research always starts with a general topic to indicate the purpose of the study. It provides a focus for investigation and a starting point for the researcher.

Sample Topic: How Buddhist monks interact with the modern world.

2. Formulate specific research questions to guide the collection of data.

These questions are further developed, or sometimes completely changed, as the research progresses. Answers to these questions might change the focus of the investigation.

> - How do Buddhists conduct their daily lives in the observed setting?
> - How do the observed Buddhists perceive and interpret the modern world?
> - How do the observed Buddhists contribute to the modern world? In what areas do they have concerns? How does it affect how they live? Why?

3. Select the participants in the study.

Participants are selected not because they represent the larger population, but because they will hopefully be the most open and informative. A Buddhist temple or organization and its members might provide the appropriate participants and setting for the sample topic presented above.

4. Collect data.

• Observation

Some research questions are best answered if the researcher observes the participants in their natural setting. For our sample study, the researcher might observe the daily life, routines, and rituals of a Buddhist monk in a monastery.

• Field Notes

They are notes taken during observation or during an interview. These notes represent what the researcher saw, heard, experienced, and even believes, as he or she collects and reflects on the findings. These notes can be descriptive and/or reflective.

> Entering the monastery I feel an air of serenity. Many monks walking about going somewhere with purpose. Wearing yellow robes to the ankles with cloth over left shoulder. Wearing sandals on their feet. Their heads are shaven. As they walk they are serious-looking and contemplative. They talk in whispers. As they pass me, they nod and sometimes smile but do not engage in conversation...

• Interview

Interviews are often used by qualitative researchers to verify the impressions gained during observation. For our sample investigation, the researcher might interview one of the monks he or she has been observing. For interviewing strategies and sample interviews, see pages 293-94.

• Case Study

A case study involves the investigation of one group, one organization, or one individual. For example, one Buddhist monk might be examined through a series of interviews and observations. Several interviews might also take place with his family, friends, and colleagues in order to collect as much detailed information as possible about him. For a sample of a case study, refer to the Community Study feature on page 204 of this chapter.

• Focus Group

This is a group interview. The focus group constitutes an interview of 10 to 12 people, designed to promote an exchange of information among individuals and a deeper understanding of the subject being investigated. There is a moderator who guides the discussion using prepared questions. The focus group method encourages participants to offer insights about a value, concept, or other element of their lives, through basic interaction with one another. For our sample investigation, it would involve, if possible, a group of Buddhist monks, or members of a Buddhist congregation.

5. Analyze data.

A qualitative researcher usually has a large amount of data to analyze. Analysis is completed both during research and at the end. The researcher looks for categories of topics and concepts, and common themes.

6. Draw conclusions.

Unlike quantitative research, where the researcher draws conclusions at the end of the study, a qualitative researcher is continuously drawing conclusions throughout the research process. A researcher will record his or her interpretations and reflections while observing.

PRACTISE IT!

1. a) In your opinion, which of the topics below would be best suited to qualitative research?
   • how Buddhists experience their religion
   • the number of Canadians practising Buddhism
   • how and why Buddhism has influenced Canadian society
   • Buddhist symbols and festivals
   • why a person with a Western religious outlook would choose Buddhism

   b) Can you think of any other topics that would be well-suited to qualitative research?

2. Examine the list of topics below. For each topic, identify three methods of research you might use in order to conduct a qualitative research study. Justify your selection.
   • how Buddhists in Canada practise their religion
   • how, in today's world, Buddhists go about attaining their goal: to end suffering
   • the challenges of being a Buddhist in a non-Buddhist society
   • the effects of meditation on students

PRACTICES, RITUALS, SYMBOLS, AND FESTIVALS

Practices and Rituals

Buddhism, like most religions, involves various rituals. Most Buddhist devotions are not performed in a temple, with a congregation, except for major festivals. Lay people have a place set aside in their house where they can complete their worship. This can be done in the morning and/or in the evening. It is also possible to go to the temple at any time, but it is more common for this to take place on festive or "special" days. There is a practice among many Buddhists, particularly in East Asia and Tibet, called **puja**. Puja honours holy beings. Reverence is shown by bowing, making an offering, and chanting.

Bowing is done on many occasions. For example, a lay person bows to monks and nuns to show respect. Monks and nuns bow to lay people and other members of the sangha. Buddhists bow before sacred objects (for example, images of the Buddha) three times to honour the Three Refuges. They can stand or kneel, with the palms of their hands joined and held to the chest or forehead. In some cases, the hands are held to the head, lips, and chest to represent respect for the mind, speech, and body.

Offerings are performed with appropriate chanting. The most common offering is flowers, because as they fade and wilt, they emphasize the notion of impermanence. Incense sticks burn in the home and in the temple to symbolize the Buddha's "odour of sanctity." Another common offering is the light of a candle or lamp as a representation of the Buddha's enlightenment (Figure 5.9).

Meditation

Monks and lay people pray through **meditation**—bowing, chanting, and receiving offerings. For the Buddhist, meditation leads to wisdom, which in turn leads to the end of suffering. The practice enables a person to be composed and calm and to follow the Buddhist precepts more closely. The purpose of meditation is to improve concentration, calm the mind, and clear it of bad thoughts caused by hatred, greed, or ignorance. Buddhists believe that meditation brings insights into truths and inner peace, which in turn lead to compassion and humility. Meditation can also improve confidence as well as general mental and physical health. To get the full benefit of meditation, an individual needs the right conditions and proper practice.

To meditate, one should, ideally, sit in the "lotus posture," that is, with crossed legs and hands; the hands are on the lap, and the soles of the feet rest on top of the thighs (Figure 5.10). The back is straight, the tongue touches the back of the upper front teeth, and the eyes are downcast with the eyelids partially closed. In this position, the meditator concentrates on breathing and the movement of the diaphragm. He or she then meditates on objects or ideas. Subjects of meditation are identified in Buddhist manuals.

Figure 5.9 *Women bow and make offerings of flowers and candles at a Buddhist temple in Bangkok, Thailand. Why do worshippers offer flowers?*

Meditation is an essential practice for monks, nuns, lay people, and novices—those who are training to become monks or nuns. Historically, the practice has not been stressed for lay people, although this has begun to change with instruction being made available to them.

Chanting Mantras

Mantras are symbolic phrases that are chanted by Buddhists to help them keep in touch with their spiritual nature. They also serve to enhance meditation. *Om Mani Padme Hum* is a six-syllable mantra (Figure 5.11); it means "Hail, the jewel in the lotus." This is the mantra of Avlokiteshvara, a Bodhisattva representing compassion who is also the "Protector from danger." Anyone who recites this phrase will be saved from all dangers.

Figure 5.10 *A monk meditates in the Lotus position. Why is meditation important in Buddhism?*

Figure 5.11 *Om Mani Padme Hum is a popular mantra in Tibetan Buddhism inscribed on prayer wheels, roads, and mountain passes.*

Practices That Contribute to Good Karma

Rituals in Buddhism can be an opportunity for gaining merit, thus creating good karma. **Karma** is the totality of one's thoughts and actions, which determines one's fate in future lives. Anything we think or do may be good, bad, or neutral, and will accordingly give good or bad karma. The amount of good or bad karma accumulated will determine the next incarnation. Everyday actions, such as making meals, shopping, and cleaning, are neutral actions.

Giving alms, or donations, to the monks from the sangha is one example of a practice that gives good karma. Traditionally, this has been done by donating cooked food to the sangha members as they walk through the streets (Figure 5.12). The lay person will bow to the monks after giving the food, as a mark of respect.

A *dana*, an occasion where lay people donate food, robes, medicines, and other necessities to the sangha, is another example of a practice that gives good karma. This ceremony often takes place at the temple, but it may also occur in private homes. A family will usually invite monks to conduct the ritual on a special occasion, such as an anniversary. Friends and other relatives may also be included. When it takes place in the home, the monks arrive around 10:00 A.M. and have their feet washed by their hosts; this is an ancient symbol of hospitality. The monks pay respect to the family's Buddhist altar, and then they sit on the floor where they chant Buddha's teachings. It is believed that the act of listening to these chants helps purify the mind. All those present at the ceremony gain merit.

The Daily Rituals of a Buddhist Monk

The daily rituals of a Buddhist monk vary according to which tradition the person belongs. The following text describes daily activities in a Korean Buddhist monastery:

The day begins at 3:00 A.M. when the monks are awakened by the sound of a wooden bell-shaped percussion instrument, called a *mokt'ak*. After washing and putting away their bedding, the monks go to the main hall for chanting. After chanting together, the meditating monks go to the meditation hall, the students go to the study hall, and the working monks to their place of work. There is more chanting and the offering of rice at 10:30 A.M. to mark the Buddha's habit of eating only once a day. At

Figure 5.12 *Donating food to the monks from the sangha contributes to good karma. Explain.*

midday, the monks eat lunch, at which time they chant to remind themselves that food is for sustaining the body and not for greed. After lunch, all monks return to their respective activities. At approximately 6:00 P.M., a temple bell announces more chanting. Quiet study or meditation follows, and the day ends at approximately 10:00 P.M.

Symbols and Icons

Buddhism is very rich in symbols, and many are recognized all over the world. As Buddhism spread from India to East Asia, it assimilated local cultures and, consequently, local images. Abstract teachings are hard for many people to grasp. One way to help clarify these teachings is by using symbols. The icons, or images, of the Buddha to which Buddhists pay homage are considered representations of

him and his teachings and are respected but not generally worshipped.

Buddha Images

Figure 5.13

Figure 5.14

Following his death, the absence of the Buddha created a need to represent him in human form as a focus of devotion. However, the first images of the Buddha did not begin to appear until 500 years after the parinirvana. Until that time, Buddhists believed that physical representations of the Buddha were not possible or appropriate. The portrayal of the Buddha differs according to the part of the world where his images are found. Figure 5.13 shows a Buddha statue from Japan while Figure 5.14 shows a figure from Thailand. He often appears standing, seated in lotus position, or reclining. He is often dressed as a monk with his left shoulder covered and his right shoulder bare. Elongated earlobes are another characteristic of Buddha images. Representations of the Buddha vary greatly in size. Some Buddha figures are enormous, while others are of human proportions. Contrary to the general impression of Westerners, Buddha figures are not always fat.

Mudras

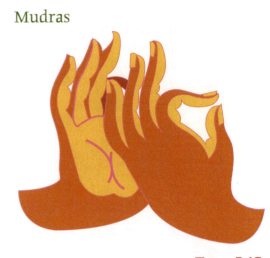

Figure 5.15

These hand gestures, which appear in images of Hindu deities, are important Buddhist icons. They are often used in meditation or seen on Buddha images. There are many *mudras*, and they symbolize different states of the mind. The underlying idea of *mudras* is that we can often tell someone's state of mind by looking at their stance or gestures; therefore, by making a certain gesture, we can generate a particular state of mind. The gesture in Figure 5.15 symbolizes the turning of the dharma wheel.

Stupa

Figure 5.16

Stupas are domed-shaped mounds that were built to house the relics of the Buddha or other holy figures. Almost every Buddhist temple has one, and monks and lay people walk around them three times when making their devotions. The inside of a stupa may be decorated with paintings or carvings illustrating the life of the Buddha. Some stupas are surrounded by beautifully carved fences that depict the life of the Buddha. Certain temple sites may also include smaller stupas; these are memorial crypts of prominent Buddhists who belonged to that particular temple. A pilgrimage to a stupa and the construction of small stupas (permanent or temporary) are considered merit-gaining activities by some Buddhists.

The Lotus Flower

Figure 5.17

Soon after his enlightenment, the Buddha had a vision of the human race as a bed of lotus flowers. Some were bogged in the mud, some were emerging from it, and others were about to bloom. In the same way, all people have the ability to develop their potential and rise from an undesirable life.

Buddhapada

Figure 5.18

These representations of Buddha's footprints, or Buddhapada, are revered in all Buddhist countries. The footprints are usually carved in stone and feature signs of the Buddha, for example, Buddha figures and sacred wheels, on the soles. The toes of the Buddhapada are all the same length. These footprints may feature 32, 108, or 132 signs of the Buddha.

Symbols
The Wheel of Life

The **Wheel of Life** is a complete visual representation of *samsara*, or the endless cycle of uncontrolled rebirths. This wheel is a visual aid to show the environments of *samsara* and all the beings who inhabit them. It is composed of four concentric circles and is thought to have been designed by the Buddha. The inner circle features three animals: a bird, a pig, and a snake. The animals represent the three basic human vices that keep the wheel turning: greed, ignorance, and hatred. The goal of Buddhists is to conquer these vices with the aim of attaining enlightenment.

The next ring shows the forms we take when we are reborn. The white half shows the heavens, where everyone is happy, and the black half shows hell, where suffering is unbearable.

The third ring shows the various regions into which one can be reborn. They represent real places and are not metaphors for states of mind. This ring includes illustrations of experiences we may have as humans, for example, sensory pleasure or suffering.

The images in the outer circle represent the twelve causes of endless rebirths: the old, blind person is ignorance; the potter creating a pot represents actions; the monkey climbing the tree of *samsara* symbolizes consciousness; the man rowing a boat represents name and form (or body); a house with six doors and windows illustrates the senses; a man and woman embracing symbolizes contact; the arrow in the eye represents feeling; the man drinking alcohol depicts craving; the monkey grabbing fruit illustrates grasping; a woman about to give birth depicts existence; a baby being born indicates birth; and, finally, a man carrying a corpse represents aging and death.

The wheel is held in the teeth of Yama, Lord of Death, and there is no single being in the wheel who is outside the control of death. Only the Buddha is outside the wheel pointing at the moon, which symbolizes nirvana. These words appear under the wheel:

Figure 5.19

Make an effort to destroy it
Enter into Buddhadharma
Eliminate the Lord of Death
As an elephant destroys a grass hut.

QUESTIONS

1. How effective is the Wheel of Life image in representing the central teachings of Buddhism? Explain.

2. Create your own Wheel of Life, using images that have meaning for you. Be prepared to explain your imagery.

Mandala

All monks in Tibetan Buddhist monasteries have to learn how to construct sand mandalas in the various traditional images. Before beginning work on a mandala, monks must engage in extensive meditation because the manadala is an exercise of meditation and prayer. The Tibetan word for mandala is *khiyl-khor*, which means "centre of the Universe in which a fully awakened being abides." According to Buddhist history, the techniques for making mandalas were taught by the Buddha Sakyamuni in the sixth century BCE. The practice has been passed on from master to disciple for 2500 years.

The basic structure of a mandala consists of a square in the centre that is enclosed by circles; this symbolizes the limits of physical space. The sand used to make the mandalas comes from the Himalayas and consists of minerals that have been ground to five degrees of fineness. Coarser grains are used for backgrounds while finer sand is used for detail. The sand is dyed traditionally with natural dyes, although today acrylic ones may be used. Monks pour the sand from cone-shaped metal tubes with a textured side similar to a file. A metal tool is grated against this ridge, and the vibrations cause the sand to exit grain by grain. Tibetan Buddhists believe that the exiting sand makes the sound of emptiness, which symbolizes the absence of an independent self-existence.

When a sand mandala is completed, monks recite chants and prayers before it is swept up and placed into a stream or body of water where it is washed away. While we might consider this a shame, to Tibetan Buddhists, it symbolizes the impermanence of the world.

Figure 5.20

Mandala means circle; it is a visual aid for concentration and a device for meditation. Mandalas may be temporary (as in sand mandalas) or permanent (as in wall hangings). They are pictorial representations of the architectural ground floor plans for the heavenly mansion of a particular deity or divine person. The viewing of a mandala generates healing energy and brings the viewer closer to enlightenment.

QUESTIONS

1. What is the purpose of a mandala?
2. Why is the sand mandala destroyed after use?

Festivals

Every year, Buddhists celebrate a number of holy days. Festivals commemorate important dates in the Buddhist calendar and the birthdays of Bodhisattvas. Many of the festivals are particular to certain sects of Buddhism, so the dates vary from country to country and among different traditions. With the exception of the Japanese, most Buddhist festivals are based on the lunar calendar. The Buddhist New Year, for example, is in late January or early February for the Chinese, Koreans and Vietnamese, while Tibetans celebrate one month later. Buddhists from Sri Lanka, Myanmar, Thailand, Laos, and Cambodia celebrate for three days in April. Other Buddhist festivals are described in the text that follows.

Visakha Puja Day (Buddha Day)

On the full-moon day of May, Buddhists celebrate Visakha Puja Day. They believe that the birth, enlightenment, and death of the Buddha all took place on that day of the year. People assemble on the grounds of the monasteries, bringing flowers, lit candles, and incense sticks. They walk around the main hall three times while reciting the Three Refuges.

Asalha Puja Day (Dhamma Day)

On the full-moon day of July, people commemorate the First Sermon in Deer Park by celebrating Asalha Puja Day. Food is offered to monks, nuns, and novices. In the evening, people give food to the poor, observe the Five Precepts, and practise meditation. The full moon figures prominently in Buddhist festivals. While there is no single explanation for this, the full moon is associated with important events in the Buddha's life, which were said to have occurred during full moons.

Magha Puja Day (Sanhga Day)

Magha Puja Day, which takes place on the full-moon day of March, commemorates two important events in the Buddha's life. The first was the proclamation of the basic principles of Buddhist teachings, and the second was a sermon called the Basis of Success. Food is offered to monks, and people engage in activities that bring them good karma. Followers observe the Five Precepts and attend a sermon at the monastery.

Songkran

This Thai Buddhist festival takes place in mid-April. During Songkran, people clean their houses, wash their clothes, and sprinkle perfumed water on monks. Fish are rescued from dry ponds and are carried in jars to the river. This act symbolizes the observance of the First Precept, which forbids harm to any living being. Participating in this ritual brings good karma.

Loy Krathong (Festival of Floating Bowls)

Loy Krathong occurs in Thailand on the full-moon night of the twelfth lunar month, when the rivers are full. During this festival, Buddhists float bowls made of leaves on the rivers (Figure 5.21). These bowls contain candles and incense sticks, and it is believed that, as the bowls float away, all bad luck disappears.

Figure 5.21 *During the festival of Loy Krathong, Buddhists in Thailand float bowls containing burning candles and incense on the rivers. What is the purpose of the floating bowls?*

Web Quest

For more information on Buddhist festivals presented in this section, visit the Friends of the Western Buddhist Order Web site at **www.fwbo.org/ festivals.html.**

Check Your Understanding

1. Briefly describe three practices or rituals that Buddhists perform. Describe one ritual, religious or otherwise, that you practise regularly.

2. Describe the practice of meditation. How is it performed and what is its significance? Why might meditation appeal to contemporary Canadians?

3. What is karma? How does one accumulate good karma? What kinds of activities do you pursue that might generate good karma?

Do you practise any activities that might generate "bad karma"?

4. What is the significance of the following Buddhist symbols?
a) Wheel of Life
b) mudras
c) lotus flower

5. a) What is the significance of the following Buddhist festivals, and what observances are associated with each: Loy Krathong, Songkran, Visakha Puja Day?
b) Which religious festivals, if any, are important in your own life? Why?

MILESTONES

Early Buddhism did not have its own rituals to mark the stages of life. People generally practised those rituals that were already in place in the Hindu traditions of India. As Buddhism spread around the world, new converts continued to practise the life-cycle rituals of their own country. Because of this, Buddhism does not have a standard set of rites to mark life's passages.

Early Life

In general, when a baby boy reaches one month of age, the parents invite monks to their house or take the baby to the temple so that his head can be shaved. Sometimes parents will take their male children to stay with the monks for an extended period of time, especially during school holidays. When a boy is brought into the temple, he comes as a novice, or a monk in training (Figure 5.22). The novice participates in all the activities of becoming a monk. In some Buddhist countries in Southeast Asia, a man can enter monkhood for a limited period of time, such as a few weeks before he gets married.

Becoming a Buddhist Monk

There are two stages in becoming a Buddhist monk. The first takes place when a boy is seven or eight years old and he enters a monastery as a novice. He undertakes the Ten Precepts and usually acts as an attendant to a senior monk. This senior monk is responsible for teaching the novice Buddhist rituals, philosophy, and scripture, as well as anything else that he deems necessary for full ordination.

The second stage, ordination, occurs when the young man reaches the age of twenty and is able to read, write, and chant a few simple texts.

Figure 5.22 *Novice monks in training at a Tibetan monastery. Could you handle the discipline of monastic life?*

Once ordained, a monk must shave his head as a sign of rejecting vanity, take a religious name, and wear the appropriate robes.

Upon ordination, Buddhist monks renounce their possessions and keep only those things that are absolutely necessary. Originally, these included the following: a robe, an alms bowl, a belt, a razor, a filter for drinking water, a staff, and a toothpick. Today, monks still receive some of these items, plus a warm jacket and, sometimes, an umbrella.

Marriage

When a couple gets married, the bride and groom go to the monastery to feed the monks in order to receive a blessing, but the monks never attend the wedding itself. For other important events, people go to the temple to seek a blessing from the monks or to gain merit, but they do not involve the monks in any of the actual ceremonies.

The Buddhist Funeral

The Buddhist funeral marks death in an elaborate and ritualized way. Buddhist practices are based on the cremation customs of India, but the involvement of the monks has marked the ceremony with strong Buddhist characteristics. Since wood in some Buddhist countries is exceedingly expensive, making cremation a costly option, burial is permitted. In general, the ceremony consists of a procession, prayers, water-pouring rituals, cremation, final prayers, and a shared meal. First, the route to the cemetery is cleared of potholes, weeds, and overgrown grass. The body is then placed into a funeral pyre so that it is hidden from view. The monks perform a short funeral service that includes chants and prayers. Everyone recites the Triple Refuge and the Five Precepts. While a prayer is chanted, holy water is poured on the body by family members and friends. The pyre is then lit, usually by the eldest son of the deceased person. On the sixth day after the death, a dharma-preaching service is held at the home, which is followed on the seventh day by a *dana*. Similar services are held again after three months and then again a year after that.

Check Your Understanding

1. In general, does Buddhism practise specific rites of passage? Why or why not?

2. What Buddhist practices mark the following stages of life?
a) childhood
b) marriage
c) death

3. Buddhist monks are required to renounce their possessions. Is renunciation possible or practical in our consumer-oriented society?

4. Describe a Buddhist funeral.

Living My Religion

How Buddhism Has Influenced My Life by Christopher Lawley

Figure 5.23

Christopher Lawley was born in 1977 in Toronto. He was a student at Jarvis Collegiate Institute, and, after graduation, he attended McGill University in Montreal. As his original intention was to enter medical school, he took courses mainly in the sciences but also in South Asian studies. At the end of his second year, Christopher took a year off to work at an orphanage in Honduras, teaching English. As he worked with people who are desperately poor in material things but rich in spirit, the experience had a profound effect on his outlook; he questioned society's materialistic attitudes. When he returned to Canada, he attended the University of Toronto to study Chinese history, religion, philosophy, and the Mandarin language. That is when he discovered Buddhism. In the 2000–2001 school year, he taught English in Beijing, China. Concerning Buddhism, Christopher writes:

Perhaps the most profound impact Buddhism has had on my life is that it has awakened me to the power and importance of compassion. Buddhist meditative practice encourages me to examine the state of the world and not to ignore the great suffering which occurs every day.

I come from a non-religious family background. My parents neither encouraged nor discouraged any religious inquiry on my part. I do not eat meat of any kind whatsoever, do not drink alcohol, and do not squash flies! I firmly believe in karma. While I have a deep interest in Buddhist scripture, I practise Buddhism for its practical benefits. I try to meditate at least once a day to help me achieve my goals. The realization that every action has an effect has had a huge impact on my daily life. In the end, my goal is to remove all negative influence (to not create evil), bring about positive change (practise only good), and realize love and compassion for all living beings (realize good for others). All this I do to achieve enlightenment. Applying the doctrine of karma to my daily life has been very liberating. I recognize that the only one responsible for my own suffering or unhappiness is myself. In this way, although I still experience unpleasantness, I am able to pinpoint its cause and hopefully avoid creating the causes for a similar experience in the future. Through taking this responsibility, I try to recognize my own part in creating the world I experience. So perhaps my daily life is best defined as an attempt to be mindful of that which I have learned through reading or contemplation, and that which I have experienced in meditation.

The extent to which I feel compassion for all living beings determines how well I can calm my mind and strengthen positive states of mind such as patience, love, and wisdom. Through generating positive states of mind, I find that I am happier and able to make decisions more easily, as the most appropriate response to a situation is more apparent. Acts of generosity and kindness also occur more naturally. Without having to think about it, my disposition toward other people is warmer and more welcoming. Therefore, Buddhist practice has affected my life on both the practical and profound levels.

QUESTIONS

1. What benefits does Christopher feel he has gained from practising Buddhism?

2. How might living in another part of the world help change a person's outlook on life, as it did for Christopher?

SACRED WRITINGS

Scriptures or sacred writings can be difficult to understand, yet they remain one of the most valuable and trustworthy vehicles we can use to gain insight into a religion. By reading scriptures directly, we are free of the interpretations of others and can discover their meaning for ourselves. Sacred writings are the central primary sources of religious belief. While they can be obscure, they can also be insightful, instructive, inspiring, and comforting. Most sacred writings have many authors and were composed over lengthy periods of time.

The main written source of Buddha's wisdom is the **Tripitaka**, or Three Baskets. It is referred to as the Three Baskets because the palm leaf manuscripts written by the Buddha's followers were kept in three different baskets. These baskets are called the Vinaya-Pitaka, the Sutta-Pitaka, and the Abhidhamma-Pitaka. Many Buddhists consider the Tripitaka to be the most accurate record of the Buddha's teachings.

The Vinaya-Pitaka, or Basket of Discipline, consists of five books that address the rules of monastic life and codes of conduct. The Sutta-Pitaka, or Basket of Discourses, is contained in five collections and incorporates the teachings of the Buddha. In general, this basket is the most important one for Buddhists. The last component is the Abhidhamma-Pitaka, or Basket of Further Teachings, which discusses the nature of consciousness and includes technical explanations of the Sutta-Pitaka.

The Sutta-Pitaka also contains the Dhammapada—a collection of 424 verses on ethics. The short verses are organized by themes. The following are two examples of these verses:

> *In this world hate never dispelled hate.*
> *Only love dispels hate.*
> *This is the law, ancient and inexhaustible.*
>
> *Anger is like a chariot careering wildly.*
> *He who curbs his anger is the true charioteer.*
> *Others merely hold the reins.*

The Mahayana school of Buddhism (see page 195) contributed to the sacred literature of Buddhism by adding more **Sutras**, or discourses attributed to the Buddha. Reciting or copying the Mahayana Sutras is believed to give merit to the participants. The statements that comprise one particular Sutra—the Karma Sutra—were referred to by the Buddha as the Golden Precepts. These statements attempt to explain an individual's situation in his or her present life, as well as how the individual's actions might affect his or her next life. Believing in and following the Karma Sutra is supposed to bring eternal prosperity and happiness.

The statements at the top of page 193 are excerpts from the Karma Sutra. The Sutra ends with the last three statements, which outline the consequences of following or not following the Golden Precepts.

Sacred Text

One of the most often translated elements of the Sutta-Pitaka is the Jatakas—a collection of 547 birth stories about the previous lives of the Buddha. The aim of these popular stories is to illustrate morality. In these stories, the Buddha takes on the identity of one of the characters, which might include a king, beggar, animal, or other being who exhibits virtue. The following is an example of one of these stories:

Jataka No. 100
Non Violence
A Mother's Wise Advice
Once upon a time, the son of Brahmadatta was ruling righteously in Benares, in northern India. It came to pass that the King of Kosala made war, killing the King of Benares, and made the Queen become his own wife.

Meanwhile, the Queen's son escaped by sneaking away through the sewers. In the countryside he eventually raised a large army and surrounded the city. He sent a message to the king, the murderer of his father and the husband of his mother. He told him to surrender the kingdom or fight a battle.

The prince's mother, the Queen of Benares, heard of this threat from her son. She was a gentle and kind woman who wanted to prevent violence and suffering and killing. So she sent a message to her son – "There is no need for the risks of battle. It would be wiser to close every entrance to the city. Eventually the lack of food, water and firewood will wear down the citizens. Then they will give the city to you without any fighting."

The prince decided to follow his mother's advice. His army blockaded the city for seven days and nights. The citizens captured their unlawful king, cut off his head, and delivered it to the prince. He entered the city triumphantly and became the new King of Benares.

The moral is: Kind advice is wise advice.

Questions

1. What are the Jatakas and what is their purpose? How would you explain their popularity?
2. Review Jataka No. 100.
   a) What is the significance of this story?
   b) Who do you think is the Buddha?
   c) Do you agree with the moral of this story? Why or why not?

- *To be miserly and unwilling to help the needy gives rise to future starvation and clothlessness.*
- *To abstain from eating meat and to pray constantly to Buddha will ensure you to be born a very intelligent child in your next incarnation.*
- *To be reborn a pig or a dog is the punishment for your deceiving and hurting others in your previous life.*
- *Whoever slanders this Sutra will not be born again a human being.*
- *Whoever carries this Sutra will be free from mishaps.*
- *Whoever recites this Sutra will be well-respected by people in his next incarnation.*

Check Your Understanding

1. What is the Tripitaka and why is it significant? Why is it referred to as the Three Baskets? Describe each of its components.

2. What is the Dhammapada? Read the excerpts from the Dhammapada on page 191. What is the theme of each verse? What is the significance of the Dhammapada?

3. What does the Karma Sutra tell a Buddhist? Why is it a good idea to practise what the Karma Sutra preaches?

4. Write your own brief story or fable to illustrate a Buddhist principle. Share it with a classmate, and see if he or she understands the belief at the centre of the story.

GROUPS AND INSTITUTIONS

As with most religions, the development of Buddhism was affected by disagreements on issues of doctrine. To trace the development of schools of Buddhist thought, it is necessary to start with the original organization—the sangha.

The sangha was the small community of monks that was established at the First Sermon in Deer Park. This community later included nuns—the bhikkhuni sangha (see page 167). During the next forty-five years, members of the sangha wandered all over India spreading the Buddha's teachings. The Buddha wanted the various local sanghas to meet on a regular basis in order to come to an agreement on such matters as lax behaviour and scriptures.

After the Buddha's passing, there were various councils called to discuss problems in the sangha. The second of these councils, in 383 BCE, was called to settle problems about what the Sutras should contain. There were two groups involved in these discussions: the Sthaviravada, who voted to leave the content unchanged, and the Mahasanghika, who wanted more literature included as sacred text. This rift led to the formation of two schools: the Theravada and the Mahayana.

The Theravada School

The **Theravada**, or Southern school of Buddhism, is found in Sri Lanka, Myanmar, Thailand, Laos, and Cambodia. The name *Theravada* means "the Way of the Elders," and it is considered the orig- inal and more conservative school of Buddhism. This school of Buddhism does not recognize any scriptures written after the Tripitaka. In Theravada Buddhism, the emphasis is on the teachings of the Buddha and not the Buddha himself.

Figure 5.24
Theravada Buddhism spread throughout Southeast Asia while the Mahayana School spread to China, Vietnam, Korea, and Japan.

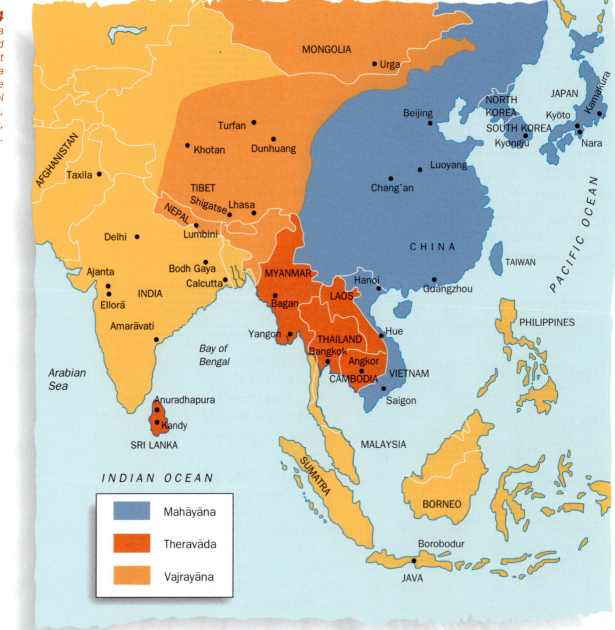

Legend:
- Mahāyāna
- Theravāda
- Vajrayāna

Theravada Buddhists do not worship the Buddha as a god; they consider him a human figure on whose teachings they pattern their lives. They rely on individual meditation and insight to attain nirvana. Those who achieve nirvana, the **Arhats**, represent the ideal of spiritual perfection.

The spread of Theravada Buddhism was the work of King Ashoka of India during the third century BCE. Ashoka met a monk, Nigrodha, who told him that he could use his power to promote peace and virtue instead of war, which he did by adopting the Buddhist attitude to life. He sent his son Mahinda and his daughter Sanghamitta to Sri Lanka to convert the ruler and his people to Buddhism. Over the next several centuries, Theravada Buddhism spread throughout Southeast Asia.

The Mahayana School

The **Mahayana**, or Northern school, spread to China, Vietnam, Korea, and Japan. The name *Mahayana* means "the Greater Vehicle," as opposed to *Hinayana* ("the Little Vehicle")—the name the movement has given to older forms of Buddhism. This more liberal school of Buddhism considers the Buddha a divine being and believes that the heavens are populated with buddhas, or divinities, to whom people can pray. Mahayana Buddhism emphasizes the role of the Bodhisattvas, or compassionate beings who have almost achieved enlightenment but choose to be reborn in one of the heavens in order to help others who pray to them. Worshippers pray to the Bodhisattvas

for blessings and assistance along their spiritual path.

One of the most important Bodhisattvas in Buddhist history is known as Avalokiteshvara, which means the "Lord who looks down." He is the Bodhisattva of compassion and is worshipped in both masculine and feminine form. In China, Mahayana Buddhists have venerated this figure as a female, under the name Kuan-yin (Figure 5.25). She has been glorified by Mahayana women, in particular, because they

Figure 5.25 *A porcelain representation of Kuan-yin, who is venerated by Mahayana Buddhists in China.*

consider her a provider and protector of children.

The main differences between the Theravada and the Mahayana schools of Buddhism are outlined in Figure 5.26.

Although the Theravada and Mahayana schools differ in many

Figure 5.26 *The differences between the Theravada and Mahayana schools are outlined in this chart.*

Theravada	Mahayana
Beliefs	
• Humans are individuals	• Humans are involved with others
• The key virtue is wisdom	• The key virtue is compassion
• Religion is for monks	• Religion is also for the lay person
• The ideal being is the Arhat	• The ideal being is the Bodhisattva
• Buddha is a saint	• Buddha is a saviour
Practices	
• Pray through meditation	• Pray for requests
Scriptures	
• Early scriptures in Pali (*dhamma, kamma*)	• Early scriptures in Sanskrit (*dharma, karma*)

ways, they both agree on the following basic points:

• The Buddha is the only master.
• One must take refuge in the Buddha, the dharma, and the sangha.
• This world was not created and ruled by a god.
• One must follow the example of the Buddha.
• One must accept the Four Noble Truths.
• All things are impermanent.

The Vajrayana School

Today, it is customary to talk of a third school, the **Vajrayana**, which is found mostly in Tibet, Bhutan, and Nepal. This school, which emerged at a later date than the other two, is also known as esoteric or Tantric Buddhism because of its emphasis on rituals, such as mantras, and on visualization in creations, such as **thangkas**, or wall hangings, and mandalas. The Vajrayana Buddhist views these visual representations with great concentration in his or her quest to achieve enlightenment.

The Buddhist religion entered Tibet around 750 CE when a Buddhist monk from India, called Padmasambhava (also referred to as Guru Rinpoche), was invited into the country to introduce the new religion.

He founded a monastery near Lhasa, the capital city. Because there was some resistance, Buddhist notions were joined to the early religion of Tibet called Bon; in this way, Buddhism became acceptable to the people. What developed in Tibet was a *theocracy*, since it became a country governed by monks. The leader was both the spiritual and worldly authority, which, after about 1600 CE, was claimed to be in the office and the person of the **Dalai Lama** (page. 200). Tibetan Buddhists believe that when a Dalai Lama dies, the newly released consciousness immediately enters the body of a newly born male child and will be discovered by monks, using a complicated set of procedures.

Most Tibetan Buddhists seek enlightenment, but Tibetan Buddhism also includes elements of Bon—Tibet's earlier religion. Worship by Tibetan Buddhists includes reciting prayers and chanting hymns to the accompaniment of shrill horns and drums (Figure 5.27). Religious rites are performed by the **lamas,** or religious leaders, three times a day and include rosaries, prayer wheels, and prayer flags.

Monks have translated most of the original Buddhist texts into Tibetan. In certain cases, these translations are the only existing copies of some scriptures.

Zen Buddhism

Buddhism was first introduced into Japan in the mid-sixth century, but it did not become a popular force in that country until the twelfth, thirteenth, and fourteenth centuries. One of the sects that emerged and became successful was **Zen.** Zen, which originally came from China where it was called Ch'an, was founded by the legendary Indian monk Bodhidharma around 520 CE. There is a story that he spent years in meditation gazing at a wall, until his legs dropped off. This story is probably not true, but it illustrates Zen's emphasis on meditation as the best method for attaining enlightenment. Good works and devotion are not discounted in Zen, but they should not become the vehicles for reaching enlightenment. Zen cannot be taught;

Figure 5.27 *Women beat a drum while they chant in a Tibetan Buddhist temple. How does music enhance religious ceremonies?*

it has to be experienced. To this end, Bodhidharma founded the Shaolin temple, where monks searched for illumination through meditation.

Although there are many schools in the Zen tradition, two schools are predominant—the Rinzai school and the Soto school.

The Rinzai School

The Rinzai school was introduced to Japan by the monk Eisai in 1191. This school emphasizes the use of non-rational statements called **koans**. These riddles, which are so puzzling to outsiders, are used to test the enlightenment of students. The students' effort to "solve" a *koan* is intended to break their sense of logic and self. The students are not permitted to dismiss the *koan* as absurd and have to bring all their mental strength to the task of solving the riddle. Reason is considered inadequate as a way to understand one's true nature. To understand it, the mind must be agitated. A koan takes the form of a dialogue between the master and the student in a private audience called a *sanzen*. What a master recognizes as a correct answer may apply only to that student, because it is not the answer that is important but the insight demonstrated by the student in obtaining it. The great twentieth-century Zen Buddhist master D. T. Suzuki said the following on the topic of *koans*:

The koan refuses to be solved under any [easy] conditions. But once solved the koan is compared to a piece of brick used to knock at a gate; when the gate is opened the brick is thrown away. The koan is useful as long as the mental doors are closed but when they are opened it may be forgotten.

The following are examples of *koans*:

- You know the sound of two hands clapping. Now what is the sound of one?
- What is the colour of wind?
- When the many are reduced to one, to what is one reduced?
- When you can do nothing, what can you do?
- How does an enlightened one return to the ordinary world? (Answer: A broken mirror never reflects again; fallen flowers never go back to the old branches.)

At some point, the student of Zen will be ready for the intuitive experience of enlightenment called **satori**. Satori, which is rather like the experience that the Buddha had under the Bodhi Tree, can come quickly to some, but it may take months or years for others. While Japanese Buddhist monks have always worked toward enlightenment, the warrior class—the samurai—were attracted to Zen as a way of fostering personal discipline and mental strength so that they could conquer the fear of death in warfare.

The Soto School

The Soto school was introduced to Japan by the Japanese monk Dogen after he visited China to study and to have his enlightenment confirmed. He returned to Japan in 1227 CE. Although he did not intend to form a new school, one arose around him because of his teachings. The Soto school prefers the achievement of enlightenment through strict discipline and *zazen*, or "sitting meditation," done in the lotus posture. This is seen as a return to the true Buddhism of the Buddha and is considered a natural and easy method, open to all. Dogen believed that meditation alone would lead to one's "awakening." Unlike the Rinzai school, which believes satori can come quickly, the Soto Buddhists believe that it comes slowly through personal effort. Historically, the Rinzai sect was supported mainly by aristocrats and the higher ranks of the samurai, while the Soto school found support among the peasants. It is sometimes referred to as Country Zen.

Check Your Understanding

1. What are the major schools of Buddhism, and where in the world are they found?

2. What are the main differences between the Theravada and Mahayana sects? What are the similarities?

3. What objects do Tibetan Buddhists use in their worship?

4. a) What are *koans* and why are they used in Zen Buddhism?
b) Take a few quiet moments to carefully consider one of the *koans* presented on page 198, and try to offer an answer. Describe the experience.

5. What is the main difference in practice between Rinzai and Soto Zen?

Profile: *The Fourteenth*

Figure 5.28

"I am a simple Buddhist monk—no more, no less."

—Fourteenth Dalai Lama

In October 1950, the Chinese Army crossed into Tibet. On 7 November 1950, Tenzin Gyatso was made the leader of Tibet by his people. The Chinese took complete control of Tibet on 23 May 1951. To avoid capture, the Dalai Lama escaped to India in March 1958, disguised as a common soldier and followed by 30 000 other Tibetans. The Indian government provided him with asylum.

Since 1960, he has resided in northern India, leading an organization calling itself the Tibetan Government in Exile. The Dalai Lama has set up educational, cultural, and religious institutions to help preserve the Tibetan identity and heritage. He spends a great deal of his time trying to resolve Tibetan issues. In 1987, he proposed that Tibet be set up as a zone of peace with its own self-governing democracy "in association with the People's Republic of China."

Unlike his predecessors, the fourteenth Dalai Lama has travelled extensively, visiting almost fifty countries. He has met with the religious leaders of all these countries and has spoken passionately about the need for a better understanding and mutual respect among different faiths of the world. The Dalai Lama has also gained a reputation as a scholar and man of peace. He has received many awards and honours, including the Nobel Peace Prize in 1989. The following are excerpts from his Nobel Peace Prize acceptance speech, which he gave in Oslo, Norway, on December 10 of that year:

The present Dalai Lama was born Lhamo Thondup on 6 July 1935, in Takster, Tibet. His family worked as peasant farmers, and Lhamo had a sister and three brothers. Lhamo Thondup was recognized as the successor to the thirteenth Dalai Lama, who had died in 1933. Lhamo was renamed Tenzin Gyatso, but Tibetans also refer to him as Yeshe Norbu, which means "Kundun—The Presence." He is considered the manifestation of the Bodhisattva of Compassion, Avalokiteshvara.

In the winter of 1940, he was taken to the Jokhang Temple in Lhasa. Here he was inducted as a novice monk and commenced his education in all aspects of Buddhist studies. Referring to that time in his life, Tenzin Gyatso recalls that "from now on, I was to be shaven-headed and attired in maroon monk's robes."

Dalai Lama: Tenzin Gyatso

Your majesty, Members of the Nobel Committee, Brothers and Sisters.

I am very happy to be here with you today to receive the Nobel Prize for Peace. I feel honored, humbled and deeply moved that you should give this important prize to a simple monk from Tibet, I am no one special. But I believe the prize is a recognition of the true value of altruism, love, compassion and non-violence which I try to practice, in accordance with the teachings of the Buddha and the great sages of India and Tibet.

I accept the prize with profound gratitude on behalf of the oppressed everywhere and for all those who struggle for freedom and work for world peace. I accept it as a tribute to the man who founded the modern tradition of non-violent action for change, Mahatma Gandhi, whose life taught and inspired me. And, of course, I accept it on behalf of the six million Tibetan people, my brave countrymen and women inside Tibet, who have suffered and continue to suffer so much. They confront a calculated and systematic strategy aimed at the destruction of their national and cultural identities. The prize reaffirms our conviction that with truth, courage and determination as our weapons, Tibet will be liberated. . . .

The suffering of our people during the past forty years of occupation is well documented. Ours has been a long struggle. We know our cause is just because violence can only breed more violence and suffering; our struggle must remain non-violent and free of hatred. We are trying to end the suffering of our people, not to inflict suffering upon others.

It is with this in mind that I proposed negotiations between Tibet and China on numerous occasions. In 1987, I made specific proposals in a Five-Point plan for the restoration of peace and human rights in Tibet. This included the conversion of the entire Tibetan plateau into a Zone of Ahimsa, a sanctuary of peace and non-violence where human beings and nature can live in peace and harmony. . . .

As a Buddhist monk, my concern extends to all members of the human family and, indeed, to all sentient beings who suffer. I believe all suffering is caused by ignorance. People inflict pain on others in the selfish pursuit of their happiness or satisfaction. Yet true happiness comes from a sense of brotherhood and sisterhood. . . .

I pray for all of us, oppressor and friend, that together we succeed in building a better world through human understanding and love, and that in doing so we may reduce the pain and suffering of all sentient beings.

Thank you.

QUESTIONS

1. What must it be like to become the leader of a country at the age of 15? Imagine that you're the 15-year-old Dalai Lama. Write a half-to-one-page journal entry describing your life, thoughts, and feelings.

2. In your opinion, did the Dalai Lama make the right decision by leaving Tibet? What other options did he have?

3. a) Review the Dalai Lama's acceptance speech and show how it reflects central Buddhist teachings.

   b) Write a one-page letter to the Dalai Lama outlining your reaction to his acceptance speech.

CULTURAL IMPACT

There are an estimated 350 million adherents of Buddhism worldwide. This makes it the fourth largest religion in the world. The following countries have the highest percentage of Buddhists:

- Thailand   95%
- Cambodia   90%
- Myanmar   88%
- Bhutan   75%
- Sri Lanka   70%
- Tibet   65%
- Laos   60%
- Vietnam   55%
- Japan   50%

The countries below are ranked according to the actual number of Buddhists that reside in them.

1. China   5. Myanmar
2. Japan   6. Sri Lanka
3. Thailand   7. South Korea
4. Vietnam

The impact of Buddhism on Vietnam was dramatic in the 1960s. In Vietnam, the sanghas are heavily involved in daily life: they run schools, orphanages, medical clinics, and homes for disabled people. During the Vietnam War, Buddhist monks and nuns protested the South Vietnamese government of the Catholic president Ngo Dhin Diem, which they felt restricted their religious freedom. Several monks and nuns burnt themselves in protest in the streets of Saigon, starting with seventy-year-old Thich Quang Duc. These events helped to bring down the Diem government. Another monk, Thich Nhat Hanh, started a movement called Engaged Buddhism, which was Buddhist wisdom melded with civil disobedience.

In Thailand, the impact of Buddhism has been less dramatic, although the influence of the religion is evident in all aspects of Thai life. The king has some monastic training, and the royal family takes part in Buddhist ceremonies. The Buddhist temples have traditionally been the place where young men learn to read and write.

The impact of Zen Buddhism on Japanese life is very evident. The simplicity of housing and surrounding areas reflects a disapproval of excess. The Zen garden is also proof of Buddhism's strong influence in Japan. The gardens are reduced to their very basic elements and attempt to express symbolically the extent of nature in a small space. The items used in this type of gardening are gravel, sand, and stones. Stones can represent a mountain or an island, while sand or gravel represents water or the sea.

There is an expression in Japanese, *Chaji*, which means "tea and Zen are one." It was the Zen monks in China who first used tea as an aid to keep awake during meditation. The monk Eisai is credited with bringing the Japanese tea ceremony to Japan (Figure 5.29). The tea ceremony, which might include a meal, is very formal. The host may spend many days ensuring that the ceremony will be perfect. The number of guests is preferably four, and the ceremony is held in a special tea room called the

Figure 5.29 *The Japanese tea ceremony was introduced to Japan by a Buddhist monk. What is the connection between the tea ceremony and Zen?*

chashitsu. There are virtually no decorations except for a Buddhist scripture on a scroll. Flowers are carefully chosen and arranged according to custom. The final presentation should embrace the Zen idea of simplicity, austerity, and devotion.

In Tibet, the prominence of Buddhism has led to very colourful architecture, painting, and carving, of which monasteries are full of examples. Tibetan medical knowledge and the Tibetan calendar have been extracted from Buddhist literature.

In the second half of the twentieth century, Tibetan Buddhism spread into the West, particularly after the Chinese takeover of Tibet in the 1950s. Since then, there has been an increased interest in the West in this form of Buddhism because the Chinese invasion attracted much attention to the religion. The attitudes of Buddhism toward peace, non-violence to living beings, and ecology have led many Westerners to adopt Buddhist principles.

Buddhism in Canada

As Buddhist people moved to the West, in particular to North America, they brought their religion with them and set up Buddhist temples and centres (Figure 5.31). Canada has many sanghas and temples in the larger urban centres. All the major sects of Buddhism are represented in Canada, and, at least three Canadian universities—the University of Toronto, the University of Western Ontario, and the University of British Columbia—have student Buddhist organizations. Many universities and colleges offer courses in Eastern studies, and there has been a growth in the number of courses on Buddhism.

Web Quest

For a list of Buddhist centres and temples in Canada, go to **www. buddhismcanada.com**

Community Study

The Chandrakirti Buddhist Centre
Toronto, Ontario

Web Quest

For more information on the Chandrakirti Buddhist Centre, go to http//:www. chandrakirti.org

Figure 5.30

The Chandrakirti Buddhist Centre follows the Kadampa Buddhist tradition within the Mahayana school. Although Kadampa Buddhism was founded in the tenth century CE, it was first introduced to the West in 1976 by the Venerable Geshe Kelsang Gyatso. Born in 1931 in Tibet, the venerable Geshe was ordained a Buddhist monk at the age of eight. He left Tibet in 1959, following the Chinese invasion, and formed the New Kadampa Tradition (NKT) in England.

All NKT centres have been established with the intention of benefiting all beings without exception. The emphasis is on integrating the Buddha's teachings into daily life to solve our human problems and to spread lasting peace and happiness throughout the world.

The Chandrakirti Centre offers instruction in Buddhist philosophy and is a place where adherents may pray and meditate. The monks at the centre offer basic programs for the beginner and more advanced courses for those who wish to train as dharma teachers.

Kelsang Phuntsog (shown standing in the photograph), who is an ordained monk, is the Education Program Coordinator. He was born in Zambia and immigrated with his family to Canada when he was three years old. His family settled in Alberta where Phuntsog went to school. After one year of study at McGill University followed by a year of study at Augustana University College in Alberta, he went in search of a spiritual teacher. Phuntsog embraced Buddhism, and because compassion was very important to him, he chose the Mahayana tradition.

Gen Kelsang Zopa (seated in the picture) is the resident teacher at Chandrakirti Buddhist Centre and the Spiritual Director for Kadampa Buddhism in Canada. He was born in Hamilton and attended York University.

QUESTIONS

1. What is Kadampa Buddhism? Describe the meaning of NKT and the objective of NKT centres.

2. What services does the Chandrakirti Centre offer to those who are interested?

Figure 5.31
This marriage ceremony is taking place at the temple of the International Buddhist Progress Society of Toronto, located in Mississauga, Ontario. What different marriage ceremonies have you attended?

Check Your Understanding

1. In what areas of the world is Buddhism concentrated?

2. How have Buddhist monks and nuns in Vietnam influenced their country on a political level?

3. In what ways has Zen Buddhism affected Japanese cultural life?

4. What evidence is there that Buddhism is playing a significant role in Canadian life?

5. Now that you have studied Buddhism, would you consider adopting some Buddhist practices or principles? Explain your answer fully.

Exploring Issues:

Figure 5.32 *Chinese police arrest a member of the Falun Gong in Tiananmen Square on January 1, 2001. Should governments have any say on religious practices? Explain.*

The Falun Gong has recently become a news item because in China, where the movement started, the government has taken measures to suppress it. Falun Gong (pronounced *fah-luhn goong*), which means "the practice of the Wheel of the Dharma," was founded in 1992 by Li Hongzhi.

Although there has been some debate about its foundation, Falun Gong incorporates Buddhist and Taoist principles together with cultivation, which is the development and transformation of one's entire being, including the mind, body, and spirit. In China alone, this movement has an estimated 70 million members, which is more than the membership of the Communist Party. The movement has an estimated 30 million followers outside of China.

In 1999, the Chinese government launched a new campaign outlawing spiritual and religious groups, including the Falun Gong, calling them a threat to social stability and the interests of the people. In response to this campaign, the Falun Gong organized a massive, but peaceful, demonstration in Beijing. Alarmed by their failure to prevent the demonstration, the Chinese government arrested hundreds of Falun Gong members. In violation of the United Nations Declaration of Human Rights, the Chinese government has detained tens of thousands of Falun Gong members and has sent thousands to labour camps.

AT ISSUE: Is the Falun Gong a subversive organization threatening the stability of Chinese society, or is it a harmless organization concerned with the bodily and spiritual well being of its members?

Each of the following articles represents one side of the issue outlined above. Article A was taken from the Chinese newspaper *The People's Daily*. Article B was written by a member of the Falun Gong movement.

Article A:

The Falun Gong cult has evolved into a reactionary political force that is doing everything possible against the Chinese government and people . . .

Since the Falun Gong cult was founded, it has carried out a steady stream of sabotage, created chaos, sought refuge with political forces hostile to China, and been a force behind outside interference in China's internal affairs . . .

A great number of facts prove that the activities of Falun Gong founder Li Hongzhi and his cult are no longer done for the purposes of improving health, seeking truth or for deepening philosophical beliefs; they are carefully organized, politically-motivated acts directed at the Chinese government and the Communist Party of China . . .

Li Hongzhi and his crowd fully abandoned national pride, threw themselves into the arms of overseas anti-China forces and were willingly used by international forces as tools to interfere in China's affairs . . .

The Falun Gong

It will be a mistake to go down in history if the Chinese cannot clearly understand the political nature of the cult and deal with it in a firm and just way . . .

Abridged from "Reactionary Nature of Falun Cult Exposed," *The People's Daily Online* http://english.peopledaily.com.cn/200010/11/eng200 01011_52291.html 11 October 2000.

Article B:

Falun Gong is a meditation practice for improving the body, mind, and spirit; it is rooted in ancient Chinese culture. Practitioners of Falun Gong live according to the principles of Truth, Compassion, and Tolerance, and do five gentle qigong exercises. These exercises, although simple, are very powerful. Falun Gong spread rapidly in China in part because of its tremendous health benefits. Governments (including China's) and non-governmental organizations around the world have honoured Falun Gong and its founder, Li Hongzhi, with over 600 awards and recognitions. Li is a three-time Nobel Peace Prize nominee.

The Chinese government's persecution of Falun Gong practitioners is born of fear and intolerance: the fear is due to the fact that the Falun Gong has outgrown the Communist Party in size, and the intolerance stems from the belief that any ideology that lies outside communist ideology is wrong. With China's totalitarian form of government, any activity not regulated by the state is branded a "political threat" or "destabilizing."

And if the government cannot control it, it seeks to destroy that activity and those involved. In order to eradicate Falun Gong, China's leadership has employed state terror: systematic torture, brainwashing, propaganda, and hate campaigns. Hundreds have been murdered in custody. Despite the grave injustice, Falun Gong's response has been one of completely non-violent resistance.

Amnesty International, Human Rights Watch, the Congress of the United States, and leading politicians in Canada, Europe, Australia, and other nations around the world have condemned this persecution and demanded that China respect the fundamental human rights of Falun Gong practitioners.

"The Persecution of Falun Gong in China" was written by Falun Gong practitioner Stephen Gregory, November 2001. For more information visit: www.faluninfo.net

---

QUESTIONS

1. In your own words, briefly summarize the two positions taken in the articles.

2. With which position do you agree personally? State your opinion in a letter to the author of either article.

Activities

Check Your Understanding

1. Indicate the meaning and importance of the following key terms by completing the organizer below: samsara, ahimsa, Bodhisattva, dharma, sangha, mantra, mandala, tripitaka, koan, bhikkhuni.

Key term / Meaning / Importance

2. Provide two examples that show the influence of Buddhism on the political development of a country.

3. Briefly describe the Tibetan form of Buddhism. What aspects of Tibetan life are the direct result of Buddhist scriptures?

4. How have the following figures contributed to the development of Buddhism: King Ashoka, Bodhidharma, Padmasambhava, Thich Nhat Hanh?

Think and Communicate

5. How do Hinduism and Buddhism differ in their beliefs on the place of women? Organize your answer by making a list for each religion and then summarizing the results.

6. Design a poster that applies Buddhist principles to contemporary Canadian society. You might visually represent one of the following:

- the Four Noble Truths
- the Noble Eightfold Path
- the Three Characteristics of Existence

7. In your opinion, is Buddhism a religion, a philosophy, a psychology, or a way of life? Organize the class into four groups, each representing one of these positions. Work within your group to prepare supporting arguments for your position. Present your arguments in a class discussion.

8. Some people call Buddhism atheistic because Buddhists do not believe in a god-creator of the universe. Buddhists are more inclined to say that Buddhism is non-theistic, that is, a god has no place in their belief system. Does this mean Buddhism is not a religion? Present your view in a letter to a religious newspaper.

9. Conduct research on one of the topics below. Use both primary sources (for example, interviews) and secondary sources (for example, books or the Internet). Present your findings in a newspaper article in which you describe the issue, events, and future prospects.
a) the place of women in Buddhism
b) the persecution of Buddhist monks
c) the Chinese occupation of Tibet
d) engaged Buddhism

10. Complete a series of visits to Web sites that provide information on Buddhism (start with ones noted in this chapter), and present a brief report to your peers. Indicate which sites appear to be most interesting or valuable and why.

Apply Your Learning

11. You are washing some lettuce for a salad, and there is an insect between the leaves that you do not see. The water washes the creature down the drain. What effect does this have on your karma? Present your view to the class orally.

12. a) Often, when faced with intense personal suffering, some people choose to commit suicide. In a few sentences, explain what a Buddhist might have to say about this decision.
b) Suppose that a person who committed suicide did so in order to protest injustice, as demonstrated by the case of Thich Quang Duc in South Vietnam in 1963. Participate in a class discussion to determine what the opinion of a Buddhist would be concerning this action.

13. Although the environmental concerns that we face today, for example, clear-cut logging, toxic spills, global warming, and water pollution, were not present in the time of the Buddha, there were ideas about how to treat the environment. In a written report, present your view on what position you think Buddhists would take on the environmental and ecological issues of today and why.

14. One of the principles behind Buddhism is that individuals can make changes in their lives. People can reduce suffering for themselves and for others. How might you apply these principles to your own life today?

Glossary

ahimsa. The doctrine of non-violence toward all living beings; represented in the First Precept.

anatta [a NATTA]. No-self; the notion that there is no permanent self, and that a person is a changing combination of components.

anicca [AH netch ah]. Impermanence; the idea that the world is in constant flux.

arhat [AR ut]. Someone who has achieved nirvana; the ideal of spiritual perfection in Theravada Buddhism.

ascetic. One who practices very strict devotions using severe self-denial.

bhikkhu [BICK you]. A fully ordained monk who has left his home and renounced all his possessions in order to follow the way of the Buddha.

bhikkhuni sangha [BICK you nee SANG ga]. The community of fully ordained nuns.

bodhisattva [boe dee SATVA]. a compassionate being who enlightens himself or herself and helps others to be enlightened

Buddha. The Enlightened or Awakened One; the founder of Buddhism, formerly Siddhartha Gautama.

Dalai Lama. The ruler and spiritual leader of Tibet.

dana [DONNA]. A ceremony that takes place at the temple or in a private home, which involves the donation of food, robes, medicines, and other necessities to the sangha. Those who participate in this ritual gain merit.

dharma [DARR muh]. The teachings of the Buddha and his idea of the "truth" concerning the "laws" of the universe.

dukkha [DOOKA]. Dissatisfaction; the idea that human suffering is inevitable.

enlightenment. Understanding the truth of life by attaining freedom from ignorance.

Five Precepts. The rules that Buddhists follow. They include abstaining from harming living beings, stealing, improper sexual activity, false speech, and taking alcohol or drugs.

Four Noble Truths. The Buddha's diagnosis of the main problem in life: suffering, the cause of suffering, elimination of suffering, and the path to ending suffering.

Four Sights. The sights that led to the Buddha's departure from his palace to help humankind: a sick man, a corpse, and old man, and a begging monk.

karma. "Action," or the law of cause and effect; the totality of one's thoughts and actions, which determines one's fate in the next life.

koan. An unsolvable riddle presented to a novice by his or her master for the purpose of mental discipline.

lama. A Tibetan religious leader; translation of "guru," or teacher.

Mahayana [ma ha YANNA]. One of the 3 major forms of Buddhism; dominant in East Asia, it is considered the most liberal and practical.

mandala [MANDA luh]. Maps, or geometrical diagrams, of the spiritual journey. Looking at them helps awaken spiritual potential.

mantras. Symbolic phrases that are chanted.

meditation. A method of calming and training the mind through concentration.

Middle Way. The path in life prescribed by the Buddha; the path between extremes.

nirvana [nur VONNA]. An everlasting state of great joy and peace resulting from the end of desire and suffering.

Noble Eightfold Path. The last of the Four Noble Truths. This is the path leading to the end of suffering.

parinirvana [perry nur VONNA]. Sometimes called the "final nirvana"; the state attained upon the death of someone who has achieved nirvana.

puja [POO juh]. Offerings to holy beings.

reincarnation. The transference of consciousness into new bodies; being born again.

samsara **[sam SARA].** The endless cycle of uncontrolled rebirths.

sangha [SANG ga]. The community of Buddhist monks and nuns.

satori [sa TORY]. Spiritual enlightenment in the Zen tradition.

Six Perfections. Giving, morality, patience, vigour, meditation and wisdom; what a Boddhisattva practises.

sutras. Scriptures establishing the teachings of Buddhism. They are represented as the discourses or sermons of the Buddha.

thangkas [TONKA]. Wall hangings found in Tibetan Buddhist temples.

Theravada [terra VODDA]. One of the three major forms of Buddhism. Dominant in Southeast Asia, it is considered to be the original and orthodox form of Buddhism.

Tripitaka [tree PETTA kah]. Known as the Three Baskets; a collection of early Buddhist scriptures.

Vajrayana [vudge rah YANNA]. One of the three major forms of Buddhism; popular in Tibet.

Wheel of Life. A complete visual representation of *samsara*, or the endless cycle of uncontrolled rebirths.

Zen. A Buddhist sect that originated in Japan. This sect favours meditation and intuition rather than scripture or rituals as the means to enlightenment.

When God began to create heaven and earth—the earth being unformed and void, with darkness over the surface of the deep and a wind from God sweeping over the water—God said, "Let there be light"; and there was light. God saw that the light was good, and God separated the light from the darkness. God called the light Day, and the darkness He called Night. And there was evening and there was morning, a first day.

Genesis 1: 1–5.

Chapter Six

Judaism

6

Look at the photograph and consider the following questions:

1. Define the word *creation*. (Use a dictionary if necessary.)

2. What is the significance of the separation of "light" from "dark" in the passage from Genesis?

Introduction

Of the recognized major world religions, Judaism is by far the smallest. The worldwide population of Jews is about 14 million. In light of this fact, the question might be: Why does a religious group with a global membership of less than half the population of Canada warrant a full chapter in a book on world religions? The answer to this question is twofold. First, Judaism has made overwhelming contributions to the development of Western religious thinking and philosophy. Second, no other religious group in the history of the world has undergone so much persecution based on its beliefs. For these reasons, Judaism is an essential component in any study of the world's religions.

Chronologically, Judaism is the first of the world's three great **monotheistic** religions. Dating back approximately 4000 years, Judaism marks the starting point of a history embraced by three separate faiths. From the story of Adam and Eve to the emergence of Abraham and Moses, Judaism gives roots to both Christianity and Islam. In fact, many of the prophets revered in the Hebrew Scriptures are also revered in the Christian and the Muslim traditions. Judaism has also maintained a tradition of scholarship that is unparalleled among the world's faiths, considering the size of the Jewish population. From Biblical scholarship to philosophy to science, Jews have offered ideas and made discoveries that have changed the way people see the world.

The tragic side of the Jewish experience is that its followers have been subjected to unprecedented persecution. From the Babylonian Captivity to the Spanish Inquisition, Jews were the target of people's disdain and hatred. The persecution of Jews reached its horrifying peak in the twentieth century when the Nazis murdered approximately 6 million Jews—one-third of the world's Jewish population.

Judaism offers the world an idea of God that is shared by other faiths. It also provides a challenge to the collective conscience of humanity. As we bear witness to the inspiring and tragic history of Judaism, we are struck by the suffering that the Jewish people have endured as well as the rich love of wisdom inherent in the Jewish faith.

Learning Goals

At the end of this chapter, you will be able to:

- identify the origins and beliefs of Judaism
- identify the major personalities who contributed to the formation of the Jewish faith, including Abraham, Isaac, Jacob, Moses, Maimonides, and Judah the Prince
- examine the major influences in the development of Judaism
- describe Jewish worship and religious movements from the era of the temple to the emergence of the synagogue
- analyze how Jewish leaders influenced events, created movements, and challenged the status quo of their times
- describe the beliefs of the Jewish faith
- identify and state the importance of Jewish beliefs related to the ideas of the chosen people, the Promised Land, and the Messiah
- describe the historic relationships between religion and the State in Judaism
- identify the origins and significance of the various practices, rituals, symbols, and festivals of Judaism
- develop an understanding of the emergence of the sacred writings of Judaism: Torah, Tanakh, and Talmud
- describe and understand the significance of the Reform, Orthodox, Conservative, and Reconstructionist branches of Judaism
- effectively communicate the results of your inquiries, using written reports and essays
- defend a thesis, using appropriate style, structure, argument, and documentation
- identify ways in which Jews are represented in Canada

1000? BCE King David/King Solomon—Solomon's Temple built

332 BCE Alexander the Great conquers Israel, Diaspora Hellenism begins

200–425 CE Mishnah compiled by Judah the Prince; Talmud compilation completed (425)

721–538 BCE Northern Kingdom taken by Assyrians (721), Hebrew population disperses; Southern Kingdom taken by Babylonians (586), Babylonian exile; Solomon's Temple destroyed; Cyrus of Persia defeats Babylonians (538), allows exiles to return

164 BCE–70 CE Maccabean uprising, temple rebuilt (164 BCE); Roman siege of Jerusalem, temple destroyed (70 CE)

1700–1280? BCE Patriarchal and Mosaic period; Jews leave Egypt (1280)

1948 CE
Declaration of the modern State of Israel

1980 First woman rabbi in Canada—Joan Friedman

2001 250 official Jewish synagogues in Canada

1933–1945 CE
Rise of Nazism and the Holocaust (Shoah); *St. Louis* incident (1939)

1768 CE First synagogue in Canada

1945–CE
Post-Holocaust immigration to Canada

1135–1204 CE
The life of Maimonides—philosopher and rabbinic scholar

1800s CE First wave of Jewish immigration to the Americas

1700–1800 CE
Tension between Hasidim and traditional legalists

Timeline

Judaism

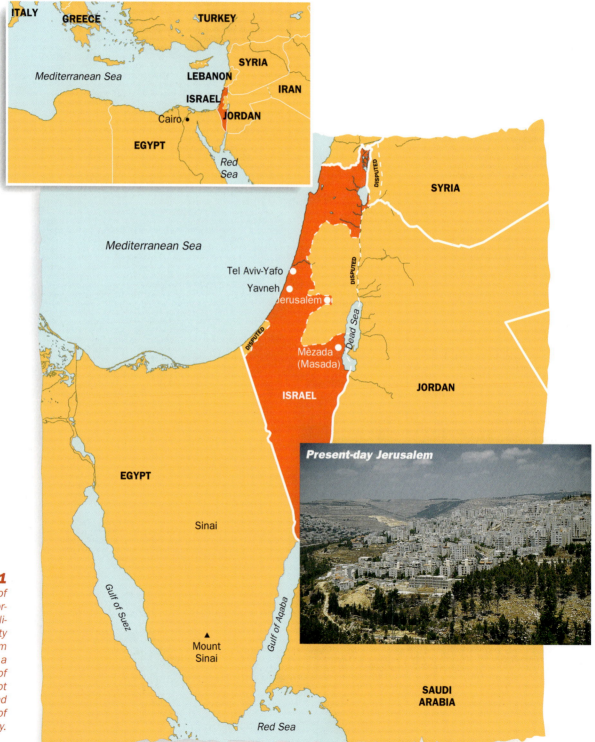

Figure 6.1
The birthplace of Judaism is also important to two other religions: Christianity (Chapter 7) and Islam (Chapter 8). Without a full understanding of Judaism, one cannot grasp the origins and teachings of Christianity.

Present-day Jerusalem

ORIGINS

The narrative of the Hebrew Bible describes the nature of God's relationship with humanity. From the rich imagery of creation to the moral lessons of the flood, the Bible is the instrument through which Jewish religious truth is recorded and communicated. While one might assume that this study should begin with Adam and Eve, it is more historically precise to begin with the patriarch of the Hebrew faith, Abraham. We start with Abraham because he represents the first steps taken in the formation of Hebrew religious practice that would eventually evolve into Judaism.

The Patriarch of the Covenant: Abraham

According to Hebrew scriptures, around 2000 BCE, Abraham received a vision from God that instructed him to leave his home in the Mesopotamian city of Ur and move to Haran and later to Canaan. The vision that Abraham received did not come from one of the many gods of polytheistic Mesopotamia; instead, he received revelation from the one God. Thus, the monotheistic tradition of the Hebrew faith came to be. In the vision, God said to Abraham:

> *Go forth from your native land and from your father's house to the land that I will show you.*
> *I will make of you a great nation,*
> *And I will bless you;.*
> *I will make your name great,*
> *And you shall be a blessing.*
>
> Genesis 12: 1–2

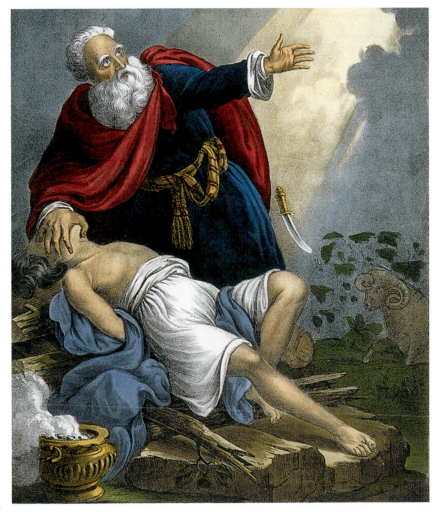

Figure 6.2
What was the nature of God's promise to Abraham?

Abraham was instructed to move to a special land to raise a nation. He did what God commanded, eventually settling in Canaan.

At this point in the history of the religion, two ideas emerged that would develop into Judaism. First, the idea arose that the Jews represented God's **chosen people**. Amid a society characterized by polytheism and idolatry, God chose Abraham and promised to bless him and make of him a "great nation." On this basis, Jews refer to themselves as God's chosen people. Second, the idea of a **Promised**

Land was established. While the idea took on added significance at the time of Moses, it was Abraham, and later his son Isaac and his grandson Jacob, who sought to keep the covenant with God and develop a community in the Promised Land.

These two ideas are the foundation of the **covenant** that God made with Abraham. A covenant is a solemn and binding agreement, similar to a contract. The covenant between God and Abraham—and, by extension, humanity—is the key to the Jewish faith. It established God as the creator and governor of all things, and the chosen people as those who would honour God's covenant.

The Law and the Covenant: Moses

According to Jewish tradition, the covenant between God and the Hebrew people took on new significance during the time of Moses. The patriarchal period of Abraham, Isaac, and Jacob had seen the establishment of a covenant wherein God agreed to love humanity and humanity agreed to love God rather than the many gods of polytheistic Mesopotamia. The Mosaic period would see God provide his people with the commandments that would allow them to keep his covenant.

When a severe drought struck Canaan, the descendants of Abraham were forced to move to Egypt. Eventually, the Egyptians turned on the Hebrews and enslaved them. By the time Ramses II became Pharaoh, slavery was a fact of Hebrew life, with liberation a distant, idealistic dream.

Often, idealistic dreams can become reality, and, as the Hebrew people longed for liberty, a liberator did emerge. Moses was born of Hebrew slaves, but was later adopted by Pharaoh's daughter and grew to manhood in the imperial court. He was favoured by Pharaoh until Moses killed an Egyptian who was harassing a Hebrew slave. Fearing the wrath of Pharaoh, Moses fled to Midian where he was received into the home of Jethro, a priest of Midian.

One day, while tending Jethro's flock of sheep, Moses came to Mount Horeb, called the mountain of God in the Book of Exodus. While at Horeb, Moses encountered God through a burning bush. God revealed that the cries of the Israelites had been heard and that they would be set free through the person of Moses. God said that they would be brought out of bondage into a "Promised Land"; indeed, it would be "a land flowing with milk and honey" (Exodus 3: 8). Moses knew that the Israelites would wonder who sent him, so he asked God what he should say. God responded by saying, *"Ehyeh-asher-Ehyeh."* The exact meaning of this name for God is uncertain, but it can be translated as one of the following: "I am in the process of becoming" or "I will be who I will be." This translation suggests that Moses would come to know God more and more as their relationship evolved.

Moses embarked on his mission and, despite the overwhelming strength of the Pharaoh and his army, led the Hebrews out of bondage.

According to tradition, God brought ten plagues on the Egyptians in order to convince the Pharaoh to let the Hebrew people go. The tenth plague called on the angel of death to descend on Egypt and take the first-born of all who lived in the region. God instructed Moses to tell the Hebrews that they could escape this plague by smearing lamb's blood over their doors. In this way, death would "pass over" their homes because the blood would be a sign that the house belonged to a descendant of Abraham. This event is celebrated in the Jewish festival of Passover (see page 235). It was the tenth plague and the death of his son that convinced the Pharaoh to set the Hebrews free.

Moses led the Hebrews out of Egypt across the Red Sea (literally, the Reed Sea) into the region of the Sinai peninsula (Figure 6.1). This mass emigration is known historically as the **Exodus**. The word *exodus* means "going out" or "departure." In this case, the Israelites left the bondage of slavery in Egypt for freedom and hope in a new land.

On Mount Sinai, God appeared to Moses again, this time sharing with him the Ten Commandments (see page 239). The Commandments emphasized the nature of God's existence as well as the laws that the people would need to follow in order to keep their covenant with God.

The Passover, the Exodus, and the Ten Commandments served as a specific renewal of the covenant between God and the people. Now, the Hebrews could draw inspiration from the example of Moses and marvel at the wonder of God, who chose to reveal his wisdom to Moses, and whom the Hebrews, in turn, chose to worship and honour. They could also conduct their lives according to the absolute laws, established by God in the Commandments, in order to live as a peaceful and faithful people.

Judges, Kings, and Prophets

The Israelites lived a nomadic existence in the Sinai for forty years until they reached the land of Canaan. This marked the beginning of the Biblical period of Judges and Kings. First, the Israelites were led by people referred to as Judges ("judges" is a translation of the Hebrew *shofetim*). Judges were like tribal leaders or chieftains who led the people through periods of crisis. They were charismatic and inspiring people—both men and women—who helped the Israelites establish a sense of identity.

By around 1000 BCE, the Hebrew people began to long for a king to lead them. Initially, God was reluctant to grant the people a king, but eventually agreed to give Saul the status of king because of growing threats from the Philistines. Saul was succeeded by David, whose kingship marked the high point of Jewish imperial history. David scored a number of military victories over his enemies and eventually established Jerusalem as his capital city. His son, Solomon, built a temple that would serve as the centre of worship for the Jewish faith for the next millennium. However, after the death of Solomon, the kingdom broke up. Around 921 BCE, the northern tribes separated from the southern tribes, taking on the name "Israel." The southern tribes, centred around

Jerusalem, became known as "Judah." The era of kings was coming to an end; outside forces would soon impose themselves on the Hebrews again.

Figure 6.3
The head of the sculpture of David, by Michelangelo. According to tradition, God favoured David by allowing him to defeat the Philistine giant, Goliath, with a sling and stone. The Philistines then retreated in shock and fear.

The end of this era was predicted by the prophets. In modern usage, the word prophet has two meanings: one who speaks on behalf of God, and one who predicts the future. In the Jewish tradition, a prophet is a person who receives a message from God and delivers that message to God's people. The message itself belongs to God; the prophet acts as God's messenger. Usually, in the Bible, the Hebrew prophets warned of a coming crisis based on the inability of the people to be true to their covenant with God.

The prophetic tradition is one that Judaism shares with Christianity and Islam. Prophecies are found throughout the Bible. They involve the belief that, at certain times, God uses specific people to deliver his divine message. The word of God, as spoken through the prophets, survives in the holy scriptures of Judaism, the **Tanakh**. The prophetic writings are a combination of practical advice, social criticism, and poetic beauty. Their ongoing refrain is, "Love God and keep the covenant with him."

The Exile

Jewish independence and autonomy would be dramatically altered by two military conquests. In 721 BCE, the Assyrians invaded and captured the territory of Israel. The invading troops not only took the land but also evicted many of the region's citizens, scattering Israel's population. Then, in 586 BCE, Babylonian invaders captured Judah and destroyed Solomon's Temple in Jerusalem. Upward of 10 000 Jewish community leaders were taken prisoner and sent into exile in Babylon. This event is known as the Exile or the Babylonian Captivity. They were held there until Cyrus the Great of Persia released them in 538 BCE, when he defeated the Babylonians.

The period of the Exile marked a shift in the manner in which the Hebrews would worship. With Solomon's Temple destroyed, the people, as a community, needed to find a new way to honour God. Sometime during the Exile, places for congregational worship, now known as **synagogues**, had been created. They grew in importance in the period after the destruction of the temple. The Exile also marked the beginning of intense scholarly analysis of scripture and the emergence of revered teachers known as **rabbis**. The rabbis sought to interpret scripture in a manner that would make the stories of the Bible more comprehensible to the average person. The emergence of the rabbis would have a profound effect on Judaism in the years to come. Finally, the period of the Exile saw the development of a belief in a divine kingship characterized by a **Messiah**, which means "anointed one." The Jews, living in captivity, hoped for the coming of a great king who would lead them out of oppression.

After the conquest of Babylon by Cyrus, the Jewish captives were encouraged to return to their homeland. The Jewish leadership, under the direction of Ezra and Nehemiah, co-operated with the Persians to facilitate the return. In 515 BCE, a second temple was completed—an outward sign of the renewal of the covenant.

During the Exile, the religion of the Jews evolved from a tribal faith to a world faith. The Jewish God acted as a force in world history, and not simply within the confines of the ancient kingdom of Israel. From this point on, the text speaks of Jews and Judaism rather than Hebrews and Israelites.

The Diaspora

Diaspora is a Greek word meaning "sowing of seed" or "dispersal." In the context of Jewish history, "the **Diaspora**" is the term used when referring to the Jewish population living outside of Israel. By the third century BCE, the majority of Jews lived in the Diaspora, so they created a new set of standards for their faith tradition. The Jews who chose to remain in Babylon rather than return from exile formed a sizable population in the region. Practical worship centred around the synagogue, and scholarly analysis of scripture continued under the direction of the rabbis. Other pockets of Jewish population sprang up in communities on the perimeter of the eastern Mediterranean Sea.

In 332 BCE, Alexander the Great conquered much of the known world including Persia, Egypt, and India. Thus, the Jewish people, particularly those in the Diaspora, fell under the influence of Greek culture, a process called **Hellenization**. Jews in Alexandria, Egypt, embraced Greek architecture, dress, and names. The Bible was translated into Greek. According to legend, seventy of Egypt's greatest Jewish scholars, independent of one another, translated the Bible into Greek. Miraculously, all seventy scholars produced independent translations of the Bible that were identical to those of their counterparts! While legendary, the story does provide a backdrop for the first translation of the Bible into Greek. This translation, known as the Septuagint, served the Jewish community of the Diaspora for centuries. Eventually, a tradition of analysis, compilation, and commentary emerged that would see the Bible reorganized into the distinct divisions of law, prophecy, poetry, and writings.

The Maccabean Revolt

The next significant event in the history of the Jews came in 168 BCE. Antiochus IV Epiphanes converted the temple into a shrine to the Greek god Zeus and installed his own candidate to the Jewish high priesthood. Drawing on the growing dissatisfaction with Greek rule among the Jewish population, a group of rebels called the Maccabees started a revolt.

Figure 6.4
A Hanukkah menorah. The events of the Maccabean revolt are celebrated each year in the festival of Hanukkah (see page 234).

By 164 BCE, the Maccabees were in control of Jerusalem, and the temple

was rededicated to God. The dynasty initiated by the Maccabees would rule until the Roman conquest of Israel.

The Romans

In 64 BCE, the Roman general Pompey entered Jerusalem as part of a campaign to expand the Roman Empire. Once again, Jews were subject to foreign domination. By this time, several distinct Jewish sects had emerged, as shown in Figure 6.5. The growing sophistication of Jewish

Figure 6.5
Sects in Judea, 64 BCE

Sect	Description
Sadduccees	• believed in co-operation with the Romans provided that religious worship was not severely restricted • represented the aristocracy and wealthy people • read the **Torah** literally (see page 238) • strictly followed the teachings of the Torah; rejected the prophetic writings • associated with temple life • believed they were the priestly descendants of Zadok, a priest from the time of David
Pharisees	• believed in co-operation with the Romans provided that religious worship was not severely restricted • represented the common people • allowed for broad interpretation of the Torah • encouraged commentary and interpretation of the Scriptures • associated with synagogue worship • sought to make Jewish law practical and compassionate
Zealots	• did not believe in co-operation with the Romans under any circumstances and sought the overthrow of Roman rule • inspired by historical victories (Maccabees, David) over invading forces • initiated the revolt of 66 CE (see page 223)
Essenes	• lived in separate, segregated communities • followed purification rites and rituals • viewed as a priestly caste • interpreted the Torah as a model for the future • beliefs centred on the coming of God's final judgment • were in possession of the Dead Sea Scrolls, discovered in 1947
Samaritans	• descendants of the northern tribes • accepted the Torah; rejected Prophets and Writings

belief, combined with the harshness of Roman rule, led to a renewed emphasis on the coming of a Messiah—one anointed by God to lead the Jews out of oppression.

Rabbinic Judaism

Jerusalem, the city was taken and the temple was destroyed. It has never been rebuilt. To this day, the only part remaining is the Western Wall, which continues to be a place of devotion and prayer for Jews (see page 225).

With the temple ruined and Jewish

Figure 6.6
King Herod's palace at Masada was built in the first century BCE. The plateau was a Jewish stronghold in the Zealots' revolt against the Romans from 66 to 73 CE. This photograph shows the ruins of the palace on the mountain overlooking the southwest shore of the Dead Sea.

A series of incidents posed a serious threat to the faith and fortitude of the Jews. First, the Jews had endured tremendous hardship at the hands of the Romans. Heavy taxation, unfair administration of justice, and Roman control of both the temple and the high priest soon proved too much to bear. In 66 CE, the Jews in Jerusalem revolted, eventually gaining control of the Temple Mount (the second temple) and, in time, the Roman fortress at Antonia just north of the temple. Jews outside Jerusalem also challenged Roman authority by attacking the occupiers in their cities.

The Romans responded with force. In 70 CE, after a five-month siege of resistance destroyed, the Jewish faith was once again faced with a potential dual fate: disintegration or reformation. The possibility of reformation came when Rabbi Yohanan ben Zakkai convinced the Romans to allow him to relocate the Sanhedrin (the supreme judicial body of the Jews) to the town of Yavneh. This provided the Jews with the opportunity to preserve their way of life and redefine themselves. In Yavneh, the Jews maintained their scriptures, wrote commentaries on the law, and developed a Jewish calendar. In other words, despite the apparent destruction of the Jews at the hands of the Romans, their will to survive prevailed.

Web Quest

A detailed timeline of the history of Judaism is provided at
http://www.usisrael.org/jsource/History/timeline.html
Click on "Judaism after the Babylonian Exile" to find out more about the second temple, Diaspora Hellenism, the Macabbean revolt, and other details of this era.

The stage was set for the emergence of rabbinic Judaism. Since the Sadduccees were a priestly caste without a temple, and the institution of the Pharisees was in need of restructuring, a new group of leaders was required to reform Judaism. The priests of old were replaced by rabbis. Synagogues, an established tradition since the Exile, became the main venue for congregational worship. Prayer practices, formerly part of temple life, found new life in the synagogues and Jewish homes. The tradition of praying three times daily while facing Jerusalem was also preserved.

The most significant contribution of the rabbinic movement was the Judaism of the dual laws: the written Torah and the interpretative tradition of the **Mishnah,** and, later, the **Talmud**. Commentary on the Bible had been a long-established tradition in Judaism. By 100 CE, the rabbis had compiled a substantial body of commentary on the Bible known as **Midrash** (which means "interpretation" or "to search out"). Midrash looks at puzzling situations presented in the Bible and poses possible explanations for these problems.

Eventually, rabbinical interpretation was extended to the law; this is where the work of the rabbis stands out. Through intense study of the Scriptures, the rabbis were able to write commentary on the law. Their interpretations were considered to be as valid as the laws written in the Torah. By around 200 CE, the Mishnah had been compiled by Judah the Prince, creating a body of commentary on the law to guide the Jews. Later, the Mishnah was expanded to form the Talmud, a vast document of Jewish law that has survived and is used to the present.

The Jewish experience from the Exile to the Roman occupation is one of inspiring fortitude and an unfailing will to preserve the faith. Behind the worldly experience of oppression, the Jews immersed themselves in coming to terms with God and the covenant. By the Middle Ages, Judaism had established deep intellectual and spiritual roots that would ensure its survival.

Check Your Understanding

1. Explain the covenant that God made with Abraham in the Bible.

2. How were the Ten Commandments a renewal of the covenant?

3. Briefly describe the role of the judges, kings, and prophets.

4. What is the significance of the Exile and the Diaspora for Judaism?

5. In your view, what is the most significant event in the early history of Judaism? Explain.

Holy Places
The Western Wall

There is no site in the world that carries so much significance for Jews as the **Western Wall** in Jerusalem. Also called the Wailing Wall, it is the part remaining after the temple was destroyed by the Romans in 70 CE. The term *Wailing Wall* was coined by European travellers who witnessed the mournful prayers that were being recited there.

It is believed that the site of the temple is near the location where Abraham built an altar on which to sacrifice his son Isaac. Three temples have occupied this site: Solomon's Temple, built around 950 BCE and destroyed by the Babylonians in 586 BCE; Zerubbabel's Temple, built in 515 BCE and plundered in 54 BCE by the Roman general Crassus; and, finally, Herod's Temple (the reconstruction of the second temple), completed in 64 CE, only six years before its total destruction by the Romans.

During the almost 2000 years of Jewish exile, the wall has stood as a symbol of the indestructibility of the Jewish people. It has become a place of prayer and pilgrimage. Prayers are also written on pieces of paper, which are then placed between the stones of the wall. Other activities, such as bar mitzvahs, take place at the wall.

There are several reasons why the wall is considered to be holy. The temple, which was inside the wall, was seen as the spiritual centre of the world for Jewish people. It is mentioned in prayer daily, and is a permanent reminder of God's presence—the fact that the Jews will never be destroyed. When the temple was still standing, Jews made three pilgrimages a year; today, the site remains a place of pilgrimage. It is the focus of prayers for Jews, as instructed in the Talmud, particularly for those living in the West, who direct their prayers toward the Western Wall. The wall also symbolizes heroism—the stones are a reminder to Jewish people that they are still thriving.

Several festivals are based on the existence of the temple. Hanukkah commemorates the rededication of the temple; Pesach (Passover), Sukkot (the autumn harvest and thanksgiving festival), and Shavout (the spring harvest festival) are the three pilgrimage holidays. While the temple was still standing, Yom Kippur was the only day when the high priest was allowed within its holiest areas.

QUESTIONS

1. Why is the Western Wall often referred to as the Wailing Wall?
2. What is the significance of the Western Wall for Jews?

Figure 6.7

BELIEFS

Jewish belief centres on the idea of the oneness of God and the compassion God shares with creation in the form of the covenant. If one can understand the Jewish vision of God and the nature of the covenant, one can understand Jewish beliefs. But first we must answer some questions.

Who Are the Jews?

A Jew is a person who is either born Jewish or converts to Judaism. In the case of birthright, Jewish heritage generally follows the matrilineal descent of the child. In other words, if a child's mother is Jewish, then the child is Jewish. In the case of some Reform and Reconstructionist Jews, as long as one of the child's parents is Jewish, the child is considered to be a Jew.

People can also choose to covert to Judaism. The process of conversion is known as *gerut*. As part of the *gerut*, candidates must reveal knowledge of Judaism, confirm their Jewish beliefs, demonstrate a will to act ethically, and show a connection with the Jewish people.

Sometimes, people identify themselves as Jews even though they do not follow the religious tenets of Judaism. They embrace the cultural aspects of Jewish life, such as art, food, and folk traditions, but do not participate in Jewish religious life.

Historically, persecution of the Jews has been based on the premise that the Jews are a genetically linked people. However, the fact that people from many different backgrounds convert to Judaism is evidence that this is a mistake.

What Do Jews Believe?

Jewish belief centres on God as the creator of everything. God governs the universe with justice and honour. Nothing happens without God, therefore humanity has an obligation to worship God. God is immaterial (not composed of material such as flesh and bones) and indivisible. Thus, the core Jewish belief is that God is One.

These beliefs concerning God can be summarized succinctly by looking at three important sources, as outlined in Figure 6.8.

Figure 6.8
Beliefs concerning God

Teaching	Source	Belief
Shema (the Jewish creed of faith)	Torah—Deuteronomy 6: 4–9	"Hear, O Israel, The Lord is our God, the Lord is One."
Five Fundamental Concepts	The philosopher Philo of Alexandria (20 BCE–50 CE)	According to Philo, a Jew believes the following: 1. There is a God. 2. There is only one God. 3. God created the world, but the world will not last forever. 4. There is only one universe. 5. God cares for the world and all of its creatures.
Thirteen Articles of Faith	The philosopher Maimonides (1135–1204 CE)	Of the Thirteen Articles of Faith, three have been accepted as absolute: • There is one God. • God is perfect Unity. • God is immaterial.

Living My Religion

Leora Wise

Leora Wise attends McGill University, majoring in Latin American studies and minoring in Jewish studies. When she was a child, Leora's parents wanted to ensure that she understood her Jewish heritage, so she attended the Baliak Hebrew Day School, a private Jewish parochial school in Toronto. In grade 8, she transferred to the Claude Watson Arts Program at Earl Haig Secondary School, majoring in visual arts. Leora would like to work in Latin America, advancing social justice and democracy. In the future, Leora is considering "making **aliyah**," or moving to Israel.

Figure 6.9

Being Jewish is very complex because so many people have different ideas on what it means to be Jewish. Some people identify with Judaism entirely as a religion, others see Judaism as a culture, and still others see Judaism as a nationality dating back to Biblical times. To me, Judaism is a combination of all three.

Though I am not an Orthodox Jew, as I do not keep **kosher** (see page 232) nor am I Shabbat [Sabbath]-observant, Judaism is always at the forefront of my mind. Ever since I was a child, Jewish practices have been a part of my routine. I received a Jewish education, attended Jewish summer camp, and had a bat mitzvah—experiences that undoubtedly helped to shape me as a Jew. Now I choose which aspects of Judaism I am going to partake in. For example, I am accustomed to having Shabbat dinner with friends and family on Friday night, and even though I am living away from home at university, I always have special plans for Shabbat. For me, the customs of eating challah [egg bread, often braided] and lighting the candles, and the sense of community created by Shabbat are important aspects of Jewish culture.

My connection to Israel is an important and daily part of my experience as a Jew. I love Israel and have visited several times. I study Hebrew literature and, consequently, Israeli culture in school. I organized an Israeli Culture Day at McGill University, the aim of which was to embrace Israeli culture separately from the Middle East politics that are often all that people know about the wonderful country. At the same time, I have a vested interest in the political situation in Israel; I studied the Arab-Israeli conflict in school and I keep myself informed.

Another facet of my Judaism is being part of a Jewish community. Being Jewish is being part of a nation, from the Exodus to the Inquisition to the shtetl [eastern European villages] and the pioneers [Jews who set up communities in Palestine after the return from exile]. Jewish nationhood is an inherent feeling. I know that wherever I am in the world, in any type of crisis, the Jewish community will always support me. Jewish solidarity transcends national borders, and the Jewish community is a security blanket for Jews worldwide.

My Jewish identity is a part of who I am. I feel hollow when there is no Jewish presence in my life, and replenish by involving myself in the religion, history, or people. There are so many facets to Judaism, and it is so unconsciously a part of my daily life, that even when there is no Jewish presence actively involving me in Judaism, I always know that I am Jewish.

QUESTIONS

1. For Leora, what is the importance of the Shabbat dinner?
2. What is the greatest benefit of being Jewish for Leora?
3. Why might a young Jew consider "making aliyah"?

The three sources in Figure 6.8 demonstrate that God is One, and not many as in the case of polytheism. This is an important distinction because if individuals are to grasp the unity of creation, they must be able to grasp the unity and oneness of God. Judaism asserts that God is responsible for all creation, is immaterial, and cares for humanity. To show this caring, God made a covenant with humanity that essentially said, "Honour Me and I shall honour you." In turn, humanity became a junior partner in God's creation.

How Do Jews Honour God?
Mitzvah

Judaism teaches that the covenant is a fact of life for all creation. It speaks to the reality that people are all connected and that, if they want fulfillment in life, they must treat life as an ongoing covenant. God created certain commandments to help people keep the covenant. Judaism holds that following the commandments allows one to see how everything is interconnected. It also provides the opportunity for individuals to actively demonstrate their devotion to God through study of the Torah, prayer, and good deeds including charity.

In the Jewish tradition, the act of performing a good deed is called a **mitzvah** (plural—**mitzvoth**). More specifically, a mitzvah is a commandment from God that gives people direction on how to live ethically while honouring God. The Bible contains a total of 613 mitzvoth: 248 positive, or "do," commandments and 365 negative, or "do not," commandments. For the Jews, it is essential that one strives to keep the covenant with God. The way to do this is by following God's commandments, particularly the Ten Commandments.

How Does God Show Commitment to the Covenant?

God has a personal relationship with humanity. According to Judaism, this was demonstrated when Moses encountered God at the burning bush. In this encounter, the name of God was revealed to Moses. The name of God is of particular significance to the Jews. The Bible refers to God as YHWH, though no one knows the exact meaning or pronunciation of YHWH. As mentioned previously, one of the interpretations of the name given to Moses at the burning bush was "I am in the process of becoming."

When Jews write or read the name of God, they use the words *Lord* or *Adonay* as substitutes, demonstrating the reverence with which they regard the name of God. Furthermore, it has become common practice to substitute the word *name* in order to avoid saying "God." There are many other names for God that have emerged over the course of the history of the Jewish faith. The names tend to be masculine in origin, which is why God is sometimes referred to as "he."

Judaism holds that, by stating his name, God was saying to humanity, "I know you, and I care for you." God demonstrated this by providing circumstances and messages that would allow people to keep their covenant with God, as illustrated in Figure 6.10.

Figure 6.10
Demonstration of the covenant

Message	Description
Chosen People	The covenant is a sign that God chose the descendants of Abraham to be God's people. In the Bible, God appeared to Abraham and gave him the message that he is the one God and that many nations would come from Abraham's family line. This event demonstrates the idea of a people chosen by God to do God's will, which necessarily means that the people must, in turn, choose to do the will of God. Therefore, the concept of "chosen" is reciprocal, with God choosing humanity and humanity choosing God. Some of the **anti-Semitism** (see page 250) that has emerged throughout history has been based, at least in part, on this idea of chosen people. The concept itself does not imply superior status; instead, it suggests a partnership between God and his people—making humanity the guardians of God's creation.
Promised Land	As part of the covenant, God promised a land to his people. Jews believe this "promised land" is Israel (Figure 6.11).
Messiah	Jews believe that God will send a great leader to the world who will bring harmony and peace. They characterize the time of the Messiah to be a period of "divine kingship" wherein the reign of God will be clearly evident.
World to Come	The Jewish faith also maintains the belief that God will provide a future time of peace and prosperity for the Jewish people.

Figure 6.11
Among Israel's 6 million people, almost 80 per cent are Jews—over half native born, and the rest from approximately seventy countries around the world.

Check Your Understanding

1. Analyze Figure 6.8. What do the three sources have in common? How are they different?

2. What is a mitzvah? Give an example.

3. List the four messages given to the Jewish people as a sign that God cares for them. Which one do you think is most important? Why?

PRACTICES, RITUALS, SYMBOLS, AND FESTIVALS

Practices and Rituals

The Jewish tradition is one that is rich in its worship and prayer practices. Worship is certainly not confined to the synagogue; the home is an important venue for worship as well.

The Synagogue

This is the communal place of worship for Jews and is considered a place of gathering, of prayer, and of study or learning. Some Jews refer to the synagogue as *shul*, which is a Yiddish word derived from the German word for "school." This emphasizes the synagogue's role as a place of study.

The Torah Scroll

The **Sefer Torah**, or Torah scroll, is the text of the five books of Moses written on parchment. It is the most sacred object of Jewish life and is essential for worship. It is always kept in a place of honour in the synagogue and is read at specific times during the service. While every synagogue needs at least one Torah scroll, most synagogues have at least three because certain rituals call for readings from two or three different sections of the Torah. This avoids delaying the service while the Torah scroll is rolled from section to section. Each scroll is either wrapped in a beautiful covering or kept in a gold or silver container. The parchment of the Torah cannot be touched while being read, so the reader uses a pointer to follow the words in the text.

According to Jewish tradition, when the Hebrews received the Ten Commandments in the desert, they were told to make an ark in which to place them. This is called the **Ark of the Covenant**. Today, the **Holy Ark** (a cabinet-like structure) sits on a raised platform in the synagogue and contains the Torah scrolls. During the service, the Torah scroll is taken from the Ark and placed on a special table called the *schulchan*, where it is unrolled and read. The *schulchan* is usually covered with a piece of decorative silk or velvet.

Figure 6.12
In addition to doors, some Holy Arks have an inner curtain. When certain prayers are recited, the doors and/or curtain of the Ark may be opened or closed by a member of the congregation. It is considered an honour when a congregant is given this responsibility.

Clergy and Laypersons

While any Jew who is knowledgeable, trained, and capable can conduct and lead a worship service, it is generally the master of prayer who does so. This is usually the rabbi. A rabbi is a trained scholar, a teacher, an interpreter of Jewish law, a counsellor, and an officiant of special ceremonies such as a bar mitzvah (see page 236). Many synagogues also have a cantor, a singer who chants the worship service and may also serve as prayer master.

Worship
Blessings

Berakhah means "blessing," which is the foundation of Jewish prayer. Through blessing, Jews believe they acknowledge, praise, thank, and petition God. It is the basis of communal worship, although it is certainly a part of private prayer as well. There are three types of blessings. The first is a blessing of thanks to God for the enjoyment of the five senses. A well-known example is the **kiddush**, a blessing recited when people drink wine that has been specially sanctified for the Sabbath or a holy day. Another type of blessing is one that is recited before performing a mitzvah to acknowledge that the commandment is divinely given and to thank God for the chance to fulfill a religious precept. A third type of blessing is recited to praise, thank, or petition God. This blessing is recited at the beginning of each festival.

Services

When Jewish people pray communally, a **minyan**, or a quorum of ten males over the age of thirteen, is required. (Reform and Reconstructionist Jews count women in a *minyan*.) There are three daily worship services held in the evening, the morning, and the afternoon. In the Jewish tradition, the day begins and ends with sunset, so the evening service is the first of the day. The morning service can be recited any time after dawn until 10 a.m. The afternoon service is a much shorter version of the morning service.

The Torah reading is the central part of certain worship services during the week. The Torah is divided into fifty-four sections. One portion is read each week (two weeks of the year have a double portion) so that the entire Torah is read from beginning to end in the course of a year. The completion of the reading cycle and the beginning of the next cycle takes place on the festival of Simkhat Torah, which celebrates this cycle.

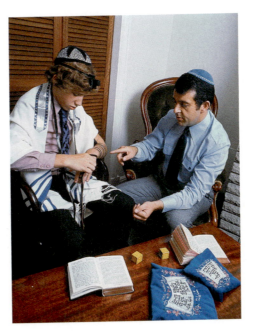

Figure 6.13
When they worship or study, Jewish men wear a head covering known as a **yarmulke**, *or* kippah, *to show their respect for God. They also wear a shawl, or* **tallis**, *while praying. The fringes of the tallis are a reminder of God's commandments and the necessity of keeping these commandments.* **Tefillin** *are either of two small leather boxes containing parchment scrolls of Biblical text. Jewish men wear the tefillin, one on the forehead and one on the arm, every day during morning prayer except on the Sabbath. Do you wear certain clothing to indicate your beliefs? Explain.*

Figure 6.14
Rabbi Harry Newmark, a full-time kosher food checker, monitors the food-manufacturing process. Kosher laws determine what foods may and may not be eaten, and how foods should be prepared and served.

Web Quest

For more information about the symbols, on page 233 go to http://www.jewfaq.org/toc.htm and click on "Signs and Symbols." You can also learn about other symbols, such as the *mezuzah*, the *chai*, and the hamesh hand at this site.

Kashruth

An active expression of adherence to the commandments is the practice of keeping kosher (Figure 6.14). The Jewish dietary laws of Kashruth serve a number of purposes. First, they establish the Jews as an identifiable group. The idea of kosher foods identifies the distinctiveness of Jews to others. Second, kosher food laws speak to the humanity and humility of the Jewish people. Humanity is revealed in the prescribed method of killing animals in the most humane manner possible. Humility enters into the equation when one considers the level of thoughtfulness and gratitude the Jews give to God for the food provided to them.

Shabbat

The Shabbat, or Sabbath, is perhaps the most important ritual of the Jewish people. It is based on the creation stories of Genesis. The Sabbath is a time to put aside work, shopping, housework, even homework! However, it is not a period of restriction, but of rejuvenation. It is an opportunity to set aside time for the important things in life—prayer, family, and friends.

At sunset on Friday, Jews go to the synagogue, where the service opens with the lighting of candles as a reminder of creation—the first act of creation was, "Let there be light." Once they return home, families sit down to the Shabbat dinner, which begins with the *kiddush* (the prayer over wine). Challah, a special egg bread, is blessed and eaten at the meal. Following the meal, particular songs are sung and the prayer of thanksgiving is recited.

Sabbath morning is spent at the synagogue in prayer and worship. At sundown, the Sabbath ends with a brief service that separates the holy Sabbath from the rest of the week. This service is often held at home. As it concludes, people greet each other by saying, "*Shavua tov*" ("May it be a good week").

The Sabbath has played an enormous role in the Jewish religion. No matter where Jews have lived, and no matter what their circumstances or conditions, the Sabbath has always sustained them as a people.

Symbols

Religious symbols are an outward representation of God. For many people, symbols help to strengthen their relationship with God. Certainly, they manifest the invisible in a visible manner. The Jewish people have numerous symbols that richly reflect their history.

Symbols

Star of David

Perhaps the best-known symbol of Judaism is the **Star of David**, also known as Magen David (shield of David). It is a six-pointed star, formed from two interlocking triangles. It is thought that this was the shape of King David's shield. While the symbol may have been used for magical and ornamental purposes in ancient times, it was not exclusively Jewish. Most experts believe that it was not until the nineteenth century that the symbol became officially accepted by Judaism.

The Star of David became even more closely identified with Judaism when it was adopted by Zionists (see page 248) as a marker of Jewish nationality in the twentieth century. Jews today see the Star of David as a symbol of the will to survive and as a source of pride in their Jewish identity. It is prominently featured on the blue and white Israeli flag. As well, in Israel, the Red Shield of David is equivalent to the Red Cross in Christian nations and the Red Crescent in Muslim countries.

Figure 6.15

Menorah

The **menorah** is a very ancient source of light. When the temple was built in Jerusalem, the seven-branched menorah became a central ritual object. After the second temple was destroyed in 70 CE, the menorah was carried off to Rome. Today, many non-Jewish people think of the menorah as the nine-branched candelabrum that is used in celebration of Hanukkah. But it is the seven-branched menorah, one branch for each of the six days of creation and one for the Sabbath, that is the authentic Jewish symbol. It is also used as the logo of the modern State of Israel.

Figure 6.16

QUESTIONS

1. What appear to be the origins of the Star of David?
2. In your opinion, is the Star of David a religious or a political symbol? Explain.
3. Why is the menorah significant to Jews?

Festivals

Festivals serve to remind people of their history and to distinguish them as a faith community. Think for a moment about the numerous events that your family celebrates. Some of these are religious in nature; others are secular, such as your birthday. Whatever the event, there is usually some planning involved; special foods are prepared, family and friends are invited, and gifts are often exchanged. For Jews, festivals mark the Jewish year and are a time for family, tradition, joy, and reflection.

Rosh Hashanah and Yom Kippur

Rosh Hashanah, the Jewish New Year, falls in September or early October. It begins a ten-day period of repentance, ending with the festival of **Yom Kippur**. The two days of Rosh Hashanah and the eight days that follow concentrate on an assessment of conduct and behaviour in the previous year. Jews request forgiveness from God and from other human beings for their mistakes and transgressions. On the Saturday evening before Rosh Hashanah, a forgiveness service is held at the synagogue. An important ritual at this service is the sounding of the shofar, the ram's horn (Figure 6.17). In Biblical times, the **shofar** was used to call people together.

Also known as the Day of Atonement, Yom Kippur is the most solemn religious day of the Jewish year, marked by a twenty-five-hour fast and prayers of repentance. Since the task of repentance is so important, regular activities are avoided on this day. Signs of comfort and luxury are not allowed; for example, women often do not wear makeup. Sexual relations between a husband and wife are not permitted. No food or drink is allowed in order to demonstrate that this day is better spent on prayer.

Hanukkah

Hanukkah, perhaps the best-known of the Jewish holidays, is the festival of dedication, or the festival of lights. This eight-day period, which usually falls in December, celebrates the events of the Maccabean revolt (see pages 221 to 222). After the small army had reclaimed the temple in Jerusalem, the ceremonies rededicating the temple took place over eight days. When the people tried to rekindle the sacred lamp in the temple, they discovered that there was only enough oil to last one day. According to legend, the oil continued to burn in the temple lamp for eight days.

As part of the celebration of Hanukkah, a candle is lit for each of the eight days in a special candelabrum, or menorah (Figure 6.4). The menorah has nine branches—one for each of the eight nights of Hanukkah and a ninth for the candle known as

Figure 6.17
One of the most important observances of Rosh Hashanah is the sounding of the shofar in the synagogue. There are four different types of shofar notes; a total of 100 notes are sounded each day.

the *shammus* (servant), which is often placed in the centre and used to light the other candles. Each night, families gather to light the candles and recite special blessings. In North America, it has become customary to exchange gifts.

Pesach

The feast of Passover is usually held in April over seven or eight days. This is an extremely important holiday because it commemorates the freeing of the Hebrews from slavery—the Exodus (see page 219).

This holiday, more than any other, celebrates the Jewish people's identity as a people of God. During the entire week of **Pesach**, Jews do no eat anything *chametz*, or leavened, in order to commemorate the haste in which the Hebrews had to flee from their oppressor. On the eve of Pesach, a ceremonial search for *chametz* takes place. This is a last chance to find any that might have been missed in the preparations for Pesach. Today, an adult often hides *chametz* somewhere in the home, then the children search for it. When it is found, a blessing is said.

Another custom is for all first-born Jewish males to fast on the first day of the festival. This is a remembrance of the first-born Egyptian males who were killed so that the Hebrews could be freed from slavery. It is considered a fast to mark history and humility.

The **Seder**, a ritual service and ceremonial dinner, is held at home on the first night of Pesach. It includes songs, special food, and prayers of praise. The events of the Exodus are told, re-enacted, and explained. The book used to explain these events is called the **Haggadah**. It is filled with Biblical quotes and interpretations of the events. It describes the rituals, symbols, objects, and food that are used during the Seder.

Check Your Understanding

1. Briefly describe the roles of a rabbi and a cantor.

2. Briefly explain the word *kosher*.

3. Why do you think it is important to Jewish people to celebrate the Sabbath?

4. Why is Pesach central to Jewish life?

5. In your opinion, which of the Jewish festivals described in this section is most important? Why?

MILESTONES

Naming a Child

In addition to a conventional name, a baby is given a formal Hebrew name, which is sometimes chosen in remembrance of a deceased relative. This signifies the importance the Jewish faith places on tradition. The formal name is usually only used in religious rituals, such as reading the Torah.

Jewish boys are circumcised on the eighth day after birth. The **circumci-**

sion is performed by a mohel, who is trained according to Jewish law. If a mohel is not present, then a trained rabbi or a doctor can perform the surgery. A boy is usually given his name during the circumcision ceremony, which takes place after morning prayers at the synagogue. Girls are given their names in the synagogue on a Sabbath shortly after their birth.

Coming of Age

When a boy turns thirteen, he celebrates his **bar mitzvah**, which means "son of the commandment." He is now considered an adult in the Jewish religion. In the months leading up to the bar mitzvah, the boy studies and prepares for the day. The bar mitzvah usually happens on the first Sabbath after his thirteenth birthday. When a girl turns twelve, she celebrates her **bat mitzvah** (Figure 6.18), which means "daughter of the commandment." Both religious services are followed by a joyful reception.

Marriage

The next big event in the life of a Jewish person is marriage. It is a very important part of life for Jewish people because the family plays such a predominant role within Jewish tradition. Although a Jewish person is not required to marry within the faith, it is usually thought to be preferable. It is believed that difficulties might arise if a Jew marries someone who does not understand and share his or her faith.

Most weddings take place in a synagogue and are conducted by a rabbi. The bride and groom stand under a special canopy called a *chuppah*, which is a symbol of the home they will share (Figure 6.22). It is often decorated with flowers. They drink from a glass of wine that has been blessed. The marriage contract, which states that the husband will look after his wife, is read and signed by the bridegroom. The groom then gives the bride a ring. At the end of the service, the groom crushes a

Figure 6.18

A member of a Conservative synagogue in Thornhill, Ontario, celebrates her bat mitzvah. In Orthodox congregations, the bat mitzvah is not always celebrated. In the Reform and Reconstructionist traditions, it is given the same importance as the bar mitzvah. During the year prior to their thirteenth birthday, boys and girls study a portion of the Torah to chant in front of the congregation. Often they also write an essay explaining their portion.

glass under his foot. This gesture is to remind the couple that they will experience bad as well as good things in their married life and must face them together. It also serves as reminder of the destruction of the temple in Jerusalem.

Divorce

Although Judaism does allow divorce, it tries very hard to discourage a couple from taking that final step. Friends and family will do their best to help the couple get through their difficulties. However, if all fails, the husband gives the wife a certificate of divorce called a *get*. If a *get* is not issued, then the marriage is not considered to be dissolved, even though the couple might be civilly divorced. Once a *get* is issued, each is free to remarry again in the Jewish religion.

Death

Funerals take place as soon as possible, usually within twenty-four hours after the death of a person. The funeral service is very simple. The body cannot be cremated because the belief is that cremation destroys what God has made. Jews believe in life after death, but it is not a very important part of their faith. They feel it is more important to focus on the present.

Shiva is the seven-day period of mourning following the funeral. This is a time when family mourners are protected from everyday problems and responsibilities. Immediately following the funeral, a shiva candle is lit in the home to symbolize the soul of the deceased. Mourners then eat a small meal, known as the meal of consolation, which is prepared by friends and neighbours. This meal symbolizes the need to continue living and to begin the healing process. While sitting shiva, family mourners do not leave the house, so friends and relatives come to visit. The mourners recite the Kaddish, known as the mourner's prayer. In some homes, the mirrors are covered so that mourners do not look at themselves, thus avoiding vanity at this time.

Check Your Understanding

1. Why is it important for Jews to give their children a Hebrew name?

2. Why did your parents choose your name?

3. What is the age you consider someone to be mature? Explain.

4. What does the *chuppah* represent?

6. Compare the funeral traditions of Judaism with those that may be practised in your family.

SACRED WRITINGS

The Torah

Figure 6.19
Rabbi Shmuel Spero, wearing a traditional prayer shawl (tallis), reads from the Torah at Anshei Minsk Synagogue in Toronto's Kensington Market.

The sacred writings of Judaism are referred to as **Torah**. *Torah* is often translated as meaning "law," but a more accurate translation is "revelation," "teaching," or "instruction." The word *Torah* is used to refer to the Law of Moses, as well as to the entire belief system of the Jewish faith. The written Torah is primarily a description of the development of God's relationship with his chosen people.

The way in which the sacred writings were assembled is interesting to note. These decisions were not taken lightly; intense study and debate preceded the selection or rejection of any book. Eventually, consensus was reached, and certain books were deemed "sacred." Coinciding with the acceptance of books into the Hebrew canon was the emergence of the body of commentary on the Scriptures known as Midrash (see page 224).

As discussed on page 224, commentary on law also emerged within Judaism dating from the time of the Exile up to approximately 500 CE. These commentaries came to be known as the Mishnah. In Babylon, the rabbis gathered both legal (Halacha) and non-legal (Haggadah) material into a compilation of literature known as the Gemara, or learning of the rabbis. Next, they combined the Gemara with the Mishnah to form the Babylonian Talmud. There is also a Palestinian Talmud that was compiled earlier, but the Babylonian Talmud has become the standard for the administration of Jewish law.

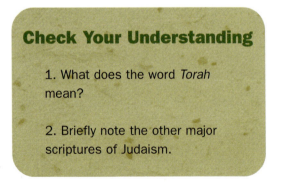

Check Your Understanding

1. What does the word *Torah* mean?

2. Briefly note the other major scriptures of Judaism.

Sacred Text

In addition to being a basic part of Judaism, the Ten Commandments have become, over time, the very foundation of the moral and legal principles that govern most nations in Western society. The tablets of the law, or *luchot*, are often used as symbols in synagogue architecture.

The Ten Commandments
Exodus 20: 2–14

I the Lord am your God who brought you out of the land of Egypt, the house of bondage: You shall have no other gods beside Me.

You shall not make for yourself a sculptured image, or any likeness of what is in the heavens above, or on the earth below, or in the waters under the earth. You shall not bow down to them or serve them. For I the Lord your God am an impassioned God, visiting the guilt of the parents upon the children, upon the third and upon the fourth generation of those who reject Me, but showing kindness to the thousandth generation who love Me and keep My commandments.

You shall not swear falsely by the name of the Lord your God; for the Lord will not clear one who swears falsely by His name.

Remember the Sabbath day and keep it holy. Six days you shall labor and do all your work, but the seventh day is a Sabbath of the Lord your God: you shall not do any work—you, your son or daughter, your male or female slave, or your cattle, or the stranger who is within your settlements. For in six days the Lord made heaven and earth and sea, and all that is in them, and He rested on the seventh day; therefore the Lord blessed the Sabbath day and hallowed it.

Honor your father and your mother, that you may long endure on the land that the Lord your God is giving to you.

You shall not murder.

You shall not commit adultery.

You shall not steal.

You shall not bear false witness against your neighbor.

You shall not covet your neighbor's house: you shall not covet your neighbor's wife, or his male or female slave, or his ox or his ass, or anything that is your neighbor's.

QUESTIONS

1. Which of these "laws" are considered important in Canada today? Why?

2. If you were asked to list these Commandments in order from most important to least important, how would you organize them? Be prepared to explain your choices.

Figure 6.20

The most distinguished philosopher in the history of Judaism was Maimonides. Born in Cordoba, Maimonides moved from Spain to Morocco to Palestine and, finally, to Cairo, Egypt.

Maimonides became the leading rabbi in Cairo; the local Jewish population referred to him as *nagid*, or head of the Egyptian Jewish community. In addition to his scholastic pursuits as a rabbi, Maimonides was the court physician for Saladin, the sultan of Egypt and Syria. His contribution to Jewish philosophy cannot be overstated. Maimonides formulated the Thirteen Articles of Jewish Faith, which clearly delineated what it meant to be a faithful Jew. He wrote *Mishnah Torah*, an exhaustive survey of Jewish law comprising fourteen books and written in Hebrew. In his *Guide for the Perplexed*, Maimonides also reconciled the perspective of rabbinic Judaism with the philosophy of Aristotle. His fame as a distinguished rabbi and scholar was paralleled by his noteworthy achievements as a physician.

The philosophical works of Maimonides brought focus to the belief system of medieval Judaism. In particular, his Thirteen Articles of Faith challenge Jewish people to know and believe in God. The Articles also call on them to recognize their responsibility to live as beings created by God in a universe created by God.

Maimonides came to be regarded as the "second Moses." Through brilliant scholarship and a burning desire to make sense of Jewish philosophy, Maimonides provided clarity and a reformed sense of purpose to Judaism, while emphasizing and honouring the power and wonder of God. The Thirteen Articles of Faith were adopted by Jews in the fourteenth century. They are now included in poetic form in the Jewish prayer book and are recited daily in services.

QUESTIONS

1. Make a point-form list of Maimonides's accomplishments.
2. Why is Maimonides referred to as the "second Moses"?

GROUPS AND INSTITUTIONS

As with other major religions, Judaism has developed into different denominations. Unlike the Jewish sects of antiquity (see page 222), these divisions are of relatively recent origin. During the Middle Ages, Jewish communities in Europe were either forced into or voluntarily lived in **ghettos**. Most followed practices and worshipped in a manner that we would regard today as Orthodox. By the latter part of the eighteenth century, Jews in western Europe were gaining civil liberties and were more inclined to associate with Gentiles (non-Jews); in the process, the rabbis lost their tight control over the Jewish people. This was also the time of the Enlightenment, which presented an opportunity for Jews to join European life more fully. Some Jews felt that they should become more assimilated into European society.

For Jews contemplating this idea, there seemed to be three possibilities: keep the old ways, assimilate fully, or introduce changes and bring Judaism into the modern world. The old ways appeared to be in conflict with the modern world, and full assimilation meant losing one's Jewish identity. Thus, the last alternative—introducing changes—offered a solution. This marked the beginning of the division of Judaism into the Orthodox, Reform, Conservative, and Reconstructionist branches.

Orthodox Judaism

Orthodox Jews accept without question that "the Torah is from Heaven." It is held to be "the word of God," as revealed by him *to* the Jewish people. The nature of this revelation is a crucial issue in the division of Judaism because it is a fundamental reason for the differences among the branches. The Orthodox view is that the written and spoken Torah combined is an evolving communication of God's will. The Torah itself is, therefore, of divine origin and has not altered in 3000 years of Jewish history. It is a source of truth, as revealed by God, handed down from generation to generation. Orthodox Judaism roots itself in the two laws and denies that humans can individually change God's teaching to suit their will and needs.

The adherence to tradition basically means that services are in Hebrew; the Sabbath is strictly observed, using the rules evolved in the interpretive tradition. Only kosher food is eaten, and traditional gender roles are often maintained whereby men are usually the leaders in worship and ritual. However, many modern North American synagogues are adapting these roles. While many Orthodox Jews have to live in today's world, they maintain Jewish practices and laws, although they may have adopted modern dress. An exception is the Hasidic community, in which many men wear beards, black hats, and long black coats, and many women cover their heads and dress very modestly.

Hasidism

The Hasidic movement started with Israel ben Eliezer (*c.* 1700–1760 CE), also known as Ba'al Shem Tov, or the "Good Master of the Name." He travelled from place to place as a children's teacher and gained a reputation as a miracle worker, healer, and mystic. Through his efforts, the Hasidic movement gained a large following, particularly in the Ukraine. The educated leaders of the Jewish communities in eastern Europe offered guidance that seemed aloof from the daily lives of their followers, who often were rural dwellers and uneducated. Ben Eliezer advised his followers to pay less attention to formal details; he believed that the best way to communicate with God was through humility, good deeds, and prayer. God's presence should be sought in everyday events—a true religion was knowledge of God in all creation. He encouraged his followers to find joy in their lives and not to mourn past miseries.

The Hasidic approach was less intellectually demanding than that of mainstream Orthodox Judaism and, therefore, more accessible. Followers became known as Hasidim, or "pious ones." Today, there are Hasidic Jews in Israel, but the largest numbers are in the United States, and their headquarters are in Brooklyn, New York.

Reform Judaism

Unlike Orthodox Judaism, the Reform movement believes that both the written and spoken Torah are human creations, and that God allows for successive generations to have a different appreciation of the truth of the Torah.

Early in the eighteenth century, there was a reinterpretation of Judaism in light of new ideas circulating in western Europe, where such reinterpretation did not conflict with the basic principles of Judaism. The leading voice in this new approach was Moses Mendelssohn, who believed that the Jews of Germany should absorb as much German culture as possible and enjoy the same intellectual freedoms as other Germans. This meant learning German and giving up Yiddish, studying secular subjects, acquiring a trade, and being ready to join the wider community. There was also a desire to revitalize Jewish public worship by introducing the vernacular (that is, the local language instead of Hebrew) into services and sermons, as well as choral and organ music.

The Reform movement spread throughout Germany and into other European countries. Today, it has followers in twenty-five countries. Reform Judaism came to North America with the immigration of European Jews. Here, in addition to using the vernacular in services, the Reform movement abolished the partition in synagogues that separated men and women. Reform accounts for 35 per cent of American Jews. In Israel, where the movement is growing, there are at least four Reform congregations and two Reform kibbutzim (collective farming settlements).

The first female rabbi, Regina Jonas, was ordained in Germany on 27 December 1935. However, it was not until 1972 that another woman, Sally Priesand, was ordained as a rabbi at Hebrew Union College in Cincinnati. In 1980, Joan Friedman of Holy Blossom Temple in Toronto became the first female rabbi to work in Canada.

In 1883, at a dinner celebrating the first graduates of Hebrew Union College, a non-kosher meal was served. It became known as the *terefah* banquet, and the outrage that resulted among traditionalists led indirectly to the development of the Conservative branch of Judaism.

Conservative Judaism

Conservative Judaism holds the middle ground between the Orthodox and Reform positions. It is a large branch and is centred in the United States. This branch recognizes the human element in revelation—that God revealed the Torah both *to* the people and *through* the people. Like Reform Jews, Conservative Jews wanted to alter the old-style Orthodoxy in order to meet the new realities of North American life. However, they could not approve of the Reform movement, which they thought was too quick to abandon practices and principles that were rooted in tradition.

Conservative synagogues maintain the traditional order of the services and conduct them mostly in Hebrew. While wanting to preserve the best of the Jewish traditions, the Conservative branch allows some flexibility in the interpretation of Jewish law. For example, men and women sit together in the synagogue; women can participate in services much as men do; and women can now become cantors as well as rabbis. At the age of twelve, a girl is permitted to become a bat mitzvah.

Reconstructionist Judaism

This is the youngest but the fastest growing of the American-centred Jewish movements. The movement, founded in the 1930s as an offshoot of Conservative Judaism, is based on the philosophy of Mordecai Kaplan (1881–1983). Its aim is to "reconstruct" Judaism by making Jewish traditions more meaningful in today's world—blending tradition with change. Reform Judaism argues that Judaism is an evolving faith and has adapted to the changing environment in the past. To explain their position, Reconstructionists say that "tradition has a vote but not a veto," promoting the view that Judaism is a "work-in-progress" rather than a finished product.

Women in Judaism

For Orthodox Jews, Jewish law provides a basic structure within which individuals may express their own personalities. This supports the notion of being different but equal. Historically, the primary vehicle of religious expression and duty for Orthodox women

Web Quest

For an in-depth look at Reconstructionist Judaism, visit http://www.jrf.org

Figure 6.21
In 1985, Amy Eilberg became the first woman to be ordained a Conservative rabbi, at the Jewish Theological Seminary in New York. Rabbi Eilberg is currently working in California. "Prayer is speech in its purest form. It is our heart speaking in its own voice, just as it needs to." In your own words, explain what Rabbi Eilberg is saying.

Figure 6.22
In all branches of Judaism, the bride and groom stand beneath a chuppah, symbolic of the home they will share. The importance of the chuppah is so great that the wedding ceremony itself is sometimes referred to as the chuppah.

has been the occupation of wife and mother. Home life is seen as a divine service and a rich world, and dedication to others is considered a virtue. Contrary to widely held belief, women can have careers outside the home. Usually, women wear modest skirts or dresses; pants may be worn for certain jobs. Most married women cover their hair in the presence of men other than their husband. Men and women do not mix during prayer because it is felt that the presence of the opposite sex could be distracting. Orthodox Judaism regards practices and activities in terms of duties and obligations, not in terms of equal rights for women. In the modern sense, most Orthodox synagogues do not claim to be egalitarian.

In the past thirty years, Conservative Judaism has changed its views on women's participation in the synagogue. Although these policies may vary by congregation, women may now publicly read the Torah, be part of a *minyan*, be called to the Torah, be ordained as a rabbi, serve as a cantor, and wear a tallis and tefillin.

The Reform movement believes in the equality of men and women and has introduced alternative mitzvoth and rituals to address the religious needs of women. Reform also allows women to initiate divorce.

Check Your Understanding

1. What are the four main divisions of Judaism?

2. What factors caused the Reform movement to emerge?

3. How do the four main denominations differ on the nature and interpretation of the Torah?

4. What event caused the emergence of the Conservative movement, and why?

5. How do the denominations regard the role and status of women within Judaism?

Skill Path Writing an Essay

For many people, the thought of writing a formal essay may be somewhat intimidating. However, if you liken essay writing to a more familiar experience, it may help you to approach the assignment more confidently. For example, think of a courtroom drama series on TV, then compare the process of writing an essay to the process that the "lawyer" in the series uses to defend a case in court. Of course, in your "case," the jury is the reader. Most of us are quite comfortable defending our point of view when necessary; essay writing is simply a more formal, written process.

An essay writer develops a thesis from a key question on a particular topic. A **thesis** is essentially an argument that you intend to prove, and the essay provides the platform for making that argument. In order to write an effective essay, you must know your topic thoroughly and carefully formulate your ideas. It is advisable to do your thinking and planning well in advance so that you can present your argument logically.

Steps in Writing an Essay

When developing your essay, follow the guidelines below, but remember that each essay topic requires a slightly different approach.

1. Analyze the question.
Read the essay question very carefully, highlighting keywords or phrases.

2. Conduct your research carefully.
Refer to the On-Line Research Skill Path on pages 104 to 105, the Qualitative Research Skill Path on pages 175 to 176, and the Quantitative Research Skill Path on pages 152 to 153 for further information.

3. Identify key points.
Make a list of the key points that you will need to explore in the essay. As a general guideline, plan on writing one paragraph per point. Arrange the points in some logical order, for example, from general to specific. Make sure that you use the results of your research to support and/or expand on these points.

4. Use graphic organizers.
Use web diagrams, T-charts, or cards to help organize and arrange your ideas. If you are examining two sides of an argument, consider arranging your thoughts in a Venn diagram. Be creative! You may wish to develop new ways of organizing your ideas by inventing your own graphic organizer.

A Venn diagram is useful for comparing arguments and determining elements they hold in common.

5. Write the first draft.
An essay assignment usually includes instructions about length, for example, "Write a 1000-word essay on . . ." The structure of the essay often depends on the essay question. Although each topic requires a different approach, there are some basic structural elements that are common to all essays:

Introduction

- Start with a statement that hooks the reader and provides a context for the essay question.
- Introduce the reader to the topic, and refer to the essay question, as well as to your previously highlighted keywords and ideas (Steps 1 and 3).
- Make sure that you clearly state your thesis, usually in the last sentence of the first paragraph.

Body

- Work through the topics from the list or diagram that you created in Step 4.
- If your essay question requires that you examine two sides of an argument, consider one of these suggestions:

i) present all points for side A, providing supporting ideas and evidence. Then follow the same procedure for side B.

ii) create an organizer that shows the points for each side of the question. Work through the points one at a time for each side, that is, present a point for side A, then respond with the counterpoint from side B.

- Remember to maintain your focus. However, you may find that you have to explore a side issue. Sometimes these side issues support your main argument, while others offer alternative views or exceptions. Find ways of inserting these side issues effectively, without confusing the flow of your ideas.

Conclusion

- Summarize your most important points and state your conclusion. You may wish to restate some keywords or phrases.
- Clearly restate your thesis, usually in the first sentence of the last paragraph.
- Be clear and concise.

6. Edit and revise.

Remember that your first draft is not the final product. A "rough draft" always leads to the important "middle" stage where you can improve your work, for example, change ideas or delete items altogether. You may wish to work with a partner so that you can edit each other's material and provide suggestions for improvement. Also consult with your teacher about possible revisions. When checking either your own material or a partner's, consider the following:

- Is it generally easy to understand?
- Has the essay question been answered?
- Is there a logical flow to the argument?
- Are the facts accurate?
- Are quotations used effectively?
- Are there better ways to word a sentence?

PRACTISE IT!

1. Write an essay comparing and contrasting two branches of Judaism with specific reference to their origins and development, central beliefs, and practices.
2. Outline the historical origins of anti-Semitism.

Credit Your Sources!
Any sources from which you have selected quotations or taken ideas must be properly credited. You may refer to the following for information on how to cite sources:

- *The Canadian Style: A Guide to Writing and Editing.* 2d. ed. (Toronto: Dundurn Press in co-operation with Public Works and Government Services Canada, 1997).
- *The Chicago Manual of Style*, 14th ed. (Chicago: The University of Chicago Press, 1993). http://www.press.uchicago.edu/Misc/Chicago/cmosfaq.html

Note: Using thoughts and ideas from others' work and failing (intentionally or unintentionally) to cite the source is known as plagiarism. Plagiarism is an academic crime that results in penalties such as automatic failure in a course or dismissal from the workplace. Remember: when in doubt, cite the source.

CULTURAL IMPACT

The story of Jewish history is more about struggle than easy triumph. The loss of and search for a homeland bracket nearly 2000 years of Jewish history. The tragedies and triumphs of the Jews marked most of the twentieth century. Much of Jewish history has been lived far from the sources of the faith, usually in territories controlled by the related, sometimes hostile, religions of Christianity and Islam. The marriage of history and faith is a potent and defining theme in Judaism.

The Sources of Anti-Semitism

Why were adherents of Judaism the target of hatred and prejudice over so many centuries? The answers are complex, but they serve as a warning about the rekindling of such powerful, unreasoned hatred in our own society today, whether aimed at Jews or any other group.

- Lacking a homeland and forced to live in widely scattered communities as a small group, Jews were the perennial outsiders.
- With very different religious customs and clothing style, the Jews were seen as strange, different, and untrustworthy.

Jewish Nobel Prize Winners

Whether it is a result of centuries of historical challenge, the Judaic focus on the world, or the support of a closely knit community, members of the Jewish faith have attained pinnacles of achievement in proportions far beyond their relatively small numbers. One small example of the creativity and impact of Judaism is reflected in the number of Jews who have been awarded the Nobel Prize. The following is only a sample:

Name	Field
Albert Einstein	Science
Elie Wiesel	Peace
Niels Bohr	Physics
Milton Friedman	Economics
Yitzhak Rabin	Peace
Isaac Bashevis Singer	Literature
Nadine Gordimer	Literature
Saul Bellow (born in Canada)	Literature
Lev Landau	Physics
Franco Modligliani	Economics
Hans Bethe	Physics
Stanley Cohen	Medicine
David Lee	Physics
Harold Kroto	Chemistry

- Their interpretation of the Bible led some Christians to blame all Jews for the brutal murder of their saviour, Jesus Christ. Attacks on Jews were often heightened during Easter. This belief has deep roots and is harboured by a small minority of extremists, even today.
- Since Jews were frequently forbidden to own land or hold citizenship, they were often on the move and had little opportunity to establish themselves as integral members of communities.
- When calamities befell nations or communities, it was common to blame the Jews and use them as scapegoats for every real or imagined problem.
- In the Middle Ages, Christians, at times, were not allowed to lend money and charge interest; when Jews did this work, they were accused of being cheats and thieves who earned a dishonest living.
- Later, when Jews received more freedoms and liberties in Europe and began to earn success in a number of fields, they were viewed with jealousy and suspicion.

Zionism

In 1896, Theodore Herzl wrote about the need for a state where Jews could truly be at home and enjoy freedom from harassment. In 1897, the World Zionist Organization was founded, and the modern struggle to reclaim the Promised Land and build a Jewish state was launched. **Zionism** is the idea and promise of the return of the people of Israel to the Promised Land. The coming twentieth century would see the fulfillment of the Zionist dream, but not before Jews faced the horrors of the Second World War and the bloody, continuing struggle to find peace in the Middle East. Zion was a dream that would be paid for in blood by both Jews and non-Jews.

The Twentieth Century

In Jewish history, the twentieth century is marked by two events of shattering magnitude and importance: the **Shoah**, or **Holocaust**, and the birth of the State of Israel. For a small community with such a long and troubled history, the twentieth century was a series of momentous, emotional events. The cultural impact of these two defining moments on both the world and Jewry continues to shape the modern world.

Perhaps the most notorious event of the twentieth century, the Holocaust (Figure 6.23) resulted in the calculated slaughter of 6 million Jews—one-half of European Jewry and one-third of world Jewry. Only the defeat of Hitler's Germany stopped the massacre. The opening of the death camps at the end of the war shocked the world, and a new term, **crimes against humanity**, was created to describe the horror.

One of the most direct and dramatic results of the Holocaust was the renewed push by Jews who survived the Holocaust to live the Zionist dream. By 1948, with increasing international support and by force of arms, the State of Israel was reborn out of Palestine. However, in the 2000 years since the Diaspora, other peoples had inhabited the region and were not ready to accept being displaced and disenfranchised by the return of the Jews. This tragic situation has resulted in continuing warfare and atrocities in the region. At times, the world itself has been brought to the brink of war because of national and religious strife in the Middle East. The tragedy of the region is that reconciliation and peace seem far away, even unattainable.

Judaism in Canada

Judaism has a long history in Canada, and Jews have had a long struggle to be accepted and treated equally. Today, the Jewish community in Canada is thriving and is an important contributor to Canadian society. The largest communities are in Toronto and Montreal.

Jews arrived on Canadian shores with the creation of New France. The first synagogue was founded in Montreal in 1768, long before Canada was a nation. By 1882, the city had three synagogues. According to the Canadian Jewish Congress, the largest wave of Jewish immigration came at the turn of the twentieth century. However, as with so many other newcomers to Canadian shores, some Jewish Canadians faced rejection and hostility (Figure 6.25). Although anti-Semitism in Canada was not like that suffered by Jews in Europe, for a country which prides itself on its multicultural roots and tolerance, Canadian history is not without the stains of prejudice and discrimination.

Figure 6.23
Aba Bayevsky's paintings of the Nazi death camps are profoundly moving. Some Jews believe that the Holocaust was both a test of faith for Jews and a commandment from God to survive.

Figure 6.24
Charles Bronfman is founding partner of birthright israel, a worldwide project that provides the gift of a first trip to Israel for Jewish youth. The organization believes it is every Jewish person's "birthright" to have the opportunity to visit Israel. Through his CRB Foundation, Bronfman has provided a challenge grant of up to $25 million to Historica, a new foundation dedicated to increasing awareness of Canada's history and people.

Figure 6.25

In 1933, a riot broke out at Toronto's Christie Pits playing field after a Nazi swastika banner was unfurled at a baseball game involving Jewish players. This scene is from the 1996 television documentary "The Riot at Christie Pitts."

Anti-Semitism

The 1930s

The tough times of the Great Depression spawned many hate groups eager to find targets to blame for the social and economic misery of the period. Several tiny Fascist parties were organized in Canada, and they imitated the Fascists in Europe with uniforms and cries of hate. The most powerful organization, the National Unity Party, was led by Adrien Arcand, a fanatical imitator of Hitler and the Nazis. Arcand was a virulent anti-Semite, who used his publishing house to spread his ideas. After the outbreak of the Second World War, Canadian Fascist organizations were made illegal, their newspapers suppressed, and Arcand was interned for the duration of the war.

In June 1939, the ocean liner *St. Louis* appeared off the east coast of Canada carrying Jewish refugees who were fleeing from Nazi-threatened Europe. They had first sought asylum in Cuba and the United States but were refused entry. When they turned to Canada, the refugees were again denied entry. The Second World War broke out shortly after the ship returned to Europe, and about half of the 907 passengers later perished in the Holocaust. Although not all Canadian politicians were anti-Semitic, many feared anti-Semitic reaction against the Jews. The refusal to accept these refugees is one of Canada's saddest historical episodes.

The Post-War Period

When the true horrors of Hitler's campaign against the Jews were revealed by the discovery of the death camps, Canada and the world were more supportive of Jewish immigration and more concerned about the protection of human rights and the suppression of hate groups. Canada received a huge post-war wave of immigration that spurred the multiculturalism that we celebrate today, as well as our human rights legislation. The Canadian Charter of Rights and Freedoms has enshrined many of the fundamental rights of Canadians. Most provinces have organized police and legal forces that combat crimes of hate. Canada is a far more tolerant and vigilant society than it was in the past. However, it is also true that each generation must be prepared to eradicate crimes of hate against any group of Canadians.

Fighting Anti-Semitism

Seven of Canada's provinces have passed legislation that marks Yom Hashoah, or Holocaust Remembrance Day, as an official day on the provincial calendar. The purpose is not simply to commemorate the terrible tragedy of the Holocaust, but also to promote increased awareness of the true nature of social evils such as racism, anti-Semitism, prejudice, and discrimination. Given the multicultural nature of Canadian society and the general Canadian support for tolerance, this day signals the continued concern Canadians express about prejudice. Held sometime in April, the day is observed across Canada, with many students participating in special educational activities.

Holocaust Education Week usually takes place in the fall and features a range of educational programs for students and the general public. Events are organized throughout Canada to educate Canadians about the Holocaust and to make sure that this brutal reality is never forgotten or denied.

Check Your Understanding

1. What evidence is there that anti-Semitism has deep historical roots?

2. Briefly describe the two most important events in twentieth-century Jewish history.

3. What specific evidence exists that some Canadians practised anti-Semitism during the 1930s?

4. How is Canada combating anti-Semitism today?

5. How do you personally respond when you see examples of prejudice and discrimination?

Community Study

Beth Tzedec Congregation
Toronto, Ontario

Figure 6.26
The sanctuary of Beth Tzedec Synagogue

Beth Tzedec was founded in 1952 by the amalgamation of two much older Jewish congregations, Goel Tzedec and Beth Hamidrash Hagadol. The synagogue was dedicated on 9 December 1955. With a congregation of 3000 families, Beth Tzedec is the largest Conservative congregation in North America. It is also multigenerational, comprising four generations—a fact that enriches the community immensely.

Beth Tzedec has a fivefold goal: to build an affirmative Judaism, to bring the miracle of the Bible into everyday lives, to cultivate a love of the Jewish tradition, to inspire respect for religious life, and to promote religious affinity among the congregation. In addition to serving the religious needs of the community, Beth Tzedec addresses two other very important areas: education and service to the community.

Hebrew education is seen as the foundation of the community's religious structure, and religious living is considered the aim of the Beth Tzedec educational program. Its objectives are to teach members the value of Jewish traditions and the

Figure 6.27 *Rabbi Baruch Frydman-Kohl*

importance of practising them. There are three parts to the educational program: the day school, which runs a full K–9 program for approximately 400 students; an after-school program, which teaches Hebrew studies to 250 students; and an adult-education program, with Bible-study and Jewish culture classes. In addition to classroom activities, school assemblies and children's services are held in the Youth Chapel. The synagogue also houses a museum, which has an impressive collection of **Judaica** and is open to the public.

Service to the community is called *hesed*, a Hebrew word meaning "loving kindness" or "justice." The Hesed Committee, made up of members of Beth Tzedec, looks after home and hospital visits, bereavement calls, and rides to the synagogue, and ensures that seniors are cared for and their rights are protected. Members of the congregation who know of someone who needs help can call the (confidential) Hesed Hotline.

Rabbi Baruch Frydman-Kohl became senior rabbi of the Beth Tzedec congregation in 1993. He emphasizes the need for everyone to be involved in Jewish life, and has a deep commitment to the provision of hesed to people who are sick, shut in, or bereaved. Since coming to the congregation, Rabbi Frydman-Kohl has "opened up" synagogue services to encourage more participation and has furthered the development of educational programs. In addition to his duties at Beth Tzedec, he is director of the Greater Toronto Jewish Federation. In 1992, the Association for Religion and Intellectual Life awarded him a Coolidge Fellowship to pursue research at the Divinity School at Harvard University.

Questions

1. What is the goal of the Beth Tzedec congregation?

2. Why is education stressed so much?

3. What does the Hesed Committee reveal about the Beth Tzedec congregation?

4. What changes has Rabbi Frydman-Kohl made to the operation of the Beth Tzedec congregation?

Exploring Issues:
Nazi War Criminals in Canada

While the majority of Canadians are clearly opposed to racism, prejudice, and the ideology of Fascism, many wish that these atrocities could be consigned to the dustbin of history. They are often surprised that people who committed crimes against humanity were admitted into Canada during the post-war immigration boom. These suspected war criminals have lived a life of comfort and freedom that they so cruelly denied to others in the Second World War. Clearly, many have died or are old and infirm. Some have led exemplary lives in Canada, working hard, raising a family, and being solid members of the community. Most of their neighbours, and even close family members, are unaware of their bloody past. Some Canadians believe that "the past is the past," and that these people should be left alone to finish out their lives and not be punished for crimes committed far away over fifty years ago.

On the other hand, these war criminals often lied or covered up their true identities when they came to Canada. They participated in crimes against humanity that saw millions of innocent people tortured and murdered. Have they "gotten away with murder"? In 1987, the Canadian government passed a law permitting the arrest and trial of war criminals in Canada. The War Crimes Unit was organized to track down these criminals and launch legal action against them, or transfer them to countries where they are still wanted. This unit was given $50 million in 1998 to strengthen and speed up investigations. However, it is a difficult process because the individuals have changed so much, and witnesses have died or their memories are not what they were. Trials can be long, difficult, and costly. Families and communities are often shocked and upset with the process. Some think the hunt for war criminals should stop; others believe that the only way to achieve even a limited justice for the victims is to bring their killers to trial.

This process is also part of the ongoing attempt to expose crimes of hate and **genocide** as one of the most despicable crimes. In fact, one result has been that Canada has pledged to bring to justice any Canadian citizen or resident suspected of war crimes in any part of the world. In 1997, it was reported that more than 300 suspected modern-day war criminals are living in Canada. Their alleged crimes were committed in places such as Rwanda, Vietnam, Cambodia the former Yugoslavia, Ethiopia, and Central America. Canadian immigration procedures have been tightened in order to prevent such undesirables from gaining entry into Canada and then seeking the protection of the Canadian justice system—actions that can make retribution a long, slow, difficult process.

QUESTIONS

1. **What arguments are there for continuing and for ending the search for and punishment of Nazi war criminals living in Canada?**

2. **If you found out that a senior citizen living on your street was suspected of committing war crimes during the Second World War, what would you do? Explain fully.**

Activities

Check Your Understanding

1. What was the nature of the covenant that God made with Abraham and Moses?

2. What was the impact of the Exile on Judaism?

3. Briefly describe the contributions of the rabbinic movement to Judaism.

4. What are the main sources of anti-Semitism?

Think and Communicate

5. Working in small groups, describe an "Exodus event" (a time when you felt you were making a new start) in your own life.

6. Which of the Ten Commandments do you think is the most difficult to follow? Explain.

7. In your opinion, how far should a religion go in making changes to its practices in order to keep up with changes in modern society? Write a brief opinion paper.

8. Judaism is seen as a religion by some people but also as a culture and a nationality by others. Prepare a position so that you can participate in a class discussion on this issue. Your answer does not necessarily have to be one of the above; you might want to argue that Judaism is a combination of two or three of these elements.

9. Working in small teams, design an ad campaign to remind people in your community about Holocaust Education Week. You might design radio ads, brochures, posters, and so on. Carefully choose and discuss your goals, and then create an effective campaign.

10. a) What do you think are the advantages and disadvantages of marrying someone of your own religion?
b) Would it be important to you to marry someone who is of the same religion? Why?
c) How do you think your family would react if you married someone who was of a different religion?

11. One of the Ten Commandments is, "Honour your father and mother." Evaluate how well you personally follow this Commandment and how useful a rule it is in your life.

Apply Your Learning

12. Using the Internet and the print media, research in detail Birthright Israel. For example: What are its goals? Who is eligible to go to Israel? How is the organization financed? Has it been successful? Are there any personal stories from people who have participated? How did they feel about the experience? What is your personal evaluation of the program?

13. Working with a partner, draw up a modern version of the Ten Commandments that you think today's Canadians could use to guide their conduct. How similar are your suggestions to the original Ten Commandments? Explain.

14. Contact your local police force and ask for information about hate crimes in your area and how you can help eradicate them. Consider inviting a member of the Hate Crimes Unit to visit your school to present a program.

15. Compose an essay on the history of the Middle East conflict, using the suggestions provided in this chapter's Skill Path feature. What lessons does this conflict reveal? Do you have any ideas for a workable solution to this tragic crisis? Explain.

Glossary

aliyah [olly AH]. Literally "going up," immigrating to Israel; generally referred to in English as "making aliyah."

anti-Semitism. Hostility and prejudice toward Jews.

Ark of the Covenant. The wooden chest that held the tablets inscribed with the Ten Commandments. The temple in Jerusalem became the home of the Ark.

bar/bat mitzvah [bar (or bat) MITS-VA]. The religious initiation ceremony of a Jewish boy who has reached the age of thirteen/a Jewish girl who has reached the age of twelve or thirteen. The term means "son/daughter of the commandment."

chosen people. The idea that God chose the Jewish people to be the keepers of his covenant on earth. The concept of "chosen" is reciprocal, with God choosing humanity and humanity choosing God.

circumcision. The cutting off of the foreskin of the penis. Abraham and his family were the first to be circumcised as a sign of the covenant.

covenant. As used in the Bible, a solemn and binding agreement between God and humanity.

crimes against humanity. Murder, extermination, enslavement, deportation, persecution, or any other inhumane act committed against a civilian population or any other identifiable group.

Diaspora [die ASPER uh]. A Greek word meaning "sowing of seed" or "dispersal." In the context of Jewish history, *Diaspora* is the word used when referring to the Jewish population living outside of Israel.

Exodus. The significant event in which Moses led the Israelites out of bondage in Egypt to freedom in the Promised Land. The word *exodus* means "going out" or "departure."

genocide. The mass extermination of a group of people, especially a race, religious group, or nation.

gerut [ger OOT]. The process of conversion to Judaism.

ghetto. An area of a city in which minority groups such as Jews were required to live. The first was in Venice in 1516.

Haggadah [ha GA dah]. The book used to explain the events of the Exodus.

Hanukkah [HONNA kuh]. The eight-day festival of lights, usually in December, commemorating the rededication of the temple.

Hellenization. The process of adopting Greek culture and language.

Holocaust. The mass murder of 6 million Jews by the Nazis during the Second World War.

Holy Ark. A cabinet-like structure in a synagogue that houses the Torah scrolls.

Judaica. The literature, customs, ritual objects, artifacts, etc., which are of particular relevance to Judaism.

kiddush [KID oosh]. A blessing recited when people drink wine that has been specially sanctified for the Sabbath or a holy day.

kippah **[KIPPA].** A small circular cap worn by Jewish men; also known as a yarmulke.

kosher [CO sher]. Fulfilling the requirements of the Jewish dietary laws of Kashruth.

menorah [men ORE   uh]. A candelabrum with seven branches, used at home and in the synagogue on the Sabbath and holidays.

Messiah [muh SIGH uh]. Means "anointed one." The Jews hope that a great king will come to lead them.

Midrash [MID rash]. Interpretation and commentary on the Bible. By 100 CE, the rabbis had compiled a sizable body of commentary on the Bible.

minyan **[MIN yun].** The quorum of ten men (or men and women) over thirteen years of age required for worship.

Mishnah [MISH nuh]. Early rabbinic teachings on how to live a life in accordance with the Torah. It was compiled around 200 CE.

mitzvah [MITS vuh]. A commandment from God; the act of performing a good deed. The most well known mitzvoth are the Ten Commandments.

monotheistic. Believing in only one God.

Pesach [PAY sack]. The Passover festival in spring commemorating the liberation of the Israelites from slavery in Egypt.

Promised Land. The area of Canaan that the Hebrews believed was promised to them by God.

prophet. A person who receives a message from God and delivers that message to God's people. The message belongs to God, with the prophet acting as God's messenger.

rabbi. A Jewish scholar or teacher, especially of the law; a person appointed as a Jewish religious leader.

Rosh Hashanah [rosh huh SHONNA]. The festival celebrating the Jewish New Year.

Seder [SAY dur]. A ritual service and ceremonial dinner for the first night or first two nights of Passover.

Sefer Torah [SAY fur TORE uh]. The text of the five books of Moses handwritten on parchment. It is the most sacred object of Jewish life and is essential for worship.

shiva [SHIVVA]. A seven-day period of mourning for the dead beginning immediately after the funeral.

Shoah [SHOW ah]. A Hebrew term for the Holocaust meaning "destruction."

shofar [SHOW fur]. A trumpet made of a ram's horn, used in religious ceremonies.

Star of David. A figure consisting of two interlaced equilateral triangles. It is used as a Jewish and Israeli symbol.

synagogue [SINNA gog]. A place for congregational worship that emerged during the Exile and became important in the period after the destruction of the temples in 586 BCE and 70 CE. Synagogues continue to be the central place of worship for Jews today.

tallis [TAL iss]. A prayer shawl.

Talmud [TAL mud]. Rabbinic teachings derived from the Mishnah. It is the main source of Jewish teaching from the medieval period to the present.

Tanakh [tuh NOCK]. The Jewish Bible, consisting of the Torah (the Law of Moses), the Prophets, and the Writings.

tefillin [tuh FILL in]. Either of two small leather boxes containing parchment scrolls of Biblical text, worn by Jewish men during morning prayer, except on the Sabbath.

Torah [TORE uh]. Refers to the Law of Moses as well as the rest of the Hebrew Scriptures and the entire belief system of the Jewish faith. The word *Torah* is often translated as meaning "law," but a more accurate translation is "teaching" or "instruction."

Western Wall. The remaining part of the wall of Herod's temple in Jerusalem where Jews traditionally pray and lament on Fridays.

yarmulke [YAR mull kuh]. A small circular cap worn by Jewish men; also known as a *kippah*.

Yom Kippur [yom ki POOR]. The most solemn religious day of the Jewish year, marked by fasting and prayers of repentence.

Zionism [ZYE in ism]. A movement originally for the re-establishment of a Jewish nation, and now for the development of a Jewish nation in what is now Israel.

"When they came to the place that is called The Skull, there they crucified him, along with the criminals—one on his right, the other on his left. . .One of the criminals who hung there hurled insults at him: "Are you not the Christ? Save yourself and us!" But the other criminal rebuked him. "Do you not fear God," he said, "since you are under the same sentence? We are punished justly, for we are getting what our deeds deserve. But this man has done nothing wrong." Then he said, "Jesus, remember me when you come into your kingdom." Jesus answered him, "I tell you the truth, today you will be with me in paradise."

Luke 23: 33-43 (NIV)

This image was taken in Quebec near Percé Rock on the Gaspé Peninsula. When Jacques Cartier landed in North America in 1534, he erected a cross in this area to claim the land for France. There has been a strong Catholic presence in this region since the time of the early French settlers who later followed Cartier.

Chapter Seven

Christianity 7

Study the photograph, and read the accompanying passage from the Bible. Consider the following questions:

1. Describe the setting of the photograph. What mood does the photograph create?
2. What is the significance of the cross shown in the picture? What does it represent?
3. What impressions do you get about Jesus Christ from the quotation?
4. How is the Crucifixion commemorated by Christians?

Introduction

Approximately one-third of the world's people consider themselves Christians, and they live on every habitable continent of the earth. Christianity, which originated in present-day Israel approximately 2000 years ago, exists in a variety of forms, including Eastern Orthodoxy, Roman Catholicism, and Protestantism. Worldwide, Christians continue to grow in numbers, despite constant division and reform. What accounts for the enduring power of this world religion?

Christianity offers both a satisfying way of life on earth, and the hope of eternal life in heaven. Christians believe that these promises were made possible by Jesus Christ, from whom the religion derives its name. Followers of Jesus believe that he is the incarnate son of God and saviour of the world. During his ministry on earth, Jesus taught people that they must love one another and practise compassion and forgiveness. This principle of love, which Jesus called "a new commandment," is central to the Christian religion. Christians also believe that Jesus died on the cross to atone for human sin, that is to "save" them. This salvation offers the possibility of everlasting life with God in heaven.

Christianity is still the religion of the majority of Canadians and is closely connected to Canadian history. Much of the settlement and early exploration of Canada was carried out by Christian missionaries, particularly in the establishment of New France. Some early political struggles in Canadian history were fought between Protestant and Catholic Christians. Today, while Canada is clearly a nation of many cultures and faiths, Christianity is still a central part of many Canadians' lives.

Learning Goals

At the end of this chapter, you will be able to:

- identify the origins of Christian beliefs regarding creation, death, God, and the afterlife
- identify influences in the development of Christianity
- identify important figures in the growth of Christianity, and explain their contributions
- evaluate the importance of such concepts as revelation, resurrection, and salvation
- understand the development of Christian institutions that govern the religious lives of Christians
- understand differences in beliefs, symbols, and practices among different Christian sects
- identify the origins, characteristics, and significant passages of the Bible's New Testament
- analyze the changing role of women in Christian institutions, practices, and sacred writings
- identify the origin and significance of Christian practices, rituals, symbols, and festivals
- understand the meanings of symbols in Christianity and their connection to practices
- identify ways in which Christian symbols are incorporated into civil practices
- identify that Canada is a diverse society with a high degree of religious pluralism
- describe how individuals have been influenced by the beliefs of Christianity to challenge the status quo of their day
- identify important rites of passage in the life of a Christian person, and understand the symbols, art, and literature associated with each
- conduct an in-depth interview using an appropriate interview format

●325 CE Council of Nicaea codifies Christian beliefs in the Nicene Creed

●50–67 CE (approximately) Paul carries Christianity into Asia Minor and Rome and writes many of the Epistles of the New Testament

●1054 CE Schism divides the Eastern Orthodox and Roman Churches

●30 CE (approximately) Crucifixion of Jesus by Roman soldiers

●70–100 CE (approximately) Mark, Matthew, Luke, and John write the four gospels of the New Testament

●4 BCE (approximately) Birth of Jesus

• **2001 CE** Organizers plan for World Youth Day when up to 750 000 young people will visit Toronto in July 2002

• **1962–1965 CE** Second Vatican Council reforms practices of the Roman Catholic Church

• **1984 CE** Pope John Paul II tours Canada

• **1870 CE** First Vatican Council declares pope infallible in matters of faith and morals

• **1925 CE** Methodists, Congregationalists, and many Presbyterians merge to form United Church of Canada

• **1517 CE** Martin Luther leads the Protestant Reformation (Lutheran Church begins)

• **1534 CE** King Henry VIII and Parliament establish the Church of England (called Anglican Church in Canada)

• **1095 CE** First of several Crusades begins

Timeline

Christianity

Figure 7.1
Christianity originated in present-day Israel approximately 2000 years ago. How is Christianity linked to Judaism?

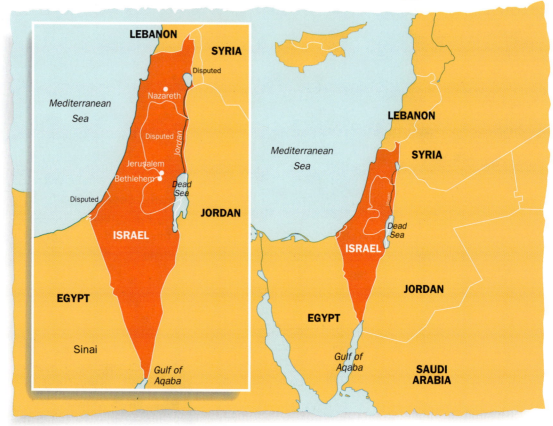

ORIGINS

Christianity must be examined in the context of its Jewish heritage. As discussed in the previous chapter, Judaism is a monotheistic religion, whose principles are based on the belief that there is only one God. According to the Judaic tradition, God created the universe and everything in it, including human beings. Through many different prophets, God promised to send a Messiah, or saviour. According to Christians, the **Messiah** was Jesus Christ, who they believe to be the son of God.

Information about Jesus Christ comes mainly from Christian followers, as well as Roman and Jewish historians and officials, and was circulated in the oral tradition until it was recorded in writing from one to three generations after his death. The source that provides the most detailed information on the life of Jesus is the New Testament of the Bible, specifically the first four books, known as the **Gospels**, or "good news" of Matthew, Mark, Luke, and John.

The Early Life of Jesus

In the reign of Caesar Augustus (31 BCE–14 CE), the Roman Empire had expanded into the region of present-day Israel (Figure 7.1), then known as Palestine. Most biblical scholars believe that Jesus was born around 4 BCE in Bethlehem. According to Christian scriptures, Jesus was conceived by the power of the Holy Spirit in the womb of a virgin named Mary, who was betrothed to Joseph. At the time of Jesus' birth, Caesar Augustus had ordered a census of the Roman empire, requiring that people travel to the town in which they were born to be recorded in the totals. Mary and Joseph came to Bethlehem, Joseph's birthplace, to register for the census. Because they could not find a place to stay, they took shelter in a stable. Mary gave birth to Jesus in the stable and placed him in a manger (Figure 7.2). Nearby, an angel appeared to shepherds who were tending their sheep, and announced the birth of Jesus:

And there were shepherds living out in the fields nearby, keeping watch over their flocks at night. An angel of the Lord appeared to them, and the glory of the Lord shone around them, and they were terrified. But the angel said to them, "Do not be afraid. I bring you good news of great joy that will be for all the people. Today in the town of David a Saviour has been born to you; he is Christ the Lord."

Luke 2: 8-11 (NIV)

The shepherds spread the news of Jesus' birth and went to worship him. These details on the birth of Jesus appear in the gospel of Luke (2:1-20). Other details on the birth of Jesus appear in the gospel of Matthew. According to Matthew's gospel, three Magi, or wise men, from the East followed a star that led them to the site where Jesus was born:

When they saw the star, they were overjoyed. On coming to the house, they saw the child with his mother Mary, and they bowed down and worshipped him. Then they opened their treasures and presented him with gifts of gold and of incense and of myrrh.

Matthew 2: 10-11 (NIV)

Little is known about Jesus' early life. His family settled in Nazareth, a town in Galilee, located in the northern part of present-day Israel. Jesus of Nazareth was a carpenter's son, and probably lacked any formal education.

Figure 7.2
This painting by Sandro Botticelli, entitled Mystic Nativity, *shows the birth of Jesus. What qualities of this birth are highlighted by the artist?*

The Baptism of Jesus

According to Christian scriptures, a prophet named John the Baptist was to prepare the way for Jesus. John immersed his followers in a river in ritual **baptism**, to wash away their sins. When Jesus came to the Jordan River to be baptized, John realized who he was and told him that Jesus should be baptizing him. After John baptized Jesus, the **Holy Spirit**, which is considered by Christians to be the life-giving presence of God, came to Jesus:

> *As soon as Jesus was baptized, he went up out of the water. At that moment heaven was opened, and he saw the Spirit of God descending like a dove and lighting on him. And a voice from heaven said, "This is my Son, whom I love; with him I am well pleased."*
>
> Matthew 3:16-17 (NIV)

Jesus' Ministry

Jesus retreated to the desert for forty days, where he fasted and was tempted by the devil. He was approximately thirty years old when he returned to the region of Galilee and began preaching in the synagogues. Although Jesus preached from a Jewish perspective, his message challenged accepted views, and was not popular in all religious circles.

Jesus gathered around him a group of **disciples**, or spiritual apprentices, and taught in smaller communities, and in large outdoor gatherings. Jesus moved comfortably among the common people and the outcasts of society. He urged people to love their neighbours and their enemies alike, and to forgive wrongs of others. He counselled and forgave even the most sinful and despised members of society. In the gospel of John, he saves a woman accused of adultery from death by stoning.

The gospels describe spectacular works, called miracles, by Jesus during his ministry. For example, Jesus changed water into wine at the wedding feast of Cana and multiplied fish and loaves of bread by the Sea of Galilee. His touch healed the faithful, including people with leprosy, the blind, and those with other afflictions. Often, Jesus spoke in **parables**, or vivid moral stories drawn from situations in life (see page 292). He used parables to emphasize values and teach lessons.

The Arrest of Jesus

As Jesus' following grew in number, so did his religious and political enemies. He strongly criticized the Pharisees—a Jewish sect who followed strict rules of dietary and ritual purity. The Jewish Sanhedrin, the governing council under Roman rule, worried that Jesus might be dangerous to them. They feared that their Roman masters might accuse the council of not maintaining a tight social order in conquered Israel. Jesus was seen as the son of God, which was considered blasphemous by religious authorities.

During Passover, in the third year of his public life, Jesus entered Jerusalem and was welcomed by the crowds who rushed to meet him with palm branches. However, religious authorities were planning his arrest. Soon after his entry into Jerusalem,

Jesus shared his last meal, the Passover meal, with his twelve **apostles**, who were his closest disciples. This event is known as the **Last Supper**. After the meal, while Jesus was praying in an olive grove, several officials consisting of religious authorities and soldiers, made their way towards him. They were led by Judas, one of Jesus' apostles, who had betrayed him.

Jesus was arrested and charged by the Sanhedrin with blasphemy, the showing of contempt for God by attributing God-like qualities to that which is not God. The council found Jesus guilty because he would not deny that he was the Messiah, or that he was God's son. They turned him over to the Roman governor, Pontius Pilate, for sentencing, but Pilate could find no fault with the prisoner. However, he bowed to the demands of the crowd, and ordered that Jesus be crucified, or nailed to a wooden cross, a method of execution that the Romans favoured to provoke fear among conquered nations.

The Death and Resurrection of Jesus

The gospels report that soldiers led Jesus to the Place of the Skull, where he was to be crucified. They made him carry the heavy cross, while many of his female disciples followed him mourning and wailing. The soldiers nailed Jesus to the wooden cross and hung a sign on it that read: This Is the King of the Jews. Jesus died on the cross that afternoon in the presence of his mother Mary and many of his female disciples, including Mary Magdalene. This event is called the **Crucifixion**, which Christians believe brought about the forgiveness of sins and the promise of eternal life (Figure 7.3).

According to Christian scriptures, Jesus' body was placed in a tomb cut out of rock. Three days after his death, Mary Magdalene, accompanied by other female disciples, went to the tomb to anoint Jesus' body with spices. When they arrived, Jesus' body was gone. An angel appeared and told them that Jesus had risen from the dead. Jesus appeared to the women and several of his followers during the days that followed. Christians call his return from the dead the **Resurrection**.

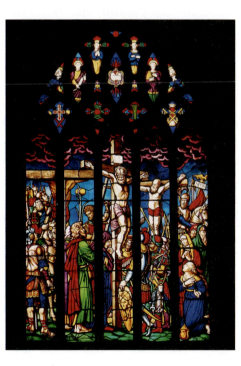

Figure 7.3
This stained-glass window representation of the Crucifixion adorns Leigh Delamere Church in Wiltshire, England. What is the significance of the Crucifixion to Christians?

The Ascension of Jesus

As the resurrected Jesus visited with his apostles, he commissioned them to baptize all nations, and spread his teachings:

> *Then Jesus came to them and said, "All authority in heaven and on earth has been given to me. Therefore go and make disciples of all nations, baptizing them in the name of the Father and of the Son and of the Holy Spirit, and teaching them to obey everything I have commanded you. And surely I am with you always, to the very end of the age."*
>
> Matthew 28:18-20 (NIV)

Christians believe that forty days after the Resurrection, Jesus ascended bodily to heaven. This event, termed the **Ascension**, ended his time on earth, and initiated two millennia of Christianity.

The Pentecost

Before the Crucifixion, Jesus had promised the apostles assistance in spreading the "good news" of his ministry: "And I will pray the Father, and he shall give you another comforter, that he may abide with you forever." (John 14:16) Christians believe that the comforter, the Holy Spirit, came on the feast that Christians call **Pentecost**, fifty days after Easter. It is believed that during this event, the Holy Spirit empowered the apostles with various spiritual gifts and abilities, including the ability to speak different languages. This enabled them to go into Jerusalem and proclaim their faith enthusiastically. Pentecost is often referred to as the birthday of the Church.

The Early Christians and the Persecutions

Some of the earliest converts to the apostles' message were Greeks, who took the name Christians, derived from Christos, which is Greek for "the Messiah." Within a generation of Jesus' death, an early missionary named Paul was actively carrying Christianity across the eastern corner of the Roman Empire. Paul spread Christianity to Cyprus, Asia Minor, Macedonia, and Greece. Paul, later called St. Paul, was so important to the development of Christianity that he is sometimes referred to as an apostle even though he was not one of the twelve original apostles of Jesus.

Both tolerance and peace encouraged the spread of Christianity. The Roman Empire was an economic arrangement supported by military power. As long as trade flowed easily along the vast road network focused on Rome, the emperor usually accepted cultural and religious differences. Rome's power resulted in relatively peaceful times, called the Pax Romana, during which Christianity multiplied rapidly. However, emperors who opposed the new religion, or sought someone to blame for the problems of their reign, sometimes persecuted Christians. Two centuries later, as Christianity flourished and the Roman Empire declined, the Emperors Decius, Valerian, and Diocletian ordered the destruction of churches, holy articles, and books. Christian **martyrs**, "witnesses" who died for their faith, were dragged to the Roman Colosseum, where they were mauled by wild animals before cheering crowds. During this period, Christians in Rome were forced to hold secret worship underground in the catacombs, or chambers where they buried their dead (Figure 7.4).

One of Diocletian's commanders, Constantine, became emperor himself, and moved the capital east to Byzantium, in modern-day Turkey. He legalized Christianity and was the first of many Christian rulers of the Roman Empire.

Figure 7.4
The Catacomb of Priscilla, in Rome, Italy, was the site of worship services by early Christians in the late second century. How were Christians persecuted?

Check Your Understanding

1. Explain the part played by each of the following in the life of Jesus:
a) Caesar Augustus
b) the Sanhedrin
c) Pontius Pilate

2. Outline factors that might help explain why the life of a good man ended in a cruel execution.

3. How did conditions during the Roman Empire both help and hinder the spread of early Christianity?

4. If it were possible to interview Jesus Christ today, what questions would you ask him? Why?

BELIEFS

Within a few generations of Jesus Christ's crucifixion, Christian communities had developed from the Middle East to Greece and Rome. In 325 CE, Emperor Constantine presided over a very important council of 300 Christian Church leaders at Nicaea, in modern-day Turkey, to settle several significant principles of the faith. This meeting produced the Nicene Creed, a statement of beliefs universally accepted by Christianity today. Although the Nicene Creed outlines the basic beliefs shared by most Christians, many differences of opinion exist among the various Christian denominations regarding some of these beliefs. These differences are discussed in the Groups and Institutions section of this chapter (page 296). The following statements of Christian belief appear as the original Nicene Creed, established in 325 CE:

We believe in one God, the Father, the Almighty, maker of heaven and earth, of all things visible and invisible; and in one Lord Jesus Christ, the only begotten Son of God, begotten of the Father before all worlds, God of God, light of light, very God of very God, begotten not made, being of one substance with the Father; by whom all things were made, who for us men and for our salvation came down from heaven, and was made flesh by the Holy Spirit of the Virgin Mary, and was made man, and was crucified for us under Pontius Pilate. He suffered and was buried, and the third day he rose again according to the Scriptures, and ascended into heaven, and sits on the right hand of the Father; and he shall come again with glory to judge both the living and the dead; whose kingdom shall have no end. And we believe in the Holy Spirit, the Lord and giver of Life, who proceeds from the Father, who with the Father and the Son together is worshipped and glorified, who spoke by the prophets. And we believe in one holy catholic and apostolic church. We acknowledge one baptism for the forgiveness of sins. And we look for the Resurrection of the dead and the life of the world to come.

Creation

The opening of the Nicene Creed explains the basic Christian belief that the whole universe is God's creation. It does not say that one must believe that God created these things step-by-step during one week, as is described in Genesis, the first book of the Bible's Old Testament.

God

Christian belief in God is derived directly from Judaism. Both religions agree that there is one God, who is an all-good Creator, responsible for the universe and all that fills it. In both faiths, God is viewed not only as a Supreme Being who rules all creation, but also as a personal God, approachable by individuals through prayer. This God is merciful, forgiving, and chooses to be a friend to people. However, God does command authority over all creation, including forces of evil. Overall, Christianity today focuses upon God's love for humanity, a love evidenced by Jesus Christ's suffering and death for the forgiveness of human sin.

The Holy Trinity

One of the issues that early Church leaders grappled with was the question of the Holy **Trinity**. While there may seem to be three different Gods in Christianity—the Father, his son Jesus, and the Holy Spirit—they are all bound together as one God in the Holy Trinity. Christians must believe that God the Father and God the son are one, and that Jesus Christ is God. There was a practical purpose to the Nicaean Council, for if Jesus was not

God, the framework of Christian doctrine would crumble, and the young Church would disintegrate. The Creed states that Jesus came down from heaven, one with God from the beginning of time. When he entered our world as a baby he became human; therefore, he was both fully human and fully divine.

The Holy Spirit

The Holy Spirit is believed to be the life-giving presence of God that helps Christians to live faithful lives and continue the work that Jesus began. Christians hold that the Holy Spirit enters into believers, dwelling there and energizing them, just as the apostles experienced at Pentecost.

Salvation and Eternal Life

Christians believe that Jesus was human, and that he suffered in his last days in order to accomplish the forgiveness of sin and human salvation. Ever since sin had entered the world, as described theologically by the story of Adam and Eve in the Old Testament, people had fallen far from harmony with God's will. Thus, Jesus' mission on earth was to bridge the gap between humanity and God, to bring about the forgiveness of sin, and to open the way to eternal life. The middle portion of the Nicene Creed outlines Christian beliefs surrounding the purpose of Christ's time on earth. The son of God came to give humans the opportunity to be "saved," that is, to attain eternal life in heaven after death (Figure 7.5).

Figure 7.5
This painting by Denis Maurice, entitled Paradise, *shows a representation of heaven. How does it reflect Christian beliefs regarding the afterlife?*

The Last Judgement

Perhaps one of the most interesting statements of the Nicene Creed is the Christian belief that Jesus will come back to earth. At that time, Jesus' purpose will be to make a **Last Judgement**, that is, to determine which humans will join him, body and soul, in heaven. This includes Christians who have died, for they will be risen from the dead to live eternally with God. In Christianity, a person is either rewarded with perfection in heaven, or punished with eternal suffering in hell, depending upon whether or not he or she has practised what Jesus taught during his ministry. This includes forgiveness, providing the poor with the basic necessities of life, and treating one another as you would like to be treated in return.

Exploring Issues:

Figure 7.6

Some people have strange ideas about the issue of cloning. They may originate from popular science fiction and comedy films, such as *Multiplicity*, in which a busy man gets clones made to help him with all of his responsibilities. People wonder if a clone would have to be born a baby or if he or she could be created as an exact duplicate of them, identical in every way, including age. Others picture a world populated with identical people, who are eerily perfect. A company called Clonaid promises that for $200 000 they can enable an individual to attain "eternal life." They have already arranged to clone the dead infant of an American couple, as soon as it becomes technologically possible.

How Cloning Works

Scientists begin with a fertilized egg of the species to be cloned. The nucleus of the egg is carefully removed, and is then replaced by a different cell nucleus taken from the clone donor. The donor could even be dead, provided that he or she has been cryogenically preserved (quickly frozen) immediately after death. The new egg is grown into an embryo, which contains "stem cells" that grow into body parts, such as bones, organs and skin. Medical scientists are mostly interested in cloning as a way to use stem cells to produce new organs and body parts as replacements for the donor if and when he or she needs them.

In 1997, researchers successfully cloned Dolly the sheep (Figure 7.6), and since then have cloned mice, pigs, cows, and most recently, a monkey. However, scientists have found that animal clones tend to suffer from a variety of physical abnormalities and genetic defects that might lead to psychological problems. Should researchers go any further with their experiments or are they playing God? And what about the potential of abusing this new technology: Could terrorists and dictators clone themselves? Would the rich have the ability to custom-design their children? Opinions on the issue vary widely.

Cloning human beings is an example of an ethical, or moral issue posed by modern science and technology. The capability to artificially reproduce human life by cloning is just around the corner.

At Issue: Should the cloning of human beings be permitted, or are we playing God?

The quotations that follow are excerpts from newspaper articles on the topic of human cloning.

"Cloning of the monkey has already been done. So the possibility of reproducing ourselves, humankind, within the next few years is really not a question of "whether" or "if you can," but a question of "who does it?"

Dr. Joseph Martin, Dean of Harvard University Medical School

"We believe that attempts to clone human beings at a time when the scientific issues of nuclear cloning have not been clarified are dangerous and irresponsible."

Rudolf Jaenisch, biologist, Massachusetts Institute of Technology

Human Cloning

"There is a push in the scientific world to go further in the field of biotechnology. But the church knows that there are deeper questions which must be asked about the impact of such technologies...we must be aware of the difference between arrogance and wisdom."

Phyllis Creighton, a Diocese of Toronto representative at the 1998 General Synod of the Anglican Church of Canada

"Who would be scandalized by the idea of bringing back to life a 10-month-old child who died accidentally? The technology allows it, the parents desire it, and I don't see any ethical problems."

Brigitte Boiseelier, chief scientist for Clonaid

QUESTIONS

1. a) Explain what Clonaid means when they state that "Cloning will enable mankind to reach eternal life."

   b) Why would Christians react in a negative way to this statement?

2. Use the Internet to research the viewpoint of Christian Churches on the issue of human cloning.

3. Should human cloning be done? Express your point of view, using a pamphlet, a poster, or some other means of personal expression.

Web Quest

For samples of Church opinion on the issue of human cloning, go to the following Church sites:

Lutheran:
http://www.elca.org/dcs/humancloning.html

Orthodox:
www.greece.org/ahepa/D5/05000eft.html

Catholic:
http://www.catholic.org/pft/magisterium/donumvitae.htm

The Role of Women in Christianity

Figure 7.7
Elizabeth Hardy is an Anglican minister at St. Michael the Archangel Church in Scarborough, Ontario.

The Bible supports equality between the sexes. Jesus himself interacted frequently with women in his public life, treating them with high regard. He protected a "sinful" woman from death at the hands of self-righteous zealots, and did not scorn her for wrong-doing. Jesus took women into his confidence, revealing his purpose on earth to them. Women, such as, Mary Magdalene, were some of Christ's most faithful disciples, following behind as he carried the cross to his crucifixion and remaining there until after he died. Jesus' female disciples were the first to learn of his resurrection when they went to visit his tomb, and Mary Magdalene was the first person to whom the resurrected Jesus appeared.

Paul's letter to the Galatians made clear the status of Christian women, and all other people baptized in Jesus' name:

> . . . *in Christ Jesus, all of you who were baptized into Christ have clothed yourselves with Christ. There is neither Jew nor Greek, slave nor free, male nor female, you are all one in Christ Jesus.*
>
> Galatians 3: 26-28 (NIV)

However, although Jesus brought a message of equality among the faithful, the Church grew in societies that were largely dominated by men with most women confined to domestic roles as obedient wives and mothers.

Modern Christianity is more open to the equality of women. The Salvation Army was the first Christian Church to recognize full status for women in its ministry, possibly because it was co-founded by a married couple, William and Catherine Booth (see page 304). Today, there are ordained female ministers in most Protestant Churches (Figure 7.7).

Check Your Understanding

1. Identify five important beliefs of Christianity that are formalized in the Nicene Creed.

2. Christianity and other faiths promise the opportunity for eternal life. Write a paragraph outlining reasons why people find this possibility so appealing.

3 . Do you believe in life after death? How do you envision the afterlife?

4. In your view, have women and men shared an equal role in Christianity? Explain.

PRACTICES, RITUALS, SYMBOLS, AND FESTIVALS

Practices and Rituals

Rituals are defined as formal, established acts and ceremonies through which believers worship their deity. They are time-honoured activities that are an important part of belonging to the faith. Most, but not all, Christian denominations have developed rituals of formal worship and prayer. Most of these rituals take place in a Christian house of worship, known as a church.

Some Christian denominations engage in simple rituals upon entering a church. Eastern Orthodox Christians cross themselves, light a candle, and kiss the icons (see page 280) depicting Jesus and other religious figures that are displayed at the entrance. Roman Catholics dip two or three fingers in the holy water font at the back of the church and bless themselves with the sign of the cross before walking to their seat.

The Christian Worship Service

The main elements of the Christian worship ritual were already in place by the second century and included the following: prayers, scripture readings, the singing of psalms from the Old Testament, the consecration of bread and wine, communion, and the collection of offerings for the poor.

Today, Christian worship takes place on Sunday in most Churches, though a growing number of Protestant Churches hold their worship service on Saturday evening. In most Christian services, there is the **liturgy of the word**, which highlights readings and preaching. Often, this portion of worship includes the recitation of core belief statements, like the Nicene Creed. Readings from scripture, particularly the gospels and epistles of the New Testament, which describe the life and teachings of Jesus, are a vital part of the liturgy of the word, and usually provide the theme for a homily, or sermon by the clergy.

The Book of Psalms, which rose out of the daily life of the Hebrews, is also important in Christian worship. Through the psalms, the Jewish people expressed their faith and trust in God. Christians often draw hymns, readings, and prayers, from the Book of Psalms for religious services and for private reflection.

Holy Communion

Most Christian worship also features a **communion** service in which the congregation is invited to share a ritual meal, as Jesus did with the apostles at the Last Supper. This is known as the liturgy of the Eucharist, and is signified by a procession, led by the clergy, bearing the gifts to the altar. It is held after the liturgy of the word, and there are two parts. First there is a sacred ritual of consecration, conducted by the priest or minister, to prepare the elements of the meal. Then, the blessed bread and wine (or grape juice), symbolizing the body and blood of Christ, is solemnly shared by the congregation. Recipients may be offered a wafer of unleavened bread, and a sip of wine, or a glass of grape juice, or they may receive a piece of bread within a spoonful of consecrated wine. They may file to the front of the church to receive communion, or the clergy (or lay leaders) may bring it to their seats. The different branches of Christianity interpret this portion of the worship ritual in very different ways, which is discussed in the Milestones section of this chapter (page 285).

Christian Prayer

Christians pray individually and in groups. The Lord's Prayer, which is the most widely used prayer in all of Christianity, is recited by the congregation at Christian worship services. In the gospel of Matthew, Jesus teaches this prayer to his followers:

> *Our Father, who art in heaven hallowed be thy name. Thy kingdom come; thy will be done, on earth as it is in heaven. Give us this day our daily bread, and forgive us our trespasses, as we forgive those who trespass against us. And lead us not into temptation, but deliver us from evil.*
>
> Matthew 6: 9-15 (NIV)

Traditionally, Roman Catholic Christians have used this prayer as part of "saying the rosary." A **rosary** (Figure 7.8) is a small chain or string that holds a cross and beads that are arranged in five "decades," or groups of ten. In saying the rosary, the worshipper begins each decade by uttering the Lord's Prayer, which is followed by the recital of additional prayers.

Contemplative Meditation

Many Christians thoughtfully read and reflect upon the Bible. Since the early days of the Church, members have been encouraged to take initiatives—through fasting, prayer, and meditation—to have mystical religious experiences that bring them closer to the presence of God.

Fasting

Fasting is abstinence from food, or certain kinds of food, for a period of time. It is often used as a way in which people seek pardon for their misdeeds, or to participate more fully in the meaning of their religious teachings. For example, Christian fasting may be used to symbolically share in the suffering of Jesus or the hungry, and as a means to set aside the money saved as an offering to the poor. Many Christians fast during Lent, before Easter, to commemorate the forty days during which Jesus fasted in the wilderness.

The Practice of Giving

Giving to others is a very important Christian practice. Christians are expected to contribute to their church financially and by service in special duties, for example, as choir members. In some churches, members may be asked to tithe, or donate up to one-tenth of their income to the church. Christian service also extends beyond the church into the local community. Members may join service clubs or organizations such as Habitat for Humanity, a Christian volunteer group that builds homes for needy families within the community and elsewhere. Finally, Christian giving should express itself in support toward the poor and those suffering from famine and disaster beyond the local community.

Christian Pilgrimage

By practising pilgrimage, Christians may want to deepen and broaden their faith, or they might be seeking some special favour from God. Pilgrims are

Figure 7.8
The rosary is used by some Christians during prayer.

religious travellers bound for a holy place, or special religious event. For example, in the summer of 2002, up to 750 000 youths from around the world are expected to converge on Toronto to hear the pope at World Youth Day. Each year, large numbers of Christians of all denominations make pilgrimages to shrines where people have experienced religious visions. They also go to the Holy Land to visit places connected to the life of Jesus.

The Church of the Holy Sepulchre

Perhaps the holiest structure in all of Christianity is the Church of the Holy Sepulchre in Jerusalem. This place of worship is believed to be located on the hill of "The Skull," identified in the gospels as the site of Jesus' crucifixion and burial. These important Biblical places were located very close together in an old stone quarry just outside the ancient city walls of Jerusalem. Early Christians knew them, and archaeological research appears to support these claims.

The first Church of the Holy Sepulchre was constructed on the site by the Emperor Constantine after the Council of Nicea in 325 CE. It replaced a city square and a temple that the Romans had built over the top of the hill about a century after the death of Christ. Persian and Arab forces partially destroyed Constantine's church in 614 and again in 1009 CE, but it was rebuilt each time. The present Church of the Holy Sepulchre was constructed from much of the original material in 1149 CE during the Christian Crusades to reclaim the Holy Land. This structure enclosed small shrines that had been built to mark the location of the Crucifixion and the burial tomb. The Grotto of St. Helena beneath the Church of the Holy Sepulchre also holds special significance. Christian tradition claims that Helena, mother of Constantine, found the wood of the cross of Jesus here when she visited during the construction of the original church.

Today, several Christian denominations share the church, and millions of visitors and pilgrims from around the world come to see it each year. Pilgrims commemorate Good Friday (see page 282) at this site by chanting prayers and reading from the gospels as they retrace Jesus' route to the site of his crucifixion.

QUESTIONS

1. Find the meaning of the word "sepulchre" in a dictionary. Why is this an appropriate name for Constantine's church in Jerusalem? Why do all types of Christians come to this holy place?

2. Make a sequential list of the different uses of the church site, starting with the original stone quarry. How would these changes have complicated the work of modern-day archaeologists?

Figure 7.9

Symbols and Icons

Like most world religions, Christianity is rich with symbols, especially those focused upon Jesus Christ. Christian Churches vary widely in their use of symbols, ranging from the ornate symbolism of Eastern Orthodoxy to the stark simplicity of some evangelical Protestant faiths.

Symbols and Icons
The Cross

Latin

Greek

Celtic

Maltese

St. Andrew's

Figure 7.10

Jesus was sentenced to a slow, painful, and public death by hanging from a cross. The gospels describe how he was nailed to it through his hands and feet. The cross reminds Christians that this cruel death was for human salvation. It symbolizes the Christian belief that God loved the people of the world so much that he offered his son for the sake of humanity.

The early Church did not use the cross as a symbol because of the horror and suffering associated with this form of execution. As time passed, it became acceptable to use the cross as a Christian symbol.

Crosses take different forms (Figure 7.10) and serve a variety of purposes. The Latin cross is used primarily by Protestants and Roman Catholics. The Greek cross is used mostly by Eastern Orthodox Christians. The Celtic cross is predominant in Ireland and Scotland, and the cross with the flared ends has been associated with Malta. Orthodox and Roman Catholic Christians make the sign of the cross on their bodies by touching their forehead, chest, and shoulders.

Religious crosses may be used in jewellery worn by believers, as grave markers in cemeteries, and on the spires and towers of Christian churches. Inside a church, the symbol of the cross might adorn the altar, the vessels used at communion, and the vestments worn by the minister or priest.

The symbol of the cross also appears in the flags of several countries that have a Christian heritage: they include Greece, Switzerland, Norway, Sweden, and Finland. The Union Jack of Britain is actually three superimposed crosses, one of them being the diagonal St. Andrew's cross, which symbolizes Scotland.

QUESTIONS

1. How do you feel about the use of the cross in national flags? Explain.
2. In Canada, how is the cross used in civil (public or state) ceremonies?

Figure 7.11

Figure 7.12

Figure 7.13

Figure 7.14

Chi Rho

Another symbol representing Jesus is the Chi Rho, which looks like a capital letter "P" with an "X" superimposed over it (Figure 7.11). These are the first two letters of the Greek word ΧΡΙΣΤΟΣ, which means "Christ." This symbol was used by the early Christians and marks vestments and other religious objects in some Christian Churches.

The Fish

The symbol of a fish, used in some Christian Churches, recalls Jesus' words to his first disciples: "Follow me and I will make you fishers of men,"(Mark 1:17). Thus, the fish symbol is linked to spreading the gospel of Jesus. The fish symbol is also associated with the ancient Greek word for fish, ΙΧΟΥΣ, which is an acronym in Greek for "Jesus Christ Son of God, Saviour," making the fish a symbol of Jesus himself (Figure 7.12). According to tradition, the fish was used as a secret sign by Christians to identify themselves to one another during periods of persecution.

Icons and Images

Icons, or images, of Christian religious figures reflect the divisions between the main branches of Christianity. Icons are stylized images rather than realistic portraits, and they are intended to show the heavenly glory of Jesus and other religious figures. Iconography, the art of making icons, was developed by the early Christians, and is done according to time-honoured rules within the Eastern Orthodox Church and the Byzantine rite of the Roman Catholic Church.

Many icons (Figure 7.13) are found within Orthodox churches for veneration by the faithful, especially on the iconostasis, an ornate screen that separates the congregation from the sanctuary. More realistic-looking images of holy subjects are not permitted in Orthodox churches, but are common in the rest of Christianity.

Three-dimensional statues and half-relief images of religious scenes in plaster, wood, and stone are most typical in Roman Catholic churches (Figure 7.14). In many Protestant churches, religious images depicting scenes from the life of Jesus appear in stained-glass windows (Figure 7.3). Stained glass is a special form of art that originated in the Middle Ages, when these colourful scenes were used to teach the common people who could not read stories from the Bible.

Festivals

The Christian cycle of holy days follows the major events in the life of Christ as presented in the gospels.

Christmas

The Christmas season begins with Advent, which starts four Sundays before Christmas, and is a time when Christians anticipate the birth of Jesus. Most Christians celebrate the birth of Jesus on December 25th, however many Eastern Orthodox and Byzantine rite Catholic denominations celebrate Christmas on January 7. Often, churches feature a manger scene, depicting the humble stable in which Jesus was born, and special song-filled worship services draw even occasional church-goers to attend.

Many of the most familiar Christmas carols were composed in the eighteenth and nineteenth centuries for Christmas Eve worship. For example, "Silent Night" was composed in 1818 by an Austrian priest named Joseph Mohr.

The tradition of gift-giving at Christmas has two different origins. The gospel of Matthew tells the story of the three Wise Men, or Magi, who followed a bright star that led them from distant lands to the infant Jesus. They brought precious gifts of gold, frankincense, and myrrh (two fragrant tree resins used for perfume and incense). Gift-giving also originates from the ancient Roman practice of year-end gifts to honour Saturn, the god of the harvest, and Mithras, god of light. The early Church adapted these Roman practices for their own religious purposes.

Epiphany

Twelve days after Christmas, on January 6, most Christians celebrate the Epiphany, which commemorates the baptism of Jesus, as well as the visit of the Magi. In some Christian countries, gift-giving takes place on this day, or is spread over the "twelve days of Christmas." The word epiphany means "manifestation" in Greek, and is used to commemorate the revelation of Jesus as God's son, as reported in the gospels, at the time of his baptism in the Jordan River.

Lent

The season of Lent begins approximately two months after Christmas and lasts for forty days, ending with

Figure 7.15
The Mardi Gras in New Orleans is a festival that has its origins in the Christian tradition of spirited celebration preceding the sombre period of Lent.

Holy Week and the festival of Easter. Lent lasts for forty days, representing the length of time Jesus spent on his meditative journey into the desert before he began his public ministry. Traditionally, Lent is a time of fasting, prayer, and spiritual self-assessment. Public festivals, such as Mardi Gras in New Orleans (Figure 7.15), or Carnivale in Rio de Janeiro, are rooted in this Christian tradition as social events before the sombre time of Lent begins. On Ash Wednesday, the day which begins the Lenten season, some Christians are marked on the forehead with ashes to remind them that they are mortals, and will return to dust upon their death.

Easter

Holy Week, the holiest period of the Christian calendar, climaxes on Easter Sunday. The Protestant and Catholic Churches celebrate Easter on the first Sunday after the first full moon after the spring equinox. The Eastern Orthodox Church usually celebrates Easter a week later, except when it coincides with the Easter of the Protestant and Catholic Churches, every four years.

Holy Week begins on the Sunday before Easter, which is known as Palm Sunday. On this day, Christians celebrate the day Jesus entered Jerusalem, and was welcomed by crowds holding palm branches, as described in the gospels. To mark this day, clergy bless and distribute palm branches to worshippers.

Holy Thursday marks the day of the Last Supper, when Jesus shared his last meal with his twelve apostles. According to the gospels, Jesus washed the feet of his apostles during the Last Supper. In some Christian traditions, a bishop or priest washes the feet of a group of priests or parishioners to reenact this deed of humble service.

Good Friday is the most solemn of Christian holy days since it commemorates the trial, crucifixion, death, and burial of Jesus. The minister or priest reads passages from the Bible describing Jesus' final hours, and in some Christian traditions, worshippers kiss a large cross and/or symbolic tomb displayed at the front of the church. Some congregations reenact the final events of Jesus' life and take a cross out on procession through the streets (Figure 7.16).

Easter Sunday, the most holy of Christian celebrations, marks the resurrection of Jesus and the events surrounding it, beginning with the female disciples' discovery of Jesus' empty tomb. In commemorating the resurrection of Jesus, Easter celebrates tri-

umph over sin and death. Worshippers celebrate this joyous occasion with a song-filled liturgy. Many Christians celebrate the eve of Easter with a vigil service where a flame, symbolizing Jesus—the light of the world—is passed from candle to candle among worshippers of the congregation.

Ascension and Pentecost

These holy days are both connected to Easter and evolved at approximately the same time as Holy Week, in early Christianity. Ascension Day takes place about forty days after Easter and celebrates Jesus' return to heaven, as witnessed by his followers. Pentecost falls ten days later. It acknowledges that the Holy Spirit filled the apostles with spiritual gifts of courage and understanding so that they could teach and spread the Christian faith.

Saints' Days

The early Christians began to direct prayer and reverence to **saints**, or holy people, and martyrs, who had died for their faith. Saints are considered to be with God in heaven and can therefore hear prayers. For many Christians, Mary holds a special place of honour because she gave birth to Jesus as part of God's plan. As the mother of Jesus, Mary is considered by some Christians to be the mother of God. Saints' days are recognized and celebrated with special parades and other rituals in many parts of the world.

In Europe, saints' days are honoured in the cultures of Greece, Italy, Spain, Portugal, and Ireland. Many nations have a patron saint that they recognize and celebrate, such as St. Patrick in Ireland, St. Andrew in Scotland, and St. Cyril in Slovakia.

In Canada, only a few saints, such as John the Baptist (a traditional holiday in Quebec), the Virgin Mary, and St. Joseph, our national patron saint, are recognized. Locally, many Christian churches acknowledge the saint's day of their particular namesake.

Check Your Understanding

1. How does the liturgy of the word differ from the communion service?

2. How does prayer differ from contemplative meditation? How are they similar?

3. Develop a list of Christian service organizations in your community (or a larger one in the region) that aim to help other people.

4. Describe the appearance and the meaning of the following Christian symbols:
a) the cross
b) the fish
c) the Chi Rho

5. In your opinion, which is the most important Christian religious festival? Why? Create a simple poster proclaiming this festival.

MILESTONES

Religious events can mark important stages in life. Christianity bestows sacraments upon individuals when they reach these stages, to identify a new beginning. Christians call these spiritual benefits grace, or "favour from God," and they represent high points in a person's religious life.

There is great variety in the recognition of sacraments among Christians, and there are some branches of Christianity that do not include sacraments as a part of their religious practices. The Eastern Orthodox and Roman Catholic Churches both celebrate seven sacraments to mark the passage of life; they include baptism, chrismation or confirmation, communion, confession, annointing the sick, ordination, and matrimony. Most Protestant Churches acknowledge two of these sacraments: baptism and communion.

Baptism

Christians believe that the act of baptism cleanses their soul and signals the beginning of their Christian lives. According to the gospels, Jesus was baptized in the Jordan River. Later in his ministry, he instructed the apostles to go out and baptize all nations, "in the name of the Father, and of the Son, and of the Holy Spirit," (Matthew 28:19). These same words are repeated in most Christian baptisms.

Early Christianity linked baptism to the Old Testament, by teaching that the sacrament removes the stain of **original sin**. According to the scripture, Adam and Eve, the first man and woman, were created by God and lived in the Garden of Eden. They were commanded not to eat the fruit of the tree of knowledge of good and evil. Their defiance of God's command left a spot on each person's soul. Baptism reclaims the soul for God by entering the person into the salvation of Christ's death and resurrection.

Today, most Christian denominations practise infant baptism. How-ever, some Protestant Churches delay baptism until adolescence, or even adulthood, as a sign of choice. In most Christian Churches, baptismal rituals include the anointing of the candidate with blessed oils, and the pouring of water over the forehead. The Eastern Orthodox Church follows the example of Christ's own baptism by having the priest immerse the infant in a font, a reservoir for blessed water. Similarly, some Protestants, such as Baptists, baptize young adults by full immersion in a pool of water.

Holy Communion

Sharing a meal is an important rite in many world religions. Most Christian Churches celebrate the Last Supper, the Passover meal that Jesus shared with his apostles the night before he was crucified. According to Christian scriptures, during the meal, Jesus passed some bread and wine to the apostles. Matthew's gospel tells the story in words that are common in the communion rituals of all Christianity:

> *While they were eating, Jesus took bread, gave thanks, broke it, and gave it to his disciples, saying, "Take and eat; this is my body." Then he took the cup, gave thanks and offered it to them, saying, "Drink from it, all of you. This is my blood of the covenant, which is poured out for many for the forgiveness of sins."*
>
> Matthew 26: 26-28 (NIV)

Early Christians met to celebrate this meal as the most important part of their worship ritual. However, as churches were built, the celebration evolved in form, so that the supper table was replaced by an altar, and the meal was replaced by a piece of bread and wine. The medieval Church taught that through the words spoken by the priest, the body and blood of Jesus Christ actually become present

Figure 7.18
These girls are preparing to enter a Catholic church to receive their first communion.

in the sacramental meal. This is the doctrine of **transubstantiation**, the belief that the bread and wine undergoes a change in substance, though not in physical appearance or chemical composition. The Orthodox and Catholic Churches believe that transubstantiation takes place through the priest's words. Most Protestant Churches celebrate the Last Supper only in a symbolic way, as a commemorative and spiritual event. They emphasize the sense of sharing of the congregation, but do not accept that the bread and wine has undergone any changes.

There is great variation in this sacrament among different Churches; the actual ritual is described on page 276 of this chapter. It is known by many different names including Holy Communion, the Mass, the Eucharist, Communion, the Lord's Supper, and the Lord's Table. It may be offered daily, weekly, monthly, quarterly, annually, or not at all. In all Churches, it is an important rite of passage to receive this sacrament for the first time (Figure 7.17).

Confession or Reconciliation

The origin of Confession, also known as Reconciliation comes from Jesus' instructions to the apostles:

> *"Receive the Holy Spirit. If you forgive the sins of any, they are forgiven them; if you retain the sins of any, they are retained."*
> John 20: 22-23 (NIV)

Members of the Orthodox and Catholic Churches, as well as some Protestant denominations, periodical-ly discuss their sins and struggles with their priest or minister; this is known as **confession**. This may be done face-to-face, or with a screen between the two for anonymity. In Eastern Orthodox Churches, confession is not done until **reconciliation** has been achieved with those who were wronged.

Chrismation or Confirmation

Many Christian denominations acknowledge the importance of attaining full participation in the Church, and conduct special rituals to recognize this, usually with young adolescents. Some Christians believe that at this time, spiritual gifts, such as wisdom and knowledge, are received from the Holy Spirit to help the individual to grow in his or her faith. In some Churches, sponsors, usually close relatives or family friends, assist the parents in preparing the person to become a young adult member of the Church. On the day of the **confirmation** ceremony, it is the sponsors, not the parents, who come forward with the young person. The anointing with oil, accompanied by the laying on of hands by a minister, bishop, or priest, are common characteristics of this rite. In the Eastern Orthodox Church, **Chrismation** rites are performed on infants at the time of baptism, and include anointing with blessed oils.

Ordination

Most Christian Churches use extensive education and formation programs at religious colleges and seminaries to prepare candidates for a life as a cleric, though a few Christian

denominations see no need for a formal clergy. Christians believe that those called to do God's work are filled with the Holy Spirit, just as the apostles were at Pentecost. The Acts of the Apostles in the New Testament describes ordination of Church leaders, which include prayer and the laying on of hands, rituals still performed today.

Matrimony

Christianity recognizes the sanctity of marriage because Jesus highlighted that it is a lasting bond before God: "For this reason a man shall leave his father and mother and be joined to his wife...So they are no longer two, but one flesh. Therefore what God has joined together, let no one separate," (Matthew 19: 5-6).

In all Christian Churches, the minister or priest functions on two levels, religious and civil, combining Christ and the law. Marriage is a sacred vow made in front of witnesses by a couple who promise to be faithful to one another, with the help of God. Some Churches consider marriage a sacrament and, therefore, a bond that cannot be dissolved. These Churches believe that the grace of the sacrament comes from God through one person in the couple to the other. Christianity usually puts the wedding into a full worship liturgy, with hymns and preaching, often including communion and a service. The Eastern Orthodox ceremony is the most distinctive in Christianity. The couple is crowned by the priest before God, and drink from a single cup to share in Holy Communion. This is followed by a triple procession around the altar table to symbolize that they have taken their first steps together in the presence of God (Figure 7.18).

Profile:
Mother Teresa of Calcutta
1910-1997

Figure 7.19

Mother Teresa was called "a living saint" by *Time Magazine*. During her lifetime, she received numerous humanitarian awards, including the Nobel Peace Prize in 1979. Her message to the world consisted of three words: "God is love." She lived this message by devoting a lifetime of work to the poor of India.

Mother Teresa was born Agnes Bojaxhui in Yugoslavia in 1910. While attending secondary school, Agnes learned about the work of missionaries in India and decided to pursue the calling. At the age of 18, she joined the Loreto nuns of Ireland and arrived in Calcutta a year later. In 1931, she took vows of poverty, chastity, and obedience, as well as the name Teresa. Fifteen years later, she had a vision in which Jesus spoke the following words to her: *"I want you to serve me among the poorest of the poor."* In 1949, she began her mission in the slums of Calcutta, India, and a year later established a new religious order—The Missionaries of Charity. Members of this religious order take a fourth vow of "wholehearted free service to the poorest of the poor."

The Missionaries of Charity expanded so quickly that at the time of Mother Teresa's death in 1997, they operated more than 600 houses in 136 countries. In fact, they recently opened a home to serve the poor in Winnipeg. The candid stories that Mother Teresa related about her work tell us a great deal about her. She often spoke frankly, with some humour, about the importance of giving dignity to the dying poor. This exerpt is taken from the book *My Life with the Poor.*

We have picked up thousands of people from the streets of Calcutta. One day I picked up a man from an open drain. Except for his face, his whole body was full of wounds.

I brought him to our house. And what did the man say? 'I have lived like an animal in the street, but now I am going to die like an angel, loved and cared for.'

We just had time to give him a bath and clean him and put him in bed. After three hours, he died with a big smile in his face and with a ticket for Saint Peter [heaven]. We gave him a special blessing by which his sins were forgiven—whatever sins he had ever committed—and he could see the face of God for all eternity. There was no complaint, there was no cursing, there was no fear."

Questions

1. What impressions do you have of Mother Teresa from this story? Explain.

2. Research the life of Mother Teresa, and then imagine that you are a journalist. Write her obituary (death notice), or prepare a headline and a newspaper article on her death.

288

Anointing the Sick or Dying

Throughout his ministry, Jesus healed the sick through prayer and the laying on of hands. Later, his followers did so in his name (James 5: 13-15), and the practice continues today in many Christian Churches. Today, Roman Catholic, Orthodox, and some Protestant Churches, anoint the sick. This ritual has certain common characteristics in different Churches. The clergy holds the patient's hand, at the same time anointing the patient's forehead with blessed oil. Prayers are said, and in some cases, communion is given to the sick or the dying. Ritual preparation for death marks the last milestone in the journey through a Christian life.

Funerals

The Christian funeral has two purposes: to commend the deceased to heaven, and to console the family and friends of the deceased. Some Christian funeral traditions come from the Romans, including cremation, a practice that has never been accepted by the Eastern Orthodox Church. Christian funeral rites can be adapted for use in the church, funeral home, cemetery chapel, or at the grave site. The religious service usually includes prayers, hymns, and other music.

Web Quest

Find information and links for Mother Teresa and the Missionaries of Charity at: http://www.categoryz.com/m/mother_teresa.htm

Check Your Understanding

1. Identify the meaning of the following terms: sacrament, original sin, transubstantiation.

2. Which two rites of passage are sacraments in most Christian Churches? Why?

3. Which Christian milestones often use the rituals indicated below?
a) cleansing with water
b) anointing with oils
c) laying on of hands

4. Prepare a scrapbook or a poster to illustrate both the religious rites of passage (if any), and secular, or non-religious, milestones that have been important events in your life.

SACRED WRITINGS

Christianity draws its sacred writings from the two sections of the Bible known as the Old Testament and the New Testament. The former is the Judaic tradition of the law and the prophets, while the latter is the Christian tradition of the apostles. Together, they form a long record of revelations, or promises of delivery or salvation, made by God to his people.

The New Testament emerged as Jesus' apostles developed a new body of writings to tell the story of Jesus Christ. The New Testament is comprised of four main components. The first component is the four gospels, the story of Jesus told by Matthew, Mark, Luke, and John. They are followed by a section called the Acts of the Apostles, which reports on the spread of Christianity after Jesus' death and resurrection. The third section contains the **epistles** (letters) written by early Christians. The last component is the book of Revelation, which contains what some believe to be prophecies about future events.

The Gospel of Mark

Mark's gospel is considered the oldest of the four, written sometime shortly before 70 CE. Some believe that Mark was an early Christian of Jewish descent, who traveled with Paul on his first missionary trip to the island of Cyprus. Mark is thought to have been with the apostle Peter in Rome, and tradition claims that this gospel contains Peter's memories. It is the shortest of the four gospels, with just 661 verses, but it forms the core of Matthew and Luke's, both written later. In fact, 600 of Mark's verses are used almost word-for-word in Matthew's gospel and 350 in Luke's. Scholars identify the gospels of Mark, Matthew, and Luke as synoptic gospels, meaning that they have a shared perspective, because of the text they share.

In the first half of Mark's gospel, Christ moves quickly from place to place, performing miraculous deeds and teaching in parables. The rest of the gospel focuses on the Crucifixion and Resurrection, showing the importance that Mark placed on these two events.

The Gospel of Matthew

Matthew's gospel was probably written around 80 CE. One of the twelve apostles, he had been a Jewish tax collector, not a popular occupation with the public. According to tradition, after Jesus' death, Matthew preached widely in North Africa and the Middle East, recording this gospel in his later years. This is the longest of the four gospels, and it has two distinct characteristics that set it apart from the others.

Matthew makes a special effort to connect Jesus with the Old Testament, using the first seventeen verses to trace Christ's family line through forty-two generations. The other important feature of the gospel of Matthew is the great detail that it provides about the teachings of Jesus. The most notable is the Sermon on the Mount, more than a hundred verses of lessons covering a wide range of topics. It is a blueprint for Christian life.

Sacred Text

The Sermon on the Mount

When Jesus taught, he was often followed by large crowds of people. In Matthew's gospel, Jesus retreated part way up a mountainside to escape this crush of followers. There, he gave important lessons about many things, like anger and forgiveness. His sermon on the mountain began by outlining the qualities, known as the "Beatitudes," needed to gain eternal life in heaven.

> *Now when he saw the crowds, he went up on a mountainside and sat down. His disciples came to him and he began to teach them, saying:*
> *"Blessed are the poor in spirit, for theirs is the kingdom of heaven.*
> *"Blessed are those who mourn, for they will be comforted.*
> *"Blessed are the meek, for they will inherit the earth.*
> *"Blessed are those who hunger and thirst for righteousness, for they will be filled.*
> *"Blessed are the merciful, for they will be shown mercy.*
> *"Blessed are the pure in heart, for they will see God.*
> *"Blessed are the peacemakers, for they will be called sons of God.*
> *"Blessed are those who are persecuted because of righteousness, for theirs is the kingdom of heaven.*
> *"Blessed are you when people insult you, persecute you and falsely say all kinds of evil against you because of me. Rejoice and be glad, because great is your reward in heaven, for in the same way they persecuted the prophets who were before you."*
>
> *Matthew 5: 1-12 (NIV)*

Questions

1. Identify the meaning of the word beatitude. Which of the beatitudes in the verses above do you think is most important today? Explain your choice.

2. Compare the Beatitudes to the Ten Commandments. How are they similar? How do they differ?

The Gospel of Luke

Scholars believe that this gospel was written between 80 and 90 CE. Traditionally, both this gospel and the Acts of the Apostles have been credited to St. Luke, though some modern scholars dispute this. Luke was an early Greek Christian, a well-educated man, and identified by his friend St. Paul as a physician. Many verses used in Luke's gospel are the same as those in Matthew's. This has led Bible scholars to two conclusions: either Luke borrowed from Matthew's work, or else both of them used another source, identified by scholars only as "Q," which has never been discovered.

As a physician, Luke highlights the message of healing by recounting parables about the poor and oppressed that are not contained in the other gospels. Stories, such as "The Good Samaritan," about a man willing to help an injured traveller, are among the best-known lessons in the New Testament. Christianity relies upon Luke's gospel for most of the details regarding Christ's early life, including much of the Christmas story.

The Gospel of John

The fourth gospel of the New Testament has been credited to John, one of the twelve apostles. It was written around 100 CE, at which time John would have been very old. This gospel differs a great deal from those of Matthew, Mark, and Luke, and scholars believe it was more likely written by followers of John, rather than the apostle himself.

John's gospel does not tell the story of Jesus biographically. Instead, he presents it theologically. John recounts Jesus' lessons and actions in long reflections that reveal his godliness. This gospel refers to Jesus as the "Word of God," the "Bread of Life," and the sacrificial "Lamb of God." These metaphors are a very important part of the Christian sacrament of Holy Communion. Another important element of this gospel is the "eleventh commandment" of loving one another. The words spoken by Jesus to his disciples represent a fundamental principle of human relationships in his time and in the present:

> *I give you a new command. Love one another. As I have loved you, so you must love one another...*
>
> John 13: 34-35 (NIV)

The Acts of the Apostles and the Epistles

Christianity considers the four gospels of paramount importance, but more than half of the New Testament contains other books of history, instruction, and warning. The Acts of the Apostles, written by Luke, outlines the beginnings of the Church, and describes the work of the apostle Peter and the early missionary Paul in spreading the Christian faith. Luke highlights the importance of the Holy Spirit in guiding the early fathers of the new Church.

The Epistles mostly come from Paul, or are attributed to him, though there are three letters from John and other letters from early leaders of the Church. Paul's letters are the earliest works of the New Testament, written from about 50 to 60 CE to the congregations that he established as he preached across a wide area of the ancient world. Paul wrote to encourage early Christians during times of persecution, and to remind them of Jesus' command that they love one another, just as they love God. The Epistles are used as sacred readings during worship services in many Christian Churches.

The Book of Revelation

The last book of the New Testament is unlike any other and has created some controversy about its true meaning. It was written around 95 CE by a persecuted Christian in exile named John, possibly, but not likely the apostle. The book of Revelation is an example of apocalyptic literature, describing, in symbolic and visionary terms, the destruction of the enemies of a persecuted people. Some Christians interpret the book of Revelation very literally to warn of a judgement day that is close at hand.

> *Then I saw another angel flying in mid-air, and beheld the eternal gospel to proclaim to those who live on the earth - to every nation, tribe, language and people. He said in a loud voice, "Fear God and give him glory, because the hour of his judgement has come. Worship him who made the heavens, the earth, the sea, and the springs of water."*
>
> Revelation 14: 6-7 (NIV)

Check Your Understanding

1. What is the major difference between the Old and New Testaments of the Bible?

2. What is the difference between the gospels and the epistles? Compare the general purposes of each type of text.

3. How are the three synoptic gospels similar to one another? How does John's gospel differ from them?

4. Read one section from the New Testament, and write a personal response of at least a half page to what you have read. Be prepared to share your comments.

Skill Path: In-depth Interview

An interview is a conversation between two or more people. Researchers value this research method because they can ask questions to obtain and clarify information on the spot. For respondents, the interview provides an often-welcome opportunity to express their views.

Structured Interview

Structured interviews are formal in nature and are designed to elicit specific answers from respondents. The researcher asks a number of prepared questions in a specific sequence, to which the respondents answer orally. Often, a researcher uses this format when testing a specific hypothesis or comparing information. For example, if a researcher is interested in discovering the religious practices of urban churches versus rural churches, he or she might ask the same specific questions during interviews with urban and rural ministers and compare the answers.

Informal Interview

Informal interviews are relaxed conversations where the researcher has not prepared particular types of questions that must be asked in a specific sequence. The main goal of this type of interview is to simply discover peoples' views on general topics. The informal interview can be the most difficult to conduct. The researcher must display an ability to be "quick on his or her feet." He or she must be able to decide instantly if the interview has become too personal; when to stop the interview; and how to maintain calm and open communication for the entire length of the exchange.

A helpful hint: Always begin the interview with non-threatening questions to establish a feeling of trust.

Retrospective Interview

A retrospective interview can be either structured or informal. The goal of the researcher is to have the person responding to the questions recall, from memory, an incident in the past. All questions reflect this goal. Retrospective interviews often do not provide the most accurate data because of the high potential for human error that might result from poor memory.

Interview Questions

There are various types of questions that a researcher might ask. They can include the following:

- **Demographic questions**

These questions relate to the background of the respondent and address topics such as age, occupation, income, and education.

- **Knowledge questions**

These questions elicit answers that reflect fact as opposed to opinion. For example, a researcher might ask a priest or minister to identify the milestones that are considered sacraments in his or her Church.

- **Experience questions**

The goal of these questions is to elicit descriptions of behaviours that might have been observed had the researcher decided to conduct an observation instead of an interview. For example, a researcher might ask: "If I were to attend an Easter Sunday service, what rituals would I observe?"

- **Opinion questions**

These questions attempt to elicit an opinion, or determine the respondent's values or beliefs.

For example: "What do you think about the Church's policy on human cloning?"

• Feelings questions

The intent of these questions is to determine how the respondent feels about a topic—what his or her emotions are with regard to experiences. For example: "How did you feel when you attended Sunday School as a child?"

Note: Often researchers confuse feelings and opinion questions. Discovering peoples' opinions on issues is not the same as probing for emotions regarding experiences. "How do you feel..." should elicit responses that reflect a respondent's likes and dislikes; whereas "What is your opinion of/What do you think about..." should elicit a respondent's point of view about an issue or policy.

Tips for a Successful Interview

- Arrive on time with all necessary equipment.
- Greet your respondent and reconfirm the purpose of your research.
- Ask your questions clearly.
- Be a good listener, and be prepared to follow-up with questions for further clarification.
- Use point-form notes to record responses, or consider taping the interview.
- When you are finished, thank the respondent and mention that you may call back for clarification of answers.

Practise It!

1. Identify each type of interview question from the list below.
- What do you think about the Church's policy on divorce?
- How did you feel during your ordination?
- How old are you?
- What vestments does a minister wear during Sunday worship?
- How often does the Church offer communion?
- What is your occupation?

2. Interview a priest, minister, or active Christian about the meaning of his or her faith in the modern world. Don't forget to choose your type of interview and questions carefully.

GROUPS AND INSTITUTIONS

For several hundred years, the Christian Church formalized its beliefs and extended its geographical boundaries. Zealous missionaries continued the work of St. Paul. St. Patrick took Christianity to Ireland, and, although he was more a warrior than a missionary, by 800 CE, King Charlemagne of the Germanic Franks had established the Holy Roman Empire, which stretched across much of Europe.

The Eastern Schism

As the Church grew larger, the forces of history began to pull it in two. When Roman Emperor Constantine shifted his capital city, he gave the empire two focal points—Rome in the west and Byzantium (Constantinople) in the east. As Christianity expanded westward into Europe, the influence of the Roman patriarch increased, and he came to be called "pope." Serious disagreement developed as the pope claimed authority over the whole Church.

There was also significant disagreement within the Church over issues of doctrine. The breaking point was the **filioque clause**, a Latin word inserted into the Nicene Creed by the Church in the west. The Roman pope added the expression "and the Son" to the end of the following statement from the original Nicene Creed of 325 CE: "And we believe in the Holy Spirit, the Lord and giver of Life, who proceeds from the Father." The western Church believed that both the Father and Son sent forth the Holy Spirit. The Eastern Church believed that the power of the Holy Spirit came only from God the Father.

In 1054 CE, the pope in Rome and the patriarch in Constantinople excommunicated, or formally expelled, one another's senior Church officials. A **schism**, or break, occurred as the Church split into two branches— the Eastern Orthodox, centred on the universal patriarch in Constantinople, and the Western Church, focused upon the pope in Rome.

The Eastern Orthodox Church

Followers of the Eastern Orthodox Church rejected the authority of the pope and any other modifications made to Christian belief after 787 CE.

Missionaries of the Greek Orthodox Church actively spread the faith into Eastern Europe and Russia. Today, the Eastern Orthodox Church is predominant in Greece, Russia, Ukraine, Serbia, Bulgaria, and Romania. Migration has spread Orthodoxy worldwide, and today it claims approximately 225 million members.

Characteristics of Orthodoxy

Typically, Eastern Orthodox Churches are constructed with a distinctive cross-shaped floor plan, where four short wings meet under a rounded central roof. Inside, they are ornately decorated with religious icons representing Jesus, Mary, the angels, and saints of the early Church (Figure 7.20). The Orthodox service, called the Divine Liturgy, is usually long and very elaborate, focused upon rituals established early in Christian history.

Figure 7.20
Christ the Saviour Cathedral in Moscow is an example of a Russian Orthodox church.

Ornate vestments, or clothing, worn by the priest, chanting, and the smell of incense burning all contribute to a sense of "other-worldliness" during the Divine Liturgy.

Today, the Eastern Churches are led by an Ecumenical Patriarch in Istanbul (formerly Constantinople). In an important symbolic healing of the East-West schism, the patriarch Athenagoras, and Pope Paul VI met in 1965 and lifted the excommunications that their predecessors had levied so long ago. However, the two Churches remain separate institutions.

Only men can be Orthodox priests, and they are allowed to have been married before their ordination; however, once ordained, they cannot marry. The Orthodox Churches have always promoted monastic life for men and women, and thousands live in monasteries around the world. Monastic priests and nuns are not permitted to have been married.

Independent Eastern Christian Churches

Several sects (Figure 7.21) in the Middle East and Africa broke from Mediterranean Christianity in the fifth and sixth centuries CE. While they worship the Holy Trinity, these Churches disagree with the decision of early Church councils that Jesus Christ was both true God and true man. About 15 million people belong to these sects, about half of them in the Ethiopian Church. This African sect is the most unusual of the Christian Churches, sharing many traditions with Judaism; for example, practicing ritual purification, keeping the Sabbath, and using a replica of the Ark of the Covenant during worship.

Figure 7.21
Independent Eastern Christian Churches

1. **East Syrian Church**—Iraq, Middle East

2. **Chaldean Church**—Iraq, Iran

3. **West Syrian Church**—Syria, Lebanon, Iraq

4. **Armenian Church**—Middle East

5. **Coptic Church**—Egypt

6. **Ethiopian Church**—Ethiopia

The Roman Catholic Church

After the schism with Orthodoxy, the Western Church expanded its influence and centralized its authority. In 1095 CE, Pope Urban II proclaimed a great expedition to recover Jerusalem and the Holy Land from Muslim rule. This began the Crusades, a "holy war" that lasted more than a century. There were at least five "waves" of crusaders, one of which even attacked and captured the Eastern Orthodox capital of Constantinople. Historians agree that in the fight against a common enemy, the Crusades unified Europe and extended the reach of the Western, or Roman Catholic Church.

The Catholic Reformation

In response to the Protestant Reformation (see page 299) the Church spent eighteen years, beginning in 1543, at the Council of Trent affirming all of its basic teachings, in what is called the Catholic Reformation. Among other things, the council identified the seven Catholic sacraments for the first time, and described three destinations for the souls of the dead—heaven, hell, and purgatory. **Purgatory** is a temporary state in which souls exist until they are cleansed of sin and can enter heaven. The Council deemed that prayers to the saints, and to Mary, are acceptable Roman Catholic practices, and it upheld the importance of both the Bible and Church tradition. During the centuries that followed the Council of Trent, missionaries and migration carried Roman Catholic beliefs to practically every corner of the world. Today, this Church has more than one billion members.

Characteristics of Catholicism

The central role of the pope is one thing that sets the Roman Catholic Church apart from the rest of Christianity. As early as the fourth century CE, the bishop of Rome claimed leadership of the Church, linking himself to the following words of Christ: "Thou art Peter [the apostle] and upon this rock I will build my church," (Matthew 16:18). Catholics believe that popes are successors to Saint Peter and that their central leadership helps hold the huge membership of the Church together. In 1870, the First Vatican Council strengthened the pope's authority by making **papal infallibility** Roman Catholic doctrine. This means, that provided the pope has consulted widely and is speaking formally as Church leader, his teachings relating to faith and morals are protected from error by God.

Vatican II, the second Vatican Council, held between 1962 and 1965, introduced many important documents that updated almost every aspect of the Church. Among other things, Latin was eliminated from worship in favour of the local language. Direct participation in the service, or the Mass, was encouraged by turning the altar and the priest to face the congregation, and by giving lay people roles as commentators and assistants in distributing Holy Communion. Since Vatican II, the Eucharist can be taken in two forms: a small, circular wafer of unleavened bread, called the host, and wine, both of which have been consecrated.

One of the major challenges facing the Roman Catholic Church today is a shortage of priests, particularly in industrialized nations, such as Canada, the United States, and Western Europe. Catholic priests must be males and they must remain both celibate, that is, abstain from marriage, and chaste, that is, abstain from sexual relations. They have a very strict personal code to maintain in an increasingly secular and individualistic society. And, it is quite unlike the Orthodox Churches where men may marry before they are ordained, or the Protestant Churches, with both married clergy and female clergy. For the past generation, the number of new Catholic priests has not been sufficient to replace retirees or to keep up with the growth of new **parishes**, or church districts. Few churches have more than one priest any more; in fact, the clustering of two or three parishes together is becoming increasingly common.

Figure 7.22
Pope John Paul II, who became the leader of the Roman Catholic Church in 1978, has been called the "people's Pope" because of his concern for the poor and his frequent world missions.

The Protestant Reformation

The second great division in the Church took place almost five hundred years after the Eastern schism, during the Renaissance, an era of social change. In 1517 CE, a German monk named Martin Luther caused a dramatic change in the Roman Catholic Church by challenging many of its medieval practices. He called for a simpler "inner faith," free from long-established rituals and outward shows of devotion. The Church excommunicated him, no longer allowing Luther membership or participation in its rites of faith. His followers established the Lutheran Church, and the **Protestant Reformation**—the reform of the western Church in protest to its practices—was underway. The Protestant Reformation also caused the Catholic Reformation, which began in 1543 as a response to the criticisms of the Protestant reformers.

The Protestant Churches

The Orthodox and Roman Churches had always focused on the importance of both faith and works, but Martin Luther introduced a new view. Salvation by faith alone turned the expectations of belief inward, rather than focusing on outward signs. While love and service to others was important, they were not necessary for salvation. Knowing God through the study of the Bible became more important than following long-established rituals of worship. This is a defining characteristic of many Protestant Churches today.

Martin Luther's translation of the Bible from Latin into German was almost as important as his new interpretation of Christianity. Soon, Luther's new Bibles were in the hands of the emerging commercial middle classes of northern and western Europe. Educated people could now read and interpret the gospels themselves, without the direction of Roman Catholic clerics. As a result, the Reformation spread rapidly, through Germany, Switzerland, Holland, Britain, and Scandinavia. New interpretations of the faith took hold, and the foundations of the Lutheran, Calvinist, and Anglican Churches were established. Later, several other Christian Churches in the Protestant tradition emerged, some of which will be discussed in this section.

The Lutheran Church

More than 75 million people in the world are Lutherans, the first of the Protestant Churches. They focus on the message of God's forgiving love and consider the Bible, rather than Church doctrine, as the sole guide to religious truth. There are two sacraments in the Lutheran Church—baptism and the Lord's Supper, or Holy Communion. Lutherans believe that in communion, Christ is present in a very real way, through consubstantiation. Consubstantiation acknowledges the presence of Christ's body and blood in the offering, but all around it, without altering the substance of the bread and wine.

The Calvinist or Reformed Churches

During the mid-sixteenth century, John Calvin, a classical scholar, experienced a sudden religious conversion in Switzerland. He developed a core of doctrine that accepted justification, but introduced new elements of belief, for example, the absolute sovereignty of God. John Knox was influenced by Calvin and carried his ideas to Scotland, where he founded the Presbyterian Church. Today, about 100 different Calvinist-based denominations belong to the World Alliance of Reformed Churches.

Calvinism stresses **sanctification**, that is purification from sin, through obedience of the Ten Commandments of the Old Testament. Members are taught to value integrity, sincerity, and hard work, since all human actions are under scrutiny from God. The liturgies of Reformed Churches are relatively free of ritual, with a strong focus upon preaching and hymn singing. The Lord's Supper is celebrated in a symbolic way, and baptism is the only other sacrament.

Profile: Martin Luther

1483-1546

Figure 7.23

Martin Luther was born in 1483 CE, and was ordained as a priest in 1507. He entered a monastery to follow an isolated life of prayer and fasting, but found that this reverence was not bringing him closer to God. Bible study led Luther to refine the idea of **justification**, that which makes a person worthy to God. While the Roman Catholic Church believed that one was justified by having faith, doing good works, receiving the sacraments, and fulfilling a number of Church demands, Luther felt that it was simpler than that. He claimed that salvation was gained "by faith alone." Furthermore, since God is kind, he looked favourably upon all people, not just the pious.

In 1517, Martin Luther posted his famous Ninety-five Theses on a church door in Wittemberg, Germany. These were points of debate about certain beliefs and practices. Some of the theses presented his radical views about salvation, but his criticism directed at selling **indulgences** angered Church authorities most of all. An indulgence was usually a formal penance of prayers done to obtain God's forgiveness for sins; however, the wealthy could simply donate money to the Church instead of praying. This challenge led to intense scholarly debate about the Ninety-five Theses with Catholic theologian Johann Eck. Luther defended his views about justification and salvation, but went even further. He denied the supremacy of the pope and declared that Church councils could commit errors of faith.

He was excommunicated and banned as "an obvious heretic." Luther translated the whole Bible into German. Later, he wrote several books and pamphlets that outlined his views of a reformed Christianity.

Luther's revised liturgy was both simpler and in the language of the people instead of Latin. Martin Luther intended to reform the Church rather than break from it, but when he died in 1546, he was already recognized as an important figure who had changed the course of Christianity.

QUESTIONS

1. How did Luther's ideas about salvation differ from those of the Roman Catholic Church?

2. Indicate with which of Luther's ideas you agree or disagree. Be prepared to explain your positions.

The Anglican Church

Anglicanism includes the original Church of England, the Anglican Church of Canada, and the Episcopalian Church in the United States. The formation of this Church was entirely political. King Henry VIII wanted his marriage to Catherine of Aragon annulled, or made void, and the Catholic Church would not comply. King Henry had the Archbishop of Canterbury annul the marriage and had Parliament pass the Act of Supremacy, which made the monarch head of the Church in England. He ordered the translation of the Bible and worship services into English, but made no other changes in doctrine. Anglicans do not recognize the authority of the pope, nor do they accept the doctrine of transubstantiation in the Eucharist (see page 286). However, their liturgy is very similar to that of Catholicism, with the result that Anglicans tend to view themselves as a "bridge" between Protestants and Roman Catholics.

The Baptist Churches

These Churches have their origin in the Anabaptist movement of sixteenth-century Protestantism. Baptists believe that becoming a Christian should be a mature and informed decision, and not a birthright. In Baptist Churches, this sacrament calls for the total immersion of adults in water, in the way John the Baptist baptized Jesus (Figure 7.24). Baptist liturgy includes the sacrament of communion, with Christ present in spirit only, as well as Bible preaching and hymn singing. Martin Luther King Jr., the American civil rights leader who championed the rights of African Americans in the 1960s was a Baptist minister. In Canada, Tommy Douglas, the founder of the Canadian medicare system and the first leader of the New Democratic Party, was also a Baptist minister.

The Methodist Churches

These Churches originated two centuries after the Protestant Reformation. In the eighteenth century, John Wesley, an Anglican priest in England, founded the movement as he and a group of friends "methodically" sought a deeper assurance of personal salvation through prayer, discussion, and reflection. He developed the following three basic principles for followers: "Do no harm; Do good; Attend to all the ordinances of God." Methodism stressed a Christian lifestyle in the world, and has often supported important social causes. Methodist Churches

Figure 7.24
This baptism is taking place in a Baptist church. What are your views on adult versus infant baptism?

vary, but all celebrate baptism, and most liturgy is a song-filled preaching service, occasionally concluded by a symbolic Lord's Supper.

The United Church of Canada, formed in 1925, is a product of a merger among the Methodist, Congregationalist, and Presbyterian Churches.

The Evangelical Movement

The Evangelical Movement, which has historic ties to the Protestant Reformation, represents a very active form of Christian belief and practice based on the literal authority of the Bible. This movement has grown rapidly in Canada to represent one of the largest communities of Protestant worshippers in the country. Evangelical Protestant Christians are very active in charitable causes, such as World Vision, which is the largest nongovernmental organization in Canada, raising some 200 million dollars for world relief.

The Mormons

In the 1820s, American Joseph Smith had visions of God the Father, Jesus Christ, and an angel he called Moroni. He claimed to have received small golden panels engraved in an ancient language that he was given the ability to translate into the Book of Mormon. The Mormon Church, known as the Church of Jesus Christ of Latter-day Saints, regards this book as divinely inspired sacred writing. Under the leadership of Brigham Young, they established Salt Lake City, the present capital of the state of Utah. This city is world headquarters to more than seven million Mormons.

Mormons do not recognize original sin; therefore, baptism only serves to receive new members into the Church. Mormons believe that a person's spirit remains on earth after death, and, therefore, family life can continue to include deceased family members. One result is that the Church of Jesus Christ of Latter-day Saints has developed a strong interest in genealogy, the study of one's ancestors. In fact, they operate the largest research library for this purpose in the world.

The Jehovah's Witnesses

This religious group began in the United States in 1868, and currently has about four million members. Jehovah's Witnesses obey the call to "witness the faith," that is bring it to others, by spreading the good news of the kingdom of God. Members personally carry out their ministry by delivering their magazines door-to-door in their home communities. They reject the idea of the Holy Trinity, and interpret the Bible in literal detail, holding it as the infallible source of the truth. One controversial aspect of this faith is its opposition to blood transfusions, even in life-threatening situations. Jehovah's Witnesses believe that it is forbidden by God to take the blood of another into one's body.

Community Study

The Salvation Army

Figure 7.25

Most Canadians are familiar with the Salvation Army in some way, for they play a very important social and religious role in many communities. You've probably seen uniformed members in shopping malls at Christmas, with bright red containers to collect donations for the poor. Perhaps you've heard their band play music on street corners or in local parades, and seen their familiar big collection boxes for used clothing and furniture. But, you may not know that the Salvation Army is also a Church, one that has been in Canada since 1882.

William and Catherine Booth, married Methodist preachers, started the Army in 1865 to bring faith to the "un-churched" in the poorest districts of London, England. It was organized along military lines, and gave completely equal status to male and female members, called "soldiers," and ministers, called "officers." To this day, members pledge themselves to spread the gospel of Jesus, particularly through charitable works, and to lead a moral life, free from alcohol, tobacco, and illegal drugs. Ministers also accept a frugal life of relative poverty. William and Catherine Booth pioneered a Christian faith with a strong tradition of music and preaching, but with very little ritual and none of the sacraments. Instead, open prayer and personal testimony, are encouraged as valuable ways to lead others toward a choice for their own salvation.

The Army has earned the respect of Canadians because of the wide range of social services that it provides to the disadvantaged (below). From the beginning, the motto of the Salvation Army has been "With heart to God, and hand to man."

Salvation Army Activity in Canada

- Clothing and furniture distribution centres called Thrift Stores
- Community food drives and food banks
- Hospitals and retirement homes for the elderly
- Counselling centres for alcohol and drug addiction
- Shelters and meals for the homeless
- Outdoor summer camps for underprivileged children
- Parole supervision for recently released prisoners
- Language instruction for new immigrants

QUESTIONS

1. Describe the role of women in the Salvation Army, and trace this role to the founders of the movement.
2. Explain how the community work of Salvation Army members is linked to the movement's origins and to their religious principles.

Check Your Understanding

1. Identify the meaning of the following terms:
a) purgatory
b) papal infallibility
c) sanctification

2. Compare the views of the Christian Churches toward a married clergy.

3. Explain the controversy of the filioque clause and its effect.

4. In your opinion, has the division of Christianity been good or bad for the faith? Explain.

5. What personal questions do you have about any of the Christian denominations described in this section? How would you go about getting your questions answered?

CULTURAL IMPACT

Numbering almost two billion people, Christians form the largest religion in the world. About one-third of the global population follows the teachings of Jesus Christ. As a result of both its huge membership and geographical distribution, Christianity has had a sizable cultural impact on Canada and the rest of the world.

Maps and statistics show that Christianity is dominant in Europe and the Western hemisphere (Figures 7.26 and 7.27). During the ages of exploration and colonization by European powers, such as Britain, France, Spain, Portugal, and the Netherlands, missionaries and immigrants carried Christianity to the Americas. Indigenous peoples in those regions were Christianized by peaceful conversion, or by show of force. In the late nineteenth century, the age of imperialism pushed European interests and Christianity deeper into Asia and Africa. Today, almost two-thirds of Roman Catholics live in the developing nations of Latin America, Asia, and Africa.

The link between Christianity and developing nations can be seen today in the activities of church-based international activities. Many Christian Churches and organizations fund and operate missions, schools, orphanages, hospitals, and other community institutions in the Third World. For example, the Christian Children's Fund uses a sponsorship plan to fund education for the children of poor families overseas. Other organizations, such as the Canadian Catholic Organization for Development and Peace, or CCODP, support community-based economic development projects in developing nations. Finally, Church groups, like the Mennonite Central Relief Committee, respond to international crises, such as, famine, flood, and hurricane destruction.

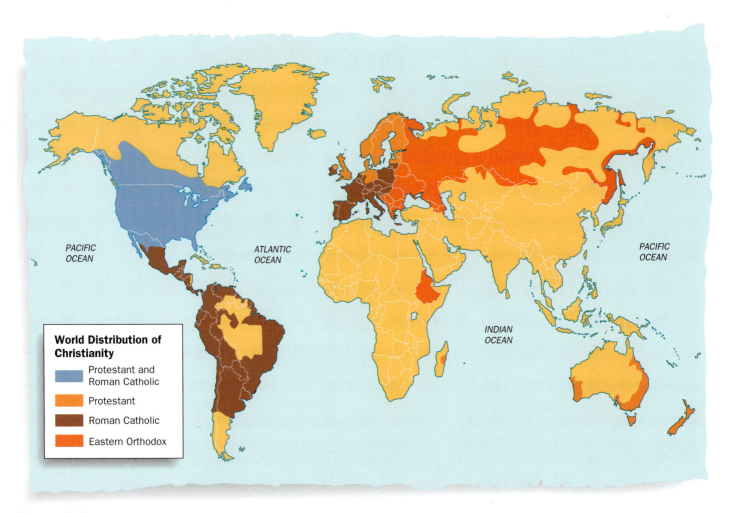

Figure 7.26 *What evidence is there that Christianity is truly a global faith?*

	Africa	Asia	Latin America	Europe	North America	Oceania	WORLD
Orthodox	33	15	1	167	7	1	224
Protestant	108	46	43	110	98	11	416
Roman Catholic	118	111	443	287	74	8	1040
Other Christians*	68	125	40	6	48	1	288
TOTALS	317	297	527	570	227	21	**1968**

* Catholics (non-Roman), marginal Protestants, Indigenous Christian Churches of Asia, Africa, and Latin America

Figure 7.27 *Christian Adherents by Continent (in millions), 1997*

Christianity in Canada

Christianity is the most widely held faith in Canada, and this has affected our society in many ways. Christian churches are the most striking buildings in many Canadian communities (Figures 7.28-7.30). The architectural landscape of our country features a range of church styles. Some of these churches are the centre of the important pilgrimage travel industry. For example, Ste. Anne de Beaupré near Quebec City, St. Joseph's Oratory in Montreal, and Martyrs' Shrine in Midland, Ontario, each draw a continuous stream of religious travellers.

The impact of Christianity is also evident in the Canadian educational system. Some provinces, such as Ontario and New Brunswick, have publicly-funded Roman Catholic school systems, first guaranteed under the terms of the 1867 British North America Act as part of the historical set of compromises that created the dominion of Canada. Religious-based schools, denominational colleges, and "Sunday school" programs aim to pass on the faith from one generation to the next.

Christianity's impact on Canada can clearly be seen with a casual reference to a map or local street directory. Many cities, towns, villages, lakes, and rivers bear Christian saints' names, particularly in Quebec. The St. Lawrence River, Sainte-Marie-Among-The-Hurons, St. Mary's and St. Thomas, Ontario, and St. George Street in Toronto are some examples of this phenomenon. Many of the holidays that we enjoy as Canadians were originally Christian holy days. These include Christmas, Easter, and Thanksgiving. Thus, although Canada is very multifaith and multicultural today, the Christian heritage is still an important feature of Canadian society.

Figure 7.29
Precious Blood Church, Winnipeg, Manitoba

Figure 7.28
St. Dunstan's Cathedral, Charlottetown, PEI

Figure 7.30
Trinity United Church, Oakville, Ontario

Living My Religion

How Christianity has Influenced my Life by Renée DesRivieres

Figure 7.31

Renée DesRivieres was born in North York, Ontario, in 1979 She spent much of her adolescence in Sarnia, Ontario, where she graduated from St. Christopher Secondary School. Before beginning university, she attended "World Youth Day 1997" in Paris, France. During this pilgrimage, the Roman Pontiff, John Paul II, challenged youth to be a voice for the voiceless in our current "culture of death." Renée felt a calling to pursue this challenge. While at the University of Western Ontario, she worked at a teen pregnancy crisis centre. Renée also held the presidential position in the university's pro-life associa-

tion, and attended the United Nations world population conference in New York City as a pro-life delegate. After graduating with a biology degree in ecology and evolution, Renée began graduate study of Catholic theology at St. Peter's Seminary, in London, Ontario. She aspires to work in a biomedical ethics field where she can combine Christian faith, biology, and medicine.

Renée states:

"The most influential effect of Christianity on my life comes from reflecting upon the life of Christ. He lived a life of perfection and calls each one of us to imitate Him. I feel this call on a daily basis. For example, if I walk by a homeless person, I am immediately reminded of Christ's words, "...just as you did not do it to the least of my brothers or sisters, you did not do it to me," (Matthew 25:45). He calls us to love our neighbour as ourselves and in doing this we are all challenged to protect the rights of the vulnerable, feed the hungry, and comfort all those in need." This practice has affected my life on both practical and profound levels.

QUESTIONS

1. Identify and describe the event that influenced Renée's commitment to the Christian faith. What activities in her life demonstrate the impact of this event upon her?

2. Think of an event that had a strong positive impact upon you. Write a paragraph detailing how this event affected you.

Social Change

Christian Churches led social reform in Canada. About a century ago, the Women's Christian Temperance Union, or WCTU, was a powerful church-based organization opposed to the widespread sale and abuse of liquor. They succeeded in outlawing the purchase of alcohol in Canada and the United States for a period of time known as Prohibition. This movement helps explain why the sale of alcohol in Canada is still carefully controlled by government.

During the Great Depression, churches stepped up their efforts to collect and distribute food and supplies for the unemployed and the desperate farmers in the Prairies. Two Christian ministers in the West, J. S. Woodsworth and William "Bible Bill" Aberhart, helped found new political parties that aimed to use political measures to end the economic problems of the times. The Co-operative Commonwealth Federation (or CCF, forerunner to today's New Democratic Party), and Aberhart's Social Credit Party were both elected in Western provinces, and introduced bold social spending programs. For example, in Saskatchewan, the CCF introduced public health care, a program available to all Canadians today.

Pastoral Ministry

One of the most important ways in which Christianity affects society can often pass unnoticed, yet its impact can be profound. Most Christian Churches in Canada have developed vital **pastoral ministries** within the Church community. Pastors and trained volunteers provide emotional support during personal and family crises; for example, bereavement counselling for family members of the deceased. Visiting programs reach the sick, the elderly, and even prison inmates. Youth ministry programs and marriage preparation courses are examples of ongoing projects carried out by several Christian denominations.

Check Your Understanding

1. Use Figure 7.27 to rank the world continents from most Christians to least. Explain this pattern.

2. Summarize three different types of activities currently supported in developing nations by Christian organizations.

3. a) Make a list of ways in which Christianity has affected Canadian society.
b) Describe the cultural impact of the following in Canada: the WCTU, the Salvation Army, J.S. Woodsworth, and William Aberhart.

4. What is pastoral ministry? Use two examples to show how it can have a significant impact upon people.

Activities

Check Your Understanding

1. Explain the part played by each of the following in the life of Jesus Christ:
a) John the Baptist
b) Judas
c) Mary Magdalene

2. Note two beliefs about the nature of God shared by Christians and Jews.

3. Compile a summary chart about four important Protestant founders as follows:

Church Founder	Church Name	Important Concepts or Activities Introduced
a. Martin Luther		
b. John Calvin		
c. Henry VIII		
d. John Wesley		

Think and Communicate

4. How important is each of the following in shaping your values: religion, school, media, parents, friends? Rank these five from most to least important, and explain your choices.

5. Do you support or reject the idea that Jesus was a rebel who challenged the status quo of his day? Explain.

6. Prepare a profile, like the one of Mother Teresa on page 288, that examines the role of an important woman, or group of women, in Christianity. Examples might include Mary Magdalene, Catherine Booth (founder of the Salvation Army), or the Women's Christian Temperance Union (WCTU).

7. Interview a church pastor or a volunteer about the pastoral counselling work that he or she performs. Try to find out the difficulties and the rewards that this person experiences with such work.

8. Examine the synoptic gospels and find three examples of the same parables contained in all of them. Then find three parables that are not found in all three gospels. Record the subjects of these parables in a chart.

9. Work with a partner to compare the style and content of the gospels of Luke and John. Summarize some important differences that you notice, using examples.

10. Use photography or sketches to collect images of different types of religious architecture in your neighbourhood or community. Arrange these pictures in an interesting display.

Apply Your Learning

11. Examine the Sermon on the Mount in the gospel of Matthew (page 291). Summarize three teachings within that passage that would be good advice in today's world. Explain each of your choices.

12. Use print and/or electronic sources to prepare a page of research about one of these topics:
a) The Crusades
b) The Coptic Churches of Egypt and/or Ethiopia
c) The American civil rights movement

13. To what degree should a person be free to practise his or her faith? Select one of the following pairs of statements and explain your point of view:
a) i) Refusal to volunteer for military service
ii) Refusal to report for the draft in time of war

b) i) Refusal to receive a blood transfusion in a medical emergency
ii) Refusal to allow a young family member an emergency transfusion

14. Work within a group to research the views of Canadian political parties on human cloning, capital punishment, abortion, euthanasia, or another contentious social issue regarding human life. Prepare a report of your findings, and present them to the class in an oral presentation.

15. Compare secular and religious celebrations held either at Christmas or Easter. Trace the origins of the secular celebration, then show how the secular and religious celebrations differ.

Glossary

apostle [a POSSLE]. One of the twelve disciples chosen by Christ to go out to teach the gospel to the world.

Ascension. Holy day that marks the bodily passing of Christ from earth to heaven on the fortieth day after Easter.

baptism. Sacrament or action that involves the sprinkling of a person with water or full immersion as a sign of washing away sin and entering the Church.

Christmas. Festival that celebrates the birth of Jesus, marked by special Church services, gifts, and greetings.

confirmation (also known as **chrismation**). Sacrament, or rite in some Churches that is a component of the initiation process into the Christian faith, which begins with baptism.

confession (also known as **reconciliation**). Sacrament in some Churches in which a person acknowledges, to a priest or a confessor, wrongs committed and receives forgiveness from God.

Crucifixion [croo suh FICK shun]. Execution of Christ on a wooden cross, in the method of the Romans; an event commemorated by Christians on Good Friday.

disciple. Follower of Jesus Christ during his public ministry; includes, but is not limited to, the twelve apostles.

Easter. Christian festival that celebrates the Resurrection of Christ.

epistles [ep PISSLE]. Letters written by Christ's apostles to instruct Churches and individuals about the faith.

filioque clause [filly O quay]. Latin word, meaning "and the son" inserted into the Nicene Creed by the Western, or Roman, Church.

gospels. Story of Jesus Christ's life and teachings told in the first four books of the Bible's New Testament.

Holy Communion /Eucharist [YUKE a rist]. Sacrament by which Christians commemorate the Last Supper.

Holy Spirit. One of the three persons in God, believed, by Christians, to bestow spiritual gifts upon individuals.

indulgences. Prayers or actions in the Roman Catholic Church that are believed to free the individual from spending a specified period of time in purgatory.

justification. Belief in some Churches that Christians are free from punishment for sin through their faith in Jesus Christ.

Last Judgement. Day of God's final judgement at the end of the world, when the faithful will go to heaven.

Last Supper. Jesus' last meal with his disciples before he was crucified; the origin of the sacrament of Holy Communion.

Lent. Forty weekdays between Ash Wednesday and Easter Sunday; a period of fasting and repentance for sin in many Christian Churches.

liturgy of the word. Portion of the Christian worship service that emphasizes Bible readings and preaching to the church congregation.

martyr [MAR tur]. Someone who has suffered or died for his or her religion or beliefs.

Messiah [muh SIGH uh]. Saviour, prophesized by the Old Testament, who would lead his people to God; Christians believe this saviour to be Jesus.

original sin. Belief of the human tendency to sin and evil, presented in scripture as a result of Adam and Eve's disobedience of God in the garden of Eden.

papal infallibility. Roman Catholic belief that the pope cannot err when speaking on matters of faith and morals in his role as head of the Church.

parable. Type of short story often used by Jesus to teach an important truth or lesson in morality.

parish. Area that has its own church and a minister or priest.

pastoral ministry. Non-ordained people who assist the clergy with many different aspects of their work.

Pentecost [PENTA cost]. Christian festival commemorating the descent of the Holy Spirit upon the apostles to help them spread the Christian faith.

Protestant Reformation. Religious movement in Europe during the sixteenth century that led to the establishment of the Protestant Churches.

Purgatory. Temporary stage in Roman Catholicism in which the souls of those who have died are purified from sin.

Resurrection. Rising of Christ from his tomb on the third day after his crucifixion.

rosary. A string of beads used for devotional prayers by some Christians.

sacrament. Ritual or ceremony that is an outward sign of spiritual benefits that are given to the recipient.

saint. Holy person that Christians venerate.

sanctification [sank tiffa KAY sh'n]. Act of being purified from sin and made right or holy in the eyes of God.

schism. Division of the Church into separate, and often hostile, groups because of strong difference of opinion.

transubstantiation [tran sub stanshy AY sh'n]. Changing of bread and wine into the substance of the body and blood of Christ during Holy Communion.

Trinity. Christian belief that there are three persons in one God: the Father, the son (Jesus Christ), and the Holy Spirit.

In the name of Allah, Most Gracious Most Merciful.
Praise be to Allah, the Cherisher and Sustainer of the
Worlds.
Most Gracious, Most Merciful.
Master of the Day of Judgement.
Thee do we worship and Thine aid we seek.
Show us the straight way.
The way of those on whom Thou hast bestowed Thy Grace,
those whose (portion) is not wrath and who go not astray.

Source: Qur'an 1:1-7

This is the first chapter of
the Qur'an, the sacred
text of Islam. It is called
al-Fatihah, which means
"the Opening," and is
recited several times when
a person prays, or performs
the salat. Muslims pray to
one God whose name is
Allah.

Chapter Eight

Islam

8

Read the text on the opposite page and the introduction below. Answer the following questions:

1. Who is Allah? What qualities does He possess?
2. What does this prayer suggest about the religion of Islam? Be specific.

Introduction

Islam is an Arabic word that means "submitting to God." A person who follows the teachings of Islam is called a Muslim, "one who submits to God and finds peace in Him." Specifically, Muslims are adherents of Islam who submit to the will of God. Islamic belief is captured in their creed, called the *Shahadah*, which states:

"There is no god but God and Muhammad is the Messenger of God."

Muslims believe that, in the seventh century, God sent a series of revelations through the Archangel Gabriel to a man named Muhammad, who is seen as the last Prophet sent to humanity by God. A **revelation** is a clear and vivid experience that teaches a profound, spiritual truth. Muslims believe that it is a special, infallible kind of inspiration reserved for only those who are appointed by God as Prophets. The revelations given to Muhammad by God proclaim the oneness of God and the need to submit to God through worship and righteous living.

Islam is the third in succession of the three great faiths born in the Middle East. One of the key figures in the Islamic tradition is the Prophet Abraham. Abraham is also a patriarch of the Jewish faith and, by extension, is a significant figure in the Christian tradition. Muslims also view Noah, Moses, and Jesus as great prophets along with the Prophet Muhammad.

Islam is the second largest and currently the fastest growing religion in the world. It lays claim to 1.2 billion adherents. Over fifty nations hold a population wherein the majority are Muslims. This range of nations stretches from Indonesia in the east to Morocco in the west, with smaller Muslim populations in Europe and the Americas. According to Statistics Canada, there were over 250 000 Muslims living in Canada in 1991. More recent statistical analysis puts the number closer to 650 000 people, with the majority residing in urban centres such as Toronto, Montreal, and Vancouver.

Learning Goals

- explain the origins of Islam beliefs regarding creation, death, God, and the afterlife
- identify the role and contributions of Muhammad and the Caliphs in the history of Islam
- explain the origins of the Qur'an
- identify key passages from the Qur'an and explain their meaning and influence
- identify the origin and significance of Islamic beliefs, practices, festivals, and rituals
- demonstrate an understanding of fasting and prayer in the Islamic faith
- examine the role of symbols in Islam
- evaluate the impact of key events in the development of Islam around the world
- describe and compare the main religious groups within Islam
- analyze issues related to the status of women within Islam
- participate effectively in a group presentation

632 CE Muhammad dies; the rule of the "Rightly-Guided" Caliphs begins

680 CE Battle of Karbala; martyrdom of Husain, the Prophet's grandson

687 CE Dome of th Rock, site of the Night Journey, built in Jerusale

624-628 CE Battles of Badr, Uhud, the Trench

610 CE Muhammad receives his first revelation; the call to Prophethood

630 CE Muhammad visits Makkah and wins the hearts of the Makkans

570 CE Muhammad born in Makkah

622 CE The *hijrah*: Muhammad moves from Makkah to Madinah

• 1930 CE Abdul Aleem Siddiqui, the first Muslim missionary and scholar in Canada dedicates the first Canadian Mosque in Edmonton, Alberta; lectures in Edmonton and Toronto as part of his world travels

• Early 1300s-1924 CE
Era of the Turkish Caliphate

• 19th–early 20th century CE Era of European Imperialism; many Muslim countries are under the rule of colonial powers.
Muslims begin to immigrate to Canada; opportunities in farming and in building the trans-national railway

• 1947 CE Areas of Muslim majority in British India form the state of Pakistan

• 1945 CE Post-war Muslim immigration to Canada; skilled labour

• 1961 CE First Islamic Centre in Toronto established by Regep Assim, founder of the Muslim Society of Toronto

• 1950-1970 CE
Muslim academics immigrate to Canada; Islamic studies established at McGill University (1952) and the University of Toronto (1962)

• 1980-2000 CE
Increased visibility of Muslim presence in Canada through growth of Muslim religious and cultural institutions (e.g., mosques, Islamic schools, funeral homes, *halal* food stores, interest-free lending institutions)

• 1969 CE First Mosque in Toronto dedicated by Dr. M. Qadeer Baig

Timeline

Islam

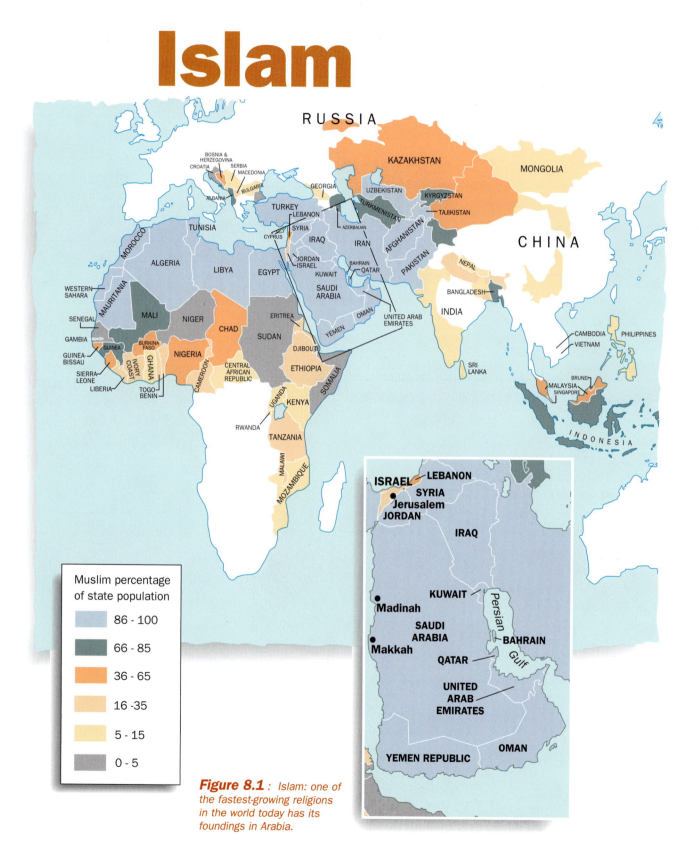

Muslim percentage of state population

- 86 - 100
- 66 - 85
- 36 - 65
- 16 - 35
- 5 - 15
- 0 - 5

Figure 8.1 : *Islam: one of the fastest-growing religions in the world today has its foundings in Arabia.*

ORIGINS

Setting the Stage

Many ideals and customs of Arabian society at the time of Muhammad were transformed by the birth and development of Islam. Three systems in particular characterized Arabia in the sixth century.

Religious System

The people of Arabia held a belief in a variety of different gods in a form of religious expression known as **polytheism**. Polytheism was actively expressed in the practice of idolatry. **Idolatry** is the worship of different objects, usually in the form of sculptures and pictures, with each representing a specific spiritual quality. By the time Muhammad was born in 570 CE, Muslims believed the **Ka'bah**, a cube-shaped building that Abraham built to honour God, was filled with idols. These idols acted as a reflection of the polytheistic tradition of the citizens of Arabia. The citizens had many patron idols and they relied on them absolutely, as a part of their belief system. They believed idols granted them favours and success in all their endeavours. For them, these idols also afforded protection from adversity in battles and from other disasters and calamities.

Social System

Arabia was divided into groupings of people called tribes. Tribes emerged because the nomadic nature of desert life meant people were forced to move from place to place to find food and

Figure 8.2
Pilgrims worship around the Ka'bah in Makkah.

water. Sometimes groups of mountain dwellers would descend upon a family, steal their goods, and evict them from their land. As a result of this, alliances were formed as families united with other families to form clans. Later, these clans united with other clans to form tribes. Tribal life led to the establishment of a tradition of rivalry and bloodshed that characterized Arabia before the advent of Islam.

Women during this time were considered to be at the bottom of the social ladder, as proven by the increasing practice of female infanticide.

Economic System

The Makkan merchants earned their livelihood through trade with various regions beyond the Arabian peninsula, and their merchant caravans faced the danger of attack by tribal Arabs at all times. They waged armed conflicts to settle family vendettas and to revenge the murder of their own members. This was an integral part of their tribal honour and served as a face-saving system of private justice.

As well, the rich loaned money and other essentials of life to the poor and the needy at an increasingly high rate of interest, which made it impossible for the borrower to ever pay off the loan and thus earn freedom from economic tyranny.

Muhammad

Muslims believe the central figure in the emergence of the religion of Islam was the Prophet Muhammad. It was he who received direct revelations from God through the Angel Gabriel. With these revelations burned into his heart, Muhammad would lead Arabia away from idolatry and into a belief in the oneness of God. Muslims regard Muhammad with great reverence, which they demonstrate by using phrases such as "peace be upon him" or the initials "pbuh" after mentioning the Prophet's name.

Muhammad was born in 570 CE. At the time, the citizens of Makkah were building their economic strength through trade, while maintaining polytheistic customs in the form of idolatry. Muhammad was born into the tribe of Quraysh, the most respected tribe in Makkah. His father died shortly before his birth and his mother died when he was just six years old. After his mother's death, the orphan Muhammad was first cared for by his paternal grandfather Abd al-Mutallib, the head of the Quraysh tribe, and later by his uncle, Abu Talib, a distinguished Quraysh merchant.

In his youth, Muhammad made journeys with his grandfather and his uncle as part of their merchant enterprises. By the time Muhammad had reached young adulthood, he had established a reputation as an honest and effective businessman, taking greater responsibility in his uncle's business. In his mid-teens, Muhammad was taking caravans to far-off places, an outward sign of how much faith his uncle and guardian, Abu Talib, had in him. Along the way, Muhammad went through a number of significant spiritual experiences. He had always demonstrated a clear preference for monotheism along with an aversion to idolatry. He saw idolatry as the poison that was inhibiting the spiritual growth of humanity. To Muhammad, idolatry was rooted in superstition and amorality; two qualities that had come to characterize his hometown of Makkah.

Muhammad also began to seek isolation for quiet reflection. The long journeys on the trade routes gave him plenty of time to think about life. When he was back in Makkah, he would retreat to the hills around the city to spend time in contemplation and meditation. It was as if the spiritual groundwork were being laid for something profound to happen.

At the age of twenty, Muhammad gained the respect of a wealthy widow named Khadijah. She engaged him to manage her business affairs. Khadijah was greatly impressed with Muhammad's honesty and integrity in his business dealings, and within a short time she found him to be completely trustworthy. So impressed was Khadijah that she proposed to Muhammad, and despite the fact that she was fifteen years older than he, they were eventually married. Khadijah and Muhammad had a very happy marriage that lasted for twenty-five years. They were devoted to each other and to their community, giving away a great deal of their wealth to the sick and impoverished of Makkah.

Revelation

Things changed dramatically one day in the year 610, in the month of Ramadan (a month of fasting), when Muhammad was on retreat in order to meditate at the cave on Mount Hira. He felt an unusual presence—a presence that Muslims regard as the Angel Gabriel—who appeared to him,

Figure 8.3
Men wait their turn to enter the cave on Mount Hira outside the city of Makkah. Inside, standing in a reverential position (du'a), another man meditates. It was in this cave that the Archangel Gabriel appeared to Muhammad.

embraced him, and commanded him to read a passage. Muhammad responded by telling Gabriel that he could not (or would not) read, but Gabriel insisted. Finally, after the third embrace and the third request to read the following words, Muhammad agreed. Those words became embedded in his heart and he read:

> *Read! In the name of thy Lord and Cherisher, Who*
> *Created man out of a (mere) clot of congealed blood:*
> *Proclaim! And thy Lord is Most Bountiful.*
> *He Who taught (the use of) the Pen*
> *Taught man that which he knew not*
>
> Qur'an 96:1-5

For the next twenty-three years, Muhammad received a series of revelations. The revelations were assembled to form the sacred text of Islam called the Qur'an.

The revelations certainly changed Muhammad. He began preaching around Makkah, sharing the revelations that he received with anyone who would listen. Early on, few would listen. Because Muhammad spoke out passionately against idolatry and for the One God, the Quraysh were extremely angered, for they saw his message as a threat to their ancestral way of life. They also saw Muhammad as a threat to their superior social status as leaders of the community.

Muhammad continued with his mission for nine difficult years until Khadijah, his wife, died in 619. His uncle, Abu Talib, also died that same year. This became known as the "Year of Sorrow." Overcome with grief and feeling personally isolated, Muhammad was faced with another problem: his fellow Makkans displayed hostility toward him because of his preachings against idolatry. Soon, it became clear that Muhammad's life was in danger. With Abu Talib gone, and along with him the protection of family and tribe, Muhammad emigrated north to the city of Yathrib, which is now called Madinah (Medina). This event is known as the **hijrah**, which means "migration."

Muslims believe that before leaving Makkah, Muhammad went through two special experiences known as the "Night Journey" and "Ascension." The Night Journey involved Muhammad, accompanied by the Angel Gabriel, travelling on a winged horse, called the Buraq, from Makkah to Jerusalem. After arriving in Jerusalem, Muhammad and Gabriel ascended through the seven heavens. The Ascension itself is known as the **Mi'raj**. In the first heaven, they met Adam, then John and Jesus in the second heaven. They went through five more heavens meeting Joseph, Enoch, Aaron, Moses, and lastly Abraham. Finally Muhammad approached the Throne of God, eventually standing "within two bow lengths" of God Himself (i.e., very close). Muhammad was profoundly affected by the experience.

Profile: *The Prophets*

According to Islamic tradition, God sent a series of prophets and messengers to guide mankind toward the Truth. The long line of prophets and messengers, numbering 140 000, begins with Adam, who God created and on whom God bestowed the first revelations. Muslims believe that there is no difference between the prophets. All of the prophets were given a message from God to deliver to humanity. There are several prophets who have influenced not only Islam, but Judaism and Christianity as well.

Prophet	Islamic Perspective	Jewish Perspective	Christian Perspective
Noah	Noah warned people of the error of their sinful ways, built an ark, survived the flood, rebuilt civilization and shared new laws governing God's creation.	Same as that of Islam.	Same as that of Islam.
Abraham	Abraham is one of seven prophets who received the Scriptures from God. He is mentioned frequently in the Qur'an. He taught people to abandon idolatry. Abraham proved to be the source of two great prophetic families: the Arab lineage through his son Ismael and Ismael's mother, Hagar. In the end, Abraham gave people a sense of their moral and religious obligations.	Abraham is seen as the patriarch of the Jewish faith. He taught people to worship the one God and abandon idolatry. Jews believe that the Hebrew line descends through Abraham's son Isaac, who was the son of Sarah. Abraham had two wives; Hagar and Sarah.	Same that of Judaism.
Moses	Moses was sent to proclaim the one God to the idolaters of Egypt. Moses, who is mentioned over 200 times in the Qur'an, is very highly regarded in Islam. Moses used miracles to demonstrate God's power over the Egyptians. He received God's law in the form of the Ten Commandments.	Agrees with the Islamic position. Also, Moses was sent by God to free the Hebrews from slavery, leading them out of bondage to the Promised Land. He was also sent to give the Jews God's law through the Ten Commandments.	Same as that of Judaism.

Prophet	Islamic Perspective	Jewish Perspective	Christian Perspective
Jesus	Jesus was born miraculously by the Virgin Mary and, over the course of his life, performed many miracles. However, the Qur'an specifically denies that Jesus was the divinely appointed son of God. The Qur'an also does not support the belief that Jesus died on the cross. Instead it holds the position that Jesus never died and ascended into heaven and will return to aid humanity again in the future.	Holds no formal view of Jesus.	Jesus is the Son of God and part of the Holy Trinity. Jesus was born of the Virgin Mary, suffered persecution, was crucified and died, and rose again after three days. He ascended into heaven and will return to judge the living and the dead.
Muhammad	Muhammad is "The Seal of the Prophets," the last of those who have come to convey the divine wisdom of God to humanity. As with every prophet he is afforded the highest spiritual prominence because he directly received the divine word of God. He instantly conveyed these Quranic revelations to all people. For Muslims, Muhammad is the last prophet, who completed the teachings of all the prophets who came before him. All the preceding prophets are regarded as "Muslims" in the sense that they all taught: a) belief in One God, and b) the importance of living a virtuous and moral life. These two fundamentals constitute "Islam" in the broadest sense of the word, i.e., submission to the Will of God.	Holds no formal view of Muhammad.	Holds no formal view of Muhammad.

QUESTIONS

1. In general, what is the special role of the prophets?
2. What evidence is there that the religions of Islam, Judaism, and Christianity have many similarities?
3. Why do Muslims consider Muhammad to be "The Seal of the Prophets"?

Muhammad in Madinah

The birth of an organized government and political system based on the religion of Islam occurred when God instructed Muhammad to move to Yathrib in 622 CE. The Muslim calendar starts from this event, known as the *hijrah* (migration). The city came to be known as al-Madinah or "the city" by the local people. Muhammad's impact was so compelling that some referred to the city as Madinah al-Nabi, which means the "City of the Prophet."

Within a short period of time, Muhammad was able to build a large community of Muslims in the city. Soon Madinah was united under the banner of Islam and the leadership of Muhammad. However, problems lay to the south. The Quraysh of Makkah were alarmed at the growing appeal of Islam. Increasingly, Muhammad was managing to persuade the pagan Arabs to give up all that they cherished—their ancestral worship of their idols upon whom they depended for their survival. They were convinced that Muhammad was bent on completely destroying them and their venerated way of life. The only solution seemed to be to annihilate Muhammad, since all other means of persuasion—offers of great wealth, absolute leadership of the Quraysh, and beautiful women—had all failed. Thus, the concern of the Quraysh, coupled with the rapid growth of Islam, led to confrontation on the battlefield.

Jihad has been translated by some to mean "holy war." This is not an accurate translation. More precisely, the term means "striving." In other words, Muslims are called to strive to follow God's commands. Early Muslims lived in an Arabia divided between the growing Muslim population of Madinah and the established Quraysh idol worshippers of Makkah.

Three battles proved to be significant in the unification of Arabia under the religion of Islam. All three battles called on Muhammad to defend Madinah and, more specifically, Islam. Here is a synopsis of the three events:

Battle	Synopsis
Badr	• Muhammad's army of 313 defeats Makkah's army of 1000.
Uhud	• Makkans return with an army of 3000 to score a victory. Despite their apparent victory, the Makkans return home instead of proceeding an additional three kilometres and sacking Madinah.
Battle of the Trench	• Makkans return with an army of 10 000. Muhammad orders his men to build a trench around the city of Madinah. The Makkans are unable to take the city, thwarted by the trench and the hot desert climate.

Web Quest

To read the entire "Farewell Sermon" see
http://www.muslim-canada.org/farewell.htm

These defensive battles solidified the position of Islam in Madinah. Disheartened, the Makkans returned home as Muhammad's star continued to rise. Now Muhammad's teachings were taken into consideration by both the people of Madinah and the people of Makkah. Muslim conversions steadily grew, many in Madinah and some in Makkah. Eventually, in 630 CE after two smaller pilgrimages, Muhammad led a group of 10 000 into Makkah, in what is commonly referred to as the "Conquest of Makkah." Few opposed Muhammad's return or his removal of idols from the Ka'bah. Before leaving the city, Muhammad appeared before the citizens of Makkah, reminded them of their ill deeds and their persecution of the Muslims of Madinah. At one point, he turned to the assembled crowd and asked, "Now what do you expect of me?" When the people lowered their heads in shame, Muhammad proclaimed, "May God pardon you. Go in peace. There shall be no responsibility on you today; you are free!" The effect of his words was felt immediately, prompting a shift in the minds of those assembled. In one remarkable moment the Makkans moved from a conquered people to a liberated people. Muhammad and his Companions left Makkah without leaving a single soldier behind. He appointed a Makkan chief to take charge of the city.

In 632, Muhammad, accompanied by 140 000 Muslims, visited Makkah to perform his last pilgrimage. He travelled south from Madinah to Makkah, stopping at Mount Arafat, where he delivered what has come to be known as his "Farewell Sermon." Dr. M. Hamidullah effectively summarizes the message of the sermon:

> *He addressed to them his celebrated sermon, in which he gave a resume of his teachings—belief in One God without images or icons; equality of all the believers without distinction of race or class; the superiority of individuals being based solely on piety; sanctity of life, property and honour; abolition of interest, and of vendettas and private justice; better treatment of women; obligatory inheritance and distribution of the property of the deceased persons among near relatives of both sexes, and removal of the possibility of the accumulation of wealth in the hands of the few. The Qur'an and the conduct of the Prophet were to serve as the bases of law and healthy criterion for every aspect of human life.*

In one sweeping and profound sermon, Muhammad offered forgiveness to those who had done wrong in the past, while summarizing the core elements of Islamic teaching.

After the pilgrimage, Muhammad returned to Madinah where he came down with a fever. While he continued to lead prayers in the Muslim place of worship, the **mosque**, for a short time, it soon became apparent that he was seriously ill. A few weeks later in June of 632, he died at the age of 63.

Profile: *The Caliphs*

The death of Muhammad brought confusion to the Muslim community. After his death, the issue of leadership came to the forefront. The Prophet had been an incredibly gifted leader and, while there were many gifted leaders in the Islamic community, it was clear that no one could replace him. There were two claims to the Muslim leadership that surfaced immediately following the Prophet's death. The first came from the supporters of Abu Bakr who claimed that he should become the inaugural "caliph," or successor, to Muhammad. Abu Bakr, who was a close friend and Companion of the Prophet, was the candidate who proved to be a strong proponent of the faith and a loyal servant of Muhammad's in both Madinah and Makkah.

The second claim came from Ali, the Prophet's cousin and son-in-law. Some believe Muhammad publicly acknowledged him as his successor on a trip between Makkah and Madinah shortly before the Prophet's death. These competing claims came to a head and eventually Abu Bakr was chosen over Ali, who some felt was unfit for leadership because he was just thirty years old. The choice of first caliph created a political rift within the Muslim community that has lasted until the present day. The following is a brief account of the four caliphs and their contributions.

Caliph	Years as Caliph	Important Contributions
Abu Bakr	632–634	• formed the separately written chapters of the Qur'an into a consolidated compilation • solidified his leadership and suppressed Arab tribes who saw the death of the Prophet as an opportunity to turn against Islam • continued the Muslim expansion initiated by the Prophet in the Middle East
Umar	634–644	• continued the expansion of Islam to Syria, Palestine, Egypt, and Persia
Uthman	644–656	• oversaw Islamic expansion west across northern Africa and east into northern India and to the border of China • was criticized for showing favouritism to his relatives even though this was never proven. In the end, Uthman was assassinated. According to some historians, he was a victim of his own kindness.
Ali	656–661	• assumed leadership of a divided Muslim community • was forced to defend his rule on the battlefield against the Ummayyad family. This marked the first time that Muslim rose against Muslim in battle. • was assassinated in 661

The first four leaders of the Muslim community are called the "Rightly-Guided Caliphs," or *Rashidin*. All four of the caliphs were close Companions of Muhammad both in Madinah and Makkah. They possessed a thorough knowledge of the Qur'an, and they proved themselves to be devout adherents of the faith. Their significance is measured by their ability to hold the Muslim community together despite the existence of internal political conflict. After the *Rashidin*, the leadership of Islam shifted to a number of family dynasties that took the Muslim community into the next phase of its evolution. While the title of caliph survived, *in varying forms*, with certain members of the ruling families, over time *the caliphate began to wane*, eventually disappearing after the devastation of World War One when it was abolished with the birth of the Turkish Republic in 1924.

QUESTIONS

1. Name the first four caliphs and outline their main accomplishments.
2. Why was Ali not chosen for the position of caliph until 656?
3. In your view, which caliph was the most important in the history of Islam? Why?

Figure 8.4
Prophet's Mosque in Madinah serves as Muhammad's place of burial (under the green dome).

Check Your Understanding

1. What is idolatry?

2. How did Muhammad win the approval and admiration of the Makkans in 630 CE?

3. What advice does Muhammad give in his Farewell Sermon?

BELIEFS

Figure 8.5
God's word, as revealed in the Qur'an, is the centrepiece of Islamic beliefs. Copying the Qur'an was the noblest of arts. This copy, transcribed in 1491 by the noted Ottoman calligrapher Shaykh Hamdullah and lavishly decorated with arabesque designs, is a worthy testament to Muslim faith.

For Muslims, beliefs are a purely personal affair. While it is regarded as a charitable act to guide others to the Truth and to dispel ignorance, Muslims are not called on to compel anyone to believe what they believe. From a Muslim perspective, to align oneself with the will of God (in order to accomplish "surrender" in the real sense of the word) is part of one's inner struggle.

Muslim belief is summarized in their creed, which is called the Shahadah (Figure 8.6):

"There is no god but God and Muhammad is the Messenger of God."

This creed is central to all of Islam. It is the organizing principle around which all other beliefs are formed.

Muslims owe their religious faith to Muhammad, the Messenger of God. One day, the Prophet Muhammad was asked about the nature of faith. He replied:

"Thou shalt believe in the One God, in His angelic messengers, in His revealed books, in His human messengers, in the Last Day (or Resurrection and final judgement) and in the determination of Good and evil by God."

Hadith literature, Bukhari and Muslim

Figure 8.6
The Arabic script of the Shahadah

God

Muslims believe God's proper name is *Allah*. The monotheistic belief in one God created a shift from the idolatry and polytheism that characterized the Arabian belief system prior to Muhammad. By the time the Prophet received his first revelation, he was already convinced that there was only one God and that idolatry did not offer anything of spiritual significance to the people of Arabia.

The belief in an omnipotent, omniscient, and omnipresent God is central to the Muslim faith. God is one, but even though He is one, He is capable of doing all sorts of things. God is not only the creator, but the master of all.

God rules over Heaven and earth; nothing moves without His knowledge and permission. It is important to remember that the word *Islam* means "submission to God" or "surrender to God's will." Therefore, Islam is not only a belief in one God, but also a practice, spiritual as well as temporal. It is a complete code of human life and a way of life. Muslims believe that humans are limited in what they are able to know, and that God is the ever-present, compassionate guide who will lead them to knowledge and fulfillment. They believe failure to recognize this is a miscalculation and that surrender to God is the only answer.

Islam has two distinctive features:

1) Equilibrium between the temporal and the spiritual (the body and the soul), permitting a full enjoyment of all the good that God has created, enjoining, at the same time on everybody, duties toward God such as worship, fasting, charity, etc. Islam was to be the religion of the masses and not merely of the elect.

Qur'an 7:32

2) A universality of the call—all the believers becoming brothers and equals without any distinction of class or race or tongue. The only superiority that it recognizes is a personal one, based on the greater fear of God and greater piety.

Qur'an 49:13

The Day of Judgement

Muslims believe that every person living on earth has a soul that lives on earth for one lifetime and, upon the death of the body, moves on to an afterlife. The motto of Islam is summed up in the expression in the Qur'an that states: "Well-being in this world and well-being in the Hereafter." Hence a Muslim should not neglect one of these for the sole profit of the other.

Muslims believe that when a soul passes into the afterlife, God will reconfigure the person's physical body so he or she can stand before Him on the Day of Judgement. It is on this day that the soul is sent to Paradise or to Hell.

Paradise is described as an eternal abode of beauty and majesty. Muslims believe it is the just reward for a person who has lived a righteous life as a believer in one God. On the other hand, Hell is described as an abode of great torment and anguish. According to Islamic tradition, God does not wish to send anyone to Hell. However, if a person chooses to live an evil life, and works against the will of God without repentance, Hell is where the soul will be sent. Hell is a destination that can be avoided by sincerely submitting to God and obeying His commands. In the end, God will judge people's actions by their intentions and motives.

Check Your Understanding

1. Why is the Shahadah such a central belief for Muslims?

2. Briefly explain the Muslim concept of God. Is it similar to your concept? Discuss.

3. What is the Day of Judgement?

4. Outline your personal views on Paradise and Hell.

PRACTICES, RITUALS, FESTIVALS, AND SYMBOLS

Practices and Rituals

Muslims place a tremendous amount of emphasis on upholding the tenets of their faith. Specifically, this is demonstrated through the Five Pillars of Islam. The Five Pillars were established in the Qur'an.

Pillar of the Faith	Description
The first pillar: **Shahadah**—Declaration of faith  *Figure 8.7*	• The *Shahadah* consists of two declarations: "There is no god but God" and "Muhammad is the Messenger of God." • The *Shahadah* is Muslims' announcement to the world that they sincerely believe in and follow the Qur'an.
The second pillar: **Salat**—Mandatory prayer five times daily  *Figure 8.8*	• Five-times-daily *salat* (prayer) is mandatory (as opposed to other voluntary forms of prayer and supplication) and takes place before dawn, mid-day, late afternoon, after sunset, and after dark. Muslims recite prayers and perform a series of movements as part of the *salat*. • Prior to *salat* prayers, a person must perform a ritual cleansing known as **wudu**, which means "making pure or radiant." • Sometimes a person may be required to clean the entire body in a process known as **ghusl**. The ritual cleansing of the entire body is mandatory after sexual intercourse, menstruation, nocturnal emissions, or childbirth. Voluntary *ghusl* is recommended on other occasions.

The third pillar:

Zakat—Mandatory almsgiving

Figure 8.9

- Paying the *zakat* alms is compliance to a divine injunction gladly performed by sincere Muslims for the sake of and in the name of God. The word *zakat* means "to purify or increase."
- Islamic law states that a person should give alms valued at 2.5 per cent of their surplus wealth over the period of one year.

The fourth pillar:

Sawm—Mandatory fasting

Figure 8.10

- For the entire month of Ramadan, Muslims are forbidden to eat, drink, smoke, or have sexual relations from dawn until dusk.
- The Ramadan fast is an act of worship wherein the Muslim community dedicates a month to considering the benevolence of God and abstaining from some of the pleasures of life in order to develop spiritual purity.
- Appropriate exemptions and concessions are given for people who are old and infirm, or on a journey, as well as for very young children.
- The fasting month ends with a one-day festival called Eid al-Fitr. (See Festivals.)

The fifth pillar:

Hajj—Mandatory pilgrimage to Makkah

Figure 8.11

- The mandatory hajj itself is undertaken by any Muslim in the world, male or female, who has the health and means to make the pilgrimage.
- The last day of the hajj commemorates the day God asked Abraham to sacrifice his son Ismael at Mina. Pilgrims throw seven pebbles at three tall stone pillars that represent Satan.

Place of Worship at the Mosque

Figure 8.12
The first Canadian mosque: Al Rashid Mosque in Edmonton

Every Friday a little after midday, Muslims offer congregational prayers (*salat*) at the Muslim place of worship called the mosque. Friday congregational prayer is mandatory.

Most mosques possess certain features such as a dome and/or a tall tower called a minaret from which the call to prayer is issued by a person (who may use a loud speaker). One element common to all mosques is a steady supply of water to perform the *wudu* before prayer begins. Before entering the interior of the mosque, Muslims take off their shoes as a sign of respect. This helps in keeping the mosque clean for prayer. There are no seats in the mosque and worshippers are required to pray on a floor covered with carpets or other floor coverings. People who are physically challenged are permitted to use chairs, if necessary. The women pray separately from the men because, according to Muslim belief, this allows both genders to avoid distractions and to concentrate more closely on God.

Inside the mosque, prayers are led by an **imam**, who delivers a sermon just before Friday prayers and after the *Eid* (festival) prayers. He speaks from an elevated platform called a *minbar*. While the imam acts as a prayer leader, he is not considered to be the Muslim equivalent of a priest. Often imams have jobs outside of the mosque and simply act as one of the members of the community who leads the prayer.

The final distinguishing feature of a mosque is a small arch on one wall that points to the Ka'bah in Makkah. This arch (commonly known as a mihrab) provides a focal point so that prayer is directed toward the Ka'bah. Congregational prayer takes place throughout the week but specifically on Friday after midday, at festivals, special occasions, and at funerals.

Living My Religion

Yasser Qurashi

Yasser Qurashi is a student at Loyola Catholic Secondary School in Mississauga, Ontario. He comes from a devout Muslim family that strives to practice their faith with as much sincerity as possible. Yasser's family immigrated to Canada when he was two years old. Both of his parents were born in the Middle East. They moved to Pakistan to pursue employment opportunities before coming to Canada. With this heritage behind him, Yasser represents a distinctive blend of traditional Muslim and Canadian Muslim culture.

Figure 8.13

Yasser honours his Muslim beliefs as faithfully as possible. Prayer is an important part of his life. Generally, Yasser prays on his own, usually in his bedroom at home, reciting his prayers aloud in Arabic while facing Makkah. While he does not speak Arabic, he does understand the words of the prayers he recites. His parents taught him the meaning of the prayers when he was very young and their teaching has remained with him throughout his life.

Yasser's parents have set a solid example of prayer and dedication for him to follow. His father, Khalid, prays regularly and attends Friday prayers at the Al-Falah mosque in Oakville, Ontario. Because the Friday prayers take place just after midday, Khalid has made arrangements with his employer to go to the mosque on his lunch hour. Yasser's mother, Huma, is quite devoted to her prayer life. Her devotion has inspired Yasser to recognize the need to maintain an awareness of God's presence at all times.

The element of the Islamic faith that has had the most profound effect on Yasser is the Ramadan fast. He has been participating in the fast since he was nine years old, even though participation in the fast is not mandatory until the age of eleven. He sees Ramadan as a time to remember the importance of his faith. Every hunger pain acts as a reminder of the sacrifice he has made for his beliefs. During Ramadan, his family wakes up between 4:30 a.m. and 6:30 a.m., depending on the time of the year, for an early meal and morning prayers. He then fasts for the day, trying to be mindful of the call for all Muslims to not only refrain from food and drink, but also to refrain from negative activities like social gossip. He ends the fast each day with a meal and evening prayers. Yasser follows the fast for the entire month of Ramadan and officially concludes the fasting month by celebrating the festival of Eid al-Fitr with his family and the Muslim community.

Yasser believes that he will always be a Muslim. While his high-school life has seen him introduced to a variety of different religious perspectives, he hopes he will maintain his belief in the truth and justice of Islam. After he finishes his education, and achieves financial security, Yasser plans on making the hajj to Makkah. Perhaps the pilgrimage to the roots of Islam will strengthen the beliefs he maintains today.

QUESTIONS

1. Why is prayer important to Yasser?

2. Where did Yasser learn to pray?

3. What element of the Islamic faith has had the most profound effect on Yasser?

Festivals

The Ramadan Fast	• The fast is celebrated during the month of Ramadan. It serves to draw Muslims closer to God and to develop spiritual piety, patience, and perseverance.
Eid al-Fitr	• The Festival of the Breaking of the Fast is held on the first day of the tenth month of the Islamic year. It celebrates the end of the fasting month of Ramadan and marks a period of spiritual and moral renewal for the Muslim community. People celebrate this day with great joy as they participate in family gatherings, giving gifts, and in giving donations to the poor.
Eid-al-Adha	• The Great Festival of Sacrifice is held on the tenth day of *Zul Hijjah* (tenth day of the twelfth month of the Islamic calendar). The occasion marks Abraham's submission to the will of God and his willingness to sacrifice his son Ismael.
Milad ul-Nabi	• The prophet Muhammad's date of birth was the 12 Rabbi 'Awwal, which is the twelvth day of the third month in the Islamic calendar. Birthday (Milad) celebrations are held throughout the month.
Mi'raj	• The *Mi'raj* celebrates the "Night Journey" or Ascension where Muhammad is taken by Gabriel from Makkah to Jerusalem and then on to Heaven. This festival is celebrated on the twenty-seventh of *Rajab* (the seventh month).
Islamic New Year	• The celebration of the New Year takes place on the first day of *Muharram*, the first month of the Islamic calendar.
The Shi'ah Observance of Muharram	• The observance of *Muharram* takes place in the first ten days of the Muslim new year and is celebrated by Shi'ahs. The festival commemorates the martyrdom of Husain, the son of Ali, who was the grandson of Muhammad and was killed at the battle of Karbala in 680. Sunnis also commemorate the tenth of *Muharram* by fasting.

Figure 8.14
In Winnipeg, Shahina Siddiqui stuffs gift bags with candy for Muslim children, who will receive the gifts at the Feast of Ramadam.

Symbols

The use of symbols as an expression of faith is not present in Islam. Muhammad made it clear that people should not revere pictures or sculptures of animals or humans. Hence, there are no human or animal representations in places of worship. He said that it was God's work to create living things and it was wrong for humans to imitate this aspect of God. For this reason, Muslim art has tended toward rich patterns and colourful designs. From superb tapestries to brilliant calligraphy, Islam is adorned with a tremendous array of beautiful art. Couple this with the unique and awe-inspiring breadth of Muslim architecture, and one can see that Muslims have derived inspiration from their faith in the area of art.

Some symbols have come to represent Muslim nations. One common example is the star and the crescent moon. This symbol is used on the national flags of Turkey and Pakistan—two Muslim nations. The history of the symbol dates back to the Roman Empire when the city of Byzantium (later Constantinople and then Istanbul) adopted the crescent moon as a symbolic tribute to Diana, goddess of the hunt. In 330 CE, Constantine added the star in honour of Mary, the mother of Jesus. By the time Constantinople became a Muslim city in 1453 CE, the star and the crescent moon were a well-established symbol for the city. Some Muslim leaders adopted the symbol and, as time passed, it came to be associated with Muslim nations. Therefore, the star and the crescent moon is more an historic symbol than a symbol of Islam.

Some believe a more fitting representation of Islam can be found in the national flag of Saudi Arabia (Figure 8.17). The Saudi Arabian flag has the *Shahadah* written in white against a solid green background. The colour green is said by some to have been the Prophet's favourite colour.

Figure 8.15
The national flag of Turkey

Figure 8.16
The national flag of Pakistan

Figure 8.17
The national flag of Saudi Arabia

Holy Places

Ka'bah and Prophet's Mosque

Figure 8.18
The Ka'bah in Makkah. Muslims revere the Ka'bah as the House of God. Their daily prayers are directed towards this cubical stone structure.

Figure 8.19
An interior view of the Prophet's Mosque in Madinah, the first mosque in Islam.

Dome of the Rock

Figure 8.20
The Dome of the Rock in Jerusalem is the third holiest site in Islam.

QUESTIONS

1. Why is the Ka'bah revered by Muslims?
2. Why is the Prophet's Mosque an important site to Muslims?

Check Your Understanding

1. What two declarations are made in the *Shahadah*?

2. Briefly describe the Five Pillars of Islam.

3. Why did Muhammad oppose the creation of symbols and icons?

4. How did the star and crescent moon come to represent some Muslim nations?

5. Why is the *Shahadah* against a green background considered by some to be a more fitting representation of Islam?

MILESTONES

Early Life

Figure 8.21
A father whispers the iqamah, the command to rise and worship into the left ear of his child.

Muslims believe that a child is born free of sin. Furthermore, the child is born pure and with a natural inclination toward goodness and virtue. As a creation of God, the child possesses an inherent understanding of the wisdom and power of God, as well as an understanding of the nature of his or her relationship with God. The ceremony that is performed after a child is born is called the *Adhan*, which is also the call to prayer that is recited from the minarets in Muslim countries. The baby is washed and then the father, or some elderly person, whispers the Call to Prayer (the *Adhan*) in his or her right ear. In the left ear, the person whispers the Command to Rise and Worship. This is called the *Iqamah*.

Aqiqah

Seven days after the birth, or earlier, a name-giving ceremony called the *Aqiqah* is performed. The naming of a baby is important for a Muslim. Muhammad made recommendations for naming a child, saying that Abdullah, meaning "servant of God," and Abdur-Rahman, meaning "servant of the Merciful One," were the most pleasing names to God.

The ceremony starts with the father, an elderly relative, or a pious person reading from the Qur'an. The announcement of the name of the child follows the reading. Muslims can choose between a family name, one of Muhammad's names, or one of the "Ninety-Nine Beautiful Names" that describe God. If one of the names of God is used, the name must be proceeded by Abd (servant) as in the name Abdullah, which was mentioned earlier.

When the hair of the child is cut or shaved for the *Aqiqah* ceremony, its weight in silver (or the equivalent in currency) is distributed to the poor. The sacrifice of either a goat or sheep is made, and one-third of the meat is distributed to the poor. In most cases, male circumcision, called *Khitan*, usually takes place in the hospital. However, in some countries, such as Morocco, the procedure takes place when the boy is three or four years old.

Marriage

A Muslim marriage is a legally sanctioned union between a man and a woman, designed to bring happiness and companionship to both parties. The marriage contract affords both partners certain rights and obligations in the hope that their union will produce a family so as to please God. The status of marriage is made clear in the Qur'an:

> *And among His Signs is this, that He created for you mates from among yourselves that ye may dwell in tranquillity with them and He has put love and mercy between your (hearts); verily in that are Signs for those who reflect.*
>
> Qur'an 30:21

The hope of the Muslim union in marriage is the emergence of a strong family; a courteous, polite, and compassionate family whose members seek to know and live the will of God.

A Muslim marriage is based on a voluntary offer and acceptance by the bride and the groom. Quite often, the parents will give advice and help in selecting a spouse for their son or daughter. However, the parents' role is simply to help by counselling, and not by making decisions for the couple. The bride and groom have the last say in the matter.

Once a suitable match is found, a contract is prepared containing the various wishes of the bride and groom regarding the relationship itself and lifestyle issues related to property and money. Because the contract reflects the wishes of the couple, no Muslim officials need to be present for the signing. However, two Muslims must witness the marriage. As well, many Muslims prefer to hold the actual marriage ceremony, which includes the signing ceremony, in a mosque or in their home with an imam or a qadi (a person authorized to solemnize marriages) who reads from the Qur'an and concludes the formal part of the proceedings. The ceremony is followed by a family celebration.

Polygamy

For modern Western society, one controversial aspect of Islamic tradition is the practice of **polygamy**. Polygamy occurs when a person is married to more than one person at the same time. Within the Islamic tradition, polygamous marriages can provide women with the opportunity to marry in societies where there are more women than men. It is also intended to provide an opportunity for widows to remarry. These situations prevailed during the time of Muhammad when some men died in battle, while others died from disease, illness, or old age. It was seen by Muslims then, as it is now, as a sign of great charity to marry a widow and spare her the hardship of having to fend for herself. Muslims believe it is a sign of great tolerance and understanding for a woman to agree to share her husband with another woman.

According to Islamic tradition, a Muslim man can marry up to four wives. Permission for this is given in the Qur'an:

> If ye fear that ye shall not be able to deal justly with the orphans (then) marry women of your choice two or three or four; but if ye fear that ye shall not be able to deal justly (with them) then only one or (a captive) that your right hands possess. That will be more suitable to prevent you from doing injustice.
>
> Qur'an 4:3

One interpretation of this verse maintains that since it can be extremely difficult, if not impossible, to give equal time, intimacy, commitment, and love to more than one wife, then one wife (the number recommended in the verse in such cases) is most appropriate.

It is important to note that first, a man must obtain permission from his first wife before taking on a second, third, or fourth wife; and second, the vast majority of Muslims maintain monogamous marriages.

Divorce

While divorce is permitted within Islam, it is regarded as a last resort for a married couple. Even Muhammad discouraged divorce saying, "The most detestable of the permitted things in the eyes of God is divorce." Accordingly, it is not in the interests of the Muslim community to force people to remain married if they cannot grow together and form productive families. Therefore, a procedure exists whereby either the man or woman can obtain a divorce from the spouse. Divorce could be unilateral (initiated by one person), bilateral (initiated by both), or could be obtained through a court of law. The Qur'an insists that the two must first refer their disputes and quarrels to arbitration before deciding to give or to obtain a divorce. The Qur'an provides a detailed account of the procedure.

Death

Muslims approach death with a sense of hope as opposed to fear. Their hope is that they will reach Paradise and attain the beautiful vision of God's own countenance.

Muslims believe that the burial should take place preferably on the day that the person has died. The body is taken to the gravesite where people who have attended the funeral procession, as well as bystanders, throw handfuls of earth into the grave while reciting chapters from the Qur'an, such as those that pertain to the Day of Judgement. After the burial, a short period of mourning is observed, usually for three days. Muslims believe that the deceased is visited by two angels who question the person about his or her life, faith, and deeds—both good and evil—while on earth.

Figure 8.22
The manuscripts of the Qur'an were never illustrated with human figures.

Check Your Understanding

1. How is a young Muslim child introduced to the faith?

2. Briefly describe the Muslim approach to marriage.

3. Outline what happens during and after a burial in the Islamic tradition.

SACRED WRITINGS

The Qur'an

The holiest book in Islam is the Qur'an. The word *Qur'an* means "recitation." Muslims usually recite or chant the Qur'an aloud rather than read it silently. Muslims believe that the revelations that Muhammad received over a twenty-three-year period form literally the "Word" of God. They believe Muhammad was directly quoting God every time he received and conveyed a revelation to his community. Because of this, criticism of the Qur'an is not permitted by anyone at anytime. The book is comprised of God's actual words and, therefore, humanity is encouraged to learn and to understand the revelations but not to make them the target of disrespect or ridicule.

The belief that the Qur'an is the actual Word of God distinguishes it from other sacred writings. It is known as *wahi*, or revelation, and was "revealed" to the Prophet Muhammad through the Angel Gabriel, the angelic messenger of God. He conveyed the divine message to Muhammad, the human messenger of God. Muslims believe therefore that the Angel Gabriel conveyed the Qur'an in its unaltered form to Muhammad and hence to all of humanity. Due to nuances in the Arabic language, even a translation of the Qur'an into another language could not be considered a true rendering of the Qur'an.

According to Muslim belief, the Qur'an was not delivered to the Prophet Muhammad in one session as a complete book, but was revealed to him bit by bit, through the Angel

Sacred Text

Allah! There is no God but He the living, the Self-subsisting Eternal. No slumber can seize Him nor sleep. His are all things in the heavens and on Earth. Who is there who can intercede in His presence except as He permitteth? He knoweth what (appeareth to his creatures as) before or after or behind them. Nor shall they compass aught of His knowledge except as He willeth. His throne doth extend over the heavens and the earth and He feeleth no fatigue in guarding and preserving them. For He is the Most High, the Supreme (in glory).

Qur'an 2:255

Figure 8.23

This passage from the Qur'an is known as the *Ayat-ul-Kursi* or the "Verse of the Throne." A throne is a symbol of power, knowledge, and authority. In this case, the throne is the seat of Allah, the Eternal and Absolute. Everything begins and ends with Allah. He is the ultimate Protector and Sustainer whose throne "extends over the heavens and the earth."

QUESTIONS

1. What does the throne represent?
2. Define the words omniscient, omnipotent, and omnipresent. How does the "Verse of the Throne" demonstrate the omniscience, omnipotence, and omnipresence of Allah?
3. In your opinion, what is the most significant characteristic of Allah? Why?

Gabriel. The Prophet would then remember the messages himself and would teach them to his Companions, so that they could also memorize them. In other words, the Qur'an was transmitted orally by the Prophet to his Companions.

Eventually a manuscript of the Qur'an was prepared. The Qur'an exists in the world today in its absolute, original purity, not only as a written text, but also in the memory of hundreds of thousands of Muslims. Muslims believe that it is impossible for anyone to change even a dot of the Qur'an because each time the text is reproduced, it must be copied in accordance with the preserved original text.

The Qur'an is made up of **surahs**, or chapters, whose titles are derived from a significant incident or word that appears within the surah's text. Each surah is made up of a number of **ayats**, or verses. *Ayats* literally means "signs." Every surah except one, the ninth chapter, begins with the words, "In the Name of Allah, the Most Compassionate, the Most Merciful."

Hadith (Sunnah)

The **Hadith** (or **Sunnah**) is the second source of Islamic Law (**Shari'ah**). The Qur'an itself is the first source of Islamic Law. There are three kinds of Hadith (Sunnah): (1) sayings directly associated with Muhammad, (2) an action or practice of Muhammad's or (3) his silent approval of someone else's actions. Using special standards, scholars classify the Hadith literature so as to determine its various grades of authenticity. Accordingly, a Hadith is classified as sound, good, weak, or infirm. The Hadith literature further clarifies Muslim religious practices such as prayer and almsgiving, which are mentioned in the Qur'an.

Check Your Understanding

1. Why do Muslims treat the Qur'an with such reverence and respect?

2. What are Hadith? Why are Hadith important?

GROUPS AND INSTITUTIONS

In the teachings of Islam, there are certain "external" duties such as prayer (*salat*), fasting, charity, and abstaining from evil and wickedness. These external aspects belong to the domain of Muslim law which contains rules and regulations that affect one's entire life. There are also "internal" duties such as faith, gratitude to God, sincerity, and freedom from egotism. The internal, or mystical, aspect is generally known as Sufism. Sufism derives its teachings and practices from the original sources of Islam, namely the Qur'an and the Hadith.

Islam has two sects: the Sunnis and the Shi'ahs. Sufism belongs to, and is practised by, both the Sunnis and the Shi'ahs. *Sufis are not considered to be a separate sect.*

Both the Sunni and the Shi'ah sects, as well as the Sufis, believe in one God and that Muhammad is the Prophet of God. This is their core belief. However, there are some differing features that are noteworthy.

Sunni	Shi'ah	Sufi
• Approximately eighty-five per cent of the world's Muslims are Sunnis. • The name is derived from the word *sunna*, which means "well-trodden path." • Sunni groups came into existence after the death of the Prophet. Over time, they have emerged as the most influential group in Islam. • They believe in building consensus within the community in order to arrive at a just and equitable society. • Sunnis follow the traditions of the Prophet as well as the four schools of Sunni law: Hanafi, Shafi'i, Hanbali and Maliki.	• Known as the "party of Ali." Shi'ahs believe that, prior to the death of Muhammad, the Prophet chose his son-in-law, Ali, as his successor. Ali was not chosen as leader in favour of Abu Bakr creating a political division within the Muslim community. Later, these developed into doctrinal differences. • Shi'ahs believe that, after the death of Muhammad, a series of infallible leaders called *Imams* were to take charge of Islam and guide the community. • The Shi'ahs are a small but noticeable group within Islam, dominating politics and religious life in Iran and representing a vocal minority in Iraq, East Africa, Pakistan, and India.	• The Arabic word *suf*, which the word *sufi* is derived from, means "wool," so it is likely that the Sufis were named after the ascetic clothing that they wore. Others say that *sufi* is derived from the word *safa* which means "purity." • Sufism developed into a mystical philosophy of Islam. • According to the Sufi tradition, the goal is to develop spiritually, both inwardly and outwardly, in order to discover the reality of God. • Sufis emphasize sincerity and excellence, performing prayers and meditations. To develop a constant and deep concentration, the Sufis employ physical methods such as playing Sufi music, chanting the name of God over and over again, or dancing, as in the case of the whirling dervishes.

Check Your Understanding

1. Who are the Sunnis? Who are the Shi'ahs?

2. What are the possible origins of the word *Sufi*?

3. Which of the groups noted above is the most appealing to you? Why?

Community Study

The Canadian Society of Muslims

Figure 8.24 Syed Mumtaz Ali

The Canadian Society of Muslims (CSM) is a non-profit Islamic organization based in Toronto. The CSM was established in the 1960s and was formally incorporated in 1980 under the direction of its founder, Dr. M. Qadeer Baig, with the following main objectives:

To promote an interest in the intellectual, philosophic, and esoteric approach to research, development and understanding of Islamic culture and civilization ... and to co-operate with other organizations ... which have objectives similar in full or in part to the objectives of the corporation."

The goal of the CSM is to provide reliable Islamic information to Muslims and non-Muslims alike. In conformity with the tenets of Islam, they try to promote tolerance and harmony, both among Muslims and non-Muslims. Their main ideology is from the Sunni-Hanafi perspective, although they do attempt occasionally to provide information from other schools of thought for informative and comparative purposes.

The current head of The Canadian Society of Muslims is Syed Mumtaz Ali, a Sufi scholar and expert on Muslim law.

QUESTIONS

1. What is the purpose of the Canadian Society of Muslims?

2. Visit the CSM Web site and read the article that is suggested in the Web Quest box. Jot down any questions that you have after reading the material. Be prepared to discuss these questions with your teacher or a representative of the Muslim community.

Web Quest

The Canadian Society of Muslims
http://www.muslim-canada.org

• An informative look at Islam from a Canadian and international perspective. Follow the links to other Muslim sites.

• The Canadian Society of Muslims recommends that students read the following article found on their web site: "An Introduction to Islam" —an excellent introduction, written by Dr. Qadeer Baig.
http://www.muslim-canada.org/introisl.htm

• Recommended book: *Elementary Teachings of Islam* by Abdul-Aleem Siddiqui
Visit http://www.muslim-canada.org/elementary_1.html

CULTURAL IMPACT

Expansion of Islam

Figure 8.25
This astrolabe (a medieval navigational device and calculator), constructed in 1712-13, is just one example of the beautifully crafted scientific instruments invented by Muslims during the golden age of Islam.

Despite the turmoil surrounding the caliphate after the death of Muhammad, Muslims gained great influence in the Middle East and beyond. Muslims maintain that the Prophet and the early caliphs were forced to engage in either defensive or preventive military activities during their leaderships. These conflicts, combined with the appeal of Islam, led to the creation of a vast Islamic empire. Within 100 years of Muhammad's death, the Muslims had established control of a vast stretch of land from northern India to Spain and Morocco. Great Muslim cities began to emerge and, while Europe slipped into the darkness of the Middle Ages, Islam thrived and became one of the most creative communities in the world: translating the works of the Greek philosophers, making strides in medical science, and establishing the Arabic system of numbers as the definitive mathematical system.

The golden age of Islam lasted for approximately 400 years. The decline of Islam was gradual, however, beginning around the thirteenth century CE and becoming most noticeable with the emergence of colonialism in the nineteenth century. During that time, countries such as Britain and France took control of many Muslim lands, resulting in what seemed like a decline in Islam under the pressure of colonial rule.

Things changed dramatically in the twentieth century. The discovery of oil brought with it wealth and power. Now the Islamic countries of the Middle East appeared to be in a position to use their trading power to control their destiny. The Islamic nations of the Middle East emerged as economic powers with the world turning increasingly to petroleum-driven machinery.

The twentieth century also saw Islam grow in areas like northern Africa and Indonesia, where Islam had already taken root in the past, but now became progressively stronger.

Skill Path Working Effectively in Groups

The generation, analysis, and communication of information is playing an increasingly important role in our economy. Consequently, interaction is a major focus in today's workplace. More and more, teams are working together on difficult problems that individual workers cannot solve alone. Thus, the development of communication and social skills has become all-important in today's complex society.

Often in everyday life, we find ourselves in situations where we have to work efficiently and productively with a wide variety of people. Collaboration and cooperation are viewed as significant life skills. How do we master these skills and accomplish the task at hand effectively? Consider the following when you work in a group:

1. Develop a strategic plan.

Set your goals by determining what you want to accomplish and how you will get there.

2. Consider the rights and responsibilities of each group member.

Each member should
- be listened to;
- be valued;
- be respected;
- be free to present his or her own opinion without insult;
- do his or her fair share of work;
- work to his or her individual strengths;
- complete tasks on time.

3. Assign a role to each group member.

Successful group work reflects the appropriate assignment of roles to individuals. Below is a list of possible roles for group members. Note that throughout the process, there can be many different roles assigned to each group member.

Recorder:
He or she records the group's ideas, decisions, and plans.

Encourager:
This positive individual supports everyone and motivates and encourages all group members.

Presenter:
The group spokesperson presents the group's work to the class.

Materials manager:
This organized individual finds and stores the group's disks, files, and other materials.

Chairperson:
He or she manages meetings and keeps the group moving forward.

Reflector:
This individual leads group members in looking back on how well they are progressing.

Question Commander:
The person in this role checks to see if anyone in the group has questions. If so, questions are asked and the group members try to respond.

In addition to the above roles, group members can take on additional roles throughout the process. For example, in order to gather appropriate research data, each member might

Use the "jigsaw" technique to help accomplish your goal.
- Identify the issue.
- The issue down into parts that correspond to the number of people in your group, e.g., five members = five parts.
- Identify each group of five students as a "home group."
- In every group, identify an "expert" for each of the five parts of the issue.
- Assign each group member a number from one to five.
- Invite all students assigned number one to meet and discuss their part of the issue. Numbers two to five follow the same procedure.
- Home groups reform and share information.

be assigned a role that reflects a different research format. For the sample topic below, Member one might be asked to interview a member of the Muslim group (see pages 294-95); Member two might be asked to create a questionnaire and distribute it to the group (see pages 153); and Member three might be asked to conduct Internet research on the group (see page 104).

Sample topic: Work in groups of three to create an informational brochure on a local Muslim group.

4. Present your group work.

There are several options for presenting group work. Options include assigning the role of spokesperson to one person in the group or having each group member present the results of his or her findings.

Remember to use visuals such as charts, diagrams, and illustrations in your presentation. Refer to these items directly when presenting your findings to the class. Try to display large copies of the visuals to ensure that all members of the class can see them. Refer to page 55 for tips on how to make an effective oral presentation.

To encourage active participation of all group members in the group presentation, you may consider assigning the following roles:

Materials distributor
Technician
Timekeeper
Checker of equal audience participation

Tips for group success

- Invite, do not confront.
- Respect the opinion and experiences of others.
- Focus on the group's strengths.
- Be organized.
- Divide work fairly among group members.
- Share and consult.

Practise It!

1. Work in groups of four or five to research the history of Islam. Remember to assign roles to each member, e.g., Internet researcher or interviewer. Present your findings to the class.

2. Work in groups of five to research and prepare an oral presentation on The Five Pillars of Islam. You may wish to refer to pages 55-56 for information on making oral presentations.

Malcolm X (1925-1965), an influential black Muslim leader in the United States, seen here with Martin Luther King Jr. (left), was assassinated in 1965.

Muslims in Canada

The Islamic presence in Canada has grown significantly since Muslim immigration began in the mid-nineteenth century. Initially, immigrants from Muslim countries were attracted to Canada by pioneering enterprises like the gold rush, farming, and the building of the Canadian Pacific Railway.

The twentieth century saw Muslim immigration grow significantly. The first wave of immigrants arrived after the Second World War as Canada shifted from a war-oriented to a peace-oriented nation. Generally, this period was characterized by skilled workers' immigrating to Canada to help in the restructuring of the economy. It also saw the emergence of academic interest in Islam with the introduction of Islamic studies at McGill University in 1952 and at the University of Toronto in 1962. By the mid-sixties, Canada's immigration laws became more favourable and many Muslims embraced the opportunity to start a new life in Canada. The increase of Muslim immigrants to Canada is evident in the following Canadian census data:

Year	Number of Muslims living in Canada
1971	33 000
1981	98 000
1991	253 000

Clearly, the Muslim presence in Canada has come a long way since the 1850s. Now boasting a population, by some estimates, of up to 650 000 people, Muslim Canadians are a clear and distinct religious minority group. Evidence of this can be seen through groups like the Canadian Society of Muslims (CSM) and the Sufi Study Circle at the University of Toronto.

Figure 8.27
Dr. M. Qadeer Baig

Both groups were founded by Dr. M. Qadeer Baig, a Sufi academic who immigrated to Canada in 1962. He was hired by the University of Toronto to conduct courses in Islamic Studies and Sufism. Shortly after arriving in Toronto, Dr. Baig founded the Sufi Study Circle and was instrumental in the establishment of the Jami Mosque of Toronto. Later, in an effort to build awareness of Islamic issues for both Muslims and non-Muslims, he founded the CSM. Dr. Baig dedicated his life to teaching. In the 1970s, he led a successful campaign to remove discriminatory material about Islam from Ontario school textbooks. Dr. Baig died in 1988, but his work continues under the leadership of Syed Mumtaz Ali.

From the mid-nineteenth century to today, it is clear that Islam is having a profound effect on Canadian society. As each generation of Canadian students becomes more exposed to the religious tenets of different faiths, the level of tolerance and understanding increases.

Check Your Understanding

1. Describe the expansion of the Islamic empire after the death of the Prophet?

2. What effect did colonialism have on the Muslim community?

3. Why is Islam such a fast-growing religion today?

4. Who was Dr. M. Qadeer Baig? What did he accomplish after coming to Canada?

5. Research the important events in the life of Malcolm X. Write your own profile feature using the profiles in this book as a model.

Exploring Issues:
Women and Islam

Figure 8.28 *A Canadian Muslim wears the hijab*

For some Canadians, the role of women in Islam is unclear. Many feel that perhaps Muslim women are not treated as equals of men. Some Canadians wonder about the clothes worn by some Muslim women. As with most issues, this requires a little understanding and explanation.

The Muslim position on the status of women is clear: in the eyes of God, as emphasized in the Qur'an, women and men are equal. Both genders should constantly seek to please God. Frequently, the Qur'an refers to "believing men and women," which further emphasizes the equality of the sexes.

Lo! men who surrender unto Allah, and women who surrender, and men who believe and women who believe, and men who obey and women who obey, and men who speak the truth and women who speak the truth, and men who persevere (in righteousness) and women who persevere, and men who are humble and women who are humble, and men who give alms and women who give alms, and men who fast and women who fast, and men who guard their chastity and women who guard their chastity, and men who remember Allah much and women who remember—Allah hath prepared for them forgiveness and a vast reward.
Qur'an 33: 35

This passage serves to demonstrate the call for both men and women to pursue the goals of charity, devotion, patience, and humility. In the end, the Qur'an calls on men to live with women "on a footing of kindness and equity." As well, women, along with men, are called upon to live modest and virtuous lives.

Most observers feel that the arrival of Islam markedly improved the conditions for women. Muslims are quite proud of the fair and equitable treatment that most women are accorded in Islam. However, non-Muslims often question the equality of women, particularly the question of dress. Contemporary Canadians enjoying much personal freedom and expression in dress, may find it hard to comprehend the conservative clothing and covering of some Muslim women. It could be that they are mistakenly "judging a book by its cover."

Judging a book by its cover: Hijab

Many Muslim women wear the **hijab** so as to be faithful to the Qur'anic suggestions dealing with modesty in their dress code. This suggestion of modesty in dress is not a demand, but rather a strong recommendation. There is no legal penalty for the neglect of this Qur'anic recommendation under the Qur'an and the Sunnah (the two main sources of law in Islam). At the time of Muhammad, while strictly obeying the recommended Qur'anic injunction of wearing the hijab, women often worked alongside men. Thus, it is not a question of "forcing" women to dress more modestly.

The hijab consists of a "veil," or head covering, similar to that worn by a Roman Catholic nun. Very few Canadian Muslims include covering the face, which is known as niqab. Many Muslims simply view the hijab as an essential part of their dress code, which is aimed at expressing a sense of modesty. As well, it is not only Muslims who prefer to adopt a more modest dress code; many religious people, whatever their faith, prefer to be conservatively dressed.

Pride and Identity

Increasingly, Muslim women in Canada declare that modesty in dress is a mark of liberation and pride in their faith and culture. They point out that modesty is a requirement for both men and women. Younger women living in the West say that the hijab enables them to maintain a distinct Muslim identity.

Many Muslims contend that a woman who dresses modestly (e.g. wears the hijab) will not attract unwanted attention to her body. Instead, attention will more likely be focussed on her personality, her ideas, and her intellect.

Judging a book by its content: Women and the Qur'an

The struggle to retain traditional religious values and practices in the modern world is a challenge for all faiths. We live in a world where freedom, personal expression and materialism seem to dominate. As part of this struggle, some religious groups may have lost sight of what truly obeying God means and have imposed harsh rules on their adherents that essentially take religious teachings to a distance far removed from what was originally intended. It could be said that Muslims have not escaped this trend either. Thus, if one is looking for oppression of women in some Muslim societies, he or she will find it.

In some cases, there is a clear disparity between the ideals expressed in the Qur'an and actual practice. There are some communities in Islam (the Taliban in Afghanistan, for example) that are regarded as being too rigid in their interpretation of Islam. In certain cases, it is apparent that Muslim women are clearly not treated equally. However, to judge an entire religion on the actions of a small minority of extremists is clearly unfair and inaccurate. The vast majority of Muslims do not support the unjust treatment of women and believe that when injustice is seen, with respect to the treatment of women in the Muslim community, it is important to return to the roots of the religion (the teachings found in the Qur'an and the Sunnah) which clearly express equality and respect. Canadian Muslims will continue to face the challenge of maintaining their faith in a nation where diversity of expression is a central feature. It is likely that both they and Canada will be enriched by the experience.

QUESTIONS

1. How does the Qur'an view women? Be specific.

2. What is the hijab? Why might some women prefer to wear it in the modern world?

3. Do you believe that most Canadian youths dress immodestly? Explain.

4. Does your school have a dress code? Do you support it?

Activities

Check Your Understanding

1. Define the following terms: Allah, Islam, Muslim, jihad, mosque, Qur'an, revelation, Shahadah.

2. Write a point form biography of Muhammad (minimum: 15 points).

Think and Communicate

3. Make a bristol board display that outlines the origins, beliefs, and practices of Islam.

4. Make a detailed timeline of important dates in Muslim history.

5. Look for articles in the newspaper that deal with Muslim people or nations. Write a brief analysis of how the article(s) reflect or do not reflect Muslim beliefs.

6. a) Using a world map, outline the expansion of Islam from the time of the Prophet to the present. Make sure you indicate Muslim immigration to Canada. b) Work in small groups to note the features of Islam that you believe explain its rapid growth and report your analysis to the class.

Apply Your Learning

7. Read the Exploring Issues feature on the hijab. Arrange a class debate that outlines the pros and cons of expressing modesty in one's appearance.

8. Compare Judaism, Christianity, and Islam in the following chart:

Origins	Key People	Beliefs	View of God

9. Visit the Web site http://www.religious tolerance.org. From the home page, select the link that will take you to the summary feature on Islam. Scroll down to the end of the article and select one of the links to another Muslim Web site. Based on your study of Islam, write a 200-300 word review of the site stating whether or not the site provides a clear and concise understanding of the main elements of Islam.

10. Find out if there is a mosque in your community. Contact the mosque and arrange to visit. Write a 300-500 word report about the visit and share the main points with your classmates.

11. Go to your school resource centre or library and research the following theme:

The treatment of the Muslim community in the popular media.

Are Muslims depicted in a fair way in major motion pictures and on television? Write a 300-500 word report or work with a partner and present your findings to the class in a 10- to 15-minute presentation.

Glossary

Allah [ALLA]. The name of God.

ayat **[I at].** Translates directly to mean "signs," but means "verses," as in the Qur'an.

ghusl **[goozle].** Ritual cleansing of the entire body; an act of purification so that an individual can participate in prayer, attend the mosque or touch the Qur'an.

Hadith [ha DEETH]. Traditions based on the teachings and sayings of the Prophet. They are the second source of law for Muslims; the Qur'an is the first source.

hajj [HADGE]. Pilgrimage to Makkah; the fifth Pillar of the Islamic Faith.

hijab [HIDGE ob]. A headscarf worn by women as a sign of modesty.

hijrah **[HIDGE ruh].** The migration of Muhammad from Makkah to Madinah. The Islamic lunar calendar begins from the lunar year of the hijrah (622 CE).

idolatry [eye DOLL a tree]. The worshipping of objects, usually sculptures or paintings, as gods.

imam [im MAM]. Muslim prayer leader.

Islam [IZ lam]. Literally means "submission" or "surrender" to the will of God; a world religion that believes in one God and that the Word of God was sent via God's holy Messenger, Muhammad.

jihad [juh HAD]. Literally means "striving"; striving to obey the commands of God; often translated by non-Muslims as "holy war."

Ka'bah [ka BA]. A cube-shaped building that Abraham built under divine inspiration and dedicated to the One God.

Mi'raj **[mirage].** The ascension of Muhammad into heaven.

mosque [MOSK]. Muslim place of worship.

Muslim. Literally means "one who submits" to the will of God; an adherent of the Islamic faith.

polygamy [puh LIGGA me]. The practice of having more than one wife at a time; under certain conditions, Islam allows for men to marry up to four wives.

polytheism. The belief in numerous gods.

Qur'an [kuh RAN]. The holy book of Islam, seen as God's word and not Muhammad's word even though Muhammad conveyed it.

revelation. A special infallible kind of inspiration (Arabic: *wahi*) reserved for only those who are appointed by God as Prophets (as distinct from a normal kind of inspiration experienced by other people).

salat [sal UT]. Ritual prayer (or service of worship) that takes place before dawn, early afternoon, late-afternoon, soon after sunset and then an hour and a half later in the evening; the second Pillar of the Islamic faith.

sawm. Mandatory fasting during Ramadan, the ninth month. Muslims may fast on several other occasions in addition to this; the fourth Pillar of the Islamic faith.

Shahadah [shaw HA da]. The Islamic creed or declaration of faith: There is no god but God and Muhammad is the Messenger of God. It is the first Pillar of the Islamic faith.

Shari'ah [sher REE ah]. Islamic law; based on the Qur'an, the Sunnah (i.e., the example set by the Prophet).

Sunnah [SOON uh]. The practices, traditions, and example set by the Prophet.

surah [SIR ah]. A chapter in the Qur'an.

wudu [WOO zoo]. Ablution; ritual cleansing of certain parts of the body performed prior to *salat* prayers, other acts of worship and other religious practices; literally and spiritually means "making pure or radiant."

zakat [za CAT]. Giving alms to the poor and needy; the third Pillar of the Islamic faith.

He who shouts at the poor
Comes to grief.
God does justice;
He looks after his devotee, Who is hon-
oured.
He who is foul-mouthed
Dies a wretched death:
He kills himself.
No one may save him.
He is talked ill of
Here and hereafter.
God saves His servants,
Holding them to His heart.
Says Nanak, submit yourself to Him
And meditate on His Word.

Guru Arjan Dev

Chapter Nine

Sikhism

9

Read the poem on the left and answer the following questions:

1. What do you think the poem is talking about?
2. How does this theme apply to your life?
3. What does the poem tell you about the Sikh religion? Be specific.

Introduction

Sikhism is one of the younger of the world's major religions. When it was founded less than five centuries ago in northwestern India, both Hinduism and Islam had long been established as the two major religions in the region. While Sikhism shares characteristics with both Hinduism and Islam, it is a unique tradition that has its own vibrancy and is rapidly becoming a global faith.

The word **sikh** means student or learner. Today, a Sikh is one who follows the teachings of the religion's founder, Guru Nanak, and his successors. One of these successors, Guru Arjan Dev, is shown in the painting on the opposite page. He was the fifth guru, from 1563-1606. These teachings include a commitment to a way of life based on the guiding principles of worship, work, and charity.

Sikhs started to emigrate to Western countries towards the beginning of the 1900s. Many Sikhs arrived and settled on the Canadian West Coast as trade between Canada and Pacific Rim nations began to flourish. However, the largest influx of Sikhs came in the 1970s. Current estimates have the Sikh population in Canada at around 400 000. Worldwide, there are fewer than 20 million Sikhs, with the majority living in the Punjab, an area now divided between India and Pakistan.

While the Punjab remains the heartland of Sikhism, there are growing North American communities, particularly in Western Canada and Ontario. Sikhism's commitment to equality and hard work has helped Sikhs become valued members of the Canadian community.

Learning Goals

At the end of this chapter, you will be able to:

- identify the origins of Sikhism
- identify the ten gurus as major influences in Sikhism
- identify the conditions that led to the formation of the belief system of Sikhism
- identify the significant sacred writings and oral teachings of Sikhism
- identify the origins and significance of the various practices, rituals, and festivals of Sikhism
- demonstrate an understanding of the role of sign and symbol in Sikhism
- describe the relationship between religion and the State in Sikhism
- identify ways in which Sikhs are represented in Canada
- identify the basic role and/or responsibility of the adherents of Sikhism
- summarize the major historical influences and events in the development of Sikhism
- demonstrate an ability to recognize prejudices associated with, and misconceptions about Sikhism
- identify Sikh religious leaders who used religion to oppose prejudice and discrimination
- distinguish between fact and opinion, belief and religion, and theory and practice, as they apply to Sikhism
- use communication technology appropriately to produce and disseminate the results of research

1919 CE The British massacre Sikhs at the festival of Baisakhi in Amritsar, India

1912 CE The first Canadian-born Sikh, Hardial Singh Atwal, is born in Vancouver

1902 CE The first Sikhs arrive in Canada, and most settle in British Columbia

1914 CE The *Komagata Maru* attempts to enter Canada with Sikh immigrants and is refused admission

1469 CE Birth of the founder of Sikhism, Guru Nanak

1908 CE The "continuous journey" legislation is passed by the Canadian federal government, bringing Sikh immigration to a halt

1469–1708 CE Era of the gurus

1845–1847 CE Two wars are fought between the Sikhs and the British; the British rule Punjab

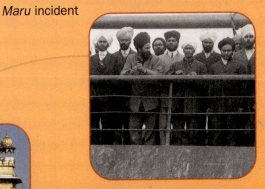

2000 CE RCMP make arrests in Air India tragedy

2000 CE Ujjal Dosanjh, a moderate Sikh, is elected first Indo-Canadian premier of British Columbia

1985 CE Air India Flight 182 bombed by terrorists. Two hundred and eighty-seven Canadians die

1993 CE The Government of Canada issues an apology to the Sikhs for the *Komagata Maru* incident

1950s–1970s CE Many Sikhs move to Canada

1919 CE A change in legislation allows families of Sikh residents to enter Canada

1984 CE Golden Temple complex is attacked by Indian security forces. Akal Takhat is badly damaged

1947 CE India is divided and a new country, Pakistan, is created. The Punjab is divided between the two countries. Most Sikhs go to India, but most of the holy sites are in Pakistan. Canada's "continuous journey" legislation is repealed. Sikhs and other people from India are given the right to vote and allowed to work as professionals

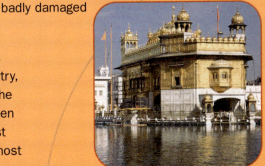

Timeline

Sikhism

Figure 9.1
The largest community of Sikhs can be found today in the Punjab, an area divided between India and Pakistan.

IRAQ

IRAN

Medina

Mecca

SAUDI ARABIA

Lahore   Amristar
PAKISTAN   Kartarpur
Nankana Sahib   Anandpur
Patna

Arabian Sea

INDIA

Hazur Sahib

Bay of Bengal

INDIAN OCEAN

ORIGINS

Figure 9.2
The founder of Sikhism, Guru Nanak

Sikhism traces its founding to Guru Nanak (Figure 9.2). He was born a Hindu in 1469, in a small village near Lahore, located in the Punjab area of present-day Pakistan (Figure 9.1). The **pandit**, or holy man, who was present at his birth, saw greatness in his horoscope. He said, "Both Hindus and Turks will reverence him, his name will become current on earth and in heaven. The ocean will give him the way, so will the earth and the skies. He will worship and acknowledge only the One Formless Lord and teach others to do so."

By his late teens, Guru Nanak was dissatisfied with formal Hinduism, especially the caste system. In Hindu society, families were divided into hereditary social classes, or castes. He married at the age of nineteen, and became the father of two sons. When he was thirty, he went through a profound spiritual experience. One day, he failed to return from his daily prayers. Since his clothes were found on the banks of a local river, the townspeople concluded that he had drowned. Three days later, he returned to the town, but remained silent. On the following day, he broke his silence, saying, "There is neither Hindu nor Muslim [followers of Islam], so whose path shall I follow? I shall follow God's path. God is neither Hindu nor Muslim, and the path which I follow is God's."

It was at this point that he was considered to be a **guru**. For Sikhs, a guru is a source of spiritual guidance from ignorance to a state of enlightenment.

Suddenly, Guru Nanak's life had gained a profound focus. He had been given a revelation from the One God. In Sikhism, there is a belief in only one God. Sikhs believe that the path to oneness with God can be revealed by the Guru.

Nanak felt compelled to share his newfound insight with those around him. One of the ways he accomplished this was by composing hymns. In one of his hymns, he proclaims:

He was here in the beginning
And before the beginning.
He is here today;
He will be here hereafter.

With the power of this revelation behind him, Guru Nanak felt compelled to deliver his message to a wider audience. He set out on a journey to teach people about the One God of Sikhism. Nanak travelled

Figure 9.3
This painting depicts one of the many stories associated with Guru Nanak.

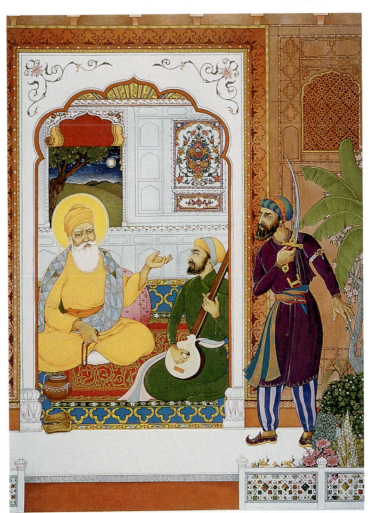

throughout India, Sri Lanka, and Tibet. He also went to the Muslim holy places of Makkah (Mecca) and Madinah (Medina), and sacred places in Iraq and Iran. Throughout his travels, he was accompanied by his friend Mardana, a talented Muslim musician who was skilled in the art of performing hymns. Guru Nanak felt Mardana's talents would be of use because most people could not read or write, and he thought learning a song was the best way to help people to remember his teachings.

There are several stories associated with Guru Nanak during this time. According to one account, Guru Nanak visited Duni Chand, who lived near Lahore. Duni Chand was a very wealthy man. Despite this, he continued to try to get richer. In the end, he was extraordinarily wealthy, but he was very unhappy. He invited Guru Nanak to his house. The Guru stayed for a period of time, and, upon his departure, he gave Duni Chand a needle. He asked him to keep the needle safe and to give it back to him when he asks for it in the next world. "But how can one carry a needle to the next world?" asked Duni Chand. Guru Nanak responded, "Then what have you collected all these riches for?"

When Duni Chand heard this, he was overwhelmed with the wisdom of the Guru and gave all his wealth to the poor. He knew his focus would have to shift from the material world to the spiritual world.

Guru Nanak travelled until 1521, when he settled in a place called Kartarpur, meaning "the abode of the Creator." There, he set up a communal farm with his sons, and all those who lived on the farm were expected to work in the fields and share the harvest. He also built a place of worship, which provided a model for the **gurdwara**, a main structure for worship in all present-day Sikh communities. Thus, it was on this farm, representing the first Sikh community, that Nanak established a way of life that still characterizes Sikhs today.

As the end of his life approached, Guru Nanak sought a successor. He bypassed both of his sons in favour of one of his followers. He gave his successor the name Angad, which means "part of me."

Guru Nanak is revered in Sikhism as the founder of the religion, and he established a line of successors to continue the legacy. For this reason, many Sikhs view him with a sense of exalted adoration.

Profile: *The Gurus*

The gurus were seen as spiritual guides, with Guru Nanak representing the embodiment of humility. The ten gurus were known for unique qualities and for accomplishing special feats. The nine consecutive gurus that followed Guru Nanak led the Sikh movement until 1708. After the death of the tenth guru, the leadership of the Sikh movement changed. At that point, the functions of the guru were passed to the community itself under the guidance of the holy text, the **Guru Granth Sahib**, which is considered to be the final guru. Also known as the **Adi Granth**, the Guru Granth Sahib is the most sacred text for Sikhs.

Figure 9.4
Guru Nanak featured with the nine gurus: Guru Angad Dev (1539-1552), Guru Amar Das (1552-1574), Guru Ram Das (1574-1581), Guru Arjan Dev (1581-1606), Guru Hargobind (1606-1644), Guru Har Rai (1644-1661), Guru Har Khrishan (1661-1664), Guru Tegh Bahadur (1664-1675), Guru Gobind Singh (1675-1708)

Profile: *The Gurus*

Figure 9.5

The Tenth Guru
Guru Gobind Singh (1675-1708)

The Wisdom of the Guru

What God has told me Himself
I tell the world.
Those who meditate on Him
Only they will go to Heaven in the
end.
God and Godmen are one

There is no difference between them
Like the tide that rises from water
And subsides in water again.

(From the hymns of
Guru Gobind Singh (Doha)

The tenth Sikh guru was Guru Gobind Singh. The divine attribute associated with him is "Royal Courage." He led the Sikhs in a time of tremendous conflict with the Mughal ruler of India, Aurangzeb. Mughal refers to the Muslim dynasty in India from the sixteenth to the nineteenth centuries. Like his father, Guru Tegh Bahadur, Guru Gobind Singh needed to find a way to oppose the Mughal emperor and his armies. In his case, the Guru chose to fight, eventually seeing his two older sons killed in battle, while his two younger sons were buried alive in the city of Sirhind's walls because they refused to convert to Islam. Guru Gobind Singh is best remembered for creating the Khalsa, a special Sikh community, and introducing the Five Ks, or signs, to Sikhism (see page 378). He is also known for ending the line of human gurus by instructing his fellow Sikhs that the holy book, the Guru Granth Sahib, should act as the final guru for all who seek oneness with God.

Interpretation of "The Wisdom of the Guru"

A true holy man is one with God. He is a pure expression of God consciousness, so much so that he has achieved total oneness with God. Guru Gobind Singh echoes the sentiments of Guru Nanak; he reaffirms the glory of one God.

After Guru Gobind Singh's death in 1708, groups of Sikhs joined together to try to fight for their own country and faith. They wanted to be free to follow their religion without persecution. However, in the fifty years after Guru Gobind Singh's death, the Sikhs endured tremendous persecution. Sikhs and Hindus were punished if they did not obey the ruling Muslim emperor, with the fate of the ninth guru, Guru Tegh Bahadur and his grandchildren acting as a painful reminder of the consequences of disobedience.

Questions

1. Why is it important for a community to remember the lives of those who have gone before them?

2. Who would you consider to be the great religious leaders in our world today? Explain why.

3. Choose one guru and do some research to identify three important details of his life.

Other Important Sikh Leaders

After the ten gurus, the next important leader for the Sikhs was Maharajah Ranjit Singh. He became the ruler of Punjab in 1799, maintaining his leadership for the next forty years. Many Sikhs opted to settle in the Punjab at this time because of the freedom from persecution provided by Ranjit Singh. After his death, a strong leader could not be found to succeed him. The Sikh army became less organized, and it began to lose ground against the British. By 1849, the British had assumed control of the Punjab. It was at this point that many Sikh soldiers became part of the British army. The British ruled the Punjab for the next 100 years.

By the mid-twentieth century, British rule of India was gradually coming to an end. The efforts of Muslim, Hindu, and Sikh nationalists resulted in the granting of independence to India in 1947. This had a profound impact on the Sikh community. Along with the creation of an independent India, came the creation of a new Muslim country called Pakistan, and the border between India and Pakistan cut Punjab in half.

In the late 1960s and the early 1970s, the concept of **Khalistan** came into existence. Khalistan was the name for a proposed independent Sikh country. Jagjit Singh Chauhan initiated the idea. He later moved to the United Kingdom, but he was a political leader in India at the time. Today, the desire for an independent Sikh homeland remains the unresolved hope of many in the Sikh community.

Check Your Understanding

1. Define the term "guru." What qualities must a guru possess?

2. Who was Guru Nanak and why is he significant to Sikhs?

3. Why would people be willing to die for what they believe?

4. What is Khalistan? Why is it likely to be a controversial political issue?

BELIEFS

Sikhs believe in one God, who is the creator of the universe and the sovereign ruler. He is known as **Waheguru**, which means "Wonderful Lord." They believe God's name should be remembered, repeated, and meditated upon continually. Although God has never walked the earth in a human body, Sikhs believe God is present everywhere, and therefore prayers can be said anywhere and at any time.

For Sikhs, equality for all is a fundamental belief. They believe all human beings are created equal and that anything that emphasizes inequality is a creation of human beings and not of God. They believe, therefore, that God made and loves all people. This belief was a clear reaction to the Hindu caste system, which categorized people into groups.

Sikhs believe in the dignity of one's labour. This is called **Kirat Karni**. A person's work must be legal and ethical, and the use of dishonest ways to accumulate wealth is regarded as sinful. Sikhs also believe in charity and serving others, which is called **seva**. They believe God forgives all sins, and that the best way to worship God is by living honestly and caring for others. Sikhs believe caring for others is a demonstration of love for God.

Sikhs also believe in the hereafter. They believe people are accountable to God for their actions and that judgement takes place soon after death. According to their beliefs, after judgement the soul experiences pleasure or pain depending on its past actions, and the cycle ends with God determining the soul's next form of life.

Sikhs believe that if people want to transcend suffering caused by repeated deaths and births, they need to turn to God. They believe that by continually being reborn, humans get caught up in the illusions of this world. Humans can, therefore, turn to God in two ways. They can listen to the **gurbani**, which is a compilation of special hymns from the sacred scripture, the Guru Granth Sahib. They can also meditate on the name of God, and worship God in the hope of achieving release from rebirth, called **mukti**.

Figure 9.6
Guru Raj Kaur Khalsa in Vancouver, BC

Women and Sikhism

Sikhs believe that women and men are born equal. The gurus were revolutionary with regard to their teaching on the status of women. They openly spoke out against the customs of **purdah** and **suttee (sati)**. Purdah is the veil usually worn by Muslim women. Suttee, or sati, is the former Hindu custom whereby a widow burned herself to death on her husband's funeral pyre. Guru Nanak and the other gurus rejected these traditions and established teachings that drew on the equality of men and women.

Women are encouraged to participate fully in religious services, even to the point of becoming **granthis** (Figure 9.6). A granthi is a reader of the holy book and a teacher, or priest. Women can also perform **kirtan**, the singing of religious hymns. They can solemnize marriages and be one of the five "beloved ones" at the Amrit ceremony, which is a ceremony of initiation. The Guru Granth Sahib clearly recognizes the importance of women as is evident in the following quote:

"It is by women we are conceived and from them that we are born. It is with them that we are betrothed and married. It is the women we befriend and it is the women who keep the race going. When one woman dies we seek another. It is with women that we become established in society. Why should women be called inferior when they give birth to great men?"

The Qualities of a Sikh

A Sikh is any person who faithfully believes in

- one Immortal Being;
- the ten gurus, from Guru Nanak Dev to Guru Gobind Singh;
- the Guru Granth Sahib, who is the last guru and holy text of Sikhism;
- the utterances and teachings of the ten gurus.

Check Your Understanding

1. Briefly explain the Sikh concept of God.

2. How do Sikhs believe is the best way to show love for God?

3. Do Sikhs believe in reincarnation? Explain.

4. What is the Sikh teaching on the status of women?

5. What Sikh belief might be valued in Canadian society?

6. Why were many of the gurus opposed to the Hindu caste system? Explain.

Skill Path Communications Technology

A good research plan includes the following steps:

- ✔ selecting a subject
- ✔ identifying sources
- ✔ collecting, evaluating, and recording information
- ✔ presenting findings
- ✔ assessing your research plan

Before you make your multimedia presentation, you should ask yourself the following questions:

- ✔ Am I presenting to inform, entertain, or persuade?
- ✔ Is the level of difficulty of my material appropriate for the audience?
- ✔ Is my material clearly organized?
- ✔ Does the use of graphics, sound, and technology enhance the presentation?
- ✔ Have I allowed for questions, equipment problems, and time constraints?

One of the final stages in the research process is the presentation of your findings. To successfully accomplish this step, start by considering the presentation methods that might be most effective with regards to the content and the intended audience. For example, you may decide to present your information in a written report, accompanied by graphics. Other options might include an oral (see pages 55-56), video, or computer presentation. Today, researchers have many options available to them, and, in all cases, technology plays a significant role.

Basic Word Processing

Word processing skills are essential for all forms of written communication. The word processing tips outlined below will help you to communicate written information effectively.

- Make your text visually appealing by selecting interesting (and appropriate) fonts and by varying the type style, e.g., bold, or italic.
- Consider adding colour to your document. Depending on your program, click Format to discover colour options.
- Ensure that the written material you present does not contain spelling or grammar errors. Depending on your program, you can have your computer do a global spelling and grammar check to help you minimize mistakes.
- Use the thesaurus feature of your program to help you avoid the repetition of words.
- Do an automatic word count of your document to make sure that your text is the appropriate length.

Charts and Graphs

You can create column charts and line, bar, or pie graphs to visually represent the results of your research. Using a spreadsheet program, such as Excel, you can easily design graphics by following the suggestions of the "Chart Wizard." Just click Insert →Object (or Chart), and make your selections. Remember, you can alter your chart by resizing it, or by editing the text; you can also present most charts that are available within the Excel program in 3-D format.

Multimedia Presentations

Multimedia presentations include more than one form of communication. An oral presentation accompanied by slides is an example of a multimedia presentation. Other more complex examples might include PowerPoint presentations (see page 371), which can incorporate sound, video, and graphics.

You can use any of the following communication methods in the creation of an effective multimedia presentation: exhibit, bulletin board display, poster, timeline, overhead, photo essay, video, simulation game, slide show, time capsule, comic strip, skit, Web page, cartoon, project cube, demonstration, computer program presentation, advertisement, book or magazine cover, scrapbook, puppet show, or brochure.

The PowerPoint Presentation

PowerPoint is a computer program that enables you to create a "slide show" presentation on your computer screen. The slides can simply include text, or they can include charts, tables, pictures, clipart, animation, sound, and video.

The PowerPoint presentation is particularly effective when it is used to explain a new idea or a complicated concept. If you know how to accomplish basic word processing tasks, then you already have some of the tools necessary for PowerPoint. You can also transfer much of the work you have created on other computer programs, such as Excel or Microsoft Word, to your PowerPoint presentation.

Video Presentation

This effective method of communication, which can be used as part of a multimedia presentation, involves a combination of visual and audio elements. When creating a video presentation, follow the steps outlined below:

- Establish goals. What do you want to show your audience? Make sure you know exactly what you want to communicate, to whom, and the desired effect of your message before you go out and shoot your video.
- Carefully consider your techniques. What mood do you want to create with the use of sound and pictures?
- Create a storyboard to represent the finished product. The storyboard details dialogue, music, sound effects, camera angles, and movements.
- Make sure members of your production team understand their roles. Does the camera person have experience shooting videos? Does the editor understand the sequence of the shots?

Practise It!

1. Create a video journal. Play the role of a reporter and visit a local gurdwara. Remember to clearly identify what you want to communicate to your classmates before you start to shoot your video. Present your findings to the class.

2. Use PowerPoint, or another presentation program, or combine an oral presentation with one of the communication methods outlined in this Skill Path, to create a multimedia presentation on the Five Ks (see page 378).

PRACTICES, RITUALS, AND FESTIVALS

Practices and Rituals

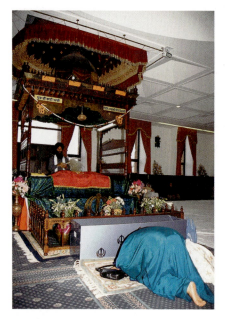

Figure 9.7
The interior of a Sikh gurdwara, showing the throne, or takht

The Gurdwara

The gurdwara is a building where Sikhs gather to worship. Gurdwara means "the door of the Guru," or "God's home." When a gurdwara is established, the first thing the community must do is appoint someone to look after it. The Sikh religion has no formal priesthood; however, they do appoint someone who can recite the scriptures, sing hymns, and perform religious rites. This person is respectfully called **Bhai Ji**, or brother. He or she is not only responsible for ceremonial tasks. The most important duty is to rise early in the morning and arrange the morning service by bringing the holy text to the main room of the gurdwara and placing it on the altar. Sikhs do not have a special day for worship, or **diwan**. However, it is usually held on Sunday by Sikhs around the world.

All gurdwaras have certain features in common. The only furniture in the worship room is a special platform at one end, which is called the **takhat**, meaning the "throne." This is where the Guru Granth Sahib (the holy text) is placed. The takht is a symbol indicating that the Guru Granth Sahib is treated with respect. A special canopy hangs over the throne. In front of the takht is a place where worshippers can leave their offerings of food, or money. As a sign of respect, before entering the worship room, people must remove their shoes, wash themselves, and cover their heads.

A kitchen and a dining room are also part of the gurdwara, and if space permits, a classroom is also included. All gurdwaras display a flag outside, called the **nishan sahib**, which shows the symbol of the **Khalsa**, a special Sikh community. The symbol is called the **Khanda**. No tobacco, alcohol, or drugs can be consumed while one is in the gurdwara.

During the Worship Service

During services, people sit on a carpeted floor and may leave at any time. According to tradition, men and women sit separately. Most of the service involves kirtan, the singing of hymns. The **ragis**, or singers, perform with the accompaniment of musical instruments.

At the end of the service, special hymns are sung. Everyone joins in the singing, before standing to say a special prayer called the **Ardas**. After the Ardas, the granthi, or reader of the holy book, opens the Guru Granth Sahib and, at random, reads a verse, which will give guidance for the day to those in attendance. At the end of the service, everyone is given **karah parshad**, a sweet pudding that worshippers eat. This is a blessed pudding given to everyone present in the congregation regardless of caste, or creed affiliation.

After the Worship Service

The service is followed by a vegetarian meal known as **langar** (Figure 9.8), meaning "free kitchen." Langar was instituted by Guru Nanak, who believed all who had travelled a long way to hear him, or who were not very wealthy, should be given food and drink. The meal is vegetarian so as not to offend those in attendance who abstain from meat. In time, the practice of langar expanded to include all who came to the service. When eating the meal, everyone is seated together in rows on the floor. This format is designed to emphasize that everyone in the room is the same, or equal. There are always volunteers to prepare and serve the meal. Serving others is very important to Sikhs; therefore, all visitors to a gurdwara are offered food and drink.

Daily Life

In many ways, Sikhs live their lives here in Canada very much like any citizen. They go to school, work, have friends, raise families, and obey the laws of the country. In addition, there are certain religious customs and codes of behaviour that they honour in their daily lives. They promise to

Figure 9.9
A family eats langar in the gurdwara.

live honest lives, to remain faithful to their spouse, and to work hard for their money. They are expected to show respect for all living things; therefore, they will not eat meat if the animal has been killed in a cruel way. Sikhs are not to drink, smoke, nor to use drugs except for medicinal reasons. They also agree not to gamble or steal.

An important aspect of their day is the reciting of daily prayers, called the **nit nem**. These set prayers are said in the morning, evening, and last thing at night. In addition to reciting the nit nem, Sikhs read the scriptures on a regular basis. Some Sikhs have a **gutka**, which is a smaller collection of hymns. It is also treated with respect, and used for daily readings. Since many homes do not have the required separate room in which to hold the Guru Granth Sahib, the gutka often becomes the daily book to which Sikhs refer. Sikhs learn about their faith both at home and at the gurdwara.

Web Quest

To learn more about the Sikh faith, a good site for students, with links noted by grade level, is **Sikhism Links for Students** http://www. studyweb.com/rel/ sikhism.htm

To serve others is one of the most important teachings of Sikhism. Serving others, known as **seva**, can be divided into three different categories: intellectual (using your mind), manual (physical work), and material (giving things). Of the three categories, the most common is material service, which usually involves some type of charitable donation called **Daswandh**. Sikhs are expected to donate one-tenth of their income to charity.

Intellectual service can refer to teaching about Sikhism; whereas manual service might include the preparation and serving of food in the langar. Serving others includes all people and is not restricted to only fellow Sikhs.

Festivals

There are two kinds of festivals. One type is connected with the lives of the gurus, called *gurpurbs*, while the other is called the *jore melas*.

Figure 9.9
Sikhs celebrate the birthday of Guru Nanak.

Gurpurb

This is a holy day that is associated with the birth or death of one of the gurus. The birthday of Guru Nanak is a gurpurb (Figure 9.9). It takes place in November and is considered to be the most important of all the gurpurbs. This celebration can last for three days. The central feature of this festival is the **akhand path**, which is the continuous reading of the Guru Granth Sahib for forty-eight hours. It is followed by a regular morning service. Throughout the festival, lectures and speeches explain the importance of the event and the Guru's contribution to the Sikh faith. There is a steady stream of visitors to the gurdwara, with processions and hymns to celebrate the festival. Langar is served throughout the festival. Those who do not participate in the reading can cook, serve, or clean. Thus, everyone is involved in some way.

Jore Melas

There are a number of these types of festivals—Baisakhi, Diwali, and Hola Mohalla. These festivals provide opportunities for Sikhs to gather together. Baisakhi and Diwali were initiated by Guru Amar Das, the third guru, who ordered followers to join him in Amritsar to celebrate. He intended to divert the worshippers from focussing on Hindu culture and, instead, encourage them to reflect on the meaning of being a Sikh. Guru Gobind Singh added the festival called Hola Mohalla.

Baisakhi

Baisakhi (Figure 9.10) usually occurs on either April 13th or 14th. Its purpose is to remind Sikhs of the saint-soldiers who were prepared to fight against injustice. On this holiday, the story of the formation of the Khalsa is told. It is a day of giving thanks to God, and to listening to the teachings of the gurus. An important part of this festival is the annual changing of the flag that flies outside every gurdwara.

This festival is celebrated all over the world, with many Sikhs gathering at Amritsar, in India, to celebrate. In 1919, at Amritsar, the British rulers of India forbade Sikhs from gathering together to celebrate Baisakhi. They believed the Sikhs would rise up against them. When the Sikhs did gather, in defiance of the authorities, the army killed hundreds of those in attendance. This tragic event, called the Amritsar Massacre, is commemorated by Sikhs all over the world when celebrating Baisakhi.

Diwali

Diwali takes place in either October or November. It celebrates the imprisonment and release of Guru Hargobind, the sixth guru, which took place in the first half of the 1600s. According to the story, during Diwali, originally a Hindu festival, the Muslim king, Jehangir, decided to release Guru Hargobind. But the Guru refused to leave unless the fifty-two Hindu princes imprisoned with him were also released. The king said only those who could pass through the narrow passage while holding onto the Guru's clothes would be set free. The passage was very narrow, and only one person at a time could travel through it. The Guru had a cloak with long tassels on the ends of it. The princes held onto the tassels, and thus all were set free that day.

Hola Mohalla

Hola Mohalla occurs in the spring, and Sikhs gather to practise their martial skills. Today, it is mainly celebrated in Punjab. It is not commonly celebrated elsewhere in the world.

Figure 9.10
Sikhs gather to celebrate Baisakhi.

Holy Places

Amritsar

Many religions have a special city that is considered sacred, a city to which its adherents travel as pilgrims. Amritsar is considered to be the most important city for Sikhs. Amritsar means "pool of nectar." This city hosts the Golden Temple complex (Figure 9.11), which was built by the fifth guru, Guru Arjan Dev. The temple has four entrances to indicate that people from all directions of the world are welcome there. It is built on a twenty metre square platform in the middle of a pool of water.

In the nineteenth century, the Sikh ruler Ranjit Singh had the temple rebuilt in marble. The top half is covered in gold leaf, which is why it is called the Golden Temple. The walls of the temple feature carved verses from the Guru Granth Sahib.

The Golden Temple is considered to be the most important building for Sikhs. It contains very old, hand-written copies of the Guru Granth Sahib. Readings from the sacred scripture begin daily at dawn and continue until late at night. A special procession takes place each morning when the Guru Granth Sahib is carried into the worship room. To be asked to take part in the procession is a great honour for Sikhs. The Golden Temple is designed in such a way that worshippers have to step down to enter it. This demonstrates the humility one must show when one comes before God.

Facing the Golden Temple, opposite the main gateway, is a structure called the Akal Takht, built by Guru Hargobind, the sixth guru.

Figure 9.11

QUESTIONS

1. Briefly describe the Golden Temple.
2. What is the Akal Takht?
3. Do some research to briefly describe other sacred sites of Sikhism.

Symbols and Icons

Khanda

The main symbol of Sikhism is the **Khanda**. There are three parts to this symbol. The two swords on the outside symbolize service to God through teaching the truth and through fighting for what is right. They date back to the time of Guru Hargobind, the sixth guru, who wore two swords symbolizing the spiritual power of God, and his desire to defend his people. The swords are called kirpans. Between the swords is a circle known as the chakkar, an ancient Indian weapon that stands for one God and the unity of people, and serves as a reminder of a God who has no beginning and no end. In the centre is the two-edged sword, also called the Khanda, which is the symbol of the power of God. It is believed that the sharpness cleaves truth from falsehood.

QUESTIONS

1. Who was responsible for introducing this symbol to Sikhism?
2. What other symbols present in our society characterize similar beliefs to those expressed in the Khanda? List at least two.

Figure 9.12

Khalsa

The tenth guru, Guru Gobind Singh, started the Khalsa because Sikhs were being persecuted for refusing to convert to Islam. In 1699, on Baisakhi, Guru Gobind Singh gathered a group of Sikhs together and asked if any were willing to die for their faith. Five individuals stepped forward. The Guru took them away, one at a time, and each time the Guru returned with a bloodstained sword. Everyone who witnessed the event believed the five were dead. However, all five returned alive! They became known as the "five cherished ones," or the **Panj Pyaras**. Each one was given the name

Figure 9.13
Sikhs who join the Khalsa must take special vows: To wear the Five Ks (see page 378); To abstain from drugs and intoxicants; To respect women; To follow the teachings of the gurus; To serve only the gurus, with arms if necessary, and only in a just cause; To regard all Khalsa members as brothers and sisters.

Singh, which means "lion." They were told to wear five special signs, indicating to the world that they were Sikhs. These signs became known as the Five Ks. Everyone present that day joined the Khalsa. All the men were given the name Singh, and all the women the name Kaur, which means "princess."

Sikhs who join the Khalsa must wear the Five Ks. Not all Sikhs choose to join the Khalsa, and therefore, are not required to wear the Five Ks. Many Sikhs choose, however, to wear some, or all of them. The wearing of the Five Ks is a visible sign to the world that the person is a practising Sikh.

The Five Ks

The visible symbols of the Sikh community have proven to be controversial for many Canadians. This is largely based on misunderstanding and confusion surrounding the Five Ks. When people think of Sikhs, they think of turbans and they think of Kirpans, the ceremonial dagger. Upon learning more about the Sikh religion, many people come to a clearer understanding of Sikhism and acknowledge there is more to this complex religion.

The Five Ks include the *kesh*, the *kangha*, the *kara*, the *kirpan*, and the *kaccha*.

Kesh

Kesh means "uncut hair." This includes all body hair. To cut and to style one's hair is seen as a sign of vanity. Sikhs care for their hair and let it grow as a sign that they work for God. However, they believe it is important to keep hair clean and tidy. This is the main reason why many men wear a turban and some enclose their beard in a net.

Kangha

The comb, known as the *kangha*, is used to keep the long hair tidy. Cleanliness is an important principle for Sikhs.

Kara

The *kara* is a plain steel bracelet worn on the right wrist; steel being a sign of strength.

Kirpan

The *kirpan* is a short sword that serves as a symbol of dignity and self-respect, as well as a reminder to fight in the defence of truth. Many Sikhs have been persecuted as a result of their faith; therefore, the sword has become a symbol of their duty to protect and defend their faith and the rights of others. It is used as a last resort, and not as a weapon of intimidation, as some people who do not know the Sikh faith assume.

Kaccha

The short pants, known as *kaccha*, were introduced in times of war because they were more practical than baggy trousers for fighting in a battle.

Living My Religion

Talwinder Khubar

Figure 9.14

Talwinder Khubar is a sixteen-year-old student who lives in Brampton, Ontario. He attends a Catholic secondary school. He and his family immigrated to Canada recently. Talwinder says that practicing his religion was easier in India than it is in Canada. Yet, in Canada, he finds people very accepting of his religion.

For him, being a teenaged Sikh means being different from others. It means not eating meat, and not drinking alcohol. However, as a Sikh he also believes that all religions are important, and he will therefore not speak in negative terms about others.

At times, his fellow students are curious about his turban. Right now, his turban is a small one, he says, but when he is older he will wear a larger one because then he will have time to care for it. The same applies for wearing the Five Ks. For now, he finds it difficult to wear them. His fellow students often asked about the kirpan. He tells them it is only used in defense of others; it is not used for fighting.

Talwinder attends the gurdwara with his family each week. He says one of the things he likes about the gurdwara is that all are welcome there. Everyone is expected to give 10 per cent of their earnings to the gurdwara. "God gave everything to us; therefore the work we do with our hands should be given back to God." For Talwinder the gurdwara is different from home. He likes the tradition of no furniture in the gurdwara he attends. He believes this tradition should not be changed because God made it that way. When people change the gurdwara, he says, this action indicates people believe they are God and they are breaking with tradition.

For Talwinder, Sikh history has been written with blood. He hopes that one day Sikhs will have their own country—Khalistan. Then, everyone will be ideally the same, and no one will be different.

QUESTIONS:

1. Why does Talwinder not wear the Five Ks?

2. What are two things that are important to him as a young Sikh?

3. What does Talwinder think of his life in Canada?

Dear child, this is your mother's blessing.
May God never be out of your mind even for a minute.
Meditation on God should be your constant concern.
It purges people from all faults.
May God the Guru be kind to you.
May you love the company of God's people.
May God robe you with honour and may your food be the singing of God's praises.

MILESTONES

There are several important stages in a Sikh person's life. Each of these stages is recognized and celebrated within the community.

Birth

A few weeks after the birth of a child, the parents visit the gurdwara to present the child before the Guru Granth Sahib. They bring a **romala**, or piece of embroidered material, for the Guru Granth Sahib. They also bring money and offer the traditional gifts of thanksgiving. The Granthi offers Ardas, or general prayers, and asks for the blessings of God and for the well-being of the child. The following hymn from the Guru Granth Sahib is often recited at the **Nam Karam**, or naming ceremony:

After the prayer, the Guru Granth Sahib is opened at random. The top hymn on the left-hand page is then read by the granthi. The first letter of the first word of the hymn forms the initial letter of the name to be proposed to the child. The family decides the name, and the granthi announces it to the congregation. Singh is added if the child is a boy; Kaur if a girl.

Sometimes a mixture of honey and water called **amrit** is prepared. A kirpan may be dipped in the amrit and then lightly placed onto the baby's tongue, reminding all present of their duty to raise the child in the faith. Then, the **Anand Sahib**, a prayer of thanksgiving, is sung. As with all celebrations, food is then distributed to all present.

Amritsanshkar

Amritsanshkar is the most important ceremony for Sikhs. It is considered a ceremony of initiation. This is the time when a person is willing to make the commitment to the Sikh faith and to become a member of the Khalsa. This is seen as a public commitment of faith.

The ceremony is reminiscent of the Panj Pyare, or "five cherished ones" ceremony. Attending the ceremony are five Sikhs, who represent the original Panj Pyare. An additional Sikh reads from the Guru Granth Sahib. One of the five recites the duties and vows of a Sikh. During the ceremony, the young person kneels in the archer position, which symbolizes the willingness to defend the Sikh religion. The ceremony begins with the opening of the scriptures and the posing of a variety of questions, such as:

- Are you willing to read, learn, and live according to the Sikh teachings?
- Will you pray only to one God?
- Will you serve the whole of humanity?

Prayers are recited and hymns are sung, then each person drinks amrit. At this point, amrit is poured onto the eyes and hair of the initiate. The rules of the Khalsa are then explained to the initiate, and after more prayers are recited, the ceremony ends with everyone eating karah parshad.

Marriage

Marriage is very important for Sikhs. Because of the significance of the institution, marriages are often arranged. It is considered important though that the possible partners be acceptable to each other. Once the arrangement has been made, there usually is a betrothal ceremony. This includes the bride's father, accompanied by a few close relatives, who meet the groom's parents and a relative. The group exchanges presents. The purpose of the ceremony is designed to notify the public of the alliance of the two families and to ensure that the promises made are kept.

The **Anand Karaj**, the actual wedding ceremony, is known as the "ceremony of bliss." A Sikh marriage can be considered a religious sacrament because the Guru Granth Sahib is a witness to the marriage. A quotation from the Guru Granth Sahib illustrates the Sikh view of marriage:

Figure 9.15
The bride, wearing clothes of red and gold to represent happiness, sits on the left side of the groom during the Sikh wedding ceremony.

> *"They are not man and wife who have only physical contact. Only they are truly wedded who have one spirit in two bodies."*

The wedding ceremony (Figure 9.15) can take place in the bride's home, or in a gurdwara. During the ceremony, the groom faces the takht, wearing a special scarf, while the bride sits on his left side. She usually wears clothes of red and gold, as the colours are associated with happiness. The couple is then told about the responsibilities of marriage. Next, the couple and their parents stand, as a prayer of blessing is recited. They bow towards the Guru Granth Sahib to show they agree to the marriage. The father of the bride puts garlands of flowers over the couple, and then places one end of the groom's scarf in the bride's hand. The Lavan, or marriage hymn, composed by Guru Ram Das, the fourth guru, is read. At the end of each of the four verses, the couple walks around the Guru Granth Sahib, always keeping it to their right-hand side. As they complete each round, they bow to the Guru Granth Sahib. The bride's parents then greet the newly married couple with sweets and garlands. The rest of the guests come forward and give gifts of money to assist the couple in achieving a good financial start to their life together. After the ceremony, everyone shares a meal.

Separation and divorce are granted in cases of desertion, habitual cruelty, insanity, or impotence. Divorce is rare, however, and it is not looked upon favourably. The family usually tries to help a couple who are having difficulties.

Funerals

Although the death of a loved one is a difficult experience, Sikhs do not believe death is the end. They believe in reincarnation, which is the view that the soul moves on to another body upon physical death, and that reincarnation can happen many times. However, it is believed one can only know God when one assumes a human form. This belief is evident in the following quotation from the Guru Granth Sahib:

> *"Worldly souls who scorn God's sweetness suffer pain because of their conceit. The thorn of death pricks deeper and deeper. Those who love God's sacred name shall break the bonds of birth and death. Thus they find the eternal one; thus they win supreme honour. I am poor and humble, keep me and save me, God most high. Grant the aid that your name can give me. Grant me the peace and joy. Grant the joy of serving all who praise God's name."*

When a person is about to die, relatives and friends try to divert the attention of the dying individual from this world, and have him or her concentrate on God. The dying person is encouraged to repeat "Waheguru, Waheguru" ("Wonderful Lord, Wonderful Lord") in order to give consolation to the departing soul. Sikhs believe death is just another form of sleep, and therefore, it is considered the end of one's life and the start of a new one. Although it is a time of mourning, friends and family are encouraged to remember the person is going on to a new life. After the person dies, the eyes and mouth are closed, the arms and hands are extended to each side of the body, and the body is covered with a plain white sheet. The body is always cremated as soon as it is possible to do so.

The coffin, covered with a plain cloth, is carried to the crematorium, where prayers for the peace of the soul are said. The granthi recites a prayer while the body is cremated.

The mourning period lasts for up to ten days. This can take place either at home, or at the gurdwara. A reading of the Guru Granth Sahib is conducted each day of the mourning period. There are no memorial stones or monuments erected to remember the person because Sikhs do not believe earth is a permanent place.

Check Your Understanding

1. According to custom, how is a Sikh child's name chosen?

2. Why is the Amritsanshkar considered to be the most important rite of passage for Sikhs? What do you consider an important rite of passage in Canadian society?

3. Briefly outline the steps taken in order to establish a Sikh marriage.

4. Why do Sikhs not erect monuments to those who have died?

SACRED WRITINGS

Figure 9.16
The Guru Granth Sahib, the sacred text of Sikhism

The sacred text of Sikhism is known as the Guru Granth Sahib. It is a collection of over 3000 hymns. In 1604, Guru Arjan, the fifth guru, assembled the official collection of hymns, the Adi Granth. Eventually, the collection came to include the hymns of Guru Nanak and those of six other Gurus, and was called the Guru Granth Sahib.

A notable feature of the holy text, which sets it apart from other holy books, is the inclusion of writings by several non-Sikhs, notably Hindus and Muslims. This demonstrates the Sikh belief in the importance of listening to the wisdom of others.

The Dasam Granth, or Tenth Collection, is a separate scripture from the Guru Granth Sahib. These holy writings were assembled by Guru Gobind Singh, the tenth guru, after the death of his father, Guru Tegh Bahadur, the ninth guru.

For Sikhs, the Guru Granth Sahib is the embodiment of the authority of God and the ten gurus; therefore it takes on special importance for the Sikh community. Formerly, all copies of the sacred text were handwritten. Special care was taken in order to ensure that no mistakes were made in the transcription. In 1852, the book was printed for the first time. At that time, Sikhs agreed that every copy was to be exactly the same. Today, every copy in the **gurmukhi** script has exactly the same number of pages with particular hymns always appearing on the same page.

The opening page of the Guru Granth Sahib captures the basic Sikh belief in God:

> *"There is one God. He is the Truth. He is the Creator, and is without fear or hate. He is beyond time, is not born, and does not die to be born again. He is known by His graces."*

This proclamation is followed by an introduction, which contains the daily prayers that are said in the morning, at dusk, and at night. Next, is the main collection of hymns, followed by the hymns from Hindus and Muslims. The Guru Granth Sahib ends with a collection of hymns by other authors. All Sikhs are encouraged to study the scriptures, first by learning to read and write the gurmukhi script in which the scriptures are written, and then by studying the lives and teachings of the gurus. Most adherents of Sikhism go to the Sikh place of worship, the gurdwara, in order to study because many do not have their own personal copy of the Guru Granth Sahib. The holy text is usually expensive and considered to be very sacred. If a person does own a copy, there must be a special room in the house just for the book. Most people have a smaller book, the gutka, for home prayer. The gutka contains the most important hymns from the sacred text and the daily prayers.

Regardless of whether Sikhs worship in the gurdwara or in their homes, certain practices must be adhered to when in the presence of the sacred word. Before a Sikh enters the room where the Guru Granth Sahib is kept, he or she must cleanse the hands, cover the head, and remove his or her shoes. The book is always kept with a special cloth covering it when it is not in use. When it is opened, it rests on a cloth and three cushions. If it is being moved, it is covered with a cloth and carried above the head. It is a great honour to be the person who carries the Guru Granth Sahib (Figure 9.17).

Figure 9.17

The Guru Granth Sahib is treated with the utmost respect. When it is in use, the book is placed on a cloth and three cushions. When not in use, it is covered with a special cloth.

Sacred Text

The Guru Granth Sahib is rich in wisdom and praise for God. Several important themes emerge as one reads through the scriptures.

Theme: Avoid Judging Others

O Nanak, if someone judges himself,
only then is he known as a real judge.
If someone understands both the disease and the medicine,
only then is he a wise physician.
Do not involve yourself in idle business on the way;
remember that you are only a guest here.
Speak with those who know the God, and renounce your evil ways

Guru Granth Sahib

Theme: The Real Hero

He alone is known as a spiritual hero,
who fights in defense of righteousness.
He may be cut apart, piece by piece,
but he never leaves the battle.

Guru Granth Sahib

Theme: The Name of God

Three things are there in the vessel; Truth, contentment and intellect. The ambrosial Name of God is added to it, The Name that is everybody's sustenance. He who absorbs and enjoys it shall be saved. One must not abandon this gift, It should ever remain dear to one's heart. The dark ocean of the world can be crossed by clinging to His feet. Nanak, it is He who is everywhere.

Guru Arjan Dev, Mundawani

God is the Master, God is Truth,
His name spelleth love divine.

Hymns of Guru Nanak

Theme: Not Humanity's Will, but God's Will

...Few, some very few,
From this havoc return home,
And others inquire of them
About their lost dear ones.
Many are lost forever,
And weeping and anguish are the lot of those who survive.
Ah, Nanak, how completely helpless mere men are!
It is God's will that is done, for ever and ever.
Hymns of Guru Nanak

Were life's span extended to the four ages
And ten times more,
Were one known over the nine shores
Ever in humanity's fore,
Were one to achieve greatness with a name noised over the earth,
If one found not favour with the Lord
What would it all be worth?

Hymns of Guru Nanak

QUESTIONS

1. What do you think is meant by the phrase "you are only a guest here," found in the first reading? If you were to follow this reading, how would it change your life?

2. According to the Guru Granth Sahib, who is a hero? Do you agree or disagree? Explain.

3. Which of these readings is closest to your own views? Explain.

Check Your Understanding

1. Who wrote or compiled the Guru Granth Sahib?

2. What special consideration is taken in publishing a copy of the Guru Granth Sahib?

3. What is meant by the expression "the Guru Granth Sahib is the final Guru"?

4. Why is it unusual for Sikhs to have a copy of the Guru Granth Sahib in their homes?

GROUPS AND INSTITUTIONS

There are numerous Sikh organizations in Canada that aim to promote and continue the Sikh tradition.

The Federation of Sikh Societies of Canada

The main objective of the Toronto organization is to promote, preserve, and maintain Sikh religion, culture, and heritage. Members actively present Sikh issues and concerns to all levels of government. The group often organizes conferences to address issues of concern to Sikhs.

The World Sikh Organization

This group primarily lobbies both the United States and Canada on issues of concern to Sikhs, with specific reference to the Punjab. It frequently speaks to the Canadian Human Rights Commission on behalf of Sikhs.

The International Sikh Youth Federation

Established in 1984, the members of this federation are devoted to the Sikh fundamentalist movement, and are committed to the freedom of the Sikh nation.

Community Study

The Ontario Khalsa Durbar

Figure 9.18

The Ontario Khalsa Durbar is the largest gurdwara in Ontario. It was established in 1974 in Malton (northwestern Toronto). In the beginning, it was housed in a portable on two acres of land. As the gurdwara grew, three more acres of land were purchased and eventually an additional three more acres were bought. As the gurdwara continued to grow, a building was erected.

Today, it includes a huge hall to provide for the needs of the congregation. In addition to the large hall, it also contains a langar kitchen and an extensive library. The library sells religious tapes, videos, and books. The gurdwara provides many functions for its members. Marriage and funeral ceremonies are conducted there. As well, the Nam Karam, or naming ceremony, is also held at the gurdwara. Essentially all festivals are celebrated here. These occasions usually accommodate crowds of 5000–7000, a much larger group than the usual Sunday crowd of approximately 1000. In August, the annual Kabadi tournament is held. This is a sporting event that attracts large crowds.

This gurdwara, like all others, has an active Board of Directors. The directors are elected officials who are responsible for the management and funding of this large gurdwara. Other gurdwaras have evolved from this one to meet the needs of the local Sikh community.

QUESTIONS

1. What does the existence of the Ontario Khalsa Durbar tell you about the Sikh religion in Canada?

2. What are some of the services offered at this gurdwara?

CULTURAL IMPACT

Sikh Migration to Canada

It is ironic that Canada's first Sikhs, whose faith stresses equality, often faced discrimination and prejudice. When Sikhs started migrating to Canada in the early 1900s, they were greeted with some hostility. At the time, there were only about 5000 Asians in all of Canada. Locals wondered about the turbans that the men wore, the South Asian dress of the women, and the colour of their skin. While some Canadians were quite hospitable, others were suspicious. In spite of considerable discrimination, Sikhs have achieved success in every sector of Canadian society. They have risen to positions of judge, professor, author, doctor, engineer, scientist, accountant, athlete, journalist, and entrepreneur. Today, Sikhs, such as Herb Dhaliwall and Gurbax Malhi, hold positions as ministers and members of legislative assemblies. In 2000, Ujjal Dosanjh, became the first Indo-Canadian premier of British Columbia.

The *Komagata Maru* Incident

In 1914, Sikhs challenged the discriminatory measures designed to halt their immigration to Canada. A ship, the *Komagata Maru,* arrived in Vancouver with 376 passengers. Most were Sikhs. They were refused entry and forced to stay on board the ship.

As Sikh and Canadian officials negotiated, the ship grew hotter and dirtier. When local police tried to board the ship, a bloody riot broke out. Finally, a Canadian warship threatened to blow up the ship if it did not leave the harbour. The *Komagata Maru* voyage ended in tragedy when it returned to India and a clash with British authorities resulted in violence and death. Sikhs in Canada were distressed with the affair. The Canadian government, pressured by Canadians, was clearly acting in a discriminatory manner. Later, a Canadian official involved in the crisis was shot and a Sikh was hanged for his murder.

The Air India Tragedy

On June 23, 1985, Air India Flight 182 exploded off the coast of Ireland, killing all 329 people on board. Two hundred and seventy-eight of the victims were Canadians. The immediate cause of the explosion was a bomb planted in a suitcase.

The Air India tragedy can be clearly linked to a number of historic events. First, Sikhs in Punjab, while active participants in the quest for Indian independence from Britain, were shut out from the bargaining table in 1947. While Hindus and

Muslims saw nations established that suited their needs, the Sikhs were left to fight for themselves, eventually seeing the Punjab cut in half by the India-Pakistan border. This resulted in the active quest for an independent Sikh nation called Khalistan.

The conflict reached a heightened level of intensity on June 8, 1984, when Indian security forces raided the Golden Temple complex at Amritsar. The Indian government claimed that the Akal Takht, a building that was a part of the Golden Temple complex, housed a group of terrorists. While the Golden Temple itself was left relatively unharmed, the Akal Takht was severely damaged, with the bodies of the militant Sikhs lying amidst the rubble.

Sikhs around the world were outraged to learn that the Indian government would go so far as to attack their most sacred shrine. This, coupled with a series of other attacks on Sikh gurdwaras around India, infuriated the Sikh community, with some Sikhs resorting to acts of terrorism to send a message to the Indian authorities. On October 31, 1984, India's prime minister, Indira Gandhi, was assassinated by two of her bodyguards. .

Two significant acts came on June 23, 1985. Disaster struck first in Japan where a suitcase bomb exploded, killing two baggage handlers. Less than an hour later, Air India Flight 182, departing from Toronto, plummeted 31 000 feet into the Atlantic Ocean.

While law enforcement officials in Canada and India had a good idea who planted the bombs, they could not gather enough evidence to lay charges. As time passed, the Indian community of Canada began to grow disillusioned with the country in which they had settled. Some felt that more would have been done if the victims had been more clearly "Canadian." It wasn't until October, 2000, that any charges were laid. Two members of British Col-umbia's Sikh community were charged, with the trial predicted to be the longest in Canadian history.

The study of the downing of Air India Flight 182 is significant for two reasons: first, it highlights a subtle discrimination that some believe continues to exist within Canada—a discrim-

Figure 9.19
Sikh emigrants on the ship Komagata Maru. A compelling footnote to the story: In 1993, the Canadian government issued an apology to the Sikh community for the Komagata Maru incident.

Web Quest

To find out more about the origins, development, philosophy and scriptures of Sikhism, visit the site **www.sikhs.org** This site also investigates contemporary issues affecting Sikhs, such as the Indian government attack on the Golden Temple complex in 1984.

ination that saw many Canadians apparently downplay the impact because the victims were seen as "immigrants." The second reason for studying the tragedy is the effect it has had on Canada's Sikh community.

When the media reported on the bombing of the plane, the perpetrators were identified as "Sikh terrorists." This had a twin effect on Sikh-Canadians: first, the reporting of the incident equated Sikhism with terrorism. Sikhs pointed out that linking the two terms was profoundly misleading. Secondly, the terrorists may have been followers of Sikhism, but their actions went directly against the teachings of the gurus and the beliefs of the greater Sikh community. In fact, after the bombing, support for the formation of Khalistan dropped noticeably.

The Air India tragedy highlights the effects that violence has on innocent people. Because of the actions of a few people, the whole Sikh community was forced to endure the suspicion of its fellow Canadians. The after-effects of the Air India bombing are still being felt today, particularly in Canada's Indian and Sikh communities.

Check Your Understanding

1. Briefly describe the *Komagata Maru* crisis.

2. What does the Air India tragedy reveal about the complexities and challenges of living in a truly multicultural society?

3. Is it more important to keep tradition, or adapt to modern times? Give one example of this type of dilemma.

Exploring Issues:
The Royal Canadian Mounted Police

Figure 9.20 *Constable Baltej Singh Dhillon, a Sikh, is shown here with fellow RCMP classmates in Regina prior to becoming the first graduate to wear a turban and sport a beard.*

For many years, Sikhs attempted to join the RCMP. Law enforcement was a role they had filled in many other countries. Sikhs have worn their turbans and their symbols in police forces throughout the world. For Sikhs, wearing the turban, keeping their hair uncut, and other Sikh symbols are all an important part of their religious tradition. However, the RCMP did not allow Sikhs to wear turbans, or other symbols if they wanted to join the force. In 1987, RCMP commissioner Norman Inkster made changes to the RCMP dress code to facilitate the entry of Sikhs into the force. This proposal was met with opposition from approximately 200 000 people. Many felt that if a Sikh RCMP officer wore his turban, he would not be met with respect or cooperation when responding to a call. In 1986, the Metro Toronto police department allowed Sikh officials to wear their turbans and other Sikh symbols while on duty. In 1990, Prime Minister Brian Mulroney expressed his support of the Sikhs on the turban issue. In 1991, Baltej Singh Dhillon (Figure 9.20) made history when he was decorated as a RCMP officer— he proudly wore a turban and other Sikh symbols at his graduating ceremony from the Regina Police Academy.

AT ISSUE: Should Sikhs be permitted to wear their religious symbols while on duty as RCMP officers?

The RCMP, also known as "the Mounties," believed that if a Sikh wore his turban, he might not be greeted with respect or taken seriously when responding to a call. Also, the RCMP uniform is an identifying feature of who they are; therefore, some believed that to allow a Sikh to wear a turban while in uniform would be a detraction from the uniform. As well, police forces prize uniformity and discipline, and some feared varieties in uniform would weaken group cohesion and discipline. Others held that the State should not be seen as endorsing any particular religious group.

The Sikhs opposed the RCMP position. Throughout the history of the Mounties, their uniform had been altered to suit the changing styles and needs of those wearing it. Also, it is believed that the Mounties' ability to do their job is not based on what they wear, but in fact is based on their intensive training. To focus on their apparel would be insulting to the commendable work that they perform. As well, Sikhs correctly pointed out that they had a long and distinguished history as reliable soldiers and police officers in many nations.

QUESTIONS
1. Why do you think people were opposed to Sikhs wearing their turbans while on duty?

2. Do you think it matters what a person wears while he or she is at work? Explain why.

CONCLUSION

Like so many other religions, the Sikh religion is a response to the mysteries of life and death. It is their attempt to live out this response in their daily lives. For the Sikh community, equality, service to others, and living a good and honourable life are essential. This is rooted in their religious tradition. In carrying this out, Sikhs have shown their commitment in their willingness to defend their religion when necessary. This commitment has been challenged many times throughout their history. It has taken the form of wars, persecution, and racism. Despite these challenges, Sikhs continue to prosper and grow in their devotion to God, and their desire to contribute to the country in which they live.

Sikhs, like all people of different religions moving to North America, adjust to a different society, and occasionally experience challenges in maintaining their faith and traditions, while at the same time recognizing the different circumstances and customs of their new home. Today, Canadian Sikhs are an integral part of Canadian society and, along with citizens of other religious traditions, are actively contributing to Canadian society.

Activities

Check Your Understanding

1. Identify and state the significance of the following key terms: Granthi, Gurbani, Gurdwara, Guru, Guru Granth Sahib, Khalistan, Khalsa, Khanda, Langar, Panj Pyare, Seva, Takht.

2. Sikhism was established by a succession of ten gurus, with the eleventh guru being the Guru Granth Sahib. These gurus are listed in the caption on page 365. Research them and make a chart outlining some of their contributions.

3. What are the Five Ks, and why are they significant to Sikhs?

4. How important is prayer in the daily life of a Sikh? Explain your answer.

Think and Communicate

5. How has your understanding of Sikhism changed since you have studied this chapter? Be specific.

6. Sikhs have been the target of a great deal of persecution since they established themselves as a religion in the 1500s. Why do you think the Sikhs have been the victims of discrimination and persecution?

Apply Your Learning

7. Imagine it is the day after the bombing of Air India Flight 182. Write two letters, one to the Hindu community and one to the Sikh community, sending your sympathy to both groups of Canadians, indicating the affect the tragedy has had on you.

8. Sikhism is a faith that entails tremendous tolerance of other religions. With specific reference to Sikh history, show how Sikhism is a friend to other religious groups.

9. Research further into the *Komagata Maru* incident and present a brief report.

10. Design a poster that will encourage people to treat women, or people of different races or religions, equally.

11. Make a chart of all the festivals Sikhs celebrate each year. Make another chart of all the ones you celebrate. Compare the dates.

12. In pairs, discuss ways at school in which you could fulfill the Sikh belief in serving the whole community. Share your ideas with the rest of the class and decide which ones you can carry out.

Glossary

Adi Granth [ADDY grunth]. Sikh holy text, more commonly known as the Guru Granth Sahib.

akhand path [a KUND path]. Continuous reading of the Sikh holy text during gurpurb.

amrit [am RIT]. A special mixture of sugar and water, which is used during certain ceremonies.

Amritsar [AM rit sir]. A holy city for Sikhs.

Anand Karaj [a NUND ca RAJ]. Sikh wedding ceremony.

Anand Sahib [a NUND sa HUB]. A Sikh prayer for thanksgiving.

Ardas [ar DASS]. Prayers said at the end of worship.

Bhai Ji [b'HAI gee]. Male or female responsible for ceremonial tasks and most importantly for bringing the Sikh holy text to main room of gurdwara before worship.

Daswandh [DUSS wunt]. The giving of charitable donations.

diwan [DEE wan]. The Sikh congregation.

granthi [GRUNTH ee]. The person who reads from Guru Granth Sahib.

gurbani [gur BONN ee]. The hymns of the Gurus in Guru Granth Sahib.

gurdwara [gurd WAR a]. A Sikh house of worship.

gurmukhi [gur MOOKY]. Script in which the Guru Granth Sahib is written.

guru. A spiritual guide, leader, or religious teacher.

Guru Granth Sahib [guru grunth sa HUB]. The Sikhs' most holy book, formerly known as the Adi Granth.

gutka [GOOT ka]. A book containing a selection of Sikh hymns.

karah parshad [KUR A pur shaad]. A sacred sweet pudding.

Karma. Totality of actions in one's life that determines your next life.

Khalistan [CALL is stan]. The name of an independent country some Sikhs hope to establish.

Khalsa [CALL SA]. A specially dedicated group within the Sikh community.

Khanda [CAN da]. The symbol of Sikhism.

kirat karni [kirit CUR nee]. To earn one's living by honest means.

kirtan [keer TAN]. The singing of hymns.

langar [LUN gar]. The free meal at the end of Sikh worship.

mukti [MOOKTY]. Release from constant rebirth.

Nam Karam [nam KAR um]. The naming ceremony.

nishan sahib [nee SHAWN sa HUB]. The Sikh flag hanging outside all gurdwaras.

pandit [PUN dit]. A holy man.

Panj Pyaras [PUNGE pee YA ra]. The first members of the Khalsa, the "five cherished ones."

purdah [PUR duh]. A veil worn by Muslim women.

ragis [ra GIS]. Singers.

romala [ru MOLLA]. Embroidered material.

seva [SAY VA]. Serving others.

sikh. A student or learner.

suttee [sut TEE]. Also known as sati; Hindu custom whereby a widow burned herself to death on husband's funeral pyre.

takhat [TACT]. The throne in a gurdwara where the Guru Granth Sahib is placed.

Waheguru [WAH heh guru]. The Sikh name of God, which means "Wonderful Lord."

Chapter Ten

Religion in the New Millennium

10

Study the painting and answer the following questions:

1. What appears to be the central message or theme of this illustration? Explain.
2. How do the circle and the fire serve to promote the message of the illustration? Be specific.
3. Identify the symbols that surround the image.

Introduction

Throughout history, religions have clashed and competed against each other. For centuries, Catholics and Protestants fought terrible wars in Europe. These religious conflicts continue today in various parts of the world. Northern Ireland has long been embroiled in a deadly struggle between Catholics and Protestants, while the Middle East continues to witness brutal conflicts among Muslims, Jews, and Christians.

However, in the last few decades the world has observed the development of a growing interfaith movement in which members of many faiths are engaged in respectful and tolerant communication. This dialogue is designed to promote harmony and understanding among different religions rather than division and conflict. This sentiment can be seen in the illustration on the opposite page, which was designed by a Sikh community in New Mexico.

Learning Goals

At the end of this chapter, you will be able to:

- demonstrate an understanding of religious pluralism as a defining characteristic of Canadian society
- identify the diverse religions represented in Canada and analyse how the high degree of religious pluralism in the population is reflected in Canadian society and culture
- explain how the religious impulse can be expressed outside formal religion
- identify some areas in which relationships between people of different beliefs, traditions, and practices can create conflict
- explain the concepts of ecumenism and interfaith dialogue
- investigate the origins of the World's Parliament of Religions and analyze the implications of its recently published statements
- demonstrate an understanding of different belief systems, e.g., humanism
- demonstrate an understanding of the term *fundamentalist*
- analyze demographic data to predict religious change in society
- compile a demographic study of the various religions within your community

Canadians are fortunate in that we live in an environment of religious pluralism, which allows us to learn about and contemplate the various faith traditions of the world.

THE NEW CENTURY— YOUR CENTURY

In spite of the wonders of new technology and the triumphs of science, it is clear that humankind still needs and wants a sense of religion. Indeed, to some observers, the technological age has spurred an increased interest in a broad range of spiritual and faith traditions. Canada is uniquely positioned to participate in this new age because its multicultural society includes active, well-established communities with diverse religious practices. The future of religion will likely feature some of the themes presented in this chapter.

Religious Extremism

Meeting the challenges of the twenty-first century is one of the objectives of most faiths. Some people have firmly accepted the interfaith path and are keen on sharing information and ideas with members of different religions. However, there are some practitioners of religion who do not approve of this kind of exchange. They propose a more fundamental view of their faith that stresses traditional practices and beliefs. These **fundamentalists** fear that too much change will lead to a great dilution of their faith and a weakening of their values and practices. They sometimes demand a more literal and thus narrower interpretation of their scriptures.

One challenge of this century is **religious extremism**. Religious extremists move far beyond fundamentalists in their interpretation of their faith. They are prepared to take violent action to defend their views and are willing to attack those who they deem enemies. At times, religious extremists may also try to spread their views across borders. In some countries, they have become politically active and attempt to use the power of the state to impose their beliefs on their fellow citizens. The Taliban in Afghanistan (Figure 10.1) are an example.

As the world changes ever more quickly and becomes increasingly multicultural, some people may choose the path of religious extremism to preserve what they feel is the truth. Most observers recognize that all major religions suffer from groups of extremists who do not fairly represent the spirit or teachings of their faith. In the twenty-first century, perhaps you will have a chance to witness the victory of tolerance and understanding over ignorance and prejudice.

Figure 10.1
In March 2001, the extremist Taliban government of Afghanistan ordered the destruction of this 1500-year-old Buddha statue in Bamiyan. Although Muslim, the Taliban are regarded as extremists by most Muslims and are not representative of Islam, which is respectful of other religious traditions.

Skill Path Demographic Study

Canada is a very multicultural and diverse country undergoing rapid changes in population. Canadians need some way to track and even predict these changes in order to understand the present and plan for the future. The study of population statistics is called demography.

Demographic data refers to facts and figures regarding population, such as age, gender, and household income. The goal of the demographer is to measure past and forecast future changes in population. Demographic researchers often collect data through methods such as surveys, questionnaires, and interviews. Sometimes they use the sampling method, which relies on a sample of the population to collect information.

As in all research, it is essential to clearly define the study group. For example, if the study group in question is the percentage of Canadians who attend religious services regularly, the researcher must clearly define the characteristics of that group before commencing his or her research. These characteristics essentially define the type of data to be collected. Frequency of occurrence (number of same responses) is generally communicated when analyzing the data through percentages rather than numbers. For example, the researcher may discover that 35 per cent of Canadians attend religious services regularly.

In order to draw conclusions about change in population, the researcher examines two factors: heads and events. The counting of "heads" refers to the population census, a common source for data. Births, deaths, and marriages might constitute important events that demographers count.

Population Census

A country's main source of information about its population comes from the population census. A census is a survey, which is taken in Canada every five years. For over 300 years, the census in Canada has provided a clear picture of Canadians, and the cities, towns, and villages in which we live. Statistics Canada, our national statistics agency, uses the data that it collects to produce statistical tables and reports. This information is available to researchers employed by communities, businesses, and governments for program development in the areas of day care, public transport, education, etc.

The questions asked in a typical Canadian census questionnaire relate to geographic, family, personal, cultural, and economic characteristics. The questionnaire might include questions about the following:

- Address
- Name
- Gender
- Age
- Marital Status
- Number of people living at residence, and their relationships to each other
- Language spoken
- Religion

The goal of the population census is to count heads as well as to identify household or family groupings. This information is particularly crucial to all those interested in assessing consumer demands.

Conducting a Survey for Demographic Research

Conducting a survey for demographic research involves the collection and analysis of data that relate to the opinions and habits of a population.

Step 1.
Determine the information you are seeking.

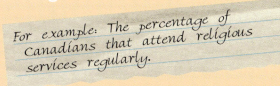

For example: The percentage of Canadians that attend religious services regularly.

2. Design the survey.

In designing the survey, follow the helpful hints below.

- Choose your audience carefully.
- Decide how to carry out the survey: in person, through mail, e-mail, telephone, or Internet site.
- Try to guarantee the anonymity of your respondents.
- Compose simple questions that can be answered quickly. You may wish to create a multiple choice, yes/no, or rank-in-order survey.

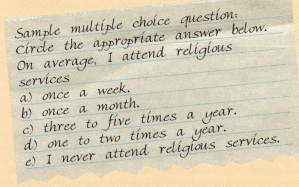

Sample multiple choice question:
Circle the appropriate answer below.
On average, I attend religious services
a) once a week.
b) once a month.
c) three to five times a year.
d) one to two times a year.
e) I never attend religious services.

3. Conduct the survey.

Before conducting the actual survey, do a test-run with a small group of people. Ask respondents to complete the survey. If conducting a survey with a large group, keep a record of all the completed surveys and store them carefully in a file. If conducting a sampling, work quickly and try to supervise the survey.

4. Analyze and represent your collected data.

Record the results on a large tally sheet. Use percentages to present your results. When data are expressed using percentages or proportions of the total population, the researcher can quickly grasp the frequency indication and more readily compare the frequency of one group with a second group. Tables and charts are often used to represent findings in a demographic study.

Practise It!

1. Conduct a demographic survey to find out the religious affiliation of the students in your school or your class. Design and conduct your survey. Analyze your data and present your findings in percentages.

2. Refer to the Population by Religion information on the Statistics Canada Web site (below) from the last two censuses. What changes do you see in Canada's population in terms of religious composition? What changes, or trends, are likely in the future?

Visit the Statistics Canada web site at www. statisticscanada.ca.

Humanism

Many people are concerned with living a good life, being ethical, and nurturing their fellow human beings. They sense an order and a rhythm to life but do not consider themselves to be religious. In fact, they may doubt or deny the existence of God, an eternal soul, or the concept of an afterlife. People who place their emphasis and concerns on humanity itself are adherents of a philosophy called **humanism**.

Humanism is a philosophy that emphasizes human welfare and dignity and is based on the belief that human beings alone are responsible for their fate. It was largely born in the exuberance of the Renaissance—a time that saw renewed interest in the arts and knowledge of the Greeks and Romans. While humanism originally existed alongside traditional religious beliefs, it became more and more opposed to official religious doctrine, superstition, and ritual. Immanuel

Kant (1724-1804), a German philosopher, argued that moral law was written on the heart of each person and that religion was not essential as a source of moral direction.

In Canada, contemporary humanists are concerned with many things, including human rights, equality, global issues, and racism. Increasingly, humanists are concerned about how our materialistic society is destroying the planet in pursuit of economic expansion and excess (see Figure 10.2). Canadian humanists are often in the forefront of issues relating to the Canadian Charter of Rights and Freedoms.

More recently, humanists and followers of religion have come to see the commonality of their concerns and are less focussed on their divisions and historical struggles. After all, the desire to lead a good and moral life and the urge to make the world a better and happier place appeals to almost everybody.

The Interfaith Age

We live in an era of great communication and dialogue within and among the world's religions. **Ecumenism** identifies the movement of denominations within Christianity to work more closely together and to foster a spirit of unity. There exists an even broader desire to reach out to other faiths. Although much of the history of the world has shown tremendous rivalry, competition, and even violence among peoples of differing faiths, there has been a growing movement based on **interfaith dialogue**, which stresses comparison and communication rather than competition. Because Canada is growing increasingly multi-cultural and multi-religious, it is natural that our country should be in the forefront of the interfaith movement (Figure 10.3).

The growth of this movement does not signal that the world's religions are merging or abandoning their unique identities, but it does mean that the search for dialogue and understanding is on-going. There are undoubtedly some commonalities among many religions, however there is clearly a rich diversity as well. This diversity is recognized and accepted in the spirit of tolerance and respect. Religious pluralism is a defining characteristic of Canadian society and is increasingly a global development as well.

The World's Parliament of Religions

In 1893, a singular event took place in the American city of Chicago. At a time when religious competition and rivalry was still very intense, a group of religious leaders from radically different faith traditions met to foster peace and harmony among their followers. It was the first ground-breaking interfaith meeting of representatives from the great Eastern and Western faith traditions. While this first meeting resulted in a certain amount of tension and attempts to demonstrate superiority, the spirit of true interfaith dialogue and tolerance was born. For some, it was the remarks and spirit of the great Hindu teacher, Swami Vivekananda that set in motion a new era among the world's religions. He spoke the following words:

The Christian is not to become a Hindu or a Buddhist, nor a Hindu or a Buddhist become a Christian. But each must assimilate the spirit of the others and yet preserve his individuality and grow according to his own law of growth.

Just as the twentieth century was coming to an end, a second **World's Parliament of Religions** was held in Chicago, in 1993.

In 1999, the third World's Parliament of Religions was convened in Capetown, South Africa, where attendees heard passionate addresses by luminaries such as Nelson Mandela and the Dalai Lama. Plans are being developed to hold another World's Parliament of Religions in 2004 to further the pace and scope of interfaith co-operation.

Figure 10.3
Interfaith discussions, like this one in Scarborough, Ontario, are more and more common across Canada. Why is Canada at the forefront of the interfaith movement?

Community Study

Scarboro Missions Interfaith Desk

Figure 10.4
The Scarboro Interfaith Desk was involved in the development and publication of the Golden Rule Poster, which features scripture passages and symbols of thirteen world religions.

With the migration of people, more regions of the world are becoming increasingly multicultural and multi-religious resulting in an encounter of religions that is new in history. At the same time, the great faiths of the world are talking to one another in a way that is innovative, challenging, and exciting. The Catholic Church has asked its members to join in this interfaith conversation.

Through its Interfaith Desk, Scarboro Missions works to bring together people of various faiths, and to promote harmony among religions, cultures, and races. Founded in 1918 by Monsignor John Mary Fraser for work in China, Scarboro Missions is now present in countries throughout Asia, Africa, Latin America, and the Caribbean, as well as in Canada. Today, Christian missions are committed to interfaith dialogue, cross-cultural encounters, and social justice in Canada as well as abroad. Scarboro Missions' priests and laity are responding enthusiastically to this challenge.

Scarboro Missions sponsored its first interfaith event in 1995 in which members of eight world religions were invited to comment on Gandhi's philosophy of non-violence from the perspective of their religions. Working with representatives of other faith traditions, the Interfaith Desk continues to sponsor and participate in several interfaith events in the Greater Toronto Area, around such themes as non-violence, ecology, and unity.

Many of these events are hosted by other religions at their place of worship, such as at a Baha'i centre, Sikh gurdwara, or Jain temple. The events usually involve observing the worship ceremony of the host faith and sharing a common meal after a day of interaction and dialogue. The Scarboro Interfaith Desk is particularly active with high-school students and teachers, and often organizes reflection days when students can meet with representatives of several world religions.

The Interfaith Desk has been recognized for its work and presented with a number of awards, including the Racial Harmony Award presented by the Community and Race Relations Committee of Toronto East. It has published several interfaith articles in its magazine, *Scarboro Missions*.

"Indeed, religious pluralism has proven to be one of the most extraordinary developments of the 20th century."

Paul McKenna (member of Interfaith Committee)

QUESTIONS

1. What are the central goals and activities of the Scarboro Missions Interfaith Desk?

2. Would you be interested in meeting members of other faiths and sharing a communal meal? Explain.

Sacred Text

In spite of the different origins and histories of the world's faiths, there is an apparent common thread that unites all believers. Once one ventures beyond the rich diversity of clothing, language, skin colour, ethnicity, religious practice, and hours of worship, he or she often finds a deeper commonality and unity of religious expression. The following are quotations from various faiths:

Confucianism

"Is there one word that sums up the basis of all good conduct? Surely it is the word loving kindness. Do not do unto others what you would not have done unto yourself."

-Confucius, Analects 15, 23

Buddhism

"Hurt not others in ways that you yourself would find hurtful."

-Udana-Varga 5.18

Christianity

"In everything, do unto others as you would have them do unto you"

-Jesus, Matthew 7:12

Aboriginal Spirituality

"We are as much as we keep the earth alive."

-Chief Dan George

Islam

"Not one of you truly believes until you wish for others what you wish for yourself."

-Muhammad, Hadith

Hinduism

"This is the sum of duty: do not do unto others what would cause pain unto you."

-Mahabharata 5:1517

Jainism

"One should treat all creatures in the world as one would like to be treated."

-Mahavira

Zoroastrianism

"That nature alone is good which refrains from doing unto another whatsoever is not good for itself."

-Dadistan-I-Dinik, 94:5

Judaism

"What is hateful to you do not do unto your neighbour. That is the entire law; all the rest is commentary."

-Hillel, Talmud-Shabbath 31a

Taoism

"Regard your neighbours gain as your own gain, regard your neighbours loss as your own loss."

-T'ai Shang Kan Ying P'ien, pp. 213-218

Bahá'í

"He should not wish for others that which he doth not wish for himself, nor promise that which he doth not fulfill."

-Tablets of Bahá'u'lláh, 71

Sikhism

"I am a stranger to no one; and no one is a stranger to me. Indeed I am a friend to all."

-Guru Granth Sahib, p. 1299

QUESTIONS

1. What appears to be the common theme that runs through most of these quotations?

2. Which quotations do you find most inspiring? Why?

Web Quest

Bahá'u'lláh, founder of the Bahá'í faith, taught that all the great religions of the world are one in their essential message of love.

To learn more about the Bahá'í faith, visit the Canadian Web site:
www.ca.bahai.org

Your Personal Journey

As you finish this book, you can take some pride in knowing that you have been introduced to numerous religious faiths, principles, and practices that may offer you some guidance and information for your very own spiritual journey through life. As a Canadian, you have access to a broad range of religious experiences within the boundaries of your country. Your neighbours and classmates are living proof of the religious diversity that surrounds you. Canada's laws and traditions protect and enhance religious expression, so you are free to grow and develop as a human being.

Hopefully, you have become more knowledgeable and tolerant of different approaches to life. Perhaps you understand your fellow Canadians a bit better and understand how enriching it can be to live and participate in such a multicultural society. Keep in mind that the completion of this book is really only the start of your personal exploration of life and its challenges. The authors of this text hope that some of the rich wisdom presented in this book will guide and inspire your personal spiritual evolution.

*No human life together
Without a world ethic for the nations
No peace among the nations
Without peace among the religions
No peace among the religions
Without dialogue among the religions*

-Hans Küng, Swiss Theologian

Figure 10.5
Young Canadians can pursue their personal spiritual journey in a nation rich in cultural and religious diversity. What faiths have made the greatest impression on you? Why?

Activities

Check Your Understanding

1. What are fundamentalists? How do they differ from religious extremists?

2. What is the appeal of humanism in today's world?

3. What is the meaning of the phrase "The Interfaith Age"?

4. What is the goal of the World's Parliament of Religions?

5. What are the most likely themes of religion in the new century?

Think and Communicate

6. Working in small groups, respond to the following question: What are the three most important things that you have learned from your study of some of the world's religions? Why?

7. Visit this Web site on the World's Parliament of Religions to analyze and report on one of the documents published by this organization. www.nycinterfaith.org/parliament.htm

8. Working in small groups, create and complete a graphic organizer on the religions that you have studied this year. Decide on at least six comparative criteria, for example, country of origin, symbols, and basic beliefs, and then complete your organizer. Be prepared to present your organizer to your peers.

9. Briefly describe where you are on your personal journey at this point in your life.

Apply Your Learning

10. Review the many symbols and icons presented in this book and design a suitable symbol for the unity of the world's faiths. Prepare a brief written statement explaining your design.

11. Working with other students, prepare an attractive guide or resource book on religious communities in your area. Include information on places and times of worship, community resources, spokespersons, activities, events, and maps, etc.

Glossary

ecumenism [eck YOU m'n ism]. The movement to bring all Christian denominations closer together and to foster mutual understanding.

fundamentalism. Strict maintenance of traditional teachings and practices of any religion.

humanism. An outlook or system of thought that views humankind as the source of all value or meaning, rather than spiritual or religious matters.

interfaith dialogue. The movement among religious communities to communicate with each other openly and in the spirit of mutual understanding, respect, and tolerance.

religious extremism. The belief in extreme religious opinions and the advocacy of extreme action in support of those opinions.

World's Parliament of Religions. Meeting of representatives of the world's religions whose aim is mutual understanding, tolerance, and discussion of important issues.

Text Credits

Every reasonable effort has been made to trace the original source of text material and photographs contained in this book. Where the attempt has been unsuccessful, the publisher would be pleased to hear from copyright holders to rectify any omissions.

10 'I Still Haven't Found What I'm Looking For' (lyrics only), U2, Universal International Music/Universal/Island Records MCA Music Publishing.

44 Excerpt from *Lame Deer, Seeker of Visions*, John Fire Lame Deer and Richard Erdoes, (New York: Simon & Schuster, 1972), pp. 14-16.

49 Excerpt from *People of the Dancing Sky* copyright © 2000 by Myron Zobel and Lorre Jensen. Reprinted by permission of Stoddart Publishing Co. Limited.

60 'The Story of the Bell Stand' from *Taoism* by Paula R. Hartz. Copyright © 1993 by Paula R. Hartz. Reprinted by permission of Facts On File, Inc.

61 Quote from *Taoism* by Paula R. Hartz. Copyright © 1993 by Paula R. Hartz. Reprinted by permission of Facts On File, Inc.

67 Yasna 30:3-6 from *An Introduction to Ancient Iranian Religion* by W.W. Malandra (Minneapolis: University of Minnesota Press, 1983). Reprinted by permission of University of Minnesota Press.

82 Excerpt from page 253 from *Our Religions* edited by Arvind Sharma. Copyright © 1993 by HarperCollins Publishers Inc. Reprinted by permission of HarperCollins Publishers, Inc.

114 Abridgement of 'Thousands in Toronto *See* Ganesha Miracle' reprinted by permission from *Indo Caribbean World*, Vol. 13, no. 3, 4 October 1995.

121 'Svetasvatara Upanishad' from *Hinduism*, 2nd Edition, by R.C. Zaehner (Oxford: Oxford University Press, 1966). Reprinted by permission of Oxford University Press.

123 Quote from *The Hindu Traditions: Readings in Oriental Thought*, Ainslie T. Ebree, ed. (New York: Vintage Books, 1972).

144 Bhagavad-Gita, Chapter 9, Verses 3-8 from *A Source Book in Indian Philosophy*, S. Radhakrishnan and C.A. Moore, eds. Copyright © 1957, renewed 1985, by Princeton University Press. Reprinted by permission of Princeton University Press.

192 Jataka No. 100, 'A Mother's Wise Advice' from http://www.geocities.com/Athens/Delphi/9241/jatak100.htm reprinted by permission of Mahindarama Sunday Pali School, Penang, Malaysia.

201 Excerpts from His Holiness the Dalai Lama's Nobel Price acceptance speech are reprinted by kind permission of the Office of His Holiness the Dalai Lama.

206 Abridged from 'Reactionary Natury of Falun Cult Exposed' from People's Daily Online, http://english.people.com.cn by permission.

207 Stephen Gregory: 'My Understanding about Falun Gong' (abridged)from http://www.clearwisdom.net/eng/clarification/common_mis.html, 9 February 2001.

212 Quotes from Genesis 1:1-5 and Exodus 20:2-14 from *The Tanakh: The New JPS Translation According to the Traditional Hebrew Text*. Copyright © 1985 by the Jewish Publication Society. Used by permission.

260, 265, 266, 268, 276, 285, 286, 291, Scripture quotations marked(NIV) are taken from the *Holy Bible*, New International Version ®. NIV ®. Copyright © 1973, 1978, 1984 by International Bible Society. Used by permission. All rights reserved.

288 Excerpt from page 90 from *My Life for the Poor: Mother Teresa's Life and Work in Her Own Words* by José Luis González-Balado and Janet N. Playfoot. Copyright © 1985 by José Luis González-Balado and Janet N. Playfoot. Reprinted by permission of HarperCollins Publishers, Inc.

314 Quotes from 1:1-7, 4:3, 30:21, 33:35, 49:13, and 96:1-5 from *The Meaning of the Holy Qur'an*, Abdullah Yusuf Ali, (Brentwood, MD: American Trust Publications, 1991) copyright holder: The Islamic Book Service.

326 Summary of Muhammad's 'Farewell Sermon' (from http://muslim-canada.org/prophetbio.html) from *Introduction to Islam*, Muhammad Hamidullah, (Paris: Centre Culturel Islamique, 1969).

358 Excerpts taken from *Sikh Gurus: Their Lives and Teachings* by K.S. Duggal published by UBS Publishers' Distributors Ltd., New Delhi. Reprinted by permission.

363 Guru Nanak: Hymn: 'He was here in the beginning…' from *The Sikh Gurus: Their Lives and Teachings*, K.S. Duggal, (New Delhi: Vikas, 1980).

369 Thompson, Jan. The Sikh Experience (London: Hodder and Stoughton, 2000).

380 Guru Granth Sahib: Hymn for a naming ceremony: 'Dear child, this is your mother's blessing…May God robe you with honour and may your food be the singing of God's praises.' from *The Sikh Gurus: Their Lives and Teachings*, K.S. Duggal, (New Delhi: Vikas, 1980), p. 486.

386 Guru Angad Dev: 'The Wisdom of the Guru' from *The Sikh Gurus: Their Lives and Teachings*, K.S. Duggal, (New Delhi: Vikas, 1980).

386 Guru Granth Sahib: 'Theme: Avoid Judging Others' from *The Sikh Gurus: Their Lives and Teachings*, K.S. Duggal, (New Delhi: Vikas, 1980).

386 Guru Granth Sahib: 'Theme: The Real Hero' from *The Sikh Gurus: Their Lives and Teachings*, K.S. Duggal, (New Delhi: Vikas, 1980).

386 Guru Nanek: Hymn: 'God is the Master, God is Truth, His name spelleth love divine.' from *The Sikh Gurus: Their Lives and Teachings*, K.S. Duggal, (New Delhi: Vikas, 1980).

387 Guru Nanak: 'Bright and brilliant is the bronze…' from *The Sikh Gurus: Their Lives and Teachings*, K.S. Duggal, (New Delhi: Vikas, 1980).

387 Guru Nanak: Hymn: '…Few, some very few…It is God's will that is done, for ever and ever.' from *The Sikh Gurus: Their Lives and Teachings*, K.S. Duggal, (New Delhi: Vikas, 1980).

387 Guru Nanak: Hymn: 'Were life's span extended…What would it all be worth?' from *The Sikh Gurus: Their Lives and Teachings*, K.S. Duggal, (New Delhi: Vikas, 1980).

Photo Credits

Bridgeman=Bridgeman Art Library, Christine Osborne=Christine Osborne Pictures/MEP, CP=CP Picture Archive, Granger=The Granger Collection, New York, NY, Corbis/Magma=CORBIS/MAGMA PHOTO

2-3 top row (l to r) Ivy Images, © Kelly-Mooney Photography/Corbis/Magma, The Toronto Star/R. Bull, **centre row (l to r)** Toronto Sun/Paul Henry/CP, © Lindsay Hebberd/Corbis/Magma, Shaun Best/CP, **bottom row (l to r)** The Toronto Star/A. Stawicki, The Toronto Star/P. Power, Christine Osborne; **4 (l)** Winnipeg Free Press/Phil Hossack/CP, **(c)** The Toronto Star/P. Power, **(r)** Christine Osborne; **8** Courtesy of VisionTV; **9** The Toronto Star/B. Weil; **12** Courtesy of Sandy Mackellar; **13** Tak Bui www.pccomix.com; **16 (l) and (c)** Everett Collection, **(r)** M. Aronowitz/New Line © 2000 New Line Cinema/Kobal Collection; **18 (l) and (r)** Granger; **22** Sheena Singh/Creative Cultural Communications; **26-27** © Macduff Everton/Corbis/Magma; **26 (t)** Wayne Glowacki/CP, **(b)** Fred Chartrand/CP; **28** Courtesy of the UBC Museum of Anthropology, Photo: W. McLennan; **29 (tl)** BC Archives, Province of BC/E-04017, **(tr)** Shaun Best/CP, **(b)** Shaney Komulainen/CP; **30 (t)** Woodland Cultural Centre, **(b)** Victor Last/Geographical Visual Arts; **36 (t)** Roy Thomas "Relationship with Nature," 1990, acrylic on canvas, 61 x 61 cm, Thunder Bay Art Gallery Collection, Thunder Bay, ON, Photography: Judy Flett, Thunder Bay, **(c)** Smithsonian Institution, **(b)** Arnold Jacobs; **37 (t)** Stanley R. Hill, **(c)** Courtesy of the UBC Museum of Anthropology, Photo: W. McLennan, **(b)** Blake Debassige; **38 (t)** © John Eastcott/Yva Momatiuk/Valan Photos, **(b)** © Kelly-Mooney Photography/Corbis/Magma; **39** Allen Sapp; **40** BC Archives, Province of BC/E-04017; **41 (t)** Woodland Cultural Centre, **(b)** Elizabeth Simpson/FPG; **42** Myron Zabol; **43** Colin Corneau; **47** Woodland Cultural Centre; **48** Paul Bailey; **50** Woodland Cultural Centre; **51** Courtesy of Sean Dolan; **53** Shaney Komulainen/CP; **54** Shaun Best/CP; **55** Colin Corneau; **60-61** © Pierre Colombel/Corbis/Magma; **62 (l)** Ann & Bury Peerless Picture Library, **(r)** Granger; **63 (l)** Granger, **(c)** © Kelly-Mooney Photography/Corbis/Magma, **(r)** Dick Hemingway; **64** Private Collection/Ann & Bury Peerless Picture Library/Bridgeman; **66** The Toronto Star/R. Bull; **68** Courtesy of Sean Dolan; **70** Dinodia Picture Agency, Bombay, India/Bridgeman; **71** Chris Sanders/Stone; **72** Ann & Bury Peerless Picture Library; **77** © Bettmann/Corbis/Magma; **80** Private Collection/Bridgeman; **81** Granger; **83** Toronto Star/Boris Spremo/CP; **87** Dick Hemingway; **89** Granger; **91** Private Collection/Bridgeman; **95** © Lindsay Hebberd/Corbis/Magma; **96** Peter Mong/Confucius Publishing Co. Ltd.; **99** Werner Forman Archive/Art Resource; **101** Victoria & Albert Museum, London/Art Resource/NY, **(inset)** © Joyce Photographics/Valan Photos; **102** Richard T. Nowitz/National Geographic Society; **107** © Kelly-Mooney Photography/Corbis/Magma; **114-115** Dick Hemingway; **116 (l)** © David Samuel Robbins/Corbis/Magma, **(r)** © India Book House Limited, 1998; **117 (t)** Dave Thomas/CP, **(b)** © Hulton-Deutsch Collection/Corbis/Magma; **119** © David Samuel Robbins/Corbis/Magma; **121** Ann & Bury Peerless Picture Library/Bridgeman; **122** Freud Museum, London, UK/Bridgeman;

127 © Hulton-Deutsch Collection/Corbis/Magma; **128** © Bettmann/Corbis/Magma; **130** The Toronto Star/A. Stawicki; **132** © Robert Holmes/Corbis/Magma; **134 (t)** National Museum of India, New Delhi/Bridgeman, **(b)** Circa Photo Library/William Holby; **135** The Toronto Star/D. Loek; **140** Ann & Bury Peerless Picture Library; **142** © India Book House Limited, 1998; **145** Private Collection/Bridgeman; **147** Dave Thomas/CP; **148** Tannis Toohey/CP; **150** Courtesy of Chaaya Raghunanan; **151** Dick Hemingway; **158-159** Friedrich Reg; **160 (l)** Giraudon/Art Resource, NY, **(c)** Martin Gray, **(r)** Private Collection/Bridgeman; **161 (tl)** Arthur Strange/Valan Photos, **(tr)** Reuters/Kamal Kishore/Archive Photos, **(bl)** Bushnell/Soifer/Stone, **(br)** Reuters/Andrew Wong/Archive Photos; **163** Giraudon/Art Resource, NY; **165** Martin Gray; **166** Borromeo/Art Resource, NY; **169** Courtesy of the New Kadampa Tradition; **173** Courtesy of Andy Weber; **179 (t)** © James Marshall/Corbis/Magma, **(b)** Archive Photos; **181 (t)** Reuters/Kamal Kishore/Archive Photos, **(b)** Ivy Images; **182 (t)** Al Harvey/The Slide Farm, **(b)** Scala/Art Resource, NY; **183** Martin Gray; **184** Courtesy of Andy Weber; **185** National Gallery of Canada, Ottawa/Gift of Max Tanenbaum, Toronto, 1980/No. 26869; **187** © R. Ian Lloyd/Masterfile; **188** Dennis Cox/First Light; **190** Courtesy of Peter Lawley; **195** Private Collection/Bridgeman; **197** Bushnell/Soifer/Stone; **200** Reuters/Kamal Kishore/Archive Photos; **203** A. Strange/Valan Photos; **204** Courtesy of Peter Lawley; **205** Toronto Star/L. Slezic; **206** Reuters/Andrew Wong/Archive Photos; **212-213** Steven Hunt/Image Bank; **214 (l)** Stapleton Collection/Bridgeman, **(r)** © Erich Lessing/Art Resource, NY; **215 (l)** Granger Collection, **(c)** Comstock, **(r)** Courtesy of Beth Tzedec Congregation; **217** Stapleton Collection/Bridgeman; **218** Christine Osborne; **220** Gallery dell' Accademia, Florence, Italy/Bridgeman; **222** Klaus Synagoga, Prague, Czech Republic/Scala/Art Resource, NY; **223** © Erich Lessing/Art Resource, NY; **225** © Steve Vidler/Comstock; **227** Courtesy of Leora Wise; **229** Comstock; **230** Archive Photos; **231** Zefa/H. Armstrong Roberts/Comstock; **232** Associated Press AP; **234** Circa Photo Library/Ged Murray; **236** Courtesy of the Marcus family; **238** Toronto Star/Andrew Stawicki/CP; **240** Granger Collection; **243** Courtesy of Rabbi Ami Eilberg; **244** Courtesy of Miriam Tessler; **249 (t)** Belsen Concentration Camp -- Malnutrition No. 2 by Aba Bayefsky/CN#10843/Canadian War Museum, **(b)** Courtesy of Mr. Charles Bronfman and birthright israel; **250** Courtesy of Breakthrough Films; **252** Courtesy of Beth Tzedec Congregation; **253** Courtesy of Rabbi Baruch Frydman-Kohl; **260-261** Sygma/Magma Photo; **262 (l)** Granger, **(c)** Leigh Delamere Church, Wiltshire, UK/Bridgeman, **(r)** Mikhail Metzel/AP Photo/CP; **263 (l)** Galleria degli Uffizi, Florence, Italy/Bridgeman, **(c)** © 1991 Winston Fraser/Ivy Images, **(r)** Reuters/Gary Hersorn/Archive Photos; **265** Granger; **267** Leigh Delamere Church, Wiltshire, UK/Bridgeman; **269** © Archivo Iconografico, S.A./Corbis/Magma; **271** © Erich Lessing/Art Resource, NY; **272** AP Photo/CP; **274** Dick Hemingway; **277** Ivy Images; **278** © Michael Nicholson/Corbis/Magma; **280 (t)** Scala/Art Resource, NY, **(bl)** Granger, **(br)** Giraudon/Art Resource, NY; **282** Andrew J. Cohoon/AP Photo/CP; **283** Ivy Images; **285** Courtesy of Maria Aprile; **287** Courtesy of Maria Christopoulos; **288** Sherwin Crasto/AP Photo/CP; **297** Mikhail Metzel/AP Photo/CP; **299** Reuters/Gary Hersorn/Archive Photos; **301** Galleria degli Uffizi,

SKILL PATH REFERENCES

Chapter 3
Carroll, Jim, and Rick Broadhead. *Canadian Internet Directory and Research Guide.* Toronto: Stoddart Publishing Co. Limited, 2001.
Wang, Wallace, and Roger C. Parker. *Microsoft Office 2000 for Windows for Dummies.* Foster City: CA: IDG Books Worldwide Inc., 1999.

Chapters 4, 5, and 7
Ary, Donald, Lucy Cheser Jacobs, and Asghar Razavieh. *Introduction to Research in Education,* 5th ed. Orlando, FL: Harcourt Brace College Publishers, 1996.
Fraenkel, Jack R., and Norman E.Wallen. *How to Design and Evaluate Research in Education,* 3rd ed. New York: McGraw Hill, 1993.

Hillway, Tyrus. *Handbook of Educational Research: A Guide to Methods and Materials.* Boston: Houghton Mifflin Company, 1992.
MacMillan, James H. *Educational Research: Fundamentals for the Consumer.* New York: Harper Collins Publishers, 1992.

Chapter 9
Wang, Wallace, and Roger C. Parker. *Microsoft Office 2000 for Windows for Dummies.* Foster City: CA: IDG Books Worldwide Inc., 1999.

Chapter 10
Hillway, Tyrus. *Handbook of Educational Research: A Guide to Methods and Materials.* Boston: Houghton Mifflin Company, 1992.
Hopkins, Charles D., and Richard L. Antes. *Educational Research: A Structure for Inquiry.* Itasca, IL: F.E. Peacock Publishers, 1992.

Index of Glossary Terms

Index